NUCLEAR HOLOCAUST
AND
CHRISTIAN HOPE

NUCLEAR HOLOCAUST AND CHRISTIAN HOPE

**Ronald J. Sider
and
Richard K. Taylor**

HODDER AND STOUGHTON
LONDON SYDNEY AUCKLAND TORONTO

British Library Cataloguing in Publication Data

Sider, Ronald
   Nuclear holocaust and Christian hope
   1. Atomic warfare.   2. War and religion
   I. Title   II. Taylor, Richard
   261.8′73   JX1974.7

   ISBN 0 340 32639 5

*Printed in Great Britain for Hodder and Stoughton Limited, Mill Road,
Dunton Green, Sevenoaks, Kent by Cox & Wyman Limited, Reading.
Photoset by Rowland Phototypesetting Limited, Bury St Edmunds,
Suffolk. Hodder and Stoughton Editorial Office: 47 Bedford Square,
London WC1B 3DP.*

To our children, in hope

Contents

Appendices

List of Figures

List of Photographs

Acknowledgments

Many people helped us with this book.

The final version is much better because of many friends, scholars and experts in several fields who read part or all of the first draft: Robert Aldridge, Barbara Allaire, D. W. Boardman, M.D., Geraldine Burd, Ellen Charry, Harvie Conn, Adam and Susan Corson-Finnerty, Peter Dyck, Frank Gaebelein, Tom Getman, Robert Hull, George Hunsinger, Bob Irwin, Homer A. Jack, Carolyn Klaus, M.D., George Lakey, Weldon Nisly, Robert Osborn, Patricia Parkman, Paul Ramsey, Sally Schreiner, Gene Sharp, Lynne Shivers, Edward F. Snyder, Jack Stewart, John Stoner, Mark Stuart, Reginald W. Toews, Charles Walker and Merold Westphal. Having stubbornly resisted their advice at times, we cannot blame them for any errors or faults that remain.

Also, Randy Bond, Darel Brubaker and George Patterson helped dig out necessary materials. Our appreciation also goes to several typists: Nancy Burwell, Eleanor Butler, Susan Letis, Bette McClelland, Alice Morrow and Robin Songer.

We owe special thanks to our wives, Arbutus Sider and Phyllis Taylor, for their advice and support. Their help, along with that of our children—Ted, Michael, Sonja, Deborah and Daniel—was crucial during the sometimes arduous labour of writing and rewriting. Arbutus, Ted and Michael even found time while on holiday to help prepare the indexes.

Preface

There can be little doubt that the two most important issues in our world today are first, its continued existence, and second, the proper distribution of its limited resources.

Ronald Sider has already become known all over the English-speaking world for his devastating critique of Christian acquiescence in the materialism of the West while millions die of starvation and disease. *Rich Christians in an Age of Hunger* is one of the most important books of conscience to be written in recent years. It was very uncomfortable to read, and flew in the face of current assumptions in Christian circles that if you paid your tithe, or something like it, you could expect the good Lord to endow you with material prosperity in return.

Now he has addressed himself to the even more crucial issue of the world's continued existence. We can by no means take it for granted. We have the power of destroying our planet many times over. And there is nothing in human history or human nature to encourage us in the hope that all will be well. It is exceedingly probable that some day some fool will press the button that will consign the world to nuclear holocaust.

Mercifully the population of the world is waking up to the reality of the dangerous precipice on which the human race is so precariously balanced. In Germany and the United States, in Britain and Australia there is widespread revulsion against the siting of nuclear missiles. Parliaments debate. Marchers demonstrate. Women surround nuclear bases with pleas of peace. But governments on the whole are unwilling to listen. The myth of deterrence based on

ever-escalating nuclear overkill holds the field. It has re-
putedly kept the peace since 1945, and seems to many to
be the only hope for the future, since we cannot close Pan-
dora's Box, opened on Hiroshima and Nagasaki in that
year. Is there any possible alternative policy? Ronald Sider
believes that there is.

His book comes hard in the wake of the Church of
England's Working Party which produced the highly con-
troversial report, *The Church and the Bomb*. Both books
argue boldly from Christian principle. And both see the
teaching and example of Jesus as pointing unequivocally to
nonviolence. In short, God is against nuclear weapons.
They ought not to be used by Christian people. Ah, say the
Western governments, that is just the point. We build these
arsenals in order that we may never have to use them. That
argument is searched in this book and found wanting.
Mutual fear is no way to build relationships in the world,
and the astronomical misuse of the earth's resources in
multiplying arsenals is the ultimate obscenity. The Bishop
of Salisbury and Professor Sider are at one on this, the most
important issue in the world. The Christian voice should be
heard loud and clear against the build-up, the threat and
the use of nuclear weapons. The old 'Just War' theory is
meaningless in a nuclear age. There *are* ways of securing
and promoting disarmament, and they are not the ways at
present fashionable in the Kremlin, Whitehall and Congress. Nonmilitary defence is a possibility which needs
careful exploration, and Ronald Sider sketches the direction it could take.

To be sure, this may necessitate unilateral disarmament.
Somebody has got to take the moral initiative, and face the
risks inherent in it. But what of the risks inherent in
increasing escalation? Yes, the Russians might take advantage of the West and walk over us. But would this be the
ultimate disaster? There would at least be a world left to
inhabit. And the Christian gospel is not inseparably allied
with any political system, nor is it committed to the glor-
ification of any nation. On the contrary, the faith of Christ

flourishes very well in wintry conditions, and has a remarkable propensity to bud in the most unlikely climates. The phenomenal growth of Christianity in Russia and China in recent decades is eloquent proof of that.

I have not always believed the position Professor Sider advances, but for the past two years I have. As I prepared to preach on the Christmas theme in 1980, I came to see that in the incarnation of Jesus Christ we have the ultimate power in the universe willingly laying aside its might and becoming the most weak and defenceless creature imaginable, a baby in a manger. The way of self-abnegation and non-retaliation against evil was the path Jesus pursued right through to the end, the bitter end on a cross. Yet it was not the end. It was followed by the resurrection, and the moral influence of that dangerous path of nonviolence has been greater and longer-lasting than any other expression of power in the history of mankind. Such is the paradox of God. Such is the teaching and example of Jesus. "Whoever would save his life will lose it; and whoever loses his life for My sake and the gospel's will save it. For what does it profit a man to gain the whole world and forfeit his life?

For what can a man give in return for his life?" (Mark 8:35f). Here is a book that could change the world. Read it. Wrestle with it. Let it become part of you. If you do, you will find that Ronald Sider gives many practical guides to appropriate action. The time is short. The issue is paramount. And here is a book that shows us a truly Christian approach. I commend it with all my heart.

Michael Green
Christmas 1982

SECTION I

The Threat of Nuclear War

Three basic questions lie behind this book. Can Christians support government policies which rely on the threat of nuclear war? Given the realities of modern war and the ethics of Jesus, can followers of Jesus Christ support or engage in war in any form? How can Christians act for peace in today's world?

This section paints a picture of what nuclear war is all about. Chapter one, a fictionalised account of a nuclear attack on a city, makes unpleasant but necessary reading. It is based on factual government reports, eyewitness testimony and scientific studies about the effects of nuclear war. Dick Taylor also visited Hiroshima and Nagasaki and talked with survivors of the atomic bombings. Chapter two describes the effect of a nuclear exchange on people, civilisation and the earth's environment. And chapter three takes a critical look at the concept of deterrence.

The second section of the book examines deterrence, nuclear war and war itself from a biblical point of view. It argues that an alternative to deterrence – and a way out of the nuclear impasse – can be found in the life and teachings of Jesus Christ, the Prince of Peace. Sections three and four explore how individual Christians and the Christian church can live out their divine call to be peacemakers.

'The present arms race is a terrifying thing, and it is almost impossible to over-estimate its potential for disaster. . . . Is a nuclear holocaust inevitable if the arms race is not stopped? Frankly, the answer is almost certainly yes. . . . I cannot see any way in which nuclear war could be branded as being God's will. Such warfare, if it ever happens, will come because of the greed and pride and covetousness of the human heart.'

Billy Graham[1]

1

The First Hour

An instant after the one-megaton warhead exploded over Moscow, a huge fireball burst upward.[2] At its centre the temperature was 150 million degrees Fahrenheit, more than eight times the heat at the centre of the sun.

In central Moscow life came to an end. The fireball itself was three-quarters of a mile wide. It vaporised steel and concrete buildings, roads, bridges, and hundreds of thousands of people. Mingled in a raging cauldron, the structures and bodies – pulverised and reduced to cinders – were sucked up into a towering, mushroom-shaped cloud. Moments later, the heavier rubble, now highly radioactive, fell back on to the shambles below. Lighter particles rose with the mushroom cloud into the upper atmosphere, from which they would later descend as radioactive dust.

The American rocket, the first to break through Moscow's anti-ballistic missile system,[3] was launched by Major Raymond Butts and Captain James Mercer, combat missile crewmen at the 341st Strategic Missile Wing, Malmstrom Air Force Base, Great Falls, Montana.

A year before World War III erupted, a Montana reporter had researched a newspaper story on US rockets. The reporter had heard Major Butts in a chance remark describe himself as a Christian.

'How can you square your faith with the frightful power of these weapons?' the reporter had asked. 'You have more killing power at your fingertips than Alexander,

Attila, Genghis Khan, Napoleon and Hitler combined!'

'Yes,' the major had replied, 'with the turn of our keys, Captain Mercer and I could fire this missile and destroy a Russian city. But that's not my source of power. My power as a Christian comes from Christ. My mission here is to prevent war by helping to keep American nuclear forces combat-ready so that the Soviet Union will be afraid to attack. In an imperfect world, that seems to me a valid way to exercise power and to serve Christ.'[4]

Major Butts had insisted that he would launch his weapon if he ever received the president's order. When the order came, he followed instructions and fired. So did hundreds of other American missile crewmen in underground silos and submarines. Soviet missile crewmen, of course, did the same.

The eye-stabbing flash of the incandescent fireball momentarily blinded the pilot of a Soviet Aeroflot jetliner on its approach to Moscow's Sheremetyevo Airport, twenty miles north of Red Square. Moments later, the plane lurched violently under the impact of the blast's shock wave. The co-pilot, who had not looked into the searing light, took the controls and banked the jet sharply away from Moscow. Passengers watched dumbfounded as a white-hot ball of fire surged up over the city like an enormous hot-air balloon.

Tourists on a suburban bus returning from a visit to the Arkhangelskoye Palace, ten miles from Moscow, were not so fortunate. The blinded driver crashed the bus into a wall at sixty miles an hour, killing all the passengers.

In central Moscow the blast and heat of the first bomb were stupefying. It was as if a hundred thousand trucks, each loaded with ten tons of dynamite, had been parked in Red Square and then detonated simultaneously. It was as if over seventy of the bombs that obliterated Hiroshima had been set off at the same moment in the same place. People were vaporised, squashed, blown apart, turned to dust.

Vasily Solunsky, an art student from Kiev who was visiting Moscow on a class trip, was one of them. At age sixteen, Vasily was a confirmed atheist and an officer in the Young Communist League. Because of this he felt a twinge of guilt at his admiration for the church icons the class had been studying at the Tretyakov Art Gallery, across the Moscow River from the Kremlin. Hadn't Lenin taught that every religious idea, every idea of God, even flirting with the idea of God, is utter vileness? Why, then, was the class spending so much time with these religious paintings?

Vasily's teacher had said, 'In our modern society, science has replaced religion. But you should still appreciate these religious masterpieces as part of our national treasure. Many were painted by humble serfs, oppressed by the Tsar. Comrade Lenin himself demanded the protection of all our artistic monuments of the past. Tretyakov Gallery now contains one of the world's greatest collections of religious icons, plus dozens of paintings and mosaics. They show scenes from the lives of Jesus, the saints and Bible figures. The gallery has over five thousand canvases, nine hundred sculptures and nearly thirty thousand drawings and engravings.'

The class had moved down the corridor, leaving Vasily standing pensively in front of a painting called 'The Dormition of the Virgin.' The fourteenth-century icon, painted in vivid colours of red, blue, orange, brown, yellow and black, showed Jesus' disciples weeping over Mary's dead body. Their sorrow touched Vasily. The disciples' devotion reminded him of the look of his grandmother's face long ago, when she had taken him to church and knelt before a statue of the Virgin. A figure of Christ, clothed in a shimmering, golden robe, stood in the painting's background.

Suddenly, the entire gallery filled with a blue-white flash, as if a thousand flash bulbs had exploded. Vasily felt a sharp pain in his back. He was astonished to see smoke begin to rise from the icon. An instant later he was thrown violently into the painting, and both were buried in twisted steel and jagged bits of marble.

On the northern side of the Moscow River, Pastor Gregor Yusupov was walking hurriedly past the Kremlin wall. He was late to a meeting of the All-Union Council of Evangelical Christian Baptists, which, in spite of maddening government restrictions and even outright persecution, claimed a nationwide constituency of five million Soviet citizens.

'But that's not very many,' he said to himself, 'when compared to the fifty million members of the Russian Orthodox Church.'

Pastor Yusupov was especially looking forward to the two-hour Communion service after the meeting. It would be attended by over a thousand believers at the packed Moscow Baptist Church.[5] He loved to assist the deacons in breaking the large, sweet-smelling loaves and passing them to the congregation, many of whom would be moved to tears. Then he would step to the wooden pulpit and offer his prayer. As was the custom, worshippers would at the same time fill the church with their own whispered petitions and praise. This reverent mingling of voices bound everyone together in a deep sense of Christ's presence.

Just as the pastor rounded a corner and saw the church in the distance, the street and buildings flashed whiter than anything he had ever seen. A moment later the bomb's fiery wind consumed him.

To the north, the Bolshoi Ballet troupe was rehearsing 'Swan Lake.' Prima ballerina Marina Popova, dressed for the part of Odetta in a white tutu and jewelled tiara, was crushed with the other dancers in the collapsing golden balconies and shattered crystal chandeliers of the theatre.

Four blocks east of the Kremlin, Trinity Church and the Moscow Synagogue were churned together as if caught in a malicious food grinder. To the northwest, the children's department store and Children's World were levelled. Children laughing at a puppet show in Gorky Park, one and a half miles southwest of the Kremlin, burned to death in the fireball's heat. The park's Rocket Sled roller coaster, full of families on holiday, careened from its track and landed upside-down.

Thousands of passengers on the underground were

buried alive under the crumpled marble walls and columns of the ornate Moscow underground. Above ground, five-hundred-mile-per-hour winds sent scorched bodies sailing through the air like waste paper, somersaulting, ripping apart, piling up like logs, slashed by splintered wood, glass and metal, which flew about like shrapnel.[6]

The warhead exploded directly above the Kremlin. Top Soviet leaders had used the half-hour warning provided by their reconnaissance satellites to escape by helicopter to command posts away from the city. Bureaucrats not on the priority list died in the Kremlin's deep underground bomb shelters when all the oxygen was sucked away by the bomb's immense heat.

Nagarekawa Church, Hiroshima, after atomic bombing of 6 August 1945. Courtesy of the National Archives.

The Kremlin's nineteen towers, with its belfries, ramparts, ancient battlements and monumental buildings, were instantly destroyed. Also pulverised, melted down and swept upward were dozens of shimmering gold crosses which had topped the onion-shaped cupolas of the Kremlin's ancient cathedrals. These magnificent churches had been built in the fifteenth and sixteenth centuries by the Tsars, such as Ivan the Terrible. The Kremlin's main open area was called Cathedral Square. The cathedrals had been used by the Communist government as art museums. They stood alongside the government buildings inside the Kremlin's walls.[7]

The blast and heat immediately and totally demolished other Kremlin buildings:

– the enormous Palace of Congresses, the Council of Ministers building, the Great Kremlin Palace, and other government edifices.

– the fifteenth-century Assumption Cathedral, whose architectural proportions were considered perfect, and whose southern doors had been covered with black lacquered copper sheets overlaid with twenty biblical scenes wrought in gold.

– the austere, gemlike Chapel of the Deposition of the Garments, a masterwork of fifteenth-century architecture, with pure white stone walls, grey roof and a round silver dome topped by a gold cross.

– the Cathedral of the Annunciation, whose priceless Byzantine frescoes, which were restored in 1947 by Soviet artists, were mostly themes from the Apocalypse.

Just outside the Kremlin walls, three hundred Soviet citizens, waiting patiently in line for a glimpse of Lenin in his red granite tomb, were evaporated and sucked into the mushroom cloud. Near by, on the south side of Red Square, the grandiose, lavishly ornamented Cathedral of St Basil the Blessed, with its exotic, multicoloured steeples and domes, was twisted like toffee and smashed to the ground. (According to legend, Ivan the Terrible had blinded the architect of St Basil's to prevent him from ever again designing anything so beautiful.) Stones from the cathedral mixed with broken pieces of concrete and steel from GUM, the largest department store in the USSR.

GUM was incinerated along with one thousand shoppers.

Within a radius of one-and-a-half miles from the centre of the explosion, nothing recognisable remained. The Pushkin Museum of Fine Arts, with its world-renowned collection of ancient Egyptian art and its modern paintings by Cézanne, Renoir, Monet and Degas, was levelled. The offices of the KGB, the secret police, collapsed with a roar, mixing the furniture of the upper levels with the awful torture instruments of the basement cells. Gone were the Historical Museum on Red Square and the Lenin Library with the largest book collections in the USSR. Gone were the Moscow Theatre of Drama and Comedy, the Light Opera Theatre, the Rossiya Cinema, the Central Children's Theatre, the Film Actors' Studio, the Tolstoi Museum. The aristocratic-looking estates and mansions of Kropotkin Street melted like butter. Along Kalinin Avenue skyscrapers twenty-five storeys high split apart and crashed to the ground. Animals died with their trainers at the Moscow State Circus. The only evidence of the former Kremlin was a ragged, triangular heap of stones showing where the massive, twelve to sixteen-foot-thick walls once had stood.

Of the one million people living, working and shopping in the area, ninety-eight per cent were killed by heat, blast or radiation. Nearly all the twenty thousand who survived had received multiple injuries and radiation poisoning.

In the area between one-and-a-half and three miles from the centre of the explosion, winds of three hundred miles per hour hurled burning trucks and cars end over end, splashing petrol and igniting new fires. Only the strongest steel and reinforced-concrete structures survived the blast, but their windows and walls were completely blown out. Fifty per cent of the one million people in the area died immediately. Forty per cent were badly injured. Only ten per cent remained unhurt.

The few who escaped injury were overwhelmed by the devastation and the casualties around them. Unspeakable horrors met their eyes. Seated in little clumps were people who had gazed directly at the flash, their faces charred and black, their eyesockets left hollow. Others staggered about aimlessly, with fixed, cataleptic stares, their clothes torn off by the force of the blast, their lacerated bodies drenched with blood.

Fire engines destroyed in Hiroshima bombimg, 6 August 1945.
Official U.S. Air Force photo.

Everywhere in the wreckage were nightmarish piles of charcoal cadavers, some with blackened arms raised stiffly upward, hands clutching the air, as if in prayer. People with singed hair and broken bones sat or limped with their limbs hanging askew. Some people, as though carrying some-thing, held out arms with oozing, raw skin, torn and hanging down like rags. Others, sickened from radiation, were bent over double, vomiting blood and foam.

Around them their familiar physical world was gone. A moment ago there had been broad boulevards, green parks and stately buildings. There had been gardeners tending

brightly coloured flower-beds; students hurrying toward
school; soldiers marching with rifles slung over their shoul-
ders; stooped, wrinkled babushkas (grandmothers) with
puffed cheeks and scarves tied under their chins pushing
children in baby carriages; street vendors selling ice-cream
and fruit.

Now everything was a nightmare of rubble, yellowish
smoke, cinders and ashes. The earth itself seemed convulsed in flames. Buses and cars, overturned and
grotesquely twisted, looked like burned beetles. The wide
roads had become narrow trails snaking through huge piles
of ruptured concrete and tortured steel. Telephone-poles
leaned at crazy angles, their wires tangled like spiders' webs
on the ground. Thousands of bricks covered the earth in
little piles, as if they had never been walls. Torn-up trolley
tracks jutted and twisted into the air like snakes. Trees
were pulled up by the roots, stripped of branches and
leaves; their trunks were mutilated as if hit by lightning,
and they hissed and smoked in the dense choking air.
Splinters of glass by the million glittered red, reflecting the
dancing sparks.

New blasts of heat scalded the survivors' skins and made
their clothes smoulder. Their ears were assaulted by the
groans and cries of the injured, the screams of those caught
in the fire, the voices of lost children calling for their
parents. Even more terrifying were the crumbling sounds
of weakened buildings and highway bridges.

Those who could rushed desperately away from the blaze
spreading out from central Moscow. They stumbled over
debris and abandoned in guilty terror people who were
pinned under chunks of concrete. They fled with the
anguished heart-rending cries of 'Help, please help me,'
ringing in their ears.

More of the injured lay in heaps among the dead. Some
had struggled to their feet. Others groped and crawled out
of demolished buildings, only to be engulfed by the gathering inferno. Small groups huddled together. Others dug
desperately through piles of tangled boards and torn plas-

Frame house destroyed in 2⅓ seconds by atomic bomb test.
(1) House before test. (2) Smouldering paint. (3) Smoke gone
before blast wave hits.

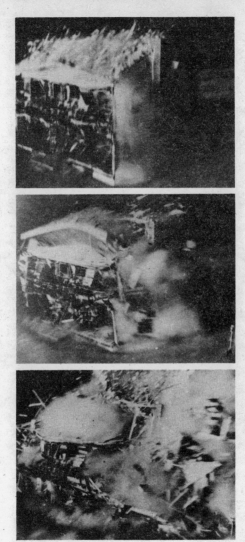

(4-6) Blast wave destroys house. Courtesy of Federal Civil Defense Administration (Federal Emergency Management Agency).

ter, searching for children, parents, brothers, sisters, friends.

To escape the terrible heat and to cool their blistering flesh, thousands of people threw themselves into the Moscow River. Soon it was almost filled with both the living and the dead.

The intense wave of heat swept out mercilessly from the centre of the explosion. Everything it touched was burned as if exposed to the flash of a gigantic, superheated sun lamp. African students walking to class at Lumumba University received third-degree flash burns and burns from the spontaneous ignition of their clothing.

The blast wave followed several seconds behind the pulse of heat. Mikhail Kramskoi, a dissident writer working near Moscow State University on a secret manuscript exposing Soviet violations of human rights, was killed by a flying piece of timber. University students studying near windows were covered from head to foot by glass fragments, which made their bodies into living pincushions.

The area three to five miles from the blast's centre suffered hurricane-force winds of well over a hundred miles per hour. Brick and wood-frame houses were totally destroyed, their walls caved in by the shock wave. Many apartment houses, factories and office buildings were knocked from their foundations. Others remained standing, but fragilely, with windows shattered and contents swept into the streets. Fires ignited by the bomb's heat and fed by crumpled oil storage tanks, overturned cars and severed gas pipelines, gutted most of the buildings that remained.

In the three to five-mile radius beyond central Moscow five per cent of the population were dead; forty-five per cent were injured; half survived unhurt.

At five to seven miles from the centre of the city, children on bicycles received second- and third-degree burns on exposed skin. Since lighter-coloured cloth reflects heat better than darker material, the pattern of their clothing was in some cases burned into their flesh.

Paint blistered off houses. The leaves of trees caught fire.
The heat passed through windows and ignited beds and
upholstery. Commercial buildings were only lightly damaged, but winds blew roofs off residential homes and
scattered fiery embers everywhere.

At this distance, a quarter of the people were injured;
three-quarters were unhurt. Many of those not hurt had
been in basements or were otherwise shielded from the
heat and debris.

Their fortune was short lived, however. Five minutes
after the rocket fired by Major Butts hit the Kremlin, other
nuclear bombs began falling. The explosions covered the
tormented city, its suburbs and outlying districts with blast,
heat and radiation. They showered on Moscow over a
thousand times more destructive power than was used
against Hiroshima and Nagasaki in 1945.

One million, five hundred and twenty thousand people
were killed by the weapon fired by Major Butts. Over four
million died in the subsequent blasts. The last bombs to fall
no longer killed anyone. They simply ground the rubble
into finer powder.

'And when it is all over what will the world be like? Our fine great buildings, our homes will exist no more. The thousands of years it took to develop our civilisation will have been in vain. Our works of art will be lost. Radio, television, newspapers will disappear. There will be no means of transport. There will be no hospitals. No help can be expected for the few mutilated survivors in any town to be sent from a neighbouring town – there will be no neighbouring towns left, no neighbours, there will be no help, there will be no hope. How can we stand by and do nothing to prevent the destruction of the world?'

Lord Louis Mountbatten[1]

'One of the best kept secrets of our day is the amount of disaster that nuclear weapons can produce.'

Fr Richard McSorley, SJ[2]

2

The Awesome Destruction

On 6 August 1945 the American B-29 bomber *Enola Gay* dropped a thirteen-kiloton atomic bomb on Hiroshima. It flattened the city and killed 130,000 people. Today the world's atomic weapons hold a lethal equivalent of over two tons of dynamite for every man, woman and child on earth, or 853,000 Hiroshimas.

In chapter one we imagined a nuclear attack on Moscow. It was a fictional account, but it was based on fact. It showed what would happen to one city in the first hour of a nuclear war. In an all-out nuclear exchange the ghastly scenario of chapter one would be repeated thousands of times. And not only Soviet targets would be hit. Soviet rockets would hit Western Europe and the USA.

In this chapter we will look at what would happen on a large scale if nuclear war broke out. As in chapter one our descriptions are based on respected scientific and governmental reports and on scholarly studies of the devastation of Hiroshima and Nagasaki.[3] Much of the most important data comes from the US government. Many careful studies (see Appendix A) describe in detail what we can expect during nuclear conflict.

The Area of Impact

What would it be like if a Soviet SS-N-8[4] rocket were exploded over the White House in Washington? Imagine a circle with a radius of one-and-a-half miles with the White House at its centre. A US government study estimates that within the circle, ninety-eight per cent of the people would die.[5] The Lincoln and Jefferson Memorials would be levelled. The Capitol would be shattered. All the national treasures and monuments in the Smithsonian Institute, the National Gallery of Art, the Library of Congress and the National Archives would be destroyed. No building would remain standing.

Outside the circle, the devastation would be enormous. Buildings would collapse and burn as far out as Georgetown University to the west and Washington National Airport to the south. People would suffer third-degree skin burns as far away as Alexandria, Virginia, and Takoma Park, Maryland. With normal prevailing winds, radioactive fallout would spread a cigar-shaped swath of sickness and death eastward across Maryland and out to Cape May, New Jersey.

In the Washington metropolitan area (beyond the blast radius), sixty thousand people would be killed and eight hundred thousand injured. Of the six thousand doctors in the area, fifteen hundred would be killed and two thousand seriously injured, leaving only two thousand five hundred to care for all the wounded. Hospital care would be minimal because Capital Hospital, DC General, and the hospitals at Howard, Georgetown and George Washington universities would be destroyed.

What if a similar bomb exploded over New York's Empire State Building? It would destroy almost every building on Manhattan Island. It would kill nearly everyone in a circle encompassing Riverside Church on the north, the World Trade Centre on the south, large sections of Brooklyn and Queens on the east, and Union City, New Jersey, on the west.

What if the much larger Soviet SS-9 rocket, with its twenty-megaton warhead, exploded at ground level in the Chicago Loop? It would crush the inner city area like a giant sledgehammer, exerting over fifteen hundred times the force of the bomb that levelled Hiroshima.[6] The blast would dig out a crater a mile and a half wide and six hundred feet deep. Its two-hundred-foot-high lip would extend almost to Lake Michigan. Buildings would be totally destroyed and nearly everyone killed up to four miles from 'ground zero' (the point of impact).

Destruction one mile from centre of Hiroshima blast. Official U.S. Air Force photo.

At seven to eight miles away, along the Stevenson Expressway, oil-storage tanks would explode. Windows would shatter and trees catch fire at Midway Airport, ten miles from the Loop. Picket fences and people's skin would burn as far away as suburban Hinsdale, sixteen miles from the centre of town.[7] The explosion would kill 4.2 million people and seriously injure 1.7 million more.[8]

These illustrations assume only one nuclear weapon falling on a city. In an actual nuclear war, the largest cities would probably receive many more. For example, the US Arms Control and Disarmament Agency estimated the effects of nuclear war with a computer simulation. The researchers assumed that the two hundred largest cities in both the United States and the USSR would each be hit by so many bombs that they would be totally destroyed. In addition, eighty per cent of all cities with populations of twenty-five thousand or more would be hit by at least one atomic bomb.[9]

In *London After the Bomb: What a nuclear attack really means* (see Appendix A), five scientists examine the consequences for London of an attack with four nuclear warheads, with two others landing near by (the scale of attack presumed in the Government's civil defence exercise, Operation Square Leg, in September 1980). The authors conclude that such an attack would result within three months in the death of 76 per cent of the population of London, or more than five million people. Square Leg postulated about 200 megatons exploding on Britain (about 13,000 Hiroshimas). But in March 1981, the Secretary for the Air Force, Mr Geoffrey Pattie, stated in a Parliamentary written answer that 'more than 1,000 megatons would be needed to destroy the ground-launched cruise missiles once they were dispersed.' That is the rough equivalent of 65,000 Hiroshimas landing on Britain. The cruise missiles are due to start arriving in Britain before Christmas 1983.[10]

Who Gets Hit

When people learn of these effects on cities, they sometimes imagine that they would be safer in rural areas. But there are almost no safe areas. In both Western Europe and the States, missiles are deployed in rural areas. Many of America's 1,052 nuclear-tipped missiles are located in farming areas outside places like Little Rock, Arkansas, Great Falls, Montana, and Wichita, Kansas. In a nuclear war these would be prime targets. The Soviet military would almost certainly try to knock them out, probably by targeting two warheads on each missile-silo.

The small town of Sedalia (population 22,000) is near the centre of a Missouri missile field. In an attack, the temperature on Main Street would rise to about 2,000°F. Sedalia and everything in it would disappear in a twenty-five-mile-high mushroom cloud.

The area that would be destroyed by such an attack would be bigger than the state of Delaware. If the wind were blowing from the west, as it usually is, the radioactive fallout would travel one hundred and seventy miles to Saint Louis, where it would kill 1.18 million people. On the way it would blanket the countryside and dozens of rural towns with deadly fallout. Given the right winds, the radioactive cloud would flow over Louisville and Cincinnati, across the Appalachians and Richmond, Virginia, and out over the Atlantic, poisoning more people on the way. This one attack on one missile field would cover about two per cent of the continental United States with radiation.[11]

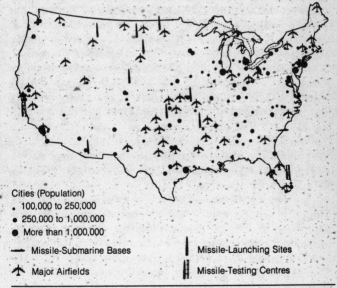

Cities (Population)
- . 100,000 to 250,000
- • 250,000 to 1,000,000
- ● More than 1,000,000

— Missile-Submarine Bases | Missile-Launching Sites

✈ Major Airfields   ⫼ Missile-Testing Centres

Figure 1. Potential Military, Population and Economic Targets in the United States. From Kevin N. Lewis, "The Prompt & Delayed Effects of Nuclear War." Copyright © July 1979 by Scientific American, Inc. All rights reserved.

Similar missile bases are in Arizona, Arkansas, Indiana, Kansas, Montana, North and South Dakota, Utah and Wyoming. In fact, there are 68 such strategic targets in the United States.[12] If we consider *all* the nuclear weapons located in the United States which Soviet rockets would probably strike, there are 121 sites in forty states.[13]

Who Would Survive

What would the world be like after a nuclear war? Some people have argued that a nuclear war could be *limited*; that is, the attack and counterattack would not be total. The nuclear powers would limit themselves to selected military or industrial targets. But even in the case of limited nuclear war, the destruction and loss of life would be immense.

Several studies have been done on the impact of a limited nuclear war. The US Office of Technology Assessment, for example, did a study to examine what would happen in a nuclear exchange where the United States and the USSR hit only oil refineries, with each country using eighty warheads.[14] Within the first hour, the report concluded, the Soviet attack would kill 3 to 5 million Americans. The American attack would kill 1 to 1.5 million Soviet citizens.[15] Sixty-four per cent of US oil-refining capacity and seventy-three per cent of Soviet capacity would be wiped out.[16] The American economy, with its heavy dependence on petroleum, would be shattered. Both countries would face the crisis of how to operate transportation and industry and how to heat homes and shops in the virtual absence of petrol and oil.

The same government study projected the result of a limited attack on each country's military installations. It concluded that under the best imaginable circumstances, more than a million people would die in each country. In less favourable circumstances, 20 million could die in the United States and 10 million in the USSR. Large portions of both countries would be covered by radioactive fallout, which would cause sickness and death for years to come.[17]

These figures, however, are based on the assumption

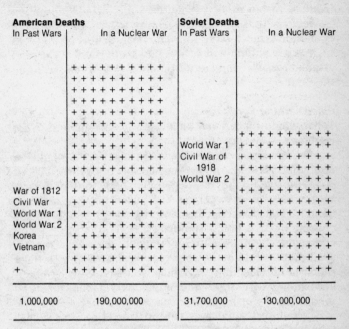

American Deaths		Soviet Deaths	
In Past Wars	In a Nuclear War	In Past Wars	In a Nuclear War
	+ + + + + + + + +		
	+ + + + + + + + +		
	+ + + + + + + + +		
	+ + + + + + + + +		
	+ + + + + + + + +		
	+ + + + + + + + +		
	+ + + + + + + + +		+ + + + + + + + +
	+ + + + + + + + +	World War 1	+ + + + + + + + +
	+ + + + + + + + +	Civil War of	+ + + + + + + + +
	+ + + + + + + + +	1918	+ + + + + + + + +
	+ + + + + + + + +	World War 2	+ + + + + + + + +
War of 1812	+ + + + + + + + +		+ + + + + + + + +
Civil War	+ + + + + + + + +	+ +	+ + + + + + + + +
World War 1	+ + + + + + + + +	+ + + + +	+ + + + + + + + +
World War 2	+ + + + + + + + +	+ + + + +	+ + + + + + + + +
Korea	+ + + + + + + + +	+ + + + +	+ + + + + + + + +
Vietnam	+ + + + + + + + +	+ + + + +	+ + + + + + + + +
	+ + + + + + + + +	+ + + + +	+ + + + + + + + +
+	+ + + + + + + + +	+ + + + +	+ + + + + + + + +
1,000,000	190,000,000	31,700,000	130,000,000

Each + represents one million people.

Figure 2. Deaths in Past Wars Compared to Estimated Casualties in a Full-Scale Nuclear War. Adapted from The Defense Monitor, *Feb. 1979, p. 8.*

that the war would be limited. But if nuclear war comes, it is likely (as we will argue in chapter three) that it will be all-out, with warheads hitting population centres as well as military and industrial targets. What would a full-scale war be like? What would be its effect on human beings? on human society? on the environment?

The Office of Technology Assessment assembled the best available estimates of what full-scale nuclear war would be like. Its report calculated that 'a very large attack

against a range of military and economic targets' would kill
from 70 to 160 million Americans and up to 100 million
Soviet citizens. If population centres, as well as military and
economic targets, were hit, American deaths could be as
high as 190 million people – eighty-six per cent of the total
population. As many as 130 million Soviet people could
die. (See figure 2.)

The World of Survivors

What would life be like for those who do survive? What
problems would they face?

Medical care and sanitation. Rescue work would be
almost impossible. In any built-up location, thousands of
survivors would be trapped under collapsed buildings.
Heavy equipment which could be used to extricate them
would be destroyed or unable to pass through streets
cluttered with rubble. Ambulances and other rescue vehicles would be unable to penetrate the clogged streets.[18]
And there would be nowhere for the ambulances to take
the injured. Hospitals and clinics would have been obliterated along with their doctors, nurses, technicians and
medicines.

The relatively small bomb dropped on Hiroshima in 1945
killed or injured 270 of the city's 298 doctors. Hiroshima's
eighteen hospitals and thirty-two first-aid stations were all
demolished or badly damaged. When ten thousand wounded people made their way to the Red Cross Hospital, only
six doctors (out of a staff of thirty doctors and two hundred
nurses) were available to help them.

If a 'small' nuclear attack hit Boston, says a US Senate
Committee study, only one hospital bed would be available
for every twenty injured people. Of the six thousand
physicians in Boston, only six hundred would be uninjured
after the attack.[19] And with medical facilities in a shambles,
what would they work with? Medical care, in most cases,
would mean treatment without laboratory equipment, x-
rays, drugs, plasma and the like.

Medical problems in the USSR would be no less severe.

Operating room of Nagasaki University Hospital after atomic bombing of 9 August 1945. Floor and balconies consumed by fire. Official U.S. Air Force photo.

A US government study of a hypothetical attack estimated that ninety-three per cent of Moscow's hospitals would be destroyed. Eighty per cent of all urban hospitals in the Soviet Union would be gone.[20]

In Western Europe as well as in the United States and the USSR, skilled medical professionals are concentrated in the areas most likely to be hit. Therefore, the most highly skilled and the most desperately needed specialists would be the ones who would die by the thousand in the urban holocausts. Medicines and medical supplies also tend to be concentrated in urban areas and so would be largely lost. Surviving doctors and nurses would be overwhelmed by the people clamouring for treatment exactly at the moment that medical supplies were sharply reduced. In addition, major stocks of drugs would be wiped out, since the pharmaceutical industry is 'one of the eight critical industries targeted for maximum destruction.'[21] John Hershey describes a Hiroshima doctor trying to cope with this overwhelming catastrophe at the Red Cross Hospital:

> The hospital was in horrible confusion: heavy partitions and ceilings had fallen on patients, beds had overturned, windows had blown in and cut people, blood was splattered on the walls and floors, instruments were everywhere, many of the patients were running about screaming, many more lay dead. . . .
>
> Dr Sasaki worked without method, taking those who were nearest him first, and he noticed soon that the corridor seemed to be getting more and more crowded. Mixed in with the abrasions and lacerations which most people in the hospital had suffered, he began to find dreadful burns. He realised then that casualties were pouring in from outdoors. . . .
>
> Tugged here and there in his stockinged feet, bewildered by the numbers, staggered by so much raw flesh, Dr Sasaki lost all sense of profession and stopped working as a skilful surgeon and sympathetic man; he became an automaton, mechanically wiping, daubing, winding, wiping, daubing, winding.[22]

Perhaps the most severe medical problems would be the burns. Under normal conditions, severe burn patients require highly skilled medical teams working in specially designed acute-care centres. 'Just to keep one such patient alive taxes us,' says Dr John Burke, director of the Massachusetts General Hospital Burn Unit.[23]

The entire United States has only twelve burn centres and facilities for a maximum of two thousand severe burn cases. But just *one* nuclear explosion could produce over *ten thousand* such cases.[24] An all-out nuclear war might create twenty-five million severe burn victims.

Most burns would be inflicted by the intense heat of the bomb, but others would be caused by fires that sprang up throughout the damaged area. The thousands of small fires would be almost impossible to fight. Fire engines and their crews would already be disabled. 'In Hiroshima, some 70% of the city's firefighting equipment was crushed in the collapse of fire stations and 80% of the firemen did not report to their posts.'[25] Those firefighters who survived unhurt would not be able to move equipment through cluttered streets. Broken water mains would not deliver the water needed to fight fires. The crews might even face a firestorm, which would be impossible to fight, because of its enormously high temperatures.

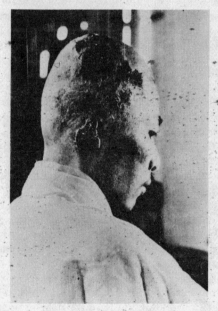

Burned survivor of Hiroshima bomb. Courtesy of the National Archives.

Sanitation would also be a major problem. Nuclear war would breach the sophisticated wall of prevention which civilisation has erected against mass epidemics. Water and sewage systems would be destroyed; raw sewage would mix with drinking water. Disease would spread from unburied corpses, and epidemics would be carried by viruses, bacteria and insects which are resistant to radiation. Old pestilences, like plague, influenza, polio, cholera, typhus and typhoid would spread throughout the world.

The impact of radiation. About twenty per cent of the people killed in an attack would die from exposure to radiation. Hospitals and first-aid stations would be swamped with people who were vomiting and wrenched with diarrhoea. Some would die almost immediately. Others would seem to improve, but in several days their hair would fall out, and they would become weak and feverish. Ulcers would form on their skin, and they would bleed internally. Their immune system would break down and massive infection would set in. If the body had been too weakened to resist, death would follow – but only after days or weeks of agony.

The particles and waves given off in an atomic explosion cause radiation disease. They enter the human body like x-rays, penetrating cell walls and damaging or destroying tissues. A nuclear explosion gives off both direct and indirect radiation. In the first few seconds the bomb produces direct radiation which kills anyone close to it by destroying brain and nerve tissue.

Indirect or residual radiation is what we refer to as fallout. Whereas direct radiation lasts a few seconds at most, fallout can be lethal for hours, days or even years. Fallout is produced when the radiation from a nuclear explosion irradiates the material pulverised by the bomb's blast. This debris is drawn up into the stem of the mushroom cloud. The heavier material falls to earth near the blast site. Smaller, dustlike particles are carried high into the air and picked up by prevailing winds which may take them hundreds of miles. The eruption of the Mt St Helen's volcano in 1980 produced nonradioactive 'fallout' which was carried completely across the continental United States.

The tiniest particles are carried into the stratosphere

from which fallout will descend in various parts of the world for months or even years after the explosion. The US Office of Technology Assessment notes that 'some fallout from US and Soviet weapons tests in the 1950s and early 1960s can still be detected.'[26]

When fallout drops to earth, its radiation has the same effect as direct radiation. It damages cells and causes sickness and death. Since radioactivity is invisible, tasteless and odourless, people hundreds of miles from an explosion may not realise that the air they are breathing, the food they are eating, or the water they are drinking has been contaminated and can kill or injure them.

People in fallout shelters receive some protection, but even the best shelters cannot completely block radiation in heavy fallout zones. Few are equipped with ventilation systems that keep out noxious gases or tiny radioactive particles. According to the US Office of Technology Assessment, therefore, the best many shelter occupants can hope for is to become very sick rather than to die.[27]

Even where immediate illness does not occur, radiation can cause cancer and future genetic problems. Leukaemia and other cancers crop up years after exposure. Japanese people exposed to the bomb, for example, developed by the mid-1950s a leukaemia death rate thirty times higher than that of the rest of Japan.[28] Scientists have established a direct correlation between exposure to nuclear radiation and the incidence of cancer of the thyroid, breast, lung and salivary glands.[29] A US government study estimated that 'cancer deaths in the millions could be expected during the forty years following a large nuclear attack, even if that attack avoided targets in population centres.'[30]

The same study estimated that, in addition to cancer, a large nuclear exchange would cause up to six million natural abortions (due to the effect of radiation on chromosomes) in the United States, eight million in the USSR, and five million in other countries. It would also cause as many as thirty-six million 'genetic effects' – for example, mutations resulting in deformed babies and increased genetic diseases – throughout the world.[31] Furthermore, these genetic effects would continue over thirty generations.[32]

One of the properties of radioactive materials is that their radiation levels 'decay'; that is, the amount of radiation they produce decreases with time. Some radioactive materials, however, are extremely long-lived. The Bikini Atoll in the Pacific, where the US Navy conducted twenty-three atomic tests between 1946 and 1958, was not declared safe for human habitation until 1968 – and there is still some debate about its safety. In spite of a $100-million government clean-up programme, the northern islands of Eniwetok Atoll, the site of forty-three nuclear tests, are off-limits for thirty more years because of the continuing high levels of radioactivity.[33]

Nuclear attacks on some civilian targets could greatly increase radiation levels from a nuclear war. A warhead striking a nuclear waste storage site would release enormous quantities of radioactivity into the atmosphere.[34] The same thing would happen if a nuclear weapon hit a nuclear power plant. This could create hundreds of Three Mile Islands with lethal radioactive releases. A 1,000-megawatt nuclear power plant contains as much radioactive material as 1,000 nuclear bombs like the one that hit Hiroshima.

Governments may try to protect their populations against radiation by building fallout shelters. The Soviet Union has already constructed an extensive system. But survival in such shelters would be very difficult. A US government study estimated that residents of Moscow who escaped into a well-built shelter during a nuclear attack would have to stay inside the shelter twenty-four hours a day for the first month. During the second month, radiation levels would still be so high that they could venture out only six hours per day.[35] Thus, if the shelter did not collapse, become superheated or allow radiation to penetrate the ventilation system, the people inside would still need a two-month supply of food, water and medicine to survive.

Governments may instead try to evacuate large cities, removing people from areas where the devastation would be greatest. The USSR has extensive evacuation plans, and the US Federal Emergency Management Agency is preparing some. If the attack came while evacuation were underway, however, people would be caught in the open and even more would die than if they had stayed inside. And relocation would just be the beginning of the problems faced by survivors.[36]

Basic human needs. Survivors would face the problem of finding food, housing, clothing and other necessities. Ninety per cent of urban (and a substantial portion of rural) housing would be destroyed. Fuel and energy for cooking meals and lighting buildings would be in extremely short supply. Heating systems would be inoperable, so a winter war would be even more devastating in more northern areas.

Food production would also be radically reduced. Damage to feed stores, grain elevators, warehouses, processing plants and transport systems would mean that food would quickly become scarce. 'If the attack takes place during the growing season,' says a US government study, 'then up to 30% of the crops could be lost . . . over half of the grazing animals would die and over a quarter of the large farm animals fed on stored food would die.'[37]

The lack of machinery, fuel, pesticides and fertilisers would undercut production, and energy to process the food would be in short supply, as would refrigeration and transport.

Industry and government. According to the US Senate Committee on Banking, industry would suffer an even more devastating blow than agriculture.[38] The missiles carried in five or six submarines have enough firepower to eliminate all the industries on which a modern economy depends. Survivors would face a fearful future. They would have to restore enough production to meet basic needs, although most factories and machinery would be damaged, destroyed or radioactive, and millions of skilled people would be dead or injured. It would be essential to do this before stocks of food and clothing and so on ran out completely. 'If production rises to the rate of consumption before stocks are exhausted,' says a government report, 'then viability has been achieved and economic recovery has begun. If not, then each postwar year would see a lower level of economic activity than the year before, and the future of civilisation itself in the nations attacked would be in doubt.'[39]

Popular Hiroshima shopping centre after atomic bombing.
Courtesy of the National Archives.

In response to the turmoil, any remaining government would either break down or resort to authoritarian methods to try to achieve order and allocate scarce resources. Cherished freedoms, legal rights and democratic political institutions would disappear in the rubble.

The environment.   Even broader than the impact of nuclear war on industry and government would be its effect on the ecosystem on which all life depends. Although controversies rage around the degree of effect, a considerable body of scientific evidence suggests that nuclear war would have a disastrous and perhaps irreparable impact on the environment.

According to these reports, a total nuclear war would seriously disrupt the ozone layer of the atmosphere. This layer, which consists of a special form of oxygen, screens out ultraviolet rays from the sun. It permits only enough rays to reach the earth to give us a sunburn.

A National Academy of Sciences' report estimates that a war using one-half of the strategic nuclear weapons held by the United States and the USSR could reduce the ozone in the Northern Hemisphere by thirty to seventy per cent.[40] Thus, a person going out in the sun for a half-hour or more would get blistering burns on any exposed skin. Many plants, animals and food crops would also be destroyed by the increased ultraviolet radiation.[41] Human skin cancer rates would also increase.[42] These harmful effects of ozone depletion would last for several years.

According to some studies, nuclear war could also alter the world's climate, possibly raising or lowering average temperatures. This could further damage agriculture and reduce already short food supplies. And radioactive fallout would affect animal populations and crops. For example, many insects can withstand much higher radiation doses than birds. So, crop-devouring insects and other pests might flourish when their natural predators were removed.[43]

When the combined effects of all these disasters are added together, some scientists conclude that all human life would come to an end after nuclear war, leaving the world to the cockroaches, which are four hundred times more resistant to radiation than human beings.[44] Others believe that 'the planet earth would eventually become inhabited by bands of roving humanoids – mutants barely recognisable as members of our species.'[45] Others believe that some humans would survive, but at a level comparable to that of the medieval period of human history.[46] A few are more optimistic, contending that even after such a shattering blow, long-term recovery to the level of a modest industrial society would be possible.[47]

No one doubts, however, that deaths and injuries would be in the millions, that industrial civilisation would be largely destroyed, and that long-term effects would create gargantuan problems for any remaining human life. As the National Academy of Sciences' study said, 'No report can portray the enormity, the utter horror which must befall the targeted areas and adjoining territories.'[48]

'The United States and all countries must find ways to control and reduce the horrifying danger that is posed by the world's stockpiles of nuclear arms. It may be only a matter of time before madness, desperation, greed or miscalculation lets loose this terrible force. . . . In an all-out nuclear war, more destructive power than in all of World War II would be unleashed every second for the long afternoon it would take for all the missiles and bombs to fall. A World War II every second – more people killed in the first few hours than all the wars of history put together.

The survivors, if any, would live in despair amid the poisoned ruins of a civilisation that had committed suicide.'

Former President Jimmy Carter[1]

3

Will Nuclear Weapons be Used?

In this chapter we must face the chilling question: Will the
nations of the world ever use nuclear weapons? To
approach that question knowledgeably, we will first look at
what nuclear weapons are and how they work. Then we will
examine some of the reasons why such incredibly destructive weapons have been built.

A Primer on Nuclear Weapons

How do strategic[2] nuclear weapons work? How do they
differ from conventional bombs? The first difference is that
over a third of the energy of a nuclear explosion is given off
in light and heat (see figure 3). The heat from a chemical
explosion is about 3000°C. The heat from a nuclear blast is
10 million°C or more. At close range, these extraordinary
temperatures incinerate both buildings and bodies. Many
miles away, the heat still causes serious skin burns. In
Hiroshima and Nagasaki today visitors can meet A-bomb
survivors whose bodies are covered with 'keloids,' the
grotesque scars caused by deep burns.

Nuclear detonation ignites secondary fires wherever
there is anything to burn. These may unite to create a
'firestorm' – a sea of fire covering many square miles with
tremendous winds and temperatures exceeding 700°C, hot
enough to melt glass and metal.

Nuclear weapons also differ from the conventional type
by producing harmful radiation. Large doses of radiation
cause rapid death. Lesser amounts can bring on a more

Cause		Effect	The Bomb's Energy
	Heat	Incineration, fires, skin burns	33%
	Blast	Bodies smashed, buildings collapsed, flying glass and other debris	50%
	Direct Nuclear Radiation	Radiation deaths	7%
	Radioactive Fallout	Radiation deaths, illnesses, and long-term effects (e.g., cancer)	10%

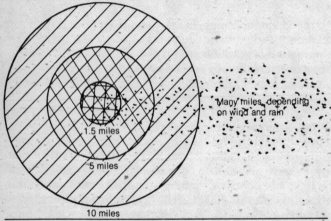

Figure 3. Effects of One-Megaton Weapon Exploded Near the Ground. From Sidney D. Drell and Frank von Hipple, "Limited Nuclear War." Copyright © November 1976 by Scientific American, Inc. All rights reserved.

lingering death, debilitating sickness or cancer which appears months or years after exposure.

The only similarity between conventional and nuclear bombs is that much of their destructive power is created by blast. Blast is produced by a high-density, high-temperature ball of gas at the centre of the explosion. The gas expands rapidly, creating pressure changes, shock waves and high winds, which sweep away from the explosion point like rings from a pebble thrown into a pond. The

Description	Destructive Power
Amount of energy released by 1,000 tons of dynamite (TNT)	1 kiloton (kt.)
Power of the warhead that destroyed Hiroshima	13 kt.
U.S. Minuteman III warhead	510 kt.
One megaton (mt.)	1,000 kt.
Equivalent destructive power of all bombs dropped during the Vietnam war	4,000 kt.
Equivalent destructive power of all U.S. bombs dropped during the Vietnam war	4,000 kt.
Soviet SS019 missile	5,000 kt.
U.S. Titan II missile	10,000 kt.
Missiles in U.S. and Soviet submarines	1,502,000 kt.
Atomic bombs in U.S. and Soviet long-range bombers	2,224,000 kt.
Warheads on U.S. and Soviet land-based missiles (ICBMs)	7,363,000 kt.
Total U.S. and Soviet long-range nuclear arsenal	11,089,000 kt.

Figure 4. Power to Destroy the World.

blast from a nuclear explosion is thousands of times more powerful than that of the largest conventional bombs. Just one Soviet SS-19 missile, for example, carries more destructive power than *all* the conventional bombs dropped during World War II (see figure 4).

The size of the explosion also distinguishes *atomic* from *hydrogen* bombs. Both can be called atomic, since their explosive power is derived from atomic reactions. In a stricter sense, however, an A-bomb is one whose detonation is caused by the splitting – or fission – of atomic nuclei (usually of plutonium or uranium) into approximately equal parts. An H-bomb, on the other hand, is detonated by the union – or fusion – of atomic nuclei of hydrogen to form nuclei of helium. A fusion bomb is more powerful than a fission bomb because, for a given weight of explosive, the energy released from the former is approximately four times as great as that from the latter. For our purposes, it is not so important to understand these complex reactions as to realise that both fission and fusion bombs release enormous quantities of energy. The United States and Western Europe and the USSR all have fission and fusion bombs in their arsenals. Both types would be used in a nuclear war.

East and West also possess both *strategic* and *tactical* nuclear weapons. Strategic weapons are those which are long-range and thus can travel from one continent to the other or which are so powerful that they can destroy huge areas at once. Both sides also possess tactical weapons which are designed for battlefield use and thus are short-range and less powerful.

In addition to these differences, nuclear bombs also vary in their means of deployment (that is, how they are launched). There are bombs which are launched from bombers, bombs which are carried by rockets launched from underground silos, and bombs which are carried on missiles fired from submarines. In the pages that follow we will examine these types of nuclear weapons.[3] What kind of nuclear firepower do East and West aim at each other?

Missile-firing submarines.   Rockets carried in nuclear-propelled submarines are the most destructive instruments ever created by the human mind. Just one submarine can carry rockets with as much destructive power as all the weapons used in World War II. Powered by a nuclear mass no larger than a baseball and capable of cruising over a hundred thousand miles while submerged, the nuclear subs are practically invulnerable. No country has yet developed effective defences against them or their missiles.

There are about ten (out of sixty-four) Soviet nuclear subs at sea at any one time.[4] Each carries enough nuclear warheads to obliterate Washington, Chicago, Dallas, San Francisco and other US cities. The United States maintains about twenty (out of forty-one) nuclear subs at sea. One of their missiles is powerful enough to destroy Moscow, Leningrad or Vladivostok. Eight French and British atomic subs are also at sea with their nuclear missiles trained on Soviet targets.

The submarine fleets of the United States and the North Atlantic Treaty Organisation (NATO) together carry about five thousand atomic warheads; the Soviet fleet carries about twelve hundred. Launched from their underwater platforms, Soviet, US and NATO rockets would land on their respective targets in fifteen minutes or less.

Land-based missiles. Also aimed at Western cities, factories and military bases are 1,398 Soviet land-based Intercontinental Ballistic Missiles (ICBMs). About half of these ICBMs carry 'packages' of three or more atomic warheads, each of which can separate from its carrier and land on a different target. Such missiles are said to be *MIRV*ed (that is, equipped with multiple, independently targetable re-entry vehicles). Thus, the Soviets have over five thousand atomic bombs mounted on their ICBMs.

For its part, the United States has 1,052 ICBMs pointed at the USSR. Over half of the Minuteman missile systems carry three nuclear warheads apiece, resulting in a total of over two thousand nuclear warheads to launch at the Soviet Union. Both East and West also possess intermediate-range and short-range missiles with nuclear warheads (IRBMs and SRBMs).

Bombers and air-launched missiles. In addition to submarines and ICBMs, the USSR has 156 long-range, piloted Bear and Bison bombers, which carry over six hundred atomic bombs, and 150 medium-to-long-range Backfire bombers capable of carrying atomic bombs. The US long-range bomber force is made up of 348 B-52 and 66 FB-111 aircraft carrying over two thousand five hundred nuclear bombs.

Because they travel more slowly than rockets, 'heavy bombers' are easier to destroy with anti-aircraft weapons and fighter planes than the land or sea-launched ICBMs, which plunge to earth from beyond the atmosphere at more than fifteen thousand miles per hour. However, the bombers are equipped with highly sophisticated defences, which make it likely that at least some would penetrate air defences and unload their bombs on target.

In addition to bombs, US long-range aircraft are being fitted with up to sixteen cruise missiles. These so-called smart rockets can be launched from under the wing of a bomber as far as fifteen hundred miles from their targets. Thus, the heavy bombers would not need to enter enemy air space to be effective. They could simply fly over the North Pole and launch their cruise missiles. It is at present almost impossible to spot cruise missiles by radar, because they fly as low as fifty feet above the ground. Enemy fighter-interceptors and defensive missiles are not effective so close to the surface. Fired by the hundred, cruise missiles would overwhelm enemy defences and some would deliver their warheads with pinpoint accuracy to preprogrammed targets. Therefore, the chilling reality is that, once nuclear war starts, there is no defence. The Soviets cannot prevent Western rockets from landing on them. We cannot prevent theirs from landing on us.

How many weapons are involved in all? In a full-scale nuclear war, the United States and the USSR have the capacity to unload over fifteen thousand atomic bombs on each other. (This is counting only strategic weapons, the kind that can travel from one continent to another. If we include tactical weapons, the type that are short-range and designed mostly for battlefield use, the total number of atomic bombs is nearly fifty thousand.) With this number of warheads, the American nuclear arsenal can destroy every major Soviet city thirty-five times. The Soviets can destroy major American cities twenty times over.

The Reagan administration has proposed vastly to increase and improve US nuclear and conventional capabilities through a five-year defence expenditure of over a trillion dollars. The Soviet Union will not want to be left behind.

Meanwhile, the 'nuclear club' is growing. Britain, France, India and China have already tested their own atomic weapons. Experts estimate that, in the next two decades, a hundred countries who do not now have nuclear weapons will possess the raw materials and knowledge necessary to produce them. Others may simply buy the weapons from countries willing to sell them.

US officials predict that Israel, Pakistan and Libya will 'go nuclear' in the 1980s. Iraq had a nuclear reactor, which was attacked in an Israeli raid, and may try to obtain nuclear weapons. South Africa either has or will soon obtain atomic weapons. Some Latin American and Asian nations, such as Brazil and South Korea, are also expected to have nuclear weapons in less than twenty years. But none of these countries have arsenals approaching the destructive power of the United States and the USSR.

Deterrence

What purpose does all that power serve? Why are the major powers of the world building more and more bombs? Why do they risk obliterating everything they have built over the years? Why do they threaten one another with weapons of such unimaginable horror?

The answer usually given is 'deterrence.' Deterrence theory holds that, if each side has enough weapons to annihilate the other, and neither could destroy all the other's weapons in a first strike, then neither side will dare to start a war. Each side says to the other, 'If you attack us, we will blast you off the face of the earth.' The two sides may have apparently irreconcilable ideologies and interests, but the prospect of mutual suicide keeps both sides from starting a nuclear war.

Many Christians accept deterrence, however much they may be appalled by basing foreign policy on the ability to kill tens of millions of people at a stroke. This 'mutually assured destruction' (MAD, as it is called) may seem a far cry from Christ's gospel of love, but a broad spectrum of Christians argue that a leader must be willing to press the nuclear button. Otherwise enemies would see weakness and take advantage of it. They might attack and plunge us into World War III.

Thus far, nuclear weapons have created a standoff fraught with peril — a balance of terror. But how safe a barrier to annihilation is this? In the following sections we will look critically at the notion of deterrence to see its weaknesses. Nuclear war *has* almost happened. We have come to within a hair's breadth of nuclear holocaust. President John F. Kennedy said in 1961, 'Every man, woman and child lives under a nuclear sword of Damocles hanging by the slenderest thread, capable of being cut at any moment by accident, miscalculation, or madness.'[5] What type of thread is deterrence?

The Cuban missile crisis shows how close we have been to actual nuclear war. This crisis occurred in October 1962. Robert Kennedy, who was constantly at President John F. Kennedy's side during this time, called it 'a confrontation between the two giant atomic nations, the US and the USSR, which brought the world to the abyss of nuclear destruction and the end of mankind.'[6]

The secret Soviet delivery of nuclear missiles and bombers to Cuba triggered the crisis. President Kennedy called the Soviet move provocative and aggressive, and he demanded that Premier Khrushchev remove the weapons.

To emphasise his determination, the president put US missile crews and armed forces around the world on alert. He ordered the B-52 bomber fleet into the air, carrying atomic bombs. Ships of the United States Navy took up blockade positions around Cuba. Robert Kennedy told Soviet Ambassador Dobrynin that the Soviets must start to remove the missile outposts within twenty-four hours or the United States would remove them with military action.

Meanwhile, Soviet ships carrying missiles were headed toward the US blockade, possibly with orders to defy it. In the White House, 'the feeling grew that . . . a direct military confrontation between the two great nuclear powers was inevitable,' according to Robert Kennedy.[7] While President John Kennedy waited for Khrushchev's response, he reflected gravely that what disturbed him most 'was the spectre of the death of the children of this country and the world – the young people who had no role, who had no say, who knew nothing even of the confrontation, but whose lives would be snuffed out like everyone else's.[8]

In Moscow, Nikita Khrushchev was agonising about the same thing. As he later put it in a conversation with journalist Norman Cousins:

> When I asked the military advisors if they could assure me that holding fast [keeping Soviet missiles in Cuba] would not result in the death of 500 million human beings, they looked at me as though I was out of my mind or, what was worse, a traitor. The biggest tragedy, as they saw it, was not that our country might be devastated and everything lost, but that the Chinese or the Albanians would accuse us of appeasement or weakness.[9]

Fortunately for the world, the Soviet premier unexpectedly pulled the weapons out of Cuba, and the crisis ended.

Deterrence and International Crises

How might deterrence work in a future world crisis and how might it break down? This question deserves close examination.

One factor which allowed a peaceful solution to the Cuban crisis was time. Although pressures on government decision-makers were extreme, the Cuban crisis developed at a pace that allowed both sides to communicate, reflect, consult and plan with a degree of thoughtfulness. Another factor was the belief in each other's basic rationality. Both President Kennedy and Premier Khrushchev believed that neither would intentionally plunge the world into nuclear war if it could be avoided.

Future international crises may arise, however, which require much quicker decisions. Under the enormous stress of hurried decisions (often based on inadequate or incomplete information), national leaders may make a fateful mistake. Even an emotionally stable person can lose his or her balance in the grip of fear or exhaustion. Humans, including national leaders, are capable of an enormous amount of evil, folly, self-centredness, error and incompetence. Who can guarantee that future Soviet and American leaders will behave rationally, especially under extreme stress? And who knows what would happen if a leader like Libya's Khadafy had nuclear weapons at his disposal at a time of international crisis?

Irrationality and mental breakdown are dangers at many levels of government. Over a hundred thousand US military personnel are involved in programmes with access to or control over nuclear weapons systems. From 1975 to 1977 the Defense Department's Personnel Reliability Program removed over fifteen thousand people from their posts for reasons such as alcohol abuse, drug abuse, and aberrant behaviour.[10] The commanders of American Trident submarines have the power to devastate the Soviet Union (using the 408 warheads on each sub's ballistic missiles). What if those commanders (or the commander of a Soviet sub) were to lose emotional balance under the pressure of a crisis? Admiral Powell Carter, Navy Director of Strategic and Theatre Nuclear Warfare, admitted to CBS reporter Bob Schieffer that US submarine commanders (it takes more than one person per ship) can under certain circumstances fire their missiles without receiving any orders to do so.[11]

The tragic irony of nuclear deterrence is that we have placed in the hands of a few sinful, fallible human beings the power to annihilate humanity. The Cuban missile crisis, of course, is not the only crisis that has occurred since 1945. World tensions rose dramatically in the autumn of 1956 when the Soviet Union brutally crushed the Hungarian uprising. The Berlin crisis of 1961 saw the confrontation of US, British and Soviet tanks at 'Check-point Charlie' and the Brandenburg gate. At that time President Kennedy warned Soviet ambassador Andrei Gromyko that the United States was ready, if necessary, to go to war over Berlin.[12] Also, during the 1973 Yom Kippur war in the Middle East, all US forces were put on alert.[13] Over one hundred wars have convulsed various parts of the world since 1945.

In such times of tension, nations fear loss of prestige or erosion of their national interests. Leaders bluff and take risks. They engage in guessing games, wondering what the other side will do. Accident or miscalculation may set in motion an irreversible chain of events moving toward war between the superpowers.

The future will hold similar crises and dangers. Even now the superpowers and their allies are duelling politically over the world's energy resources, especially the oil of the Middle East. Each country faces a growing demand for energy which puts pressure on scarce reserves of petroleum, coal, natural gas and uranium. Industrial nations believe that their survival depends upon the accessibility of energy. Seeing nothing but catastrophic depression ahead, if energy is cut off, leaders of industrial nations may consider using desperate measures to keep their factories running.[14]

An estimated two-thirds of the oil reserves on which the Western world depends are in the Middle East.[15] President Carter declared in his 1980 State of the Union address: 'Any attempt by outside force to gain control of the Persian Gulf region will be regarded as an assault on the vital interests of the United States of America. And such an assault will be repelled by any means necessary, including military force.' President Reagan has firmly reinforced this commitment, and military advisers admit that because of the lack of US bases in the area, tactical nuclear weapons might have to be used.[16]

The Soviet Union, which has until recently been self-sufficient in oil, may someday be required to import it. A greater role in the Persian Gulf is very much in the Soviet Union's interest, as it would help to satisfy both its own and its allies' energy needs. And greater control over the oil reserves would give the USSR the ability to deny this vital resource to its enemies. As the nations of the Middle East become nuclear powers, the possibility of nuclear war resulting from Middle Eastern tensions will increase even more.

And the Middle East is just one of the many areas of the world where conflict between the superpowers could erupt. While conflict has erupted since 1945 without involving nuclear weapons, the chances exist that human fallibility will sooner or later allow a nuclear conflict to begin. How can we support a military policy (nuclear deterrence) which allows even a single chance of annihilation?

Deterrence and Technological Malfunction

Human fallibility is not the only weak link in the policy of deterrence. It is ironic that the superpowers' defence systems rely on a highly sophisticated technology which is also subject to breakdown. A recent example of this was the computer foul-up at the North American Aerospace Defence Command (NORAD) on 9 November 1979. NORAD is a computer and tracking centre in Colorado which receives satellite, radar and other information about possible Soviet attacks and signals appropriate US responses. One of the exercises carried out at NORAD is a computer simulation of a Soviet missile launch. This kind of computerised 'war game' helps military planners think through responses to various attacks.

On November 9 a computer tape simulating a Soviet attack from a submarine in the Pacific Ocean was broadcast inadvertently throughout the system.[17] US military forces were placed on alert, and Air Force fighters and interceptors took off in search of the missiles. Commercial aeroplanes were notified to prepare to land.

Seven months later, on 3 June 1980, another computer error warned that the Soviet Union had launched submarine and land-based missiles at the United States.[18] US defences were put on alert. Three days later a computer malfunction gave the false signal that the United States was being attacked by Soviet ICBMs and submarine-launched missiles.[19] It was discovered later that an electronic 'chip' costing forty-six cents had caused the false alarms.[20]

Fortunately, in all these cases the computer errors were discovered within three to six minutes through the checking and re-checking procedures which were, as one might imagine, immediately carried out. Nevertheless, we must pause to consider the consequences of an error's occurring at the height of an international crisis. These errors took three to six minutes to discover, and a missile fired from a Soviet submarine off the East Coast can land on Washington, DC, in five minutes.

Of course, Soviet computers undoubtedly also give false signals of attacks. In fact, Soviet computers may be more subject to failure than those used in the West.[21]

Such foul-ups are by no means unique. There have been other false alarms, including cases of geese flying across radar fields or shadows from the moon setting off the system.[22] A report issued by Senator Barry Goldwater (R-Ariz.) and Senator Gary Hart (D-Colo.), both of whom serve on the Senate Armed Services Committee, said that the US air defence system received 147 false alarms in a recent eighteen-month period. Random failures within air defence computers may happen as often as two or three times a year and can be expected to continue.[23] The question is whether the safeguards and double-checks provided can ever be considered adequate so long as we possess the power to annihilate the human race. (And the knowledge of these computer malfunctions is a devastating argument against the 'launch on warning' system which is being discussed at present. Such a system would fire retaliatory rockets upon receiving the warning that attack missiles were coming.)

Despite the systems of checks and safeguards, imperfect technology remains a weak link in the policy called deterrence.

Deterrence and First-Strike Capability

A final weakness in deterrence policy is its assumption that neither side would dare launch an atomic attack because of the surety of a devastating counterblow. But both West and

East are deploying highly accurate missiles which might be able to wipe out all the enemy's missiles before they could be launched.[24] Precisely guided missiles are now being produced that are accurate to within one hundred feet after a flight of eight thousand miles. Military planners can target them to destroy missile silos, command posts, communications systems, bomber bases and submarine pens. Both sides are developing antisubmarine weapons which, when combined with underwater sensing devices, might be able to locate and destroy subs at sea.

The ability of one country to destroy *all* the enemy's bombers, land-based missiles and nuclear submarines before they have a chance to react to an attack would defeat the concept of deterrence. 'Improvements in US and Soviet ICBM accuracy increase the vulnerability of fixed-launcher ICBM forces of both sides and . . . could provide an incentive, in an extreme crisis, for one side or the other to strike first.'[25] Once one or both sides possess super-accurate missiles the temptation will be nearly overwhelming during an international crisis to attack first and totally disarm the opponent. Thus, the next generation of nuclear weapons will make deterrence all the more unstable.

Limited War?

If deterrence fails, and nuclear war breaks out, could the war be 'limited'? Some military strategists argue that war would not necessarily escalate into a wholly devastating exchange of strategic weapons.[26] The superpowers would use only conventional forces or tactical (short-range) nuclear weapons aimed at purely military targets. The much discussed neutron bomb, for example, is a tactical weapon designed to destroy more soldiers and fewer buildings than present nuclear bombs of the same size. Thus, if deterrence broke down temporarily, it is argued, there would be a limited nuclear exchange, but not necessarily total nuclear war.

Fighting a limited nuclear war, however, is something like agreeing to fight with one arm held behind your back – that arm comes out pretty quickly if you get a bloody nose. Most government officials admit that a nuclear war which remains small (or limited to military targets) is improbable.

Former President Carter's defence secretary, Harold Brown, said of limited war: 'To me it seems very unlikely, almost to the point of impossibility. . . . It is much more likely to me that if a few strategic weapons were fired it would then escalate to larger and larger exchanges that would end up in an all-out thermonuclear war that would destroy both countries.'[27] And as British Admiral Lord Mountbatten said, 'I can see no use for any nuclear weapons which would not end in escalation, with consequences no one can conceive.'[28]

Could deterrence break down? The answer is yes. Any number of factors – an escalating crisis, technological malfunction, or the ability to strike first without retaliation – could upset the precarious balance of terror. When Billy Graham visited the Nazi concentration camp at Auschwitz, he said:

Is a nuclear holocaust inevitable if the arms race is not stopped? Frankly, the answer is almost certainly yes. Now I know that some people feel human beings are so terrified of a nuclear war that no one would dare start one. I wish I could accept that. But neither history nor the Bible gives much reason for optimism. . . . The present insanity of the global arms race, if continued, will lead inevitably to a conflagration so great that Auschwitz will seem like a minor rehearsal.[29]

US Admiral Hyman G. Rickover, so-called father of the nuclear navy, agrees. Commenting on the current arms race in his farewell speech to Congress in February 1982, he said: 'I think probably we will destroy ourselves.'[30]

What should be the response of Christian people in the nuclear age? Is it biblical to support a defence policy which relies on the ability to kill in vast numbers? Can Christians support nuclear deterrence when it involves a willingness to retaliate by killing millions of men, women and children? Should we lend ourselves to a policy which year by year brings us closer to scenes such as those described in chapters one and two? Is there an alternative to nuclear deterrence? Is there a defence beyond deterrence? If we refuse to threaten nuclear death, how can we witness for life in the power of the Spirit?

The rest of our book is our attempt to answer these questions.

SECTION II

Biblical-Theological Perspectives

How should Christians respond to the growing danger of nuclear war? Is there a word from God for us who live in the most dangerous decade in the history of planet Earth?

Nuclear war is new, but war itself is as old as history. Over the centuries, Christians have responded to the evil of war in two major ways. A minority have believed that Christians ought never to participate in lethal violence. The majority have assumed a 'just war' stance, asserting that although war is always horrible it may sometimes be the lesser of two evils. Criteria which have developed over many centuries of careful reflection enable Christians to judge whether a particular war is just or unjust.

Both the authors of this book belong to the first tradition. But we have the deepest respect for Christians taking the just war position. Christians equally committed to Christ and the authority of Scripture disagree on the question of war.

Disagreement over the validity of conventional warfare, however, should not conceal one exceedingly important development. Christians from both traditions are coming to the same conclusion about nuclear war. Whether one begins as a Christian in the just war tradition or as a Christian in the nonviolence tradition, the judgment about nuclear war is the same.

'A war between the United States and the Soviet Union . . . would be terribly destructive and might actually eradicate human civilisation or human life itself. [But] our nation's only hope of remaining free is to be prepared to go to war to defend itself, even at the risk of being destroyed. . . . Christians [may be] the free world's hope of remaining free, for it is we alone who can dare to risk losing much or all in war to forestall what we consider a still greater evil, the world domination of a totalitarian, atheistic system.'

Harold O. J. Brown[1]

'Any act of war aimed indiscriminately at the destruction of entire cities or of extensive areas along with their population is a crime against God and man himself. It merits unequivocal and unhesitating condemnation.'

Vatican II[4]

'We threaten evil in order not to do it, and the doing of it would be so terrible that the threat seems in comparison to be morally defensible.'

Michael Walzer[2]

'Every Christian, whatever he may think of the possibility of a 'just' use of conventional weapons, must be a nuclear pacifist.'

John R. W. Stott[3]

4

The Just War Tradition

In this chapter we want to apply the just war criteria to the question of nuclear war. In the next chapter we will examine some weaknesses of the just war tradition, but for the present we will simply assume the validity of this approach held by the majority of Christians over the centuries.[5] What then are the criteria Christians have used to determine under what circumstances war is justified?[6] In *War and Conscience in America* Edward L. Long offers an exceptionally lucid and concise statement of the just war tradition.[7] Seven criteria, which pertain both to the cause for fighting and the means used in battle, are most common.

1. *Last resort.* 'All other means to the morally just solution of a conflict must be exhausted before resort to arms can be regarded as legitimate.'[8] War must be the last resort, but that does not mean that an unjust solution must be accepted.

2. *Just cause.* 'War can be just only if employed to defend a stable order or morally preferable cause against threats of destruction or the use of injustice.'[9] The goals for which one fights must be just. And the opponent must be clearly unjust, even though one recognises moral ambiguity even in oneself.

3. *Right attitudes.* 'War must be carried out with the right attitudes.'[10] The intention must be the restoration of justice, not retaliation. Anger and revenge have no part in just wars.

4. *Prior declaration of war.* 'War must be explicitly declared by a legitimate authority.'[11] Individual citizens must not take up arms as self-appointed defenders of justice. A formal declaration of war must precede armed conflict so that the opponent has an opportunity to abandon unjust activity and prevent war.

5. *Reasonable hope of success.* 'War may be conducted only by military means that promise a reasonable attainment of the moral and political objectives being sought.'[12] If there is not a reasonable chance of success, then it is wrong to fight no matter how just one's cause. Nor does this simply mean that one must think one can win. There must be a reasonable probability that the things for which one is fighting will not be destroyed in the process.

6. *Noncombatant immunity.* 'The just war theory has also entailed selective immunity for certain parts of the enemy's population, particularly for noncombatants.'[13] Noncombatants are all those not directly involved in the manufacture, direction or use of weapons.[14] In a just war, no military action may be aimed directly at noncombatants. That is not to say that civilians may never be injured. If an army justly destroys a military target and nearby noncombatants are killed, that is an unintended side effect (called double-effect) which is permissible within limits. But the principle of proportionality applies here.

7. *Proportionality.* Finally, the principle of proportionality specifies that there must be a reasonable expectation that the good results of the war will exceed the horrible evils involved. This principle applies both to the whole enterprise of the war and to specific tactics in the course of battle.[15] For example, if the unintended double-effect of attacking a legitimate military target involves killing a disproportionate number of noncombatants, then the action is immoral.

According to the just war tradition, a particular war is justified only if all the above criteria are met. Both the cause for which one goes to war and the methods by which one fights must be just. In the light of this tradition, which the majority of Christians since Augustine have accepted, how should we evaluate the legitimacy of nuclear war?

To answer this question, we must look at how modern nuclear war would be carried out. One key question is: On what targets should we drop the bombs? Should they be aimed only at military installations and perhaps related industrial, communications and transportation facilities? Should large cities also be targeted? We can distinguish three basic scenarios for the use of nuclear weapons based on different projected targets and varying weapon size and number: (1) an all-out nuclear war in which both sides shoot most of their nuclear weapons at all significant enemy targets including cities (an all-out counterpopulation war); (2) a limited nuclear war in which both sides destroy only a few enemy cities (a limited counterpopulation war); and (3) a limited nuclear war in which both sides target only military (and related) installations (a limited counterforce war).

Some Christians believe all three of the above would be justified. Others accept only one or two. And some propose a fourth option: that it would be morally wrong to *use* nuclear weapons, but we should keep our nuclear stockpiles (and develop new weapons) for the sake of deterrence. As we apply the just war criteria to nuclear war, it is important to distinguish these four options.

Total Nuclear War

A large number of world missiles are aimed at targets that include large population centres. Since the early 1950s, the United States has repeatedly warned the Soviet Union that a nuclear attack would trigger a large-scale, retaliatory nuclear attack on the Soviet Union. In order to protect Western Europe, the USA has also threatened a nuclear attack if the USSR invaded Western Europe with conventional weapons. This would mean that the United States would be the first to use nuclear weapons – a first-strike possibility that American presidents have repeatedly refused to deny.

In the seventies, US policy shifted somewhat. More Soviet military installations were targeted, and heated debate about the possibility and validity of limited nuclear war erupted.[16] But a massive retaliatory attack on the Soviet Union, killing perhaps one hundred million people, continues as the cornerstone of US national defence.

There is absolutely no uncertainty about the current declared policy of the United States, France and Great Britain. Top government leaders have repeatedly declared that if attacked we would unleash nearly total nuclear destruction on the Soviet Union. In 1958, President Eisenhower said that US bombers 'present to any attacker the prospect of *virtual annihilation* of his own country. Even if we assume a surprise attack on our own bases, our bombers would immediately be on their way in *sufficient strength* to accomplish the *mission of retaliation*.'[17] A British government white paper of 1958 declared: 'The strategy of NATO is based on the frank recognition that a full-scale Soviet attack could not be repelled without resort to a *massive nuclear bombardment* of the sources of power in *Russia*.'[18] On 21 October 1981, President Reagan reaffirmed this strategy.[19] In February 1964, the British minister of defence said: 'Governments know that major war would mean the *destruction of the world*. . . . So the only defence we have is the ability to strike back against the enemy with some indestructible form of retaliation.'[20] As US Secretary of Defence Robert McNamara told Congress in 1968: '[It is] the clear and present ability to destroy the attacker as a twentieth-century nation and *an unwavering will to use those forces in retaliation* to a nuclear attack that provides the deterrent.'[21]

In January 1980, Ron Sider had breakfast in the family room of the White House along with about fifteen other evangelicals. President Carter assured them that if the USSR launched an attack, he would promptly launch a counterstrike. Mutually assured destruction is our declared policy.[22]

How do the criteria for a just war apply to a comprehensive nuclear war? We shall discover that the most significant criteria are the demands for a reasonable hope of success, noncombatant immunity and proportionality. But we will look briefly at the other four criteria first.

Let us suppose a scenario in which the Soviet Union launches a massive first strike on the United States. In such a case the first demand, that war be a last resort, would be satisfied.

We believe that the second criterion, of a just cause, would also be met. The political and religious freedoms enjoyed in Western democratic societies are highly treasured values. This is not to say that the United States is wholly right. As diplomat George F. Kennan has said: 'We must remember that it has been we Americans who, at almost every step . . . , have taken the lead in the development of this sort of weaponry. It was we who first produced and tested such a device; . . . we who introduced the multiple warhead; we who declined every proposal for the renunciation of the principle of 'first use'; and we alone, so help us God, who have used the weapon in anger against others.'[23] Yet in spite of mistakes and injustice both at home and abroad, we believe that Western democracy is morally preferable to Soviet totalitarianism.

A massive retaliatory strike could never meet the third demand that the intention must be restoration of justice, not retaliation, revenge or anger. Repeatedly leaders have talked of retaliation. The 1979 study of the US Office of Technology Assessment (OTA), entitled *The Effects of Nuclear War*, made it unmistakably clear that total war would virtually annihilate both societies.[24] Thus a massive retaliatory attack could never be launched with the intention of restoring justice.

The technology of the nuclear age seems to make the fourth demand (for a prior declaration of war) almost irrelevant. Missiles take only twenty-four minutes to travel between Moscow and Washington. Hence there is no time for Congress to fulfil its constitutional role (which it cannot delegate) of declaring war. One might, however, plausibly argue that repeated warnings of retaliation if attacked function as a declaration of war if we are attacked first. But the demand for a declaration of war (which is designed to give the aggressor time for reconsideration) unequivocally prohibits any first-strike policy.

The fifth criterion (a reasonable hope of success) stipulates that there be a likelihood not just of winning but also of preserving that for which one is fighting. Thus when Harold O. J. Brown implies that we should fight an all-out war even though it is likely, as he himself says, 'to eradicate human civilisation or human life itself,' he violates one of the central criteria of the just war tradition.[25] In the chaos and disorder after a total nuclear war, all the things for which we had fought – a peaceful, productive society, freedom, democracy, the rule of law – would almost certainly disappear in the inevitable totalitarianism. The OTA study details the ghastly obliteration of both countries, suggesting that, at best, a life equivalent to that of the Middle Ages might emerge.[26] 'The survivors, if any,' President Carter warned in his farewell speech to the nation, 'would live in despair amid the poisoned ruins of a civilisation that had committed suicide.'[27] In an all-out nuclear war, there is absolutely no reasonable hope of preserving what we are trying to defend. Perhaps Pope John XXIII has put it best: 'In this age of ours, which prides itself on its atomic power, it is irrational to think that war is a proper way to obtain justice for violated rights.'[28]

The sixth criterion, noncombatant immunity, is particularly important. Most Christians from all Christian traditions – whether evangelical Protestant, mainline Protestant or Catholic – who have carefully applied just war criteria to the problem of nuclear war have concluded that the principle of noncombatant immunity absolutely prohibits all-out nuclear war. According to the US Office of Technology Assessment, a large attack even on military and economic targets would kill 70 to 160 million Americans and 100 million Soviet citizens. With population centres also targeted, 190 million Americans and 130 million Soviet citizens would die – virtually all of them noncombatants.[29]

Writing in *Christianity Today*, the internationally known evangelical John Stott concluded: 'I believe the same principle [of noncombatant immunity] is sufficient to condemn the use of strategic nuclear weapons. Because they are indiscriminate in their effects, destroying combatants and noncombatants alike, it seems clear to me that they are ethically indefensible, and that every Christian, whatever he may think of the possibility of a 'just' use of conventional weapons, must be a nuclear pacifist.'[30]

In the official documents from Vatican II, the Roman Catholic church also sharply condemned weapons which would indiscriminately destroy large numbers of noncombatants: 'Any act of war aimed indiscriminately at the destruction of entire cities or of extensive areas along with their population is a crime against God and man himself. It merits unequivocal and unhesitating condemnation.'[31] We can catch the gravity of Vatican II's sharp condemnation when we realise that the word *condemnation* was used only once in 103,000 words of official documents.[32] As Bryan Hehir points out, this statement by the council effectively prohibits the use of all present strategic (that is, intercontinental) nuclear weapons because they would kill so many civilians.[33] In 1976 the US Catholic bishops added that it was morally wrong even to threaten to use such weapons against noncombatants.[34]

A harsh denunciation of the present declared policy of the United States comes from two people who defend the use of nuclear weapons under some circumstances. Dr Fred Ikle, director of the US Arms Control and Disarmament Agency in the 1970s, issued a blistering attack on the long-standing strategy of mutually assured destruction (often called MAD). Decrying our plans to unleash 'widespread genocide,' Ikle insists that 'our method for preventing nuclear war rests on a form of warfare universally condemned since the Dark Ages – the mass killing of hostages.'[35]

No Christian ethicist today has devoted more careful thought to the problem of the just war and nuclear weapons than Paul Ramsey. Ramsey believes that the use of nuclear weapons against military targets is justifiable. But Ramsey insists that the present policy of targeting nuclear weapons on population centres is totally immoral. Even after our cities had been attacked, destroying Soviet cities would be like shooting the children of a criminal. 'It would be an act of pure purposeless punishment and retrospective vengeance.'[36] The 'purpose' of nuclear weapons was to deter nuclear attack. If our cities were already destroyed by a Soviet first strike, the only reason for obliterating their population centres would be vengeance – a motive the Christian faith and the just war tradition unequivocally condemn. One might argue that we should knock out the remaining Soviet missiles to prevent a second Soviet strike. But this would be futile since it is impossible to destroy the large Russian fleet of nuclear submarines.[37]

Ramsey thinks massive nuclear retaliation would be 'the most immoral, because [it is] the most stupid and politically purposeless [act], in the whole history of warfare.'[38]

To press the button in counter-retaliation will also be the most unloving deed in the history of mankind, only exceeded by those who, for the sake of some concern of theirs, cause the little ones to stumble and fall into hell. I had rather be a pagan suckled in a creed outworn, . . . than a skilful artisan of technical reason devising plans to carry out such a deed. I also doubt if any man not wholly dispossessed of humanity can actually purpose and will to do any such thing.[39]

But that unthinkable act is the oft-repeated, publicly announced policy of the leaders we elect.

Finally, the criterion of proportionality demands that the good results outweigh the evils of war. The purpose of a just war is the restoration of just relationships between two societies. Obviously if one or both societies are destroyed in the process of trying to restore right relationships between them, the means have lost all proportion to the ends.[40] Surely the murder of 190 million Americans and 130 million Russians (not to mention the death of millions in other nations because of fallout, long-term ecological damage, and so on) is a greater evil than whatever would result from not fighting an all-out war. Historian Herbert Butterfield correctly reminds us that 'with modern weapons we could easily put civilisation back a thousand years while the course of a single century can produce a colossal transition from despotic regimes to a system of liberty.'[41]

Some, however, disagree. Like Harold O. J. Brown, they truly believe the slogan 'Better dead than red.'[42] Certainly Russian totalitarianism is a ghastly evil that has destroyed millions of people. In no way do we pretend otherwise. In fact the authors of this book would expect to be among those to suffer if the Soviets were to take over the United States. But it is bad history and worse theology to claim that Soviet control of the world would destroy Christianity. Christians have flourished under totalitarian regimes before. Despotic Roman emperors could not destroy Christianity or even prevent its rapid growth. Modern totalitarians in Russia and China have been no more successful. A higher percentage of the population attends church each Sunday morning in the USSR than in Western Europe.[43]

Even Billy Graham no longer believes that the present differences between East and West would justify a nuclear war: 'The opportunities I have had to visit Yugoslavia, Hungary, and Poland have been very significant. I went with many stereotypes in my mind, but I came away with a new understanding especially of how the church exists and in some instances thrives in these societies – and a new awareness of their concern for peace. . . . No. I do not think the present differences are worth nuclear war.'[44]

One must conclude that, according to just war principles, an all-out nuclear attack would be a totally immoral, sinful act. Christians dare not participate in it or even prepare for it. And since, as Secretary of Defence McNamara and his successors have said, the ability and unwavering will to do precisely that is at the heart of current US and Western European strategies, as it is at the heart of Soviet policy, all Christians in all places must join together to say no to such Satanic plans.

A Limited Nuclear Attack on Cities

In his books on nuclear strategy, Herman Kahn discusses 'controlled city reprisal.'[45] If, for instance, the Russians obliterated Detroit, the United States might annihilate Leningrad. 'If the only alternatives are between the all-out mutually homicidal war and the city exchange, bizarre and unpleasant as the city exchange is, it is not as bizarre and unpleasant as complete mutual homicide.'[46]

Would the just war tradition permit such an approach? Paul Ramsey says absolutely not. The mere fact that completely destroying one or five cities is not as bad as destroying five hundred cities does not mean the former is acceptable. Nor does the fact that raping one woman is less evil than raping fifty women justify one rape.

The just war's demand for noncombatant immunity rules out any policy which directly targets population centres. All the condemnations against killing noncombatants in an all-out war apply with equal validity to a limited city 'exchange.' According to the just war tradition, *directly targeting noncombatants is simply murder*.

It is frightening to notice the language which Kahn uses. Obliterating one or several cities in a 'controlled city exchange' is merely 'bizarre and unpleasant.' To speak of 'exchange' when one is referring to the deaths of several million citizens of Detroit and Leningrad is to betray deadly callousness. To describe their planned murder as merely 'bizarre and unpleasant' rather than immoral and sinful is to descend to Satanic doublethink.

The principles of the just war tradition exclude limited nuclear attacks on cities just as they prohibit all-out nuclear war. Might it not be possible, however, to justify limited nuclear warfare if we targeted only military targets? In recent years military strategists and ethicists have debated this question vigorously, calling this limited counterforce warfare.

Limited Nuclear Attack on Military Targets
Limited counterforce nuclear warfare could involve the use of tactical or strategic nuclear weapons. Tactical nuclear weapons are smaller-yield, shorter-range weapons which, for example, Western forces in Europe could use against invading Soviet armies. Strategic nuclear weapons, on the other hand, if used in a limited counterforce strategy, would be intercontinental weapons hitting military targets in the Soviet Union.

Although the United States has persistently refused to commit itself not to use nuclear weapons first, it was generally assumed until the 1970s that it was United States policy to launch a nuclear attack on the USSR only if it invaded Western Europe or attacked the United States. In that case the United States would launch a massive nuclear attack on population centres in the Soviet Union. In the '70s, however, a new policy emerged.[47] The idea of targeting significant numbers of US strategic nuclear weapons on Soviet military installations was elaborated in the Rand Corporation in the late 1950s. Secretary of Defence Robert McNamara floated the idea briefly in 1962 and then abandoned it. But by 1973 when James Schlesinger became President Nixon's secretary of defence and an ardent advocate of counterforce strategy, vast sums were already being spent on research and development of counterforce weapons. The new guidance systems of the cruise and MX missiles which give them incredible accuracy (within a few hundred feet) enable these missiles to be aimed at specific military targets rather than general populated areas. President Carter's Presidential Order No. 59 in 1979 simply confirmed that limited counterforce warfare had become an official part of United States nuclear policy.[48]

Why did this change occur?[49] The sheer pace of technological development was undoubtedly one reason. Technology made possible the development of lower-yield, precisely targeted nuclear weapons that could destroy military targets. Another reason was that the consequences of massive nuclear retaliation are so horrible that it has always seemed impossible. Would the United States really annihilate the USSR if the latter invaded Western Europe? Deterrence works only if the other side believes we will do what we threaten. For this and other reasons, policymakers such as James Schlesinger believed that deterrence might fail. In that case, they wanted other options in addition to total nuclear war. If the United States could respond by destroying military targets without destroying large numbers of Soviet civilians, it might be possible to punish a Soviet attack without the mutually assured destruction of both countries.[50] Worried nuclear strategists saw limited counterforce warfare as something that would be less horrible and therefore more thinkable. Hence, our threat to do it would be more credible and deterrence would be strengthened.[51]

Also important was the obvious immorality of planning to kill millions of innocent noncombatants. As we have seen, Ramsey believed that hitting cities would be murder. Furthermore, if it would be murder to do that some time in the future, then planning for and intending to do it is also murderous. 'If deterrence rests upon genuinely intending massive retaliation [against cities], it is clearly wrong, no matter how much peace results.'[52]

Ramsey believes, however, that deterrence can be so designed that it does not rest on immoral threats.[53] *Limited* nuclear attacks against specific military targets could be justified on the basis of the just war tradition. Ramsey argues that if the USSR invaded Western Europe, it would be morally acceptable to use tactical nuclear weapons first against the invading troops after they cross the border. He also argues that it would be permissible to use strategic nuclear weapons against military targets in the Soviet

Union in response to their first use of nuclear weapons.[54]

Ramsey's defence of counterforce nuclear warfare merits careful scrutiny.[55] He believes that a counterforce policy would provide sufficient deterrence to prevent a Soviet attack in three ways. First, Ramsey knows that any attack on military targets would inevitably have the unintended double-effect of killing civilians. But just war theorists have always recognised that some noncombatants will be killed. Their deaths are foreseen but not intended. What distinguishes justified destruction of noncombatants from murder is the intention. 'This distinction is not determined by the amount of the devastation or the number of deaths but . . . by what is deliberately intended.'[56] Because the moral intention is good, Ramsey prefers counterforce warfare 'even if the damage proves as extensive or more' than counterpopulation warfare.[57] He adds, of course, that the principle of proportionality also applies.[58] But he seems to imply that the death of twenty-five million Americans (and presumably a comparable number of Russians) would be an acceptable upper limit of deaths from just counterforce nuclear war.[59]

But are not that many deaths disproportionate in terms of just war theory? Many would say yes, and we agree.[60] Furthermore, the notion of unintended effects, or double-effect, has validity only if the evil side-effects 'do not constitute a foreseen *means* of the good ones (for, of course, if they did, they, themselves, must needs be intended).'[61] But that appears to be what Ramsey's position does. As Michael Walzer argues:

> [Ramsey] wants, like other deterrent theorists, to prevent nuclear attack by threatening to kill very large numbers of innocent civilians, but unlike other deterrent theorists, he expects to kill those people without aiming at them. . . . If counterforce warfare had no collateral effects, or had minor and controllable effects, then it could play no part in Ramsey's strategy. . . . Surely anyone designing such a strategy must accept moral

responsibility for the effects on which he is so radically dependent.[62]

This sounds like 'double-think about double-effect.'[63] It would seem then that Ramsey's deterrence still depends on the threat to kill noncombatants which, he himself argues, is murder according to the just war tradition.

Ramsey sees a second kind of legitimate deterrence in the possession of nuclear weapons. No matter how often we declare that we will use them only against military targets, they *could* be used against cities. 'No matter how often we declare, and quite sincerely declare, that our targets are an enemy's forces, he can never be quite *certain* that in the fury or in the fog of war his cities may not be destroyed.'[64] To underline this uncertainty, Ramsey quotes the military strategist T. C. Schelling: 'It is our sheer inability to predict the consequences of our actions and to keep things under control, and the enemy's similar inability, that can intimidate the enemy.'[65]

But surely this statement points to one of the strongest arguments against Ramsey's viewpoint. He admits that we have an 'inability to control' limited nuclear warfare. Yet Ramsey still wants to justify this means of deterrence. Is not our lack of control – our inability to prevent limited nuclear war from becoming unlimited nuclear war – an exceedingly strong reason for rejecting the idea of limited nuclear war?[66]

Top government officials believe that limited nuclear war would not stay limited. As we already saw in chapter three, former secretary of defence Harold Brown admitted: 'To me it seems very unlikely, almost to the point of impossibility. . . . It is much more likely . . . that it would escalate to larger and larger exchanges that would end up in an all-out thermonuclear war that would destroy both countries.'[67]

Escalation could occur in a vast number of ways: computer failure, unforeseen effects of nuclear blasts, a desperate attempt to avoid defeat, or human irrationality in a situation of nearly total panic and chaos. In 1979 the United

States Arms Control and Disarmament Agency (ACDA) pointed to possible unforeseen developments in the course of an actual nuclear exchange. In earlier nuclear tests, it was discovered that the high-altitude bursts 'wiped out long-distance radio communications for hours at distances up to 600 miles from the burst point.'[68] What would happen if the soldiers in nuclear submarines and ICBM silos could not communicate with headquarters for hours at the height of a nuclear crisis? The ACDA also noted that earlier tests showed that electromagnetic pulses from a blast can play havoc with the electrical equipment (such as computers) that controls the nuclear arms.[69] Only at our peril dare we ignore the ACDA's warning that many unforeseen dangers could arise during the course of limited nuclear war.

Escalation could occur in other ways. Whoever appeared to be losing a limited nuclear war might become desperate. As Arthur Waskow so aptly described it:

Once the threshold of atomic weaponry is crossed in battle, the pressure for use of 'just one level higher' of atomic force will be practically irresistible. The side badly hurt by atomic artillery shells will respond by dropping medium-sized atomic bombs on the offending artillery emplacements. The answer to that will be larger bombs or medium-range missiles against the airfields from which the tactical atomic strikes come. Quickly the side less equipped with tactical nuclear weapons . . . will feel pressed to resort to thermonuclear attack.[70]

Bryan Hehir, a leading Catholic ethicist, concludes that we must understand the psychological dynamic of our situation. Any use of nuclear weapons makes it pyschologically easier to move to a higher level of nuclear exchange. Therefore we must have an ethical 'firebreak' between the use of conventional and nuclear weapons. Even though tactical nuclear weapons can perhaps be justified in terms of the criteria of discrimination and proportionality, they dare not be used because of the psychological danger of escalation.[71]

Furthermore, strategic planners who foresee a rationally controlled, calculated nuclear exchange that comes to a reasonable halt after ten or twenty million casualties must have a naive view of human nature. According to the Christian view of persons, sinful people often choose evil things even under the best of circumstances. Is it probable that human rationality would remain in control during intense confusion, panic, misinformation and anger?[72]

Ramsey's call for a policy of deterrence based on a willingness to fight limited, counterforce nuclear war runs the risk of escalation. In fact his argument uses precisely the possibility of the loss of control which would lead to escalation as a part of the deterrence he wills.

For the sake of deterrence, he chooses a situation that he acknowledges may be uncontrollable.[73] Is that responsible and moral?

We have seen that Ramsey believes that a counterforce nuclear policy would provide deterrence both because of the unintended destruction of noncombatants and the possibility (in spite of what the government says) of using nuclear weapons against cities. But if that is not enough deterrence, Ramsey offers a third possibility. He distinguishes between a declared and a real intention, between the appearance and the actuality of being committed to destroy cities. The West can be ambiguous about its intentions. It may even make an 'apparent resolution to wage war irrationally' – that is, to target enemy cities – as long as it does not really intend to do it. Ramsey defends this deception by saying that lying is not as bad as murder and that at any rate our enemies have no right to this information.[74]

Quite apart from the ethics of lying, Ramsey's proposal is problematic. The careful deception about announced plans to attack Soviet cities would have to be a country's most carefully guarded national secret. The threat of a massive attack on cities deters, as McNamara said, only if we convince the USSR of the unwavering intention to carry out the threat. Only a tiny handful of people in the West could know of the deception. All the soldiers manning nuclear installations, all the scientists and workers building nuclear weapons, all the strategists designing defence policy, all the citizens paying for nuclear policy would have to do so under the assumption that they were helping to prepare for a massive attack on Soviet cities.[75] But such an attack, according to Ramsey, would be mass murder. And intending to murder is also murderous. Therefore Ramsey's proposal would involve the entire public in a murderous intention.

One final objection to a limited counterforce policy should be noted. Quite possibly this approach would actually increase the danger of nuclear war. It might mislead both the Russians and ourselves.[76]

Counterforce weapons (like the cruise and MX missiles) are precision instruments of incredible accuracy. And they are to be targeted on Soviet nuclear weapons. We may never intend to use them in a first strike, but they increase our ability to launch a first strike. The USSR, which obviously trusts us no more than we trust them, will suspect us of planning a first strike. To avoid that, they might try to beat us to the punch and launch their own first strike.

A launch-on-warning policy also becomes more likely in this case, since the Soviet Union would not want to have their nuclear weapons destroyed on the ground.[77] They might, fearing a possible first strike, launch their missiles at the first warning, without waiting for careful confirmation. Thus counterforce policy increases the danger that computer failure or human mistake could lead to nuclear war.

Herbert Scoville (a former CIA officer and senior scientist with the Atomic Energy Commission) also fears that a counterforce policy might make us more willing to use nuclear weapons. Because the consequences of using a lower-yield, precisely targeted nuclear weapon are not as awesomely catastrophic as all-out nuclear war, limited nuclear war becomes more acceptable, and therefore more likely.

One must conclude that Ramsey's heroic effort to condemn unlimited nuclear war but justify deterrence based on limited, counterforce nuclear war is a failure. In what has been described as the best book on the just war tradition in the twentieth century, Michael Walzer summarises his evaluation of Ramsey's position:

> He multiplies distinctions like a Ptolemaic astronomer with his epicycles and comes very close at the end to what G. E. M. Anscombe has called 'double-think about double-effect.' . . . To draw insignificant lines, to maintain the formal categories of double-effect, collateral damage, noncombatant immunity, and so on, when so little moral content remains is to corrupt the argument for justice as a whole and to render it suspect.[78]

But Professor Ramsey is no straw man. His work represents the most articulate, careful and extensive attempt by a prominent Christian ethicist to defend limited nuclear war today. If he cannot do it, can it be done?

Deterrence without Use?

The only remaining possibility would seem to be unilateral rejection of nuclear weapons by all Christians. But such a proposal seems almost unthinkable. Politically, it appears highly unlikely that Western nations would be willing to do that, at least without sweeping changes in public opinion. Furthermore, it is quite plausible to argue that deterrence has worked since 1945. Certainly there has been superpower rivalry and devastating regional wars. But World War III has not happened. Nuclear war has been avoided. The essential presupposition of deterrent theory is, as Herbert Scoville says, that 'nuclear war can be prevented today only by making the consequences of its initiation clearly unacceptable to all parties.'[79] It is plausible to argue, as many do, that deterrence 'is the basis for most of the stability that we have in the world today.'[80]

But is deterrence compatible with the just war tradition? Only, it is generally agreed, if it avoids both immoral hypothetical decisions and immoral risks.[81] We have seen that just war theorists condemn as immoral the hypothetical decision to unleash massive retaliation against noncombatants if the Soviets attack. But current deterrence policy intends precisely that. Bryan Hehir discusses how problematic this is for Catholics who want to defend deterrence. Vatican II, Hehir admits, prohibited the use of weapons that 'cause the kind of damage nuclear weapons produce in a civilian area.'[82] Unfortunately, the credibility of deterrence rests on the enemy's belief that we will use precisely those nuclear weapons which the Catholic Church prohibits. In 1976 the US Catholic bishops explicitly said it was wrong even to *threaten* to attack population centres as part of a strategy of deterrence. Thus 'the success of deterrence is tied . . . to doing something that is morally prohibited by contemporary Catholic teaching.'[83]

The situation is, of course, the same for non-Catholic just war theorists. The kind of nuclear weapons that provide genuine deterrence are those that would, if used, destroy a disproportionate number of noncombatants. (There are very small tactical nuclear weapons that would not do that, but they do not act as an effective deterrent in an age of multimegaton weapons.) Deterrence seems to rest on immoral hypothetical decisions – on the decision, 'here and now, to murder, there and then.'[84]

Is there no alternative to unilateral abandonment of nuclear arms? Hehir thinks there is. He believes it would always be wrong to *use* nuclear weapons. But it is not wrong to develop, stockpile and install them.[85] He calls himself a nuclear pacifist on the *use* of nuclear weapons, but he wants us to keep a nuclear arsenal for the sake of deterrence. 'The mere possession of a devastating deterrent means that the adversary can never be sure it will not be used. In any rational calculation, that should be enough to deter. If it is not, I cannot find it morally justifiable to compound his irrationality with a nuclear response.'[86] If one never intends to use nuclear weapons, it is not immoral to possess them. Nuclear pacifists like Walter Stein, therefore, cannot argue that it is immoral to possess them because they are indiscriminate in their effects. That is irrelevant, because their function is to deter, not to strike.[87]

Hehir's position is tempting, and would be attractive if one could be very certain that deterrence would continue to prevent nuclear war. The prospect of Soviet totalitarianism encompassing the globe is truly terrifying. If we could be very certain nuclear deterrence would prevent this tragedy *without* leading to nuclear war, then living with deterrence might be ethically defensible. In fact, it may be that we have come to live comfortably with the awful reality of nuclear weapons precisely because we believe we will never use them.[88]

Hehir's position, however, seems profoundly problematic at three points. First, it tends to letitimise current policy without changing it. Second, it destroys the credibility of deterrence by announcing that we will not really use nuclear weapons. And, finally, it increases the risk of accidental nuclear war because of continued development and installation of nuclear weapons.

No current government has indicated the slightest openness to accepting Hehir's approach of 'possession without use.' Thus theologians who take this position end up offering a rationale for maintaining the possession of nuclear weapons (and the arms race) without changing the government's intent to *use* nuclear weapons. The practical effect, therefore, is to offer justification for current policy.

Every public figure who comments on deterrence makes it clear that deterrence works only if the Soviets believe we will use nuclear weapons. Former American Secretary of Defence Robert McNamara reflected that general view when he said: 'It is the clear and present ability to destroy the attacker as a 20th-century nation and an *unwavering* will to *use those forces in retaliation* for a nuclear attack that provides the deterrent.'[89] Hehir is, of course, painfully aware of the problem. He admits: 'Undoubtedly, to render deterrence credible, it must appear that the determination to use nuclear weapons is *beyond question*.'[90] Thus Hehir's proposal to possess but never use nuclear weapons destroys the very deterrence he hopes to preserve.

The only way out would be to keep our intention not to use them a presidential secret. But, as we saw earlier, that entangles everyone (except a handful of persons around the president) in the immoral position of preparing for what Hehir and other just war theorists call mass murder.

There is another even more serious objection to Hehir's position. The validity of Hehir's stance rests on the assumption that continuing to possess nuclear weapons does not involve us in immoral risks. Unfortunately, the evidence would suggest otherwise. As we saw in chapter three, the risks of nuclear war increase year by year. We came to the very brink of nuclear holocaust during the Cuban missile crisis. In 1979 and 1980 computer failures resulted in three instances where the central US command believed for three to six minutes that the Soviet Union had launched a nuclear attack. Republican Senator Barry Goldwater reported that the US air defence system received 147 false alarms during a recent eighteen-month period.[91]

A chilling article in the *Bulletin of the Atomic Scientists* of November 1980 shows how human error could lead to a nuclear catastrophe. Because of emotional problems, drug use and so on, about five thousand military personnel already working with the US nuclear weapons programme are removed every year. One army code specialist reported: 'Missile soldiers sometimes were high when they attached nuclear warheads to the missiles. So were soldiers who connected the two pieces up to make the missile operational.'[92] On September 18, 1980, a technician accidentally dropped a wrench seventy feet onto the fuel tank of a multimegaton Titan missile. The resulting explosion pulverised the silo's 750-ton door and dug a 250-foot crater. Although the nuclear warhead may have been hurled several hundred feet from the silo (its final position was not made public), it did not explode.[93] The report of near catastrophes goes on. No one reading this carefully documented article can feel any optimism about indefinitely avoiding nuclear war.

The pace of technological change also tends to destabilise the situation and undermine deterrence. Both sides mistrust each other. Both fear the other may make a technological breakthrough that would give a significant advantage. Therefore, both continue feverishly to develop ever more sophisticated, ever more deadly nuclear weapons. And a major technological breakthrough could make things even more dangerous. One country might be tempted to strike first while it possessed technological superiority. On the other hand, the elaborate spying networks of both sides almost guarantee that the other side would pick up enough information about the breakthrough to be exceedingly frightened – perhaps so frightened that it would strike before the other side made use of its advantage.[94]

Hehir himself points out how the pace of technological change increases the problem of control. In 1971, the United States had 1,656 deliverable warheads. Three years later it had 8,000. The reason: the new technology of MIRV. Multiple, independently targeted re-entry vehicles (MIRVs) enable each existing missile to carry several separately targeted warheads. Since 'MIRVing' missiles was technically possible, it was done. But it did not make anyone safer. The Russians soon learned how to do it too. Now it is far more difficult to know precisely how many warheads the opponent actually has. As a result, Hehir says, 'The possibility exists that he has achieved a superior position. . . . This in turn tends to give a certain plausibility to first-strike scenarios, either because of the temptation to use superior striking power, or more likely, the fear of the party which feels it has lost strategic parity and is now politically threatened.'[95]

More recent technological developments which make

possible the cruise and MX missiles will further destabilise deterrence. Cruise missiles are so small (twenty feet) that large numbers of them can be concealed. Their deadly accuracy against enemy missiles encourages a launch-on-warning policy. In late 1981 the Reagan administration announced plans to deploy 384 long-range cruise missiles with nuclear warheads on ships and submarines.[96] At the same time 1,480 almost identical cruise missiles with conventional (non-nuclear) warheads will be built. Even Secretary of Defence Caspar Weinberger admitted that it would be 'extremely difficult' to tell the difference between the two kinds of missiles.

The chief negotiators for both Salt I and Salt II are worried. If the United States proceeds, this development would be the first installation of cruise missiles on ships. Because of their small size, any small ship, including fishing boats, could be a strategic nuclear delivery vehicle. Experts believe that the decision could devastate efforts to control the arms race.

Why this new development? Technological change makes it possible. But the result is greater danger, not increased security.

Robert McNamara was surely correct when he spoke of the 'mad momentum intrinsic to the development of all new nuclear weaponry.'[97] Every year that we continue the present policy of adopting new nuclear weapons as soon as technology makes them possible, we edge closer to the day when deterrence will fail. James Schlesinger, President Nixon's defence secretary, called for a limited war strategy because he feared that deterrence *would* fail. To gamble on deterrence working indefinitely is to cling to an increasingly shaky reed.

It is striking that those who propose some variation of Hehir's position urge it as an 'interim' approach. John Bennett did that in 1961. He rejected any use of nuclear retaliation against noncombatants and admitted that the logical conclusion might seem to be unilateral nuclear disarmament. Such a position, however, seemed 'psycholo-

gically and politically' impossible. Therefore, he argued
that 'there is an *interim situation* which does provide a basis
for the possession of nuclear weapons.'[98] In 1977 Pierce S.
Corden of the US Arms Control and Disarmament Agency
took a similar position, pleading for the '*temporary* possession of weapons of mass destruction.'[99] Bryan Hehir takes
the same stand in 1982.

But how long will this increasingly dangerous 'interim'
situation last? Every year the danger of nuclear war increases. It is time to reject an upwardly spiralling nuclear
arms race justified in the name of deterrence.

More and more Christians of all theological traditions
are doing precisely that. More and more Christians within
the just war tradition have come to the conclusion that
nuclear war could never be justified. In 1978 many prominent Protestant and Catholic leaders signed 'A Call to
Faithfulness' declaring,

> Our primary allegiance to Jesus Christ and his kingdom
> commits us to total abolition of nuclear weapons. There
> can be no qualifying or conditioning used. We, the
> signers of this declaration, commit ourselves to non-
> cooperation with our country's preparations for nuclear
> war. On all levels – research, development, testing, pro-
> duction, deployment, and actual use of nuclear
> weapons – we commit ourselves to resist in the name of
> Jesus.[100]

Signers included prominent Protestants such as Robert
McAfee Brown and Eugene R. Stockwell, and well-known
Catholics such as Henri Nouwen, Bishop Thomas Gumble-
ton and Dorothy Day. More surprising perhaps was the
large proportion of prominent evangelical signers: Joseph
Bayly of David C. Cook; Ted. W. Engstrom of World
Vision; Jay Kesler, the president of Youth for Christ;
theologian Clark Pinnock; Richard Halverson, now chap-
lain of the US Senate; Frank Gaebelein, former coeditor of

Christianity Today; and Vernon Grounds of Conservative
Baptist Theological Seminary.

In January 1982, *Newsweek* reported that twenty-nine
US Catholic bishops had recently declared that 'even to
possess [nuclear weapons] is wrong.' The president of the
National Conference of Catholic Bishops, Archbishop
John Roach, recently said that the church 'needs to say
"no" clearly and decisively to the use of nuclear weapons.'
Fifty-four of the United States' 301 Catholic bishops are
members of the Catholic peace movement Pax Christi.[101]

Prominent evangelical theologian John Stott has said:
'Every Christian, whatever he may think of the possibility
of a "just" use of conventional weapons, must be a nuclear
pacifist.'[102]

Even President Reagan's pastor, Rev. Donn Moomaw,
has preached about the immorality of nuclear war: 'Because nuclear weapons are so destructive, so devastating,
so final, so widespread, they are ethically and morally
indefensible. . . . I must be a nuclear pacifist.'[103]

'If praise of God dies out in the Soviet Union, this will be the result, not of communist persecution, but of a strike with thousands of the nuclear bombs generally accepted by church-going people in the West.'

Dale Aukerman[1]

5

Is the Just War Tradition Adequate?

In the last chapter we simply accepted the validity of the just war tradition. But Christians today are beginning to have second thoughts. In 1951 the Church of Scotland declared that 'the methods of modern war are so different from those in the minds of the formulators of the traditional doctrine [of the just war] as to render many of their arguments irrelevant.'[2] For the same reason, Vatican II called for an entirely new attitude:

> The horror and perversity of war are immensely magnified by the multiplication of scientific weapons. . . . If the kinds of instruments which can now be found in the armouries of the great nations were to be employed to their fullest, an almost total and altogether reciprocal slaughter of each side by the other would follow. . . . All these considerations compel us to undertake an evaluation of war *with an entirely new attitude*.[3]

In his important book on the just war tradition, Michael Walzer asserts that 'nuclear weapons explode the theory of just war.' Nuclear weapons, Walzer says, 'are the first of mankind's technological innovations that are simply not encompassable within the familiar moral world.'[4] Even more pointed is the recent comment of Catholic Archbishop Raymond G. Hunthausen of Seattle:

> Wasn't it Einstein who made the observation that everything has changed with the advent of atomic explosions,

everything except our way of thinking? I don't know that
we have adjusted to that. The church has got to indicate
that the principles that govern the Just War theory are
shattered, and that there is no way that we can accommo-
date ourselves to that, given the weapons of destruction
now available to us.[5]

To many people, nuclear weapons seem to challenge the
validity or relevance of the just war tradition.[6]

In addition to the horror of modern war, four other
factors raise questions about the validity of the just war
tradition: the long tragic history of Christians killing Christians; the failure to implement just war criteria; the peaceful
witness of the early church before Constantine; and a
scholarly study of the teachings of Jesus. We will examine
the first three issues in this chapter and explore the fourth in
chapters six, seven and eight.

Readers who find the just war tradition's approach to our
problem fully adequate may want to skip chapters five to
eight. In those chapters we develop the approach to the
problem of nuclear war in the *other* major Christian tradition which addresses the issue of war.

Christians Killing Christians
All Christians are members of Christ's body. 'For by one
Spirit we were all baptised into one body – Jews or Greeks,
slaves or free' (1 Cor 12:13). The same verse might be
applied to Germans and Ethiopians, Britons and Chinese,
North Americans and Russians. Unless we deny our Lord,
our loyalty to Christ's worldwide body of brothers and
sisters must far exceed any loyalty to nation or country. 'If
one member suffers, all suffer together; if one member is
honoured, all rejoice together' (1 Cor 12:26).

Has not the long tragic history of European wars made a
mockery of this biblical belief in the unity of Christ's body?
German Christians have destroyed French and Dutch
Christians. English Christians have obliterated German
and Italian Christians. Over the centuries, European

Christians have slaughtered their brothers and sisters in Christ by the millions.

Now we have plans to do it by tens of millions. A higher percentage of the total population attends church in the USSR each Sunday than in Western Europe.[7] Atheistic Communism has not been able to halt the expansion of Christianity in the Soviet Union. If Christianity perishes there, it will not be due to atheistic Communism. It will happen because European and American Christians approved a nuclear policy that culminated in a holocaust destroying the 70 million Soviet Christians.

Do we not crucify Christ anew when we kill other members of his body? If Paul's doctrine of the church is valid, should not our loyalty to Soviet members of Christ's body exceed our loyalty to any secular nation?[8]

Failure to Apply the Criteria

A second significant reservation arises from the fact that in practice the just war tradition has been singularly ineffective in preventing unjust warfare. Christians have, with painfully few exceptions, defended their own nations' wars. They have condemned and then accepted every new escalation of military technology. And they have developed no mechanism independent of the state to evaluate the justice of specific wars. Obviously, failure to implement a theory does not necessarily invalidate it. But consistent, widespread failure should raise serious questions about its usefulness and prompt further consideration of its validity.

Because they involve a human judgment about a particular war (something a completely nonviolent stance avoids), the just war criteria are especially vulnerable to societal pressures and nationalism. This becomes clear when we look at the various ways just war theory has been applied in the past.

On the basis of the just war tradition, it is assumed that at least one side in each conflict is fighting for an unjust cause. Yet in both world wars and in the hundreds of European battles in previous centuries, Christians fought on both sides. If the just war tradition had functioned effectively, the Christians fighting on the wrong side should frequently have realised their country's injustice and opposed the nation's military activities. In fact, the acid test of belief in the just war tradition would seem to be a willingness to fight *against* one's country when it fights unjust wars.[9] Apart from isolated individuals, however, there are very few examples even of effective verbal opposition, much less enlistment in the army of the enemy.

The German church's response to Hitler underlines this failure. If allied opposition to Hitler is the classic example of a just war, then Hitler's attacks provide the classic example of unjust war. What did German Christians do? Only a tiny minority opposed Hitler.

After a careful study of the German Catholic response to Hitler, Gordon Zahn showed that 'German Catholics with but the rarest of exceptions did support the Hitler war effort.'[10] In 1941 the combined South German (Bavarian) hierarchy urged each Catholic 'to fulfil his duty fully and willingly and loyally' and 'to devote your full efforts to the service of the *Vaterland* and the precious *Heimat* [homeland].'[11] A prominent German Catholic theologian wrote a pamphlet urging Catholics *not* to raise the question of the just war. The question of the justice of the war, he argued, could only be answered 'scientifically' after the war when all documents were available. Therefore, each individual should 'do his best with faith in the cause of his *Volk* [nation].'[12]

Christians at other times and places have not been much more discerning in the heat of national conflict. In *The Origin and Development of the Moral Ideas*, Edward Westermarck says of Protestants: 'It would be impossible to find a single instance of a war waged by a Protestant country from any motive, to which the bulk of its clergy have not given their sanction and support.'[13] The historian W. E. H. Lecky, in his *History of European Morals*, likewise observes: 'We may look in vain for any period since Constantine in which the clergy, as a body, exerted themselves

. . . to prevent or abridge a particular war.'[14] (Perhaps Christian opposition to the war in Vietnam is an exception.)

Reinhold Niebuhr points to the explanation. Human finitude and sin are such that it is extremely difficult to transcend our personal nationalistic feelings and rightly evaluate the justice of our nation's actions. 'Every appeal to moral standards thus degenerates into a moral justification of the self against the enemy.'[15]

Even in the case of the classic illustration of an unjust war, the overwhelming majority of Christians could not faithfully apply the criteria of the just war tradition. That raises serious questions about the usefulness of the entire approach. Perhaps this consistent pattern of nationalistic rationalisation suggests that the hope of faithfully applying just war criteria rests on a naive view of human nature. Might consistent nonviolence be a more realistic response to this essential human sinfulness?[16]

The church has also throughout history denounced and then accepted each new advance in the methods of warfare. In the tenth to twelfth centuries, the more deadly crossbow gradually replaced the short bow. In 1139, the Second Lateran Council condemned the crossbow.[17] But Christians continued to use it. Christian opposition to gunpowder apparently delayed its development in the West – but only for a time. When the first submarine successfully torpedoed and drowned twenty-five hundred men, people denounced it as a terrible crime – and 'immediately set out to improve on it.'[18]

When Germany first attacked the British civilian population in aerial raids, British Christians denounced this gross immorality and vowed not to retaliate in kind. A prominent British churchman, Dr J. H. Oldham, said in 1940: 'The deliberate killing of noncombatants is murder. If war degenerates into wilful slaughter of the innocent, Christians must either become pacifists or give up their religion.'[19] Three years later, he concluded that the line 'between attacks on military targets, on the one hand, and indiscriminate slaughter and wanton destruction, on the other' was of 'secondary importance.' The government could choose whatever military necessity demanded.[20] And in fact Christian pilots participated in the allied firebombing of German cities, including Dresden where over 100,000 non-combatants perished in one day in a huge firestorm. Just war criteria about just means for fighting have often produced verbal objections to the development of new weapons. But they have never prevented either the development or use of whatever was technologically feasible.

The process of decision making is another reason for the failure of the just war criteria. According to the just war tradition, the government has the responsibility to decide whether a particular war will be just or unjust. The classical just war theorists all assumed that the 'Christian sovereigns of Europe' would faithfully apply the criteria. The individual soldier could presume that the war was just if the prince ordered him into battle. Only if the war was clearly unjust should he refuse.[21] It is doubtful that this Constantinian arrangement where the state was assumed to be Christian and therefore competent to decide for Christians was ever adequate. But it has become increasingly obvious that it is not.

In the modern world of sovereign nation states, there is no world authority which can objectively declare particular wars just or unjust. Therefore each individual nation acts as both prosecutor and judge of the actions of its opponents. If human sinfulness is too great to enable the individual citizen to function honestly and objectively as both prosecutor and judge, surely the same is true of nations.[22]

Furthermore, modern secular governments are not Christian even in whatever limited sense they might have been in medieval Europe. But in the twentieth century it is still widely assumed by Christians in the just war tradition that the government is to decide whether a given war is just or not.[23] How can we assume that a secular government in Western Europe, composed of Christians, Jews, secular humanists and agnostics, will faithfully apply the just war criteria in a way satisfactory to devout Christians? How can we assume that Hitler's elite or the atheistic rulers of the USSR could apply these criteria satisfactorily for German or Soviet Christians? Obviously every government will always say that the current war it is fighting or intends to fight is just and necessary.

Only in recent decades have the churches stressed more clearly the individual's right and obligation to evaluate particular wars. Both Protestants and Catholics have supported selective conscientious objection to particular wars on the part of individual Christians.[24]

But surely this approach is too individualistic. The individual Christian needs the help and insight of other Christians in such complex issues. Within those churches that still accept the just war tradition, there ought to be a specific, well-developed mechanism for assembling the insights of ethicists, theologians, social scientists and so on, to examine carefully the validity of possible wars that the nation might plausibly consider fighting. Individual Christians, of course, would still need to reach their own personal conclusions. But decisions as weighty as war and peace require the collective wisdom of the corporate body of believers.

The isolated individual needs help to understand complex issues and withstand nationalistic propaganda. Secular governments will always rationalise current plans and narrow national self-interest. Only if churches in the just war tradition develop sophisticated, functioning mechanisms for evaluating the validity of the wars their members may be called to fight will the just war tradition maintain credibility. The absence of such mechanisms is one measure of the failure of that tradition.

The Early Church's Attitude toward War

At a time when both the weapons of mass destruction and the ineffectiveness of the just war tradition seem to make Christian participation in war more and more questionable, it becomes increasingly important to examine the witness of the early church.

Modern historical scholarship indicates that for three centuries all known Christian writings condemned war. In his careful scholarly study entitled *Christian Attitudes toward War and Peace*, Roland Bainton notes that until the early fourth century there is not a single existing Christian writing which supports Christian participation in warfare.[25] Paul Ramsey, the leading contemporary just war theorist, admits that 'for almost two centuries of the history of the early church, Christians were universally pacifists.'[26] And Ramsey attributes their opposition to war to their theology of the cross: 'How could anyone, who knew himself to be classed with transgressors and the enemies of God whom Christ came to die to save, love his own life and seek to save it more than that of his own enemy or murderer?'[27]

When the Emperor Constantine baptised his troops and adopted Christianity in AD 313, however, rapid change occurred. Christianity became the official religion of the Empire, and masses of people flocked into the church. Theologians rethought the unanimous stance of the previous three centuries in order to allow Christians to fight for the 'Christian' emperors. By the early fifth century, only Christians could serve in the army.

Even before Constantine, to be sure, there had been a few Christians in the army. Eight epitaphs of dead soldiers represent the primary evidence of Christians in the army for the almost three hundred years prior to Constantine.[28] Writing in AD 197 Tertullian rebuked Christians who were in the army, thus acknowledging that some were there. Many, he added, withdrew at conversion.[29] It is clear from the pagan author Celsus in 170 that their numbers were very few. Celsus condemned Christianity on the grounds that if everyone became Christian, there would be no army![30]

Part of the explanation for the presence of limited numbers of Christians in the army is its police function. Bainton points out that 'a soldier might serve for a lifetime without killing in an empire at peace where the army was vested with the functions of a police force.'[31] In Rome one military unit was responsible for fire protection and keeping the peace. Christians apparently distinguished between service in the army in peacetime and in war. There is evidence of Christians participating in branches of the military devoted primarily to police work. The Canons of Hippolytus, an official church document from the early third century, makes it clear that such service was not to include killing: 'A [Christian] soldier of the civil authority must be taught not to kill men and to refuse to do so if he is commanded.'[32]

By the late third century, more Christians were in the army. In the great persecution of 303–4, some of those martyred for their Christian faith were soldiers. But even then the numbers were probably still not large.[33]

Why were the unanimous teaching and the predominant practice of the church in the first three centuries opposed to Christian participation in war? Some have argued that it was because of widespread idolatry (worship of the emperor) in the army rather than opposition to killing. But only officers had to sacrifice to the emperor. Since the church allowed soldiers who became Christians to remain in the army as long as they did not kill, idolatry in the army was not the main problem.[34]

Again and again the sources make it clear the early church believed that Jesus' teaching excluded killing. Tertullian (AD 160–220) taught that Jesus' summons to love enemies was the 'principal precept.'[35] He believed that in disarming Peter in the garden of Gethsemane, Jesus 'ungirded every soldier.' He asked, 'How shall a Christian wage war? Nay, how shall he even be a soldier in peacetime without the sword which the Lord had taken away?'[36]

In the middle of the third century, Origen (AD 183–254) said: We Christians no longer take up sword against nation, nor do we learn to make war any more, having become children of peace for the sake of Jesus who is our leader. . . .

To those who ask us where you have come from or who is our commander, we say that we have come in accordance with the counsels of Jesus to cut down our warlike and arrogant swords of dispute into ploughshares, and we convert into sickles the spears we formerly used in fighting. For we no longer take sword against a nation, nor do we learn any more to make war, having become sons of peace for the sake of Jesus, who is our commander.[37]

In the middle of the previous century, Justin Martyr (martyred in AD 165) had said the same thing: 'We who were filled with war and mutual slaughter and all wickedness have each and all throughout the earth changed our instruments of war, our swords into ploughshares and our spears into farming-tools, and cultivate piety, justice, love of mankind, faith and the hope which we have from the Father through the Crucified One.'[38] A constant stream of Christian writers in the second and third centuries – Tatian, Athenagoras, Irenaeus, Clement of Alexandria, Cyprian, Minucius, Felix, Lactantius – all unanimously condemned Christian participation in war.[39]

Does this early Christian witness have any relevance for our thermonuclear age? Does nuclear war, perhaps, disclose more clearly than ever before what the early church believed about war? All Christians agree that the root of war is sin – humanity's idolatrous rebellion against God. Instead of accepting God, Adam and Eve and all their descendants have placed themselves at the centre of the universe. This egocentrism has led, since the time of Cain, to a terrible willingness to kill one's neighbour for the sake of one's own interests, values or nation.

The consequence has been an unending spiral of violence. Clubs gave way to slingshots; longbows to cannon; firebombs to twenty-megaton nuclear warheads. Each new weapon, its creators promised, would preserve the peace. And they usually said it would never be used. But military necessity dictated otherwise. Horrified by each escalation, Christians regularly protested and then reluctantly decided that temporarily, in a fallen world, the new weapons could be used to preserve the peace. But each act of violence led to another. One war always spawned another. Unconditional surrender in World War I led to World War II. Defeating Hitler with the help of Stalin led to the establishment of two armed superpowers capable of destroying the planet with nuclear weapons.

War has always involved a sinful willingness to destroy a neighbour for the sake of one's own interests. Now we contemplate destroying not just a few thousand neighbours, or a few million neighbours, but hundreds of millions of neighbours, perhaps all neighbours. As Karl Barth has said: 'It only needed the atom and hydrogen bomb to complete the self-disclosure of war.'[40] Formerly there were limits on the evil sinful persons could inflict. Now the limits have virtually disappeared.

The serpent promised we would be like God. And he was almost correct. The ultimate result of the Satanic spiral of violence is our twenty-megaton bomb whose explosion has an initial temperature of 150 million degrees Fahrenheit. That is eight times the temperature at the centre of the sun. We have become almost like God in our awesome power to destroy.

Why has God allowed us to develop such awful weapons? Undoubtedly because God takes our sinful, stubborn desire to create our own kind of peace and security through violence so seriously that he is willing to let it reach even to nuclear holocaust – unless our desperate predicament forces us to learn that we cannot live without him and that peace and security come not from more deadly weapons but from trust in God. 'Why, under God's sovereignty, the Bomb? Because God chose to let our rebellion be limitless; because He has chosen to give this culminating disclosure that apart from Him we are doomed; because He is, in this dread time, calling all peoples to recognise that "There is salvation in no one else, for there is no other name under heaven given among men by which we must be saved' (Acts 4:12)."[41]

The way of escalating violence has led to a terrifying impasse. Our only hope lies in trying a new direction. In the late twentieth century, at the most awesome impasse in human history, is it not time to re-examine the whole issue of war and peace? Might there be more hope in the road walked by the Christians of the first three centuries? Might they perhaps have understood the mind of Christ more clearly than subsequent generations?

Next we will look at what Jesus and the New Testament say about war and peace.

'Love your enemies.'
Matthew 5:43

6

Jesus and Violence

'Peace among men on earth,' the angels sang when God's Son came into our midst as a helpless infant. The Jews of Jesus' day had long awaited the messianic age of peace foreseen by the prophets. But they expected that peaceful age only after the Messiah had violently overthrown their Roman oppressors.

The babe of Bethlehem claimed to be the Messiah. He announced that the long-expected messianic age of peace and righteousness was indeed breaking into the present evil age in his own person and work. But he disappointed passionate nationalists with his summons to love enemies, even hated Roman oppressors. He grounded this radical demand in the very nature of God, who also loves his enemies. As Messiah and Son of God, he claimed divine authority to dispense forgiveness. And he pointed to his death and resurrection as keys to understanding these otherwise blasphemous claims and revolutionary ideas.

After the resurrection, his followers continued to teach and live his nonviolent way. They also offered to a divided, broken world a new community of peace where hostile walls between Jews and Gentiles, slaves and masters were crumbling. Like Jesus, they grounded their radical message and revolutionary social order in the atonement. They loved their enemies because God himself had reconciled his sinful enemies when his incarnate Son died on the cross for our sins. Jesus' self-sacrificial death for others was for them both the unrepeatable ground of unconditional acceptance before God and the central ethical standard for how to treat friend and foe. Those who want to be children of the heavenly Father who loved a sinful world so much that he gave his only Son must be ready to take the way of the cross in a fallen, violent world.

Before Easter this way of love seemed impossible, even to the disciples like Peter. But the resurrection and Pentecost removed all doubt that the new messianic age had truly invaded this old age. In the power of the Spirit, Jesus' peaceful approach to enemies was a present possibility.

That, in brief, is the essence of the New Testament gospel of peace to be developed in this chapter and the next. Such a view grounds its opposition to war and its commitment to nonviolence and peacemaking in the very heart of orthodox Christian confession.[1] Some critics have argued that pacifism rests on theological liberalism.[2] In fact, many pacifists have been theological liberals. We, however, believe that an adequate understanding of nonviolence can only be grounded in the heart of historical Christian orthodoxy. Conversely, we believe that a high Christology and a belief in the substitutionary atonement lead inexorably to a total rejection of war. We need to examine this thesis in detail.

The Old Testament Hope for Peace

Shalom, the Old Testament term for peace, is a rich, comprehensive word.[3] 'Well-being' and 'wholeness' are good synonyms. Shalom refers to wholeness in every area: material abundance, national prosperity, right relationships among persons in society. Leviticus 26:3–6 paints a glorious picture of this comprehensive shalom which God will give Israel if the people walk in his law. The earth will yield rich harvests; wild animals will not ravage the countryside, and 'the sword shall not go through your land.' Tragically, Israel disobeyed God and terrible destruction resulted.

Beyond national disaster, however, the prophets foresaw a new age of shalom. They looked for a messianic age when a Davidic Messiah would restore peace in all its richness. In the latter days, the prophets foretold, all nations would learn God's ways.

> And they shall beat their swords into ploughshares,
>   and their spears into pruning hooks;
> nation shall not lift up sword against nation,
>   neither shall they learn war any more. (Is 2:4; Mic 4:3)

The prophets expected the Messiah to usher in this age of peace. In 'the latter time' (the messianic age), the boot of the tramping warrior and the battle garments rolled in blood will disappear (Is 9:5).

> For to us a child is born,
>   to us a son is given;
> and the government will be upon his shoulder,
>   and his name will be called
> 'Wonderful Counsellor, Mighty God,
>   Everlasting Father, Prince of Peace.'
> Of the increase of his government and of peace
>   there will be no end,
> upon the throne of David, and over his kingdom,
>   to establish it, and to uphold it
> with justice and with righteousness
>   from this time forth and for evermore. (Is 9:6–7)

Although the word *peace* is not used, the vision of messianic shalom in Isaiah 11 is at least as breathtaking. When the messianic shoot from the stump of Jesse comes forth, he will judge the poor with righteousness (v. 4). Peace and harmony will prevail throughout the earth.

> The wolf shall dwell with the lamb,
>   and the leopard shall lie down with the kid,
> and the calf and the lion and the fatling together,
>   and a little child shall lead them. . . .
> They shall not hurt or destroy
>   in all my holy mountain;

for the earth shall be full of the knowledge of the LORD
as the waters cover the sea. (Is 11:6, 9)

Von Rad summarises the Messiah's role in the prophetic
hope for shalom: 'The Messiah is the Guarantor and Guar-
dian of peace in the coming Messianic kingdom.'[4]

In both these messianic passages, peace, justice and
righteousness are a central part of the expected messianic
age. Elsewhere, Isaiah points out that peace is the result of
justice and righteousness (32:16–17).[5] The prophets, then,
foresaw a time when God's Messiah would come to restore
Israel and to establish justice and peace.

The early church declared Jesus to be the fulfilment of
these messianic prophecies. Matthew 4:15–16 quotes
Isaiah 9:1–2 in connection with the beginning of Jesus'
proclamation of the coming of the messianic kingdom. Paul
refers to Isaiah 11:1 and 10 in Romans 15:12. In Luke
1:68–79, Zechariah announces that John the Baptist will
prepare the way for Jesus, the Messiah. Quoting Isaiah 9:2,
Zechariah points with eager anticipation to the Messiah
who will 'guide our feet into the way of peace' (Lk 1:79).
When the angels (Lk 2:14) announce Jesus' birth with the
choral shout 'peace among men,' they simply confirm the
fulfilment of the prophetic vision of messianic peace.[6]

Exactly the same claim appears in the church fathers of
the first three centuries. As we saw in chapter five, all
Christian writers of the first three centuries taught that
Jesus' way of shalom was incompatible with killing. Repeatedly they asserted that the messianic prophecies of
Isaiah 2:4 and Micah 4:3 were fulfilled in Jesus' prohibition
against killing. 'We have come in accordance with the
counsels of Jesus to cut down our warlike and arrogant
swords of dispute into ploughshares, and we convert into
sickles the spears we formerly used in fighting. For we no
longer take sword against a nation, nor do we learn any
more to make war.'[7]

The Messianic Kingdom Arrives

The Gospels summarise Jesus' message with words that must have sent shivers of excitement racing through first-century Jewish folk: 'The time is fulfilled, and the kingdom of God is at hand; repent, and believe in the gospel' (Mk 1:15).[8] What did he mean? There is increasing scholarly agreement that Jesus meant two things: He meant he was the long-expected Messiah, and he meant the Messianic age was breaking into the present.[9]

Vigorous debate has raged over whether Jesus thought the kingdom was entirely future or entirely present, or partially future and partially present. Some scholars have argued that the kingdom was entirely present in his life and work. Others have insisted that for Jesus the kingdom was exclusively future. It would come only at the end of the age.[10] But there is a growing consensus that, in striking contrast to contemporary Jewish thought, Jesus viewed the kingdom as both present and future. Jewish eschatology (belief about the 'last things') looked forward to a super-natural convulsion when the Messiah would come to destroy Israel's national enemies in a bloody battle and initiate the new age of messianic peace. In Jewish expectation, there was a radical, almost total break, between the old age and the new messianic age. Jesus, on the other hand, taught that the messianic age had actually broken into the old age. Its powers were already at work in this old age in his person and work, even though the kingdom would come in its fullness only at the end of history.

Several incidents from the Gospels support the contention that Jesus considered the messianic kingdom to be present already.[11] Luke places the programmatic account of the visit to the synagogue at Nazareth at the beginning of Jesus' public ministry. There Jesus read from Isaiah 61:1–2, widely accepted as a messianic passage. A tremor of anticipation must have surged through the synagogue as they listened to the words about the coming Messiah who would release captives, heal the blind and liberate the oppressed. When he was finished, Jesus informed the audience, 'Today this scripture has been fulfilled in your hearing' (Lk 4:21).

Jesus made a similar claim when John the Baptist sent some of his disciples to ask if he was 'he who is to come' (that is, the Messiah). Jesus' answer contained clear allusions to messianic prophecies: 'Go and tell John what you hear and see: the blind receive their sight and the lame walk, lepers are cleansed and the deaf hear, and the dead are raised up and the poor have good news preached to them' (Mt 11:4–5).[12] His actions, Jesus said, demonstrated that he was fulfilling messianic expectation. After a dispute with the Pharisees about the source of his power over demons, Jesus declared: 'If it is by the Spirit of God that I cast out demons, then the kingdom of God *has come upon you*' (Mt 12:28).[13]

Yet Jesus recognised that the kingdom had not reached its culmination. Sin and evil continued to flourish, so Jesus looked ahead to a time of eschatological fulfilment when, at the close of the age, the kingdom would come in its fullness.[14]

If the presence of the kingdom evoked delight, the demands of the kingdom provoked dismay. Jesus challenged the status quo wherever it was wrong.

He upset men who were happy with the easy divorce laws that enabled them to dismiss their wives for many reasons. Instead he insisted that God intended one man and one woman to live together in lifelong, joyful union. Jesus also disregarded social patterns that treated women as inferior. According to Jews of the time, a woman's word had no authority in court.[15] It was a disgrace for men to appear publicly with women. A widely used prayer recommended for daily use by the Jewish male thanked God that he had not been created a Gentile, an ignorant man or a woman.[16] Jesus, on the other hand, appeared publicly with women (Jn 4:27), taught them theology (Lk 10:38–42) and honoured them with his first resurrection appearance.

Jesus upset political rulers, smugly satisfied with their domination of their subjects. In the dawning messianic age,

servanthood must replace domination.[17] The greatest in
the kingdom is the Messiah who is a servant of all. Therefore those who aspire to leadership in Jesus' kingdom must
likewise be humble servants rather than domineering masters.

Jesus terrified the economic establishment of his day. It
would be easier for a camel to squeeze through the eye of a
needle, he insisted, than for a rich person to enter the
kingdom (Mt 19:24). He summoned those with capital to
lend to the needy even if they had no hope of recovering
their investment (Lk 6:30, 34; Mt 5:42).[18] He recognised in
the rich young ruler that idolatrous materialism that
plagues many rich people. Therefore he summoned him –
and presumably all others who worship the same idol – to
give all his wealth to the poor (Mt 19:21). And he denounced those who oppress poor widows. If, as an increasing number of scholars have argued, Luke 4:18–19 represents Jesus' announcement of the Jubilee, that simply
underlines his call for the most radical changes in economic
life.[19]

In a daring act that led to his arrest, Jesus attacked the
economic oppression and the religious desecration going
on in the temple. Many people see only the religious side of
Jesus' cleansing of the temple. But the text explicitly says
that Jesus objected to both the sacrilege and the robbery:
'It is written, "My house shall be a house of prayer"; but
you have made it a den of robbers' (Lk 19:46). The chief
priests and their collaborators with Rome had a monopoly
on the sale of sacrificial animals, which Jewish worshippers
who came from any distance had to purchase in order to
sacrifice. Apparently they turned the Temple's Court of the
Gentiles into a profitable stockyard where they charged
very high prices. Jesus denounces their desecration of the
Gentiles' place of prayer for the sake of economic
oppression.[20]

It is hardly surprising that the authorities moved quickly
(Lk 19:47) to dispose of him. A person demanding such
radical change from the rich and powerful was a dangerous

revolutionary. Jesus' uncompromising attack on the status quo wherever it was wrong was *one* fundamental reason he was crucified.

Conflicting Messianic Strategies

Equally astounding and unconventional was Jesus' method of bringing the kingdom. Almost all the Jews of Jesus' day longed for the time of the Messiah. But they had fundamentally contradictory ideas about how to prepare for his coming. The Essenes of the Qumran community had a ritualistic approach. Ritual purity was the way to prepare for the messianic age. The Pharisees offered a legalistic strategy. If everyone would obey the law perfectly, the Messiah would come. The Zealots demanded violence. They genuinely believed that if they could persuade the entire Jewish nation to rebel against Rome, the Messiah would come.[21]

Violent Messianic Hopes.   The Zealots were not alone in expecting bloody conflict with the Romans. The 'peaceful' Essenes opposed violent resistance to Rome for a time, but their War Scroll reveals violent expectations. When God himself would intervene at the end of the age, all the devout would join him in a holy war of total annihilation of the wicked.[22] The unsophisticated masses, for their part, yearned for a military Messiah like David:

> How beautiful is the king, the messiah, who will arise from those who are of the house of Judah! He girds up his loins and goes forth and orders the battle array against his enemies and slays the kings along with their overlords, and no king or overlord can stand before him; he reddens the mountains with the blood of their slain, his clothing is dipped in blood like a winepress.[23]

The expectation of widespread violence at the appearance of the Messiah was prevalent. 'According to the unanimous judgment of the historians Josephus, Tacitus and Suetonius, such martial messianic expectations were one of the major causes of the outbreak of the Jewish War.'[24]

To understand the depth of these violent nationalistic visions and the charged political climate they created, it is essential to recall briefly the history of the two centuries before Christ.

For much of the three hundred years preceding Jesus' birth, Greek and then Roman foreigners ruled Palestine. They exacted heavy taxation and imposed Hellenistic cultural values.[25] In 167 BC the Hellenistic conquerors pushed too fast in their zeal to transform Jerusalem into a Hellenistic city. When they and apostate Jewish collaborators desecrated the Temple, forbade worship there and prohibited the observance of the Torah, devout Jews rebelled. Drawing on the tradition of the holy war and appealing to Jewish nationalism, the Maccabeans drove the Greek conquerors out of Palestine in a series of bloody battles and secured one hundred years of political freedom. But that was not to last. In 63 BC Pompey's Roman soldiers conquered Palestine, inaugurating many centuries of Roman rule.

Apart from the question of political freedom and national independence for which the Jews eagerly yearned, Roman rule was hardly benign. Herod the Great, who ruled as a client king of Rome until 4 BC, turned large portions of Palestine into personal estates worked by tenants – an oppressive arrangement depicted in Jesus' parables. After AD 6, when Judea became a directly governed Roman province, governors were often oppressive. Pilate, according to a first-century contemporary, was 'of hard disposition, brutal and pitiless.' His administration was full of 'corruption, violence, robbery, brutality, extortion and execution without trial.'[26] Hated collaborating tax collectors exacted heavy taxes. And there was the ongoing danger that Jewish religious life would be violated – witness, for instance, Emperor Caligula's attempt to set up his statue in the temple in AD 41.

That apocalyptic, messianic expectation was widespread

and intense among nationalistic Jews in the first century AD is hardly surprising. Almost everyone longed for the dawning of the new age when the Messiah would come to end the rule of the hated foreign oppressors. Given the common assumption of all messianic expectation that the Messiah would end Roman rule, the Romans naturally took a dim view of messianic claims. They viewed the succession of messianic pretenders who appeared in the first century AD as dangerous political enemies guilty of treason against Roman rule.

And they had good reason for concern. When Herod the Great died, just after Jesus' birth, three different messianic pretenders provoked armed rebellion. The Roman governor of Syria came to Jerusalem and crucified two thousand rebels. Judas, who was probably a founder of the Zealots a few years later, attacked an arsenal of Herod's three miles from Jesus' home town of Nazareth.[27] 'Messianic expectations had grown particularly intense during the reign of Herod, and . . . Jewish Palestine had become a politico-religious tinderbox.'[28]

In AD 6, when Judea became a Roman province, an underground organisation of violent, nationalistic revolutionaries emerged. The Zealots were full of ardent zeal for the law and intense messianic expectation. Deeply religious, they believed that God would intervene to usher in the new age if they could provoke a popular rebellion against Rome. According to the Zealots, slaying the godless was a religious duty.

The Zealots' mixture of fiery nationalism, religious zeal and concern for justice had significant popular appeal. In AD 6 a popular uprising led by Judas was only narrowly averted. Partially suppressed, the Zealots operated as guerrilla bands from their strongholds in the caves of the Judean desert. Occasionally, they raided Jerusalem, kidnapping prominent persons to exchange for prisoners. During the forties, two sons of Judas were crucified as Zealots. Finally in AD 66 the Zealots achieved sufficient support to conquer Jerusalem and begin the Jewish war.

The result was the total destruction of the city.[29]

In Jesus' time, the question of violent revolution was a burning issue – probably the political issue of the day. And the Zealot answer was popular.

To be sure, not all Jews favoured armed rebellion. The Sadducees and high priestly aristocracy preferred to collaborate with the Romans. The clan of Annas held the office of high priest almost all of the time between AD 6 and 41. They used some of the vast sums earned from their monopoly on the sale of animals for Temple sacrifices to offer huge bribes to the Roman governors. The moderate Pharisees also opposed rebellion, and the Essenes preferred to retreat into the Judean caves to wait quietly for the day of vengeance.

The German New Testament scholar Martin Hengel summarises this background of imperialist violence, foreign oppression and passionate nationalism so full of surprising parallels to the injustice, violence and nationalism of our own time:

> For the unsophisticated Jewish population, it was almost entirely a history of oppressive exploitation, wars of indescribable brutality and disappointed hopes. The rule of Herod and his sons and the corrupt regime of the procurators – Pilate not least among them – had made the situation in Jewish Palestine so intolerable that apparently only three possibilities remained: armed revolutionary resistance, more or less opportunistic accommodation to the establishment – leaving open the possibility of mental reservations – and patient passive endurance.[30]

It was into that maelstrom of oppression, violence and intense messianic expectation that Jesus of Nazareth stepped to proclaim and incarnate a fourth possibility – the way of suffering servanthood and unconditional love for enemies grounded in God's unmerited mercy toward sinners.

These two crucial elements of Jesus' messianic strategy –

unconditional love, even toward enemies, and unmerited forgiveness, even toward the worst of sinners – contrasted sharply with popular expectation. And both, as we shall see, were grounded in the very nature of God, who loves even his enemies.

Forgiveness as a sign of the kingdom.   Entry into the messianic kingdom, Jesus announced, was through divine forgiveness. It was not, as the Pharisees believed, through careful observance of the law and consequent merit. The kingdom of heaven, Jesus said, is like a merciful king who freely forgives a huge debt when his servant cannot repay it (Mt 18:23–35). To the horror of the Pharisees, Jesus eagerly forgave even the most notorious offenders – prostitutes, the woman caught in adultery and hated tax-collectors profiting from collaboration with the foreign oppressors. To underline his acceptance, he shared table-fellowship with those social outcasts. When the self-righteous protested indignantly, he retorted that he came, not to call the righteous, but sinners (Mk 2:17).

Jesus forgave sinners in this radical, prodigal way because he knew that God is like the forgiving father in the parable of the prodigal son. In parable after parable, Jesus taught that God takes the initiative to forgive sinners.

> Throughout all the parables, God appears in constantly new variations as the one who is generous: as the magnanimous, merciful king, as the lender generously cancelling a debt, as the shepherd seeking the sheep, as the woman searching for the lost coin, as the Father rushing out to meet his son, as the judge hearing the prayer of the tax-collector. Again and again he is seen afresh as the God of infinite mercy.[31]

We in turn – as the parable about the forgiving servant so vividly shows – are to imitate God's radical forgiveness in our relationships with others (Mt 18:23–35).

Jesus not only taught about a forgiving God. He also claimed personal authority to forgive sins. No Jewish sources speak of the Messiah forgiving sins on his own authority.[32] But Jesus boldly claimed that authority. Jesus forgave the sins of the paralytic seeking healing. When the religious leaders objected to this blasphemous infringement of God's sole authority to forgive sins, he retorted: 'That you may know that the Son of man has authority on earth to forgive sins . . . I say to you, rise, take up your pallet and go home' (Mk 2:10–11). It is striking that Jesus calls himself the 'Son of man' in this passage on forgiveness.[33] The Son of man as described in Daniel was a heavenly messianic figure who would come on the clouds of heaven to judge the earth and usher in the kingdom.[34] As the messianic Son of man, Jesus does indeed bring the kingdom. But he brings it through dispensing forgiveness rather than judgment.

It is possible that Jesus saw himself fulfilling the messianic prophecy of Jeremiah. Jeremiah foretold a time when God would make a new covenant with his people and would write his law on their hearts. This messianic passage culminates with the promise of forgiveness: 'For I will forgive their iniquity, and I will remember their sin no more' (Jer 31:34).[35] Jesus understood his offer of forgiveness as a fundamental element of the kingdom that was breaking into history in his person and work.[36] Forgiveness, not vengeance, was the sign of his messianic kingdom.

Suffering servanthood instead of violence. No image more powerfully contrasts Jesus' peaceful, messianic conception with violent contemporary expectations than that of the Suffering Servant. Popular Jewish thought hoped for a warlike, Davidic Messiah who would destroy the heathen oppressors. The early church taught that the Jewish messianic hope had been fulfilled in the humble Suffering Servant foreseen in Isaiah 53. This Old Testament passage spoke of a lowly servant who would suffer rather than kill: 'He was wounded for our transgressions, he was bruised for our iniquities; upon him was the chastisement that made us whole' (Is 53:5). In his careful study, Jeremias concludes that from the beginning the early Christians saw Jesus as the fulfilment of Isaiah's 'servant of God.'[37]

Jeremias also holds that Jesus understood himself and his death in terms of Isaiah 53.[38] There are repeated indications in the Gospels that Jesus expected to die violently.[39] Mark 10:45, which probably contains an allusion to Isaiah 53, indicates that he saw his death as a ransom for others.[40] The word *ransom* probably refers to the offering for sin of Isaiah 53:10.[41] At the Last Supper, Jesus spoke of his death for others in words that also probably allude to Isaiah 53.[42] Understanding his messianic role in the light of Isaiah 53, Jesus expected to die for others rather than to destroy the wicked.

Only in this context can we adequately understand Jesus' important teaching about peacemaking. It is the one who comes as Israel's true Messiah but then totally rejects all violent messianic visions who rebukes Peter for using the sword. It is the one who faces the burning political question of his day and rejects violence as the way to usher in the messianic kingdom who says, 'Turn the other cheek.' It is the Messiah whose kingdom has already begun in dramatic acts of divine forgiveness who says, 'Love your enemies . . . . so that you may be sons of your Father who is in heaven.'

Jesus' Nonviolent Life

In both actions and words Jesus rejected lethal violence. At the triumphal entry Jesus clearly disclosed his nonviolent messianic conception. Both Matthew 21:5 and John 12:15 quote Zechariah 9:9 to underline their belief that Jesus' action fulfilled this Old Testament prophecy. Modern commentators agree that Jesus consciously chose to fulfil the eschatological prophecy of Zechariah precisely because it depicted a humble, peaceful Messiah.[43] Zechariah's peaceful vision contrasts sharply with most messianic expectations:

Lo, your king comes to you;
    triumphant and victorious is he,
humble and riding on an ass,
    on a colt the foal of an ass.
I will cut off the chariot from Ephraim
    and the war horse from Jerusalem;
and the battle bow shall be cut off,
    and he shall command peace to the nations.
        Zech 9:9–10)

Here is a picture of the Messiah riding not a warhorse but a humble donkey. Echoing many prophets who had denounced Israel's reliance on chariots and cavalry, the text foresees the abolition of instruments of war. Messianic peace prevails.

This is the messianic picture which Jesus chooses to fulfil. The phrase 'peace in heaven' in Luke's account of the triumphal entry (19:38) means that the messianic peace which God in heaven initiates is now present.[44] The excited crowds spread garments in homage to a king and shout messianic slogans: 'Blessed is the King' (Lk 19:38), 'Hosanna to the Son of David' (Mt 21:9). They are not mistaken in thinking Jesus is making a clear messianic claim. The crowds probably hoped he would at last give the signal for the final eschatological war. Sadly, however, they discover that Jesus' ideas differ radically from theirs. Vincent Taylor summarises the incident and the crowd's eventual disappointment:

Jesus must have observed the growing Messianic tension among His disciples and have realised that His teaching about a suffering Messiah had failed. . . . By previous arrangement He sends two disciples for the colt, intending to fulfil Zechariah's prophecy. Unable to deny that He is the promised Messiah, He seeks to show to His disciples and to the crowd the kind of Messiah He is, no man of war, but lowly and riding upon an ass. The crowd is puzzled, but penetrates His meaning to see that He is not to be the Messiah of their hopes. That is why they turned against Him.[45]

❧

In the final crisis, Jesus persisted in his rejection of the sword. He rebuked Peter for attacking those who came to arrest him: 'All who take the sword will perish by the sword' (Mt 26:52). Not even the defensive sword should be used. We find it significant that Jesus' rebuke to Peter gives a general reason for not using the sword, not just an objection to use in this special case. 'He is obviously not thinking of just this special situation since he takes pains to lay down the general truth that they who take the sword shall perish with it.'[46]

Similarly, Jesus informed Pilate that his kingdom was not of this world *in one specific way* – namely, that his followers do not use violence: 'My kingship is not of this world; if my kingship were of this world, my servants would fight, that I might not be handed over to the Jews; but my kingship is not from the world' (Jn 18:36).[47] Jesus obviously did not mean that the messianic kingdom he had begun had nothing to do with this world. That would have contradicted the kingdom values he announced, and it would have made nonsense of the very prayer he taught his disciples: 'Thy kingdom come *on earth* as it is in heaven.'

Jesus' high priestly prayer is perhaps the best commentary: 'The world has hated them because they are not of the world, even as I am not of the world. I do not pray that thou shouldst take them out of the world, but that thou shouldst keep them from the evil one' (Jn 17:14–15).

In this statement, as in John 18:36, the preposition *of* points to the source, not the location, of authority, methods and norms.[48] This Gospel-of-the-Word-become-flesh would never have said that Jesus was not very much *in* this world. But his authority and methods did not derive from the fallen order. Fighting – even defensive violence to prevent the most unjust arrest in human history – belongs to the old sinful order. Jesus' followers, however, must live according to the norms of the new messianic age. Therefore, Jesus says, they will not fight.

Jesus' Nonviolent Teaching

Jesus not only lived the way of nonviolence, he also taught it. Matthew 5:38–48 is the central passage:[49]

> You have heard that it was said, 'An eye for an eye and a tooth for a tooth.' But I say to you, Do not resist one who is evil. But if any one strikes you on the right cheek, turn to him the other also; and if any one would sue you and take your coat, let him have your cloak as well; and if any one forces you to go one mile, go with him two miles. Give to him who begs from you, and do not refuse him who would borrow from you. You have heard that it was said, 'You shall love your neighbour and hate your enemy.' But I say to you, Love your enemies and pray for those who persecute you, so that you may be sons of your Father who is in heaven; for he makes his sun rise on the evil and on the good, and sends rain on the just and on the unjust. For if you love those who love you, what reward have you? Do not even the tax-collectors do the same? And if you salute only your brethren, what more are you doing than others? Do not even the Gentiles do the same? You, therefore, must be perfect, as your heavenly Father is perfect.

To a people so oppressed by foreign conquerors that over the previous two centuries they had repeatedly resorted to violent rebellion, Jesus gave the unprecedented command: 'Love your enemies.' Martin Hengel believes that Jesus formulated this command to love one's enemies in conscious contrast to the teaching and practice of the Zealots.[50] Thus Jesus rejected one currently popular political method in favour of a radically different approach.

Jesus' command to love one's enemies contrasts sharply with widespread views that Jesus summarises in verse 43: 'You have heard that it was said, "You shall love your

neighbour and hate your enemy."' The first part of this
verse is a direct quotation from Leviticus 19:18: 'You shall
love your neighbour as yourself.' But who is one's neighbour? The first part of Leviticus 19:18 indicates that the
neighbour is a 'son of our own people'. This was the normal
Jewish viewpoint. New Testament scholar John Piper, in
his extensive study of pre-Christian thinking about love for
neighbour, shows that in Jewish thought the neighbour that
one was obligated to love was normally understood to be a
fellow Israelite.[51] Thus love for neighbour had clear ethnic,
religious limitations. A different attitude toward Gentiles
was expected. Seldom, however, did the Old Testament
command or sanction hatred of foreigners or enemies.[52]
But Jewish contemporaries of Jesus did. The Zealots believed that 'slaying of the godless enemy out of zeal for
God's cause was a fundamental commandment, true to the
rabbinic maxim: "Whoever spills the blood of one of the
godless is like one who offers a sacrifice."' And the Qumran community's Manual of Discipline urged people to
'love all the sons of light . . . and . . . hate all the sons of
darkness.'[53]

Jesus' way was radically different. Loving those who love
you (v. 46), Jesus says, is relatively easy – even great
sinners like tax-collectors can do that. In fact even the
pagan Gentiles act kindly toward the people in their own
ethnic group. Jesus totally rejects that kind of ethnic or
religious limitation on love.

For the members of Jesus' messianic kingdom, neighbour love must extend beyond the limited circle of the
people of Israel, beyond the limited circle of the new
people of God. This text says explicitly what the parable of
the Good Samaritan (Lk 10:29–37) suggests: All people
everywhere are neighbours to Jesus' followers and therefore are to be actively loved. And that includes enemies –
even violent, oppressive, foreign conquerors!

The difficulty of actually implementing this command
has led to many attempts to weaken its radical demand.
Martin Luther did that with his two-kingdom analysis. He

restricted the application of these verses on love of enemies to the personal sphere and denied their application to the Christian in public life. Luther went so far as to tell Christians that in their roles as public officials, 'You do not have to ask Christ about your duty.'[54] The emperor supplies the ethic for public life. Exegetically, however, that seems highly questionable. As Eduard Schweizer says in his commentary on Matthew, 'There is not the slightest hint of any realm where the disciple is not bound by the words of Jesus.'[55] The context demonstrates clearly that Jesus intends the command to apply to the public sphere. In verses 39–41, Jesus discusses issues that clearly pertain to the public sphere of the legal system and the authorised demands of the Roman rulers.

When Jesus rejects the principle of 'an eye for an eye,' he is not merely offering some admonitions for private, interpersonal relationships, but rather he is transcending a basic legal principle of the Mosaic and other near-Eastern legal systems (see, for example, Ex 21:24).[56] (Obviously Jesus understood his action as the fulfilment of the law. In the next chapter we will deal at length with the relationship between Jesus' teaching and the Old Testament.) Instead of demanding what the law permitted, namely, full retaliation, Jesus commanded a loving response governed by the needs of the other person. One should even submit to further damage and suffering rather than exact equal pain or loss from the unfair, guilty aggressor. In no way should we allow the other person's response to govern our action. Verse 40 ('If anyone would sue you and take your coat, let him have your cloak as well') also clearly speaks of how one should respond in the public arena of the judicial system.

Verse 41 ('If anyone forces you to go one mile, go with him two miles') deals with how to respond to Roman rulers who demand forced labour. The verb translated as 'force' is a technical term used to refer to the requisition of services by civil and military authorities.[57] Josephus used the word to speak of compulsory carrying of military supplies.[58] The Roman rulers could and did demand that civilians in con-

quered lands perform such services. Thus they had the right
to demand that Simon of Cyrene carry Jesus' cross (Mt
27:32). The Latin origin of the word *mile* confirms the fact
that Jesus refers to the requisitioning of forced labour by
the Romans. It is hardly surprising that the Zealots urged
Jews to refuse this kind of forced labour.[59] Jesus, on the
other hand, condemns the Zealots' violent, angry response, even to the Romans' unjust demands.

Nonresistance or Nonviolence?

But this raises a pressing problem. Is Jesus forbidding all
forms of resistance to evil? It seems some forms of coercion
are fully compatible with love and respect for the other
person as a free moral agent while others are not. In the
home with children, in the church in disciplining brothers
and sisters, and in the marketplace with economic boycotts,
coercion can be applied which still respects the other
person's freedom to say no and accept the consequences.
Lethal violence is different. When one engages in lethal
violence, one cannot lovingly appeal to the other person as
a free moral agent responsible to God to choose to repent
and change.[60]

When Jesus said 'Do not resist one who is evil,' did he
mean to forbid all forms of resistance? To interpret Matthew 5:39 in that way is surely to prove too much. If we are
to interpret it literally, then we must consistently apply it in
a literal fashion in every area. If the text calls for literal
nonresistance, then that means absolute nonresistance toward evil persons in the home and in the congregation just
as much as in the search for justice in the marketplace or in
the political arena. It is plainly inconsistent to apply the text
literally to conclude that Jesus' nonresistance forbids
boycotts and strikes and then to apply the text in a less rigid
fashion with regard to the home and the congregation.

Jesus' own actions demonstrate that he did not intend to
forbid all forms of resistance. Jesus constantly opposed evil
persons in a forthright, vigorous fashion. He unleashed a
blistering attack on the Pharisees. Denouncing them as

blind guides, fools, hypocrites and a brood of vipers, he uttered a harsh public condemnation of their many errors, including their preoccupation with tithing in small matters while neglecting more important things like justice and mercy (Mt 23:13–33).

Nor was Jesus nonresistant when he cleansed the temple, driving the animals out with a whip, dumping the money tables upside down and denouncing the moneychangers as robbers. If Matthew 5:39 means that all forms of resistance to evil are forbidden, then Jesus contradicted his own teaching. Jesus certainly did not kill the moneychangers. Indeed, we doubt that he even used his whip on them. But he certainly resisted their evil in a dramatic act of nonviolent resistance.

Nor did Jesus silently submit to aggression at his trial when a soldier unjustly struck him on the cheek (Jn 18:19 –24). Instead of turning the other cheek, he protested! 'If I have spoken wrongly, bear witness to the wrong; but if I have spoken rightly, why do you strike me?' Apparently Jesus thought that protesting against police brutality or engaging in civil disobedience in a nonviolent fashion was entirely consistent with his command not to resist one who is evil. We assume Jesus did not disobey his own teaching. Therefore we must make some kind of distinction between lethal violence and nonviolent coercion even though the text of Matthew 5:38–48 does not explicitly contain this distinction.

What then does Matthew 5:39 mean? It means four very radical things: 1) that one should not respond to an evil person by placing him or her in the category of enemy; 2) that one should not retaliate, but rather respond according to the needs of the offending person, regardless of his offensive attitude or action; 3) that regardless of the offending person's response, one must continue to love because love does not depend on reciprocity; 4) that one should act in these ways even at great personal cost.

The needs – not necessarily the wants – of the person or persons with whom I am dealing must determine my relation to them. Whatever the damage that is done me, I must respond not in similar terms but in terms of the good of the persons involved. This is not a passive principle of supine submission, but the active effort to express the divine love by seeking my enemies' good. This active effort injects a redemptive factor of goodness into a situation which otherwise is dominated by evil.[61]

The good of the other person, not one's own needs or rights, are decisive.[62]

Jesus' command not to resist evil must be understood in the light of the preceding verse. To exact an eye for an eye was the accepted norm. Its fundamental principle was retaliation – limited to be sure by the nature of the offence. But Jesus rejected all retaliation. Instead of hating or retaliating, Jesus' followers are to respond lovingly according to the need of the other person. And that love is to be so clear and costly and so single-mindedly focused on the needs of the other that it will even accept additional insult and injury from the aggressor – even a blow with the back of the hand, the most insulting of all physical blows in Jesus' day. But that does not mean that we cannot offer any form of resistance to the evil person. That would contradict Jesus' own actions. Rather it means costly, aggressive love, controlled by the genuine needs of the other person. The members of Jesus' new messianic kingdom are to love opponents, even oppressive persecuting enemies, so deeply that they can wholeheartedly pray for their well-being and actively demonstrate their love in actions that exceed unjust demands.

We have seen that Jesus' call for nonretaliatory love does not exclude nonlethal resistance to evil. Does it exclude punishment? Not necessarily. One can distinguish retributive punishment, whose purpose is retribution, revenge or retaliation, from disciplinary punishment, whose purpose is reconciliation and restoration. Disciplinary punishment is designed to correct, educate and improve. Matthew 18:15–18 calls for vigorous church discipline. As Paul explicitly says (Gal 6:1–2; 1 Cor 5:5), however, the purpose of church discipline is reconciliation and restoration of the straying person, not retribution. The same is – or should be – true of parental punishment.

Whether in the home with children, in the church with brothers and sisters, or in the state with citizens, Jesus' followers can engage in disciplinary punishment. Retributive punishment and retaliatory vengeance, on the other hand, are excluded for Jesus' followers by the Sermon on the Mount. Only God, as Paul says in Romans 12:19, should execute retribution.[63]

Weakening Jesus' Costly Call

Until the time of Constantine in the fourth century, all Christian writings reflect the belief that Jesus clearly and explicitly forbids Christians to participate in war and capital punishment. Since that time, however, many Christians have thought otherwise.

Some version of ethical dualism lies behind almost all these arguments. In the Middle Ages many distinguished between the commands which apply to all Christians and the counsels of perfection (for example, 'Love your enemies'), which apply only to the particularly devout such as monks and nuns. In Luther's view of the two kingdoms, the love ethic of Jesus applies to the inner disposition of the heart of the individual believer, who never kills in his role as a member of the kingdom of Christ. But in his role as public official in the kingdom of the world, he rightly kills via capital punishment and war.[64] Some dispensationalists relegate the application of the Sermon on the Mount to the millennium. Reinhold Niebuhr, who believed that Jesus himself rejected all violence, considered Jesus' teaching an impossible ideal in a sinful world.[65]

Especially common is the dualistic distinction between the personal and public roles of the Christian. In his personal role, it is argued, the Christian must always refuse to retaliate or kill. But the same person acting in the public role of judge or soldier rightly does both. Jesus then was not forbidding capital punishment or war on the part of duly authorised Christian executioners and soldiers. He was merely forbidding private retaliation on the part of individuals who want to take the law into their own hands.[66]

The view of the authors stands in fundamental contrast to all these versions of ethical dualism. We do not believe God has a double ethic. We do not believe that God ordains a higher ethic for especially devout folk and a lower ethic for the masses. We do not believe that God intends Christians to wait until the millennium to obey the Sermon on the Mount. We do not believe God commands one thing for the individual and another for that same person as public official.

Space prevents a detailed response to each of these views. But the last, because it is widely held, demands careful attention. One might support this view by pointing to the Old Testament. The Old Testament clearly condemns murder, but it also commands capital punishment and war. Unless one supposes a fundamental contradiction, one must assume some kind of distinction between what one does as a person or individual and what one does as a public official. Although the distinction may not be explicitly stated, the material in the Old Testament seems to demand it.

Nor is there any explicit rejection of this kind of distinction in the New Testament. In fact, one standard interpretation of Romans 12:14–13:7 supports it. In Romans 12:19 Paul forbids vengeance, which belongs only to God. Then in 13:4 Paul says government bears the sword in order to execute God's wrath. In the first instance, it is argued, Paul speaks to individuals forbidding personal vengeance. In the second instance, he speaks about the institution of government and authorises all people, including Christians, to use the sword for the protection of the neighbour in their public roles as government officials.

For several reasons we do not believe that Christ urges the individual Christian in a personal role to love enemies but then authorises that same person as public official to kill them. This thesis, we believe, ignores the historical context of Jesus' teaching. It overlooks the most natural meaning of the text. It also relies on pragmatism. Historically it has led to very bad consequences. Finally, it neglects the first three centuries of Christian teaching.

In his historical context, Jesus came as the Messiah of Israel with a plan and an ethic for the entire Jewish people. He advocated love toward (political!) enemies as his specific political response to centuries of violence. His radical nonviolence was a conscious alternative to the contemporary Zealots' call for violent revolution to usher in the messianic kingdom. There is no hint that Jesus' reason for objecting to the Zealots was that they were unauthorised individuals whose violent sword would have been legitimate if the Sanhedrin had only given the order. On the contrary, his point was that the Zealots' whole approach to enemies, even unjust oppressive enemies, was fundamentally wrong. The Zealots offered one political approach; Jesus offered another. But both appealed to the entire Jewish nation.

The many premonitions of national disaster in the Gospels indicate that Jesus realised that the only way to avoid destruction and attain messianic shalom was through a forthright rejection of the Zealot call to arms.[67] In fact, Luke places the moving passage about Jesus' weeping over Jerusalem immediately after the triumphal entry – just after Jesus had disappointed popular hopes with his insistence on a peaceful messianic strategy: 'And when he drew near and saw the city he wept over it, saying, "Would that even today you knew the things that make for *peace*! But now they are hid from your eyes. For the days shall come upon you, when your enemies will cast up a bank about you and . . . will not leave one stone upon another"' (Lk 19:42–44).

Zealot violence, Jesus knew, would lead to national

destruction. It was an illusion – albeit one that constantly tempts humanity – to look for peace through violence. The way of the Suffering Servant was the only way to messianic shalom. Jesus' invitation to the entire Jewish people was to believe that the messianic kingdom was already breaking into the present. Therefore, if they would accept God's forgiveness and follow his Messiah, they could begin now to live according to the peaceful values of the messianic age. Understood in this historical setting, Jesus' call to love enemies can hardly be limited to the personal sphere of private life.

Second, the personal-public distinction also seems to go against the most natural, literal meaning of the text. There is no hint whatsoever in the text of such a distinction. In fact, as we have seen, the text is full of references to *public* life. 'Resist not evil' applies, Jesus says, when people take you to court (v. 40) and when foreign rulers legally demand forced labour (v. 41). Indeed, the basic norm Jesus transcends (an eye for an eye) was a fundamental principle of the legal system. We can safely assume that members of the Sanhedrin and other officials heard Jesus' words. The most natural conclusion is that Jesus intended his words to be normative not just in private but also in public life. The burden of proof would seem to rest on those who want to argue that Jesus was speaking only of the way the individual should act in his private role.

Third, an essentially pragmatic presupposition often underlies the argument that Jesus could not have meant his followers never to use lethal violence. In a sinful world which often tramples on gentle, loving persons, it is argued, violence is necessary to defend oneself and others. Love will simply not work. The factual claim may or may not be right. What is surely most important for Christians, however, is the essential pragmatism of the argument. Surely the *pragmatic* question of whether Jesus' ethic works – that is, whether it enables us and others to avoid suffering – dare not be decisive in our analyses of what Jesus actually meant.[68]

Fourth, the consequences of this dualistic distinction have often been disastrous. Christian soldiers have justified their participation in terrible evil on the pretext that it is not appropriate for them to challenge official orders. The failure of most German Protestants to oppose Hitler's atrocities is often attributed in part to Luther's two-kingdom ethic.[69] In 1933, German Christians argued that 'the church is obliged to obey the state in every earthly matter.' And they concluded that 'unconditional allegiance' to the Nazi state was fully compatible with allegiance to Christ.[70]

Finally, the first three centuries of the Christian church offer weighty evidence against the personal-public distinction. Every one of the many Christian writers who then discussed the problem of war and capital punishment thought that Jesus' teaching explicitly forbade Christians from participation in both. Repeatedly they rejected the view that Christians could kill people in the public role of soldier or executioner. If, as was suggested, the Old Testament data requires some kind of distinction between the personal and public roles with regard to capital punishment and murder, then something unusual must have happened to produce such a dramatic reversal of thinking. The early Christian writers constantly point to Jesus' Sermon on the Mount as the explanation. If they were mistaken, from where did such a novel view arise?

We are convinced that the only adequate explanation for the vigorous rejection of lethal violence by the early Christians is that Christ himself commanded it. If so, Christians ought to forsake the diverse dualistic ethical systems developed since the fourth century and return to Jesus' teaching on nonretaliatory, suffering love.

Three Brief Objections

But would that not lead to anarchy? Furthermore, doesn't the call to implement Jesus' radical kingdom ethics assume that the kingdom has already fully come when obviously it

has not? Finally, how can sinful, secular society live according to Jesus' kingdom ethics?

Our view in no way advocates anarchy. It does not
require that we abolish the police or the law courts. Rather
it suggests that police ought to develop nonviolent ways to
restrain criminals and that the law courts should apply
disciplinary rather than retributive punishment.

It is sometimes claimed that Jesus' kingdom ethic is
impossible to practise until the kingdom comes in its fullness. Since that will not happen until the return of Christ,
responsible realists must sadly use retaliation and violence.
Actually to eliminate the legal principle of 'an eye for an
eye' or to refuse to suppress evil through warfare, it is
claimed, 'must presuppose that not only those who are
injured can return good for evil, but that also no one will do
evil in the first place. In other words its *entire* elimination
presupposes the overcoming of *all* hardness of heart in *all*
men. It presupposes the glorious new age, the consumma-
tion of the Kingdom of God.'[71]

Such a view appears exceedingly plausible – until one
remembers that it contradicts Jesus' specific teaching.
Jesus' words make it clear that he is talking about this
present sinful world. It is precisely in this fallen order where
terrible evil does still exist that we meet hostile people who
slap us on the cheek, greedy folk who wrongly take our
cloaks, and oppressive governments which make unjust
demands. It is precisely in this kind of world that Jesus calls
his followers to love their enemies and reject retaliation. In
fact Jesus adds that unless we do that, we continue to act
like all the other sinners in the fallen world – surely a
gratuitous comment if he intends us to obey these commands only when all evil disappears in the consummated
kingdom. Jesus may have been naive, idealistic or stupid to
suggest that we ought to reject retaliation and lethal violence. But that seems to be what he said.

But can non-Christians obey Jesus' kingdom ethics? Of
course not. But they ought to! The fact that non-Christians
cannot fully obey Jesus' high standards on sexuality and

marriage does not mean that those norms do not apply to them. God does not have one ethic for Christians and a different ethic for others.

Certainly non-Christians will be able to follow kingdom ethics only very imperfectly. But they ought to. And to a certain degree, as the story of Gandhi shows, they can. To the limited extent that non-Christian and secular societies actually approximate Jesus' ethical teaching, to that extent they will enjoy greater justice, wholeness and peace. Truly living out Jesus' call to love one's enemies, however, is possible only by grace. Jesus never thought that such striking love would be possible for fallen humanity. His constant stress on God's radical forgiveness demonstrates that God takes the initiative. It is because Jesus knew that the prophetic promise of a new messianic age when God would write his law on our hearts was being fulfilled in his own person and work that he dared to call people to begin living out the radical, costly values of his new kingdom.[72] Because the powers of the new age are already at work in those who follow Jesus, it is now possible to live radically differently from the fallen world. It is possible even to love one's enemies.

'While we were enemies we were reconciled to God by the death of his Son.'

Romans 5:10

'The sign of the nuclear age is the Bomb. The sign of Christ is the Cross. The Bomb is the countersign to the Cross; it arrogantly threatens to undo the work that the Cross has done. In the Cross, all things are reconciled; in the Bomb, all things are destroyed. In the Cross, violence is defeated; in the Bomb, violence is victorious. In the Cross, evil has been overcome; in the Bomb, evil has dominion. In the Cross, death is swallowed up; in the Bomb, death reigns supreme. Which will hold sway in our times?'

Jim Wallis[1]

7

The Way of the Cross

We have looked at Jesus' life and teaching in its historical setting. What an utterly astounding person this Nazarene carpenter was! He went about the country tenderly ministering to the poor, sick and oppressed. He announced that the messianic age had broken into the present. Therefore the people of God were to begin living out the radical values of the new age. He claimed to be the long-expected Messiah and said he would usher in his kingdom with love (even for enemies) rather than the sword. Indeed he went further, setting his own personal authority above that of Moses, claiming divine authority to forgive sins and acknowledging that he was the Son of God. What exciting good news – if it were really true. What megalomania and blasphemy if it were false.

Cross and Resurrection
And then he died on a cross – as an impious blasphemer, a religious heretic, a social radical and a royal pretender.[2] He suffered the most despicable death possible. Paul's quotation from the Torah 'Cursed be every one who hangs on a tree' (Deut 21:23; Gal 3:13) expressed the Jewish viewpoint. As for the brutally efficient Romans, they knew how to put down political threats. They regularly crucified political criminals, especially the constant stream of rebellious Jewish messianic pretenders. And it worked too. Crucifixion had a decisive way of squelching messianic megalomaniacs. Jesus was finished. Perhaps the disciples and some of the poor masses may have begun to understand

and accept a little of Jesus' fantastic vision and claims. But the Roman and Jewish establishments did not believe such nonsense for a moment. And they killed him to prove they were right.

Jürgen Moltmann is surely correct in insisting that the cross decisively destroyed the credibility of Jesus' message and claims:

> He who proclaimed that the kingdom was near died abandoned by God. He who anticipated the future of God in miracles and in casting out demons died helpless on the cross. He who revealed the righteousness of God with an authority greater than Moses died according to the provision of the law as a blasphemer. He who spread the love of God in his fellowship with the poor and the sinners met his end between two criminals on the cross. . . . For the disciples who had followed Jesus to Jerusalem, his shameful death was not the consummation of his obedience to God nor a demonstration of martyrdom for his truth, but the rejection of his claim. It did not confirm their hopes in him, but permanently destroyed them.[3]

Then he rose from the dead.[4] It was the resurrection which restored the hope of the discouraged disciples. In spite of the cross, Jesus' claims and his announcement of the messianic kingdom were still valid – because he had risen!

Jewish eschatological expectation looked for a general resurrection and the pouring out of God's Spirit at the beginning of the new age. As Paul reflected on Jesus' resurrection, he realised that one instance of this eschatological resurrection had actually occurred in the old age. Thus he referred to Jesus' resurrection as the 'first fruits' (1 Cor 15:20–23) of that final general resurrection.[5] Jesus' resurrection then was decisive evidence that the new age had truly invaded the old.[6]

Pentecost further demonstrated the truth of Jesus' teaching that the eschatological kingdom had invaded the old age. The early church saw the coming of the Holy Spirit as the fulfilment of Joel's prophecy: 'And in the last days it shall be, God declares, that I will pour out my Spirit upon all flesh' (Acts 2:17; Joel 2:28). The dramatic outpouring of the Holy Spirit was the 'first fruits' (Rom 8:23) or 'down payment' (2 Cor 1:22; 5:5; Eph 1:13–14) of the ultimate fulfilment.[7] Pentecost both demonstrated that the powers of the new age were already at work and also guaranteed that the eschatological kingdom would finally come in its fullness and completion. Thus both the resurrection and Pentecost were powerful signs indicating that Jesus' messianic kingdom had truly begun. The Carpenter was truly Israel's Messiah.

Indeed even more lofty titles seemed appropriate after his resurrection. According to the Fourth Gospel, the sceptical Thomas lost all doubt when he saw the risen Jesus. 'My Lord and my God' (Jn 20:28) was his awesome response. Throughout Acts and the Epistles, it is clear that the resurrection convinced the disciples that Jesus was truly the Son of God (Rom 1:4; Acts 2:32–36). The word *kyrios* (Lord), used in the Septuagint (the Greek translation of the Old Testament) to translate the word *Yahweh*, now became one of the most frequently used titles for the man from Nazareth. In Philippians 2, Paul applies to Jesus words which the monotheistic prophet uses for Yahweh. After mocking the idols, Yahweh insists in Isaiah 45:23 that he alone is God: 'To me every knee shall bow, every tongue shall swear' (Is 45:23). Paul takes those words from the mouth of Yahweh and applies them to Jesus, declaring that 'at the name of Jesus every knee should bow, in heaven and on earth and under the earth, and every tongue confess that Jesus Christ is Lord' (Phil 2:10–11).

Not until we understand that *that* is who the Crucified One was do we begin to penetrate to the full meaning of the cross. The crucified criminal hanging limp on the middle cross was the eternal Word, who in the beginning was with God and indeed was God, but for our sakes became flesh and dwelt among us. The Crucified One was he 'who had always been God by nature [yet] did not cling to his prerogatives as God's equal, but stripped himself of all privilege by consenting to be a slave' (Phil 2:6–7 Phillips). Only when we grasp that that is who the Crucified One was do we begin to fathom the depth of Jesus' teaching that God's way of dealing with enemies is the way of suffering love.

The Cross as Foundation for Nonviolence

The foundation of Christian nonviolence lies not in some calculation of effectiveness. It rests in the cross. The ultimate ground of biblical opposition to taking life is the nature of God revealed first in Jesus' teaching and life and then most fully in his death.

There is one central aspect of Matthew 5:38–48 that we have not yet explored. What, according to Jesus, is the theological foundation of his call for costly, nonretaliatory love, even for enemies? Jesus did not say that one should practise loving nonviolence because it would always transform vicious enemies into bosom friends. The cross stands as a harsh reminder that love for enemies does not always work – at least not in the short run. Jesus grounds his call to love enemies, not in the hope of reciprocity, but rather in the very nature of God:[8] 'Love your enemies and pray for those who persecute you, *so that* you may be sons of your Father who is in heaven; for he makes his sun rise on the evil and on the good, and sends rain on the just and on the unjust.' (Mt 5:44–45). Jesus said the same thing in the Beatitudes: 'Blessed are the peacemakers, for they shall be called sons of God' (Mt 5:9).[9] God loves his enemies. Instead of promptly destroying sinners, he continues to shower the good gifts of creation upon them. Since that is the way God acts, those who want to be his sons and daughters must do likewise.[10] Conversely, the text implies that those who do not love their enemies are not the children of God. 'You, therefore, must be perfect, as your heavenly Father is perfect' (Mt 5:48). One fundamental aspect of the holiness and perfection of God is that he loves his enemies. Those who by his grace seek to reflect his holiness will likewise love their enemies – even when it involves a cross.

Earlier we discussed both Jesus' unconventional teaching on God's prodigal forgiveness and also his unorthodox view of a suffering Messiah à la Isaiah 53. The link between these central affirmations of Jesus and his teaching on nonviolence now becomes more clear. The divine Father so eager to forgive repentant sinners is the One whose love for enemies we are summoned to imitate. Jürgen Moltmann underlines this crucial connection: 'Everything that can be categorised as "non-violence" in the sayings and actions of Jesus can ultimately be derived from this "revolution in the concept of God" which he set forth: namely, that God comes not to carry out just revenge upon the evil, but to justify sinners by grace, whether they are Zealots or tax collectors, Pharisees or sinners.'[11] Jesus' teaching on forgiveness clearly shows that God loves and accepts sinners even though they deserve to be his enemies.

But Jesus' conception of the suffering Messiah who goes to the cross as a ransom for sinners takes us still further in our understanding of God's way of dealing with enemies. At the Last Supper, Jesus stated unequivocally that he was going to die for the sake of others.[12] All four versions of the Eucharistic words,[13] carefully prepared and handed down in the early church's oral tradition, contain this central notion. 'This is my body which is for you' (1 Cor 11:24). 'This is my blood of the covenant, which is poured out for many for the forgiveness of sins' (Mt 26:28). Jesus' death was the sacrificial inaugural of a new covenant.[14] It is the One who had claimed divine authority (blasphemously, his enemies charged) to forgive sinners who now dies for others at the demand of those very enemies. It is the One who taught his followers to imitate God's love for enemies who now dies with a forgiving prayer on his lips for the enemies who send him to the cross (Lk 23:34).

That the cross is the ultimate demonstration that God deals with his enemies through suffering love receives its clearest theological expression in Paul. 'God shows his love for us in that while we were yet *sinners* Christ died for us. . . . While we were *enemies* we were reconciled to God by the death of his Son' (Rom 5:8, 10). Jesus' vicarious cross for sinners is the foundation and deepest expression of Jesus' command to love one's enemies. As the substitutionary view of the atonement indicates, we are enemies in the double sense that sinful persons are hostile to God and that the just, holy Creator hates sin (Rom 1:18).[15] For those who know the law, failure to obey it results in a divine curse. But Christ redeemed us from that curse by becoming a curse for us (Gal 3:10–14). Jesus' blood on the cross was an expiation (Rom 5:18) for us sinful enemies of God because the One who knew no sin was made sin for us on the cross (2 Cor 5:21).

Nothing discloses the horror of sin as fully as the cross. The cross is no cheap declaration of 'indulgent amnesty.'[16] Sin is an outrageous affront to God's holiness. It would be a horrible, intolerable world if sin, evil and injustice could continue to rampage and destroy, forever unpunished. The cross demonstrates that the holy Sovereign of the universe will not tolerate that. Sin's penalty must be paid.

But the cross is not the sacrifice of a human victim on the altar of an angry, hostile deity. That would deny the doctrines of the Incarnation and the Trinity. God himself suffers. God himself bears the penalty of sin. He himself bears the awful consequences of sin. Leon Morris puts it well:

The absolute oneness between the Father and the Son in the work of atonement must not for a moment be lost sight of. When God substitutes for sinful man in his death, that is God Himself bearing the consequences of sin, God saving man at cost to Himself, not at cost to someone else. As Leonard Hodgson puts it, 'He wills that sin shall be punished, but He does not will that sin shall be punished without also willing that the punishment shall fall on Himself.'[17]

Jesus' vicarious death for sinful enemies of God leads, we believe, to nonviolence. It was because the incarnate One knew that God was loving and merciful, even toward the worst of sinners, that he associated with sinners, forgave their sins and completed his messianic mission by dying for the sins of the world. And it was precisely the same understanding of God that prompted him to command his followers to love their enemies.

At the cross God himself suffered for his enemies. Certainly we can never fathom all the mystery there. But it is precisely because the One hanging limp on the cross was the Word who became flesh that we are absolutely sure of two interrelated things: first, that a just God mercifully accepts sinful enemies, and second that he wants us to go and treat all our enemies in the same merciful, self-sacrificial way.

Since Jesus commanded his followers to love their enemies and then died as the Incarnate Son to demonstrate that God reconciles his enemies by suffering love, any rejection of the nonviolent way in human relations seems to us to involve an inadequate doctrine of the atonement.[18] If God in Christ reconciled his enemies by suffering servanthood, should not those who want to follow Christ also treat their enemies in the same way?

It is a tragedy of our time that many of those who appropriate the biblical understanding of Christ's vicarious cross fail to see its direct implications for the problem of war and violence. And it is equally tragic that some of those who emphasise pacifism and nonviolence fail to ground it in Christ's atonement. The sentimental view of Jesus as merely a noble martyr to truth and peace is an inadequate ground for nonviolence. The cross is much more than 'Christ's witness to the weakness and folly of the sword,'[19] although it certainly is that. In fact the cross is such a witness only because the incarnate Word's death for our sins demonstrates that the Sovereign of the universe is a merciful Father who reconciles his enemies through self-sacrificial love.

This statement in no way denies God's holiness, justice and wrath. Pacifists who ignore this aspect of biblical teaching are mistaken. Jesus did not teach that God's 'Fatherhood replaces Kingship.'[20] Jesus apparently did not think affirming God's wrath and punishment of sin was incompatible with teaching love for enemies. In fact the majority of the Bible's teaching about eternal punishment comes from the lips of Jesus.[21]

The relationship between God's love and wrath is certainly a mystery we will never fully fathom. But we dare not deny either. For our purposes, however, the most important fact is that while the New Testament repeatedly commands us to imitate God's love, it explicitly prohibits us from imitating his wrath. Paul could not have stated the prohibition more clearly: 'Beloved, never avenge yourselves, but leave it to the wrath of God; for it is written, "Vengeance is mine, I will repay, says the Lord"' (Rom 12:19).[22] There is no New Testament data which remotely suggests that Christians should imitate God's wrath.[23] Everywhere, on the other hand, we meet the command to imitate God's love revealed in Christ's cross. What a paradoxical tragedy that Christians have often reversed the biblical approach, seeming so eager that we 'imitate the transcendent God in his cosmic wrath; and so loath that we should imitate the cross of God incarnate in the Man Jesus!'[24]

Imitating Christ at the Cross

In response to God's loving self-sacrifice, the early Christians sought to make the cross the pattern for their lives. The New Testament writers repeatedly called Christians to imitate Christ at the cross.

That is not to say that the early Christians thought they could or should duplicate every aspect of Christ's cross.[25] His once-for-all sacrifice for the sins of the world can never be repeated. Reformed theologian Loraine Boettner is quite correct in insisting that 'Christ's *expiatory* death is no more an object for our imitation than is the creation of the world.'[26] But that fact never prevented the New Testament writers from discerning in the cross a decisive ethical pattern.

The call to imitate Jesus goes back to the Master himself. More than once the Gospels report Jesus' costly invitation: 'If any man would come after me, let him deny himself and take up his cross and follow me' (Mt 16:24). Imitation of Christ at the cross is a constant theme in the epistles: 'Be kind to one another, tenderhearted, forgiving one another, as God in Christ forgave you. Therefore be imitators of God, as beloved children. And walk in love, as Christ loved us and gave himself up for us, a fragrant offering and sacrifice to God' (Eph 4:32–5:2).[27] Paul even dared to urge Christians to imitate him as he imitated Christ (1 Cor 11:1; 1 Thess 1:6). Indeed, in his affliction and persecution, he spoke of 'carrying in [his] body the death of Jesus' (2 Cor 4:10).

So central was the theme of imitating Christ that we see it applied to the Christian's life in every major area of activity – the home, the church, the marketplace and the state.

The recipients of the Epistle to the Ephesians lived in a male-dominated Hellenistic society. But that did not deter the author from urging husbands to treat their wives with the same self-sacrificing love that Jesus incarnated at the cross. 'Husbands, love your wives, as Christ loved the church and gave himself up for her' (Eph 5:25). What quiet agony, what aching unfulfilment, would be avoided if Christian husbands followed the way of the cross in their homes. The way of the cross is not merely the exciting nonviolent stance that God sometimes permits a Gandhi or a Martin Luther King to use so successfully to change history. It is also God's way to peace and fulfilment in the persistent struggles of every marriage.

Similarly, the Epistles hold up the way of the cross as the means to accord and harmony in the church. To illustrate the kind of humility and unselfish concern for others that Christians ought to show toward one another Paul makes use of a marvellous hymn (Phil 2:6–11) about Jesus' self-emptying, his taking the form of a slave and his obeying even to death on the cross. 'The attitude you should have is the one that Christ Jesus had' (Phil 2:5, Good News). John duplicates Paul's idea with equal power: 'By this we know love, that he laid down his life for us; and we ought to lay down our lives for the brethren' (1 Jn 3:16, also 4:10–11). Much division and scandal throughout the church's history could have been prevented had Christians followed this admonition to pattern their relationships with one another after the model of Christ's cross.

But the cross as model for human relationships is not limited to family and church. The epistles also stress love for enemies in public matters. Paul's famous passage on government in Romans 13 is framed by a vigorous statement which, although it does not explictly refer to the cross, clearly echoes Jesus' command to love one's enemies: 'Bless those who persecute you; bless and do not curse them. . . . Repay no one evil for evil. . . . Beloved, never avenge yourselves, but leave it to the wrath of God. . . . No, "if your enemy is hungry, feed him." . . . Do not be overcome by evil, but overcome evil with good' (Rom 12:14–21).

Then after dealing with the topic of submission to governmental authorities, Paul returns to the theme of love for neighbour and insists that 'love does no wrong to a neighbour' (13:10). Whatever Paul's statement about the government's sword may mean – and we will examine that question in the next chapter – it hardly means participating in lethal governmental violence. Paul had just insisted that the way of love meant forsaking vengeance and loving one's enemies. Thus the way of the cross also applies to the Christian's relationships with government.

Finally, 1 Peter 2 calls on oppressed slaves who have become Christians to submit not only to kind owners but also to cruel masters:

For one is approved if, mindful of God, he endures pain while suffering unjustly. . . . For to this you have been

called, because Christ also suffered for you, leaving you
an example, that you should follow in his steps. He
committed no sin; no guile was found on his lips. When
he was reviled, he did not revile in return; when he
suffered, he did not threaten; but he trusted to him who
judges justly. He himself bore our sins in his body on the
tree, that we might die to sin and live to righteousness.
By his wounds you have been healed. (1 Pet 2:19, 21–24)

By pondering the nature of God revealed most fully in
Jesus' suffering, Christians can learn to endure even unjustly inflicted suffering. With direct references to the Suffering
Servant of Isaiah 53, Peter here explicitly commands
Christians to imitate Jesus on the cross when they confront
unjust oppressors. That does not mean that oppressed
slaves or contemporary victims of systemic injustice must
acquiesce in their oppression. But it does mean that if they
obey the biblical command to follow Christ's example, they
will refuse to regard oppressors as enemies to be reviled
and hated. Instead, as they remember that Christ died for
their sins while they were still enemies of God, they will
imitate God's love for enemies.

The Early Church's Gospel of Peace
The angels' song of peace on earth reverberates throughout
the New Testament. It is hardly surprising that peace
became a central motif for the earliest Christians. They
believed that the eschatological age of peace had broken
into the present. Jesus the Messiah was the fulfilment of the
prophetic vision of messianic shalom. In Christ, they experienced peace with God, peace with Christian brothers
and sisters in the new messianic community, and inner
peace of mind. The word *peace* is everywhere. So prominent is the concept of peace that early Christians occasionally describe their entire gospel message as the 'gospel of
peace' (Eph 6:15). Again and again, Paul describes God as
the 'God of peace.'[28] Continually and in every way, the
Lord gives peace. 'Now may the Lord of peace himself give
you peace *at all times in all ways*" (2 Thess 3:16).

Since the word *shalom* was a form of greeting in Jewish life, one would expect Paul to use it at the beginning and the close of letters. But his regular greeting of shalom at the beginning of his epistles signifies far more than an ordinary 'hello.' 'Grace and peace' or 'grace and peace from God our Father' reminded the readers of God's entire work of reconciliation in Jesus Christ.

In Paul's thinking about reconciliation, his teaching on peace with God comes together with his teaching on peace in the church.[29] The basic notion of reconciliation is 'making peace after a quarrel, or bridging over an enmity.'[30] The word Paul uses appears in Greek marriage records to refer to the repairing of estranged relationships between husband and wife.[31] Hostility and estrangement exist between God and sinners (Col 1:21; Rom 5:8–10). Sinners are rebels against God. And the God of justice hates sin. Forgiveness of our guilt through Christ's vicarious death is, of course, central to the ending of the hostility. But God wants to do more than merely forgive our sins. He wants to end the hostility. He wants to restore a relationship of harmony and personal intimacy.

When betrayal severs an intimate relationship between persons, reconciliation is possible only if both persons agree to end the hostility. One person can take the initiative. One person can even decide to forgive the other regardless of the other's response. Such an act is lovely, but it cannot produce reconciliation. Only if both persons willingly embrace a restored relationship will there be reconciliation.

No amount of force or power can successfully demand or create reconciliation. This is true both in God's relationship with persons and in our relationship with each other. Husbands can, perhaps, coerce wives into some form of submission that produces temporary domestic tranquillity. Wives can, perhaps, do the same with their husbands. But only a genuine healing of past hurt and a mutual decision to end the hostile relationship can produce true reconciliation. Since God chose to create free, personal communion, he cannot force reconciliation. Instead, he offers at the cross a costly demonstration of divine love (1 Jn 3:16; 4:9–10; 2 Cor 5:17–21).

Reconciliation starts with cancellation of punishment and forensic justification through the substitutionary atonement. At the cross Christ became sin for us to atone for our guilt and reckon pardon on us. Reconciliation, however, does not end there: 'There can be no question that in reconciliation more takes place than a mere removal of the relationship of guilt.'[32]

Paul urges us to be reconciled to God. 'We beseech you on behalf of Christ, be reconciled to God' (2 Cor 5:20). Certainly God takes initiatives that we could never take. But Paul still begs and pleads with us to take action, to be reconciled to God. Hostility ends and reconciliation occurs only when we respond. When we do, the result is peace, shalom, wholeness. Everything is different. There is a whole new creation (2 Cor 5:17). When reconciliation occurs, there is peace (Eph 2:13–16; Col 1:19–20). The messianic shalom of the new age bursts forth in the present.

The peace which comes from reconciliation with God has three interrelated aspects. As we have seen, it includes divine forgiveness of our sinful guilt (Rom 5:1; Eph 2:14 –17). It also includes a new reconciled relationship of love and obedience toward God. We who are reconciled to God are controlled by our love for him rather than selfish desire. Third, reconciliation with God involves peace between formerly hostile groups in the body of Christ. The ancient world's most glaring social hostility existed between Jews and Gentiles. In the classic passage on reconciliation (Eph 2), we see that peace with God through the cross also creates peace between Jews and Gentiles. Formerly the Gentiles were far from God,

> but now in Christ Jesus you who once were far off have been brought near in the blood of Christ. For he is *our peace*, who has made us both one, and has broken down the dividing wall of hostility, by abolishing in his flesh the

law of commandments and ordinances, that he might create in himself one new man in place of the two, *so making peace*, and might reconcile us both to God in one body through the cross, thereby bringing the hostility to an end. And he came and preached *peace* to you who were far off and *peace* to those who were near; for through him we both have access in one Spirit to the Father. (Eph 2:13–18)

Because Jews and Gentiles have peace with God through the same sacrifice, they are brought together in Christ's one body as brothers and sisters. There is one new peaceful community instead of two hostile, warring ethnic groups. The history of the early church, to be sure, demonstrates that the hostility did not end instantly. But in Christ the ancient world's most hostile division experienced dramatic, visible healing.[33]

This new multiethnic shalom is an important part of the gospel. In chapter three of Ephesians, Paul proceeds to discuss the 'mystery of Christ.' Verse 6 defines the mystery: 'that is, how the Gentiles are fellow heirs, members of the same body, and partakers of the promise in Christ Jesus through the gospel.' And then, in verses 7–9, Paul adds that this mystery is the gospel he preaches. Peace between Jews and Gentiles in the church is part of the gospel. Reconciliation between warring social groups – whether Jews and Gentiles, or slaves and masters, or men and women – is a central part of Paul's gospel. No wonder Paul speaks of the 'gospel of peace' (Eph 6:15; cf. Acts 10:36).

The early Christians experienced a dramatically new community where the old age's dividing walls crumbled. They transcended ethnic, sexual, economic and cultural barriers. They shared economically across two continents.[34] In the power of the Holy Spirit, the down payment of the new age, they learned how to live in peace across all the barriers that have produced hate and war in human history. That the kingdom Jesus announced had not fully come is clear from the fact that many of the passages are appeals to Christians to overcome their divisions. (Paul has to beg them to live in peace!) But Jesus' messianic kingdom had truly begun. Its shalom was visible in his new community.[35]

The Way of the Cross Today

What an incredible story. The Sovereign of the universe became flesh in the person of his only Son. He came to tell us that since he loves his enemies, he also wants us to love our enemies. But he spoke with more than words. He spoke through the most astounding act of love in the history of the universe. At the cross, God inflicted on himself all the guilty torment that our awful rebellion deserved. The God of the universe suffered the most painful, the most disgraceful agony conceivable to pay his enemies' just penalty and to draw them back into an intimate, reconciled embrace.

Now he beckons us to show this kind of sacrificial love in our relationships with others – in the home, the church, the marketplace and the state. He calls us to imitate his Son at the cross. Certainly it is a wicked violent world where the law of the jungle still reigns. But he invites us to believe that already in this vicious vale of tears we can imitate Christ's self-giving love for others. We, in and of ourselves, are of course not capable of such love. The New Testament never even hints at such utopianism. It is consistently pessimistic about sinful humanity. But it is equally optimistic about divine grace. All things are possible with God. All things are possible for those who believe God's Messiah has truly come.

All New Testament ethical teaching presupposes this eschatological framework. The new messianic age announced by Jesus has truly begun. The resurrection and Pentecost are proof for those with eyes to see. In the power of the Holy Spirit it is now possible to follow the way of the cross. When we do, by God's grace, the messianic shalom of Jesus' dawning kingdom bursts forth. It breaks joyfully into broken homes, divided churches, cutthroat companies and even secular societies.

Certainly shalom penetrates secular life far less than it does in the church. Secular society and secular people do not enjoy divine forgiveness, sanctifying grace and the renewing support of Jesus' new messianic body, although Christians are sometimes put to shame by the loving deeds of non-Christians. At best, though, non-Christians manage to follow the teaching of Jesus only from afar with stumbling steps. But when they do follow it, however imperfectly, human institutions experience less brokenness and more shalom. It has been possible to end slavery. It may be possible to abolish nuclear weapons. But we should never suppose that secular society will practise Jesus' ethic very faithfully. War and rumours of war will not cease until the Lord returns.

Surely, however, that does not mean that Christians must wait till the millennium to practise what Jesus taught. We do not wait to implement Jesus' sexual ethics until sinners stop fornicating. We dare not wait to obey his call to love enemies until all enemies are eliminated from the final, consummated kingdom.

It is in this fallen world that our Messiah calls his disciples to love even their national enemies. He urges his followers to say no to verbal and nonverbal, personal and national retaliation. He pleads with his church to be ministers of reconciliation in a hostile world at the brink of annihilation.

Nuclear weapons are the last mile along the Zealots' violent road. In our time, the Zealot option threatens to destroy not just Jerusalem but the planet. Jesus still weeps over Jerusalem and over all the cities of the world. He pleads with us to see the things that make for peace. He begs us to see that the way of the cross is the only hope for our nuclear age. Will his people believe him this time?

'Thus says the LORD of hosts, ". . . utterly destroy all that they have; do not spare them, but kill both man and woman, infant and suckling."'

1 Samuel 15:2–3

'But I say to you, Love your enemies and pray for those who persecute you.'

Matthew 5:44

8

Some Critical Objections

What about the numerous wars in the Old Testament which God commanded Israel to fight? What about Paul's command to obey the government which, he taught, does not bear the sword in vain? In fact, what about Jesus' advice to the disciples to go and buy a sword (Lk 22:36)? And his violent cleansing of the Temple? And his failure to condemn soldiers who came to him? Finally, didn't Reinhold Niebuhr show decades ago that 'pacifism' is merely a naive notion of liberal theology that is totally unrealistic in a fallen world?

These are significant objections to the view we have presented thus far. We want to face them honestly here. We will first explore the problem of war in the Old Testament, then examine several key New Testament texts used to support war, and finally look briefly at the charge that nonviolence is an unrealistic liberal belief.

War in the Old Testament

In the Old Testament, God repeatedly commands Israel to fight, ordering them to annihilate the enemy, including women, children and animals. Joshua 6:17 gives God's instructions for the battle of Jericho: 'The city and all that is within it shall be devoted to the LORD for destruction.' The people obeyed and God was pleased: 'Then they utterly destroyed all in the city, both men and women, young and old, oxen, sheep, and asses, with the edge of the sword. . . . So the LORD was with Joshua' (Josh 6:21, 27). How does this Old Testament teaching relate to what we have discovered in Jesus?

Inadequate solutions.   Over the centuries, many Christians have wrestled with what appears to be a fundamental contradiction between the Old and New Testaments on the problem of war. In the second century, Marcion simply rejected the Old Testament. The early church fathers adopted an allegorical approach to it. Many modern folk deny God said what the text indicates. On the other hand, some Christian defenders of war gladly endorse the Old Testament's call to arms.

The heretic Marcion taught that the warlike God of the Old Testament was a different deity from the loving, merciful Father of Jesus Christ. Marcion therefore refused to accept the Old Testament in the Christian canon of authoritative books. The church, however, rightly rejected Marcion's radical solution as heretical.[1]

The church fathers of the first three centuries consistently taught that Jesus rejected all warfare. They adopted an allegorical approach to the Old Testament, interpreting passages about warfare figuratively rather than literally.[2] Again, such a view is not an option for us. We rightly seek to understand the literal, historical intent in the text.

In one way or another, many modern thinkers have argued that these problematic passages are not really God's word. The people of Israel misunderstood God. They genuinely thought that he ordered them to fight and massacre, but they were mistaken.[3] Some base this assertion on an evolutionary view of the development of Israel's religion. The call for massacre of the enemy was the barbarian idea of a primitive people. Later, evolving religious thought transcended these early notions.

This solution, however, has serious problems. The assertion that Yahweh is a warrior who fights for his people and orders them into battle is a common, central affirmation of early Israelite belief.[4] It appears again and again in the Old Testament. To be sure, if one believes that the Old Testament is merely a human account of a primitive people's search for God, or perhaps a confused mixture of divine revelation and mistaken human theological reflection, such a view poses no problems. But if one believes that both the Old and the New Testaments are God's authoritative revelation, this solution is unsatisfactory.

Does the Old Testament support the just war tradition? Another option, of course, is simply to argue that the Old Testament's call to arms is still normative. Christians through the ages have done that. The Crusaders' favourite text was Jeremiah 48:10: 'Cursed is he who keeps back his sword from bloodshed.' The Crusaders conquered Jerusalem on 15 July 1099 after enormous bloodshed. Christian chroniclers joyfully reported that the Christian troops then beheaded ten thousand Muslims in the great Mosque, choking the area with blood and corpses.[5]

In his defence of warfare, Loraine Boettner insists that the Old Testament's endorsement of warfare is still normative for Christians. The Scriptures, our only rule of faith and practice, teach one consistent doctrine. In dozens of places in the Old Testament, God commands war for righteous ends. The Canaanites' horrible sexual practices and human sacrifice justified their slaughter by Israel. In the light of Canaanite crimes, 'their forthright execution by the Hebrews seems manly and dignified, if not even merciful.' They were 'too degraded and sinful to live.'[6] The New Testament, Boettner argues, is silent on warfare because the Old Testament had already revealed God's final word about war.

This view, however, is hardly less problematic than the former. It assumes, contrary to the overwhelming evidence we have just examined, that Jesus and the apostles said nothing about the basic problem of violence. The church of the first three centuries certainly thought otherwise. But it also mistakenly supposes that the Old Testament teaching on war supports the traditional just war tradition of the church. Taken at face value, the Old Testament proves both vastly too much and vastly too little to serve as a support for Christians in the just war tradition.

Certainly it proves too much. As we have seen, the immunity of noncombatants is a central element of the just war tradition. The same is true of proper treatment of prisoners of war. To kill civilians and prisoners of war is murder according to the just war tradition. But the Old Testament's holy-war teaching commands almost exactly the opposite. Joshua 10:40 says God told the invading Israelites to wipe out 'all that breathes.' Samuel told Saul to defeat Amalek and to annihilate all survivors: 'And Samuel said to Saul, "The LORD sent me to anoint you king over his people Israel; now therefore hearken to the words of the LORD. Thus says the LORD of hosts, '. . . Now go and smite Amalek, and utterly destroy all that they have; do not spare them, but kill both man and woman, infant and suckling, ox and sheep, camel and ass' "' (1 Sam 15:1–3).[7] No contemporary Christian ethicist believes Christians should treat noncombatants and prisoners of war that way.

The Old Testament also records God's command to destroy Israelites for idolatry and sexual misconduct. When Moses discovered that the people were worshipping idols, he ordered the Levites to slay thousands of Israelites: 'Thus says the LORD God of Israel, "Put every man his sword on his side, and go to and fro from gate to gate throughout the camp, and slay every man his brother, and every man his companion, and every man his neighbour"' (Ex 32:27). Judges 19–20 says Yahweh ordered the tribal armies to punish a gross sexual offence in the tribe of Benjamin. 'And the LORD defeated Benjamin before Israel; and the men of Israel destroyed twenty-five thousand one hundred men of Benjamin that day' (20:35).[8] Christians today do not believe that we should kill heretics, adherents of other religions or sexual offenders.

The Old Testament proves entirely too much for those who seek its endorsement for killing. But it also proves much too little. Old Testament scholar Millard C. Lind has recently explored the theology of warfare in ancient Israel.[9] He shows that at the heart of Israel's holy-war tradition is the belief that Yahweh himself miraculously intervenes to fight for Israel. Often Israel did not lift an armed finger. When God wanted the people themselves to fight, he summoned them to battle by a prophetic word. Even then it was very clear that victory was by divine act, 'not by your sword or by your bow' (Josh 24:12). 'Faith meant that Israel should rely upon Yahweh's miracle for her defence, rather than upon soldiers and weapons. The human agent in the work of Yahweh was not so much the warrior as the prophet.'[10]

The miraculous deliverance at the exodus was the basic paradigm. The very early poem in Exodus 15:1–18 says the escaping Israelites did not fight at all when the Egyptian army drowned in the sea. There are numerous accounts where divine intervention alone brought victory.[11] When Yahweh's prophet ordered Israel to fight, it was still abundantly clear that the victory came from God, as Israel's defeat of Jericho, Gideon's defeat of the Midianites, and David's defeat of Goliath show. The text of Judges explicitly explains that God pared down Gideon's army so that the Israelites could take no credit for the victory (7:2–3).

Lind summarises this early Israelite theology of warfare as follows: 'Obedience to Yahweh's word and trust in his miracle are alone decisive. Israel's faith in Yahweh as warrior led her to reject the military expediency of developing sophisticated weaponry such as horses and chariots even to the time of David, weapons that would have made Israel competitive with her Philistine and Canaanite enemies.'[12]

Later, Israel rejected Yahweh's kingship and asked for a human king to lead them into battle. The kings militarised Israelite society with standing armies, cavalry and chariots. But the prophets denounced this trust in advanced military technology.[13] Psalms 20:7 reflects this view: 'Some boast of chariots, and some of horses; but we boast of the name of the LORD our God.' Hosea, like other prophets, harshly condemned Israel's trust in military might:

You have ploughed iniquity,
   you have reaped injustice,
   you have eaten the fruit of lies.
Because you have trusted in your chariots
   and in the multitude of your warriors.
(Hos 10:13)

Since God himself fights for Israel, she need not rely on chariots, horses and a large army. Even three hundred soldiers armed with torches and pitchers will do if Yahweh leads the host.

That is the heart of the Old Testament's theology of warfare. Such a theology, if it is normative for Christians today, hardly authorises them to support our current national reliance on ever more sophisticated, ever more powerful and destructive weapons. 'Imagine what an uproar there would be if a United States President announced that God had promised victory for the United States provided we did away with our nuclear weapons and fought only with horns, pitchers and torches.'[14]

The holy-war tradition is almost as problematic for Christians in the just war tradition as it is for Christians who reject all war. It demands what the just war tradition forbids in its summons to annihilate civilians and prisoners of war. And it forbids what the just war tradition supports in its call to trust in Yahweh rather than sophisticated military technology. If the biblical holy-war tradition is still normative today, then we have done many things that we ought not to have done and we have not done many things that we ought to have done.

The mystery of God's justice and love. The fundamental problem, however, still remains. The Old Testament Scriptures tell us that in Israel's history God did many things that seem incompatible with the nature of the God revealed at the cross. How can we reconcile this picture of God with the New Testament teaching that God is love?

First, we must recognise that the God portrayed in the New Testament is not a God whose only characteristics are love and mercy. The New Testament, just as much as the Old, insists that God both restrains and punishes sin. God restrains evil lest it destroy his good creation. Further, both within history and at its culmination, God executes divine wrath and retributive punishment against sin. The world's supreme messenger of God's love, our Lord Jesus, consistently taught that at the last judgment, sinners will face God's just wrath and punishment for sin. Paul is equally clear: Those who stubbornly disobey God store up wrath for the final day of judgment where there will be 'wrath and fury' against sin (Rom 2:5, 8).

This aspect of God seems understandable and just. If there were not a natural order of regularity in nature, human freedom and responsibility would have no meaning. Moral order in the universe is essential. If defiance of the moral order had no consequences, human freedom and responsibility would have little meaning. Both Testaments insist that there is a moral order. The wages of sin is death – both now and later.[15] God punishes sin both within history, as the consequences of evil choices unfold, and at the final judgment. This divine maintenance of a moral order makes sense. As philosopher A. E. Taylor says, 'The retributive character of punishment . . . [is] a doctrine really indispensable to a sound ethics.'[16] But God's ways remain mysterious and unfathomable. Why he suddenly punishes the lies of Ananias and Sapphira (Acts 5:1–11) and withholds punishment from worse sinners we cannot explain.

We can only acknowledge that the sovereign Creator is different from us. As the Creator of all life, he can give or take life as he chooses. He has chosen to create a world where he withdraws the gift of life through earthquakes and floods, disease and old age. He also withdraws life, the Scriptures say, as punishment for sin.

Some say that they cannot believe in a God who takes life. Do they, then, believe that God gives life, that God alone is Creator? That all life is in God's hands? Do they believe that all life belongs to God: that life continues with God after this time of testing is over? These truths about conditions of life assert God's sovereignty over life. If we do not believe them, we do not believe there is a God.[17]

Even so, our questions and doubts refuse to depart. Why God would repeatedly order the annihilation of men, women and children we do not understand. Certainly it helps to remember that the Old Testament gives reasons. The abominable sexual practices and hideous human sacrifices of the Canaanites merited punishment (Num 33:50 –56; Deut 18:9–14). And God did not want their idolatrous practices to seduce Israel into idolatry (Deut 20:17–18).

Yet we still struggle. Were these sinful practices sufficient reason to destroy entire cities? Only God has the right to make such decisions. We can only confess in faith that he is the sovereign Creator and Lord of life. He promises us that he is both just and merciful. And we know that his justice and love met at the cross.

We also know that in the final revelation given by his incarnate Son, God summons us to love our enemies. And he explicitly commands us to leave vengeance to him (Rom 12:19). We dare not confuse these two issues. To insist that the Sovereign of the universe has the right to execute vengeance and retribution on sinners is one thing. To claim that we should imitate that aspect of God is quite another.

How did Jesus fulfil the Old Testament? One final aspect of our question about the Old Testament and war requires exploration. Matthew says Jesus did not come to abolish the Law and the prophets but to fulfil them. 'For truly, I say to you, till heaven and earth pass away, not an iota, not a dot, will pass from the law until all is accomplished' (Mt 5:18; see also Lk 16:17).[18] In what sense does Jesus' teaching about love for enemies fulfil the Law?

Jesus understood the Old Testament to be the very Word of God (Mk 7:8–13). At the same time, Jesus clearly did not hesitate to set aside specific Mosaic teaching.[19] He abolished dietary laws, set aside Mosaic provisions for divorce and rejected the *lex talionis*, a central foundation of Old Testament jurisprudence.

Jesus taught that it is not what a person eats but what he says that defiles him: 'There is nothing outside a man which by going into him can defile him' (Mk 7:15; see also Mt 15:11). In his editorial comment, Mark specifically asserts that this teaching of Jesus abolished the old covenant's dietary laws: 'Thus he declared all foods clean' (Mk 7:19).

Jesus also set aside the Mosaic provision for divorce (Mk 10:2–9).[20] When the Pharisees raised the topic, Jesus asked what Moses taught. But when the Pharisees quoted the Mosaic 'commandment' permitting divorce (Deut 24:1), Jesus refused to accept it as still normative. He appealed to God's original intention at creation in his rejection of divorce. The old covenant permitted it because of the hardness of their hearts, but Jesus abolished the Mosaic exception. Matthew 5:31–32 is a shorter repetition of the same teaching: 'It was also said, "Whoever divorces his wife, let him give her a certificate of divorce" [Deut 24:1]. But I say to you that every one who divorces his wife, except on the ground of unchastity, makes her an adulteress.'

In the previous chapter, we saw that Jesus also set aside 'an eye for an eye,' which was a central principle of Mosaic Law. He also forbade oaths even though the Old Testament explicitly allowed them (Deut 10:20; Mt 5:33–37). Thus Jesus declared that certain aspects of the Mosaic Law were no longer normative. How does that fit with his insistence that not the smallest part of the Law would pass away until 'all is accomplished'? Schweizer notes that the word translated *is accomplished* 'always refers in Matthew to the realisation of a promise within the life of Jesus (1:22; 21:4; 26:56) and is always equated with "come true" or "be fulfilled." '[21] Thus the meaning is that the true intention of the Law is being fulfilled in Jesus' teaching and ministry.

Jesus is not rejecting or denouncing the Law. He is fulfilling it. Sometimes this means moving from the letter (the physical act of adultery) to the inner spirit (lust). Sometimes it means actually setting aside provisions of the Mosaic Law. But always it means genuine fulfilment.

> To our Lord, the new was as superior to the old as a son is greater in authority and significance than servants. In the Old Testament, God sent his servants; now he sends his Son (Matt. 21:33ff; cf. Heb. 1:1–2). But while inferior to the new, the old is vitally related to the new as stepping stone and preparation. . . . Jesus is to the prophets as noonday sun to breaking dawn; he is what they pointed to.[22]

Paul's attitude toward the Law provides a parallel illustration of the way the new covenant fulfils the old. Paul sharply contrasted the old way of righteousness based on keeping the Law with the new way of righteousness based on faith in Christ (Rom 9:30–32; Gal 2:16; 5:2–6). The basis of one's relationship to God is different in the two covenants: 'The law does not rest on faith, for [quoting Lev 18:5] "He who does them shall live by them"' (Gal 3:12; see also 4:21–31). But Paul still insists that the new covenant's teaching on justification by faith and the transforming presence of the Spirit is the *fulfilment* of the Law (Rom 3:31; 8:4).

It is striking to note the way the New Testament quotes the Old to demonstrate the claim that the one fulfils the other. Paul cites selected passages from the Old Testament to argue that the Old Testament already pointed to that righteousness based on faith which was clearly revealed in Christ.[23] Piper points out that this selective citation of the Old Testament reappears in the passages on love for enemies.[24] There were, of course, numerous passages from the Old Testament that could have been cited against Jesus' teaching. The New Testament selected only those that supported Jesus' call to love enemies. And then it insisted that Jesus' love command was the fulfilment of the Law.[25] The New Testament must interpret the Old, not vice versa.

That the new covenant brings fundamental change is

clear. Christ's unique sacrifice at Calvary replaces repeated sacrifices in the temple. Sunday replaces the sabbath. Righteousness based on faith replaces righteousness based on law. Costly, self-sacrificial, nonretaliatory love even for enemies replaces 'an eye for an eye.' As the book of Hebrews insists, the new covenant makes the old obsolete (Heb 8:13). But the New Testament does not destroy the Old, it fulfils it.

This New Testament teaching on the way it fulfils the Old provides the framework for a Christian understanding of the statements on war in the Old Testament. We do not deny that God commanded the Israelites to go to war. Jesus, however, taught a different way, a way which refuses to retaliate against or kill opponents, even oppressive imperialists. Jesus' teaching about nonviolence, however, does not destroy the Old Testament any more than Calvary and righteousness based on faith destroy the law. In fact Christ pointed precisely to the nonviolent Suffering Servant of Isaiah 53 and the peaceful Messiah of Zechariah to indicate the character of his messianic mission. Christ fulfils that to which the Old Testament pointed.

Should Christians adopt the just war tradition on the authority of the Old Testament? By no means. Only if we were to justify massacring civilians and prisoners of war, only if we were so drastically to reduce our weaponry that 'In God We Trust' became a reality, only then could we claim to live within the general framework and central assumptions of the Old Testament teaching on war. The Old Testament stands in sharp condemnation of those who trust in atomic chariots and thermonuclear cavalry.

But what about the New Testament?

New Testament Texts Used to Justify War

'*Render unto Caesar . . .*' When the Jewish leaders asked Jesus if he believed in paying Roman taxes, he replied: 'Render to Caesar the things that are Caesar's, and to God the things that are God's' (Mk 12:17; see also Mt 22:15–22, Lk 20:20–26).

Many Christians simply assume that in this encounter Jesus supported payment of Roman taxes.[26] Many also assume that his statement obligates Christians to obey the government's call to arms. In religious matters, we discern God's will in the church; in issues pertaining to the state, we obey the government. Therefore 'Render to Caesar the things that are Caesar's' means going to war when the state issues the orders.

Such an interpretation, however, begs the question. Christians have always been ready to die for the belief that 'we must obey God rather than men' (Acts 5:29).[27] Jesus' statement about Caesar says nothing explicit about war. Therefore we must ask first whether participation in war is contrary to God's will. Only if it is not, could Christians consider military service, for instance, something we must render to Caesar. The text throws no light whatsoever on that question.[28] Since we have argued on other grounds that war is unacceptable to God, we find this text requires Christians to oppose war, not to join in it.

'*Let every person be subject . . .*'   Are defenders of war on better ground in Romans 13? After urging Christians to be subject to government, Paul says that Government 'does not bear the sword in vain' (v. 4). Does that not mean that God has authorised government to fight just wars? Should not Christians, who obey Paul's command to be subject, therefore willingly participate in legal killing (capital punishment and war) when governments issue the call?

It is surely striking that on both sides of this statement on subjection to government (13:1–7) we find clear, vigorous statements on agape love. The verses immediately preceding contain the strongest statement in Paul's letters on the Christian duty of loving enemies. He starts with the positive command to bless persecutors rather than to curse them (12:14). Then he forbids retaliation: 'Repay no one evil for evil' (12:17). He explicitly orders Christians to leave vengeance to God (12:19). Instead, we should overcome evil with good by feeding and clothing our enemies (12:20 –21).

Then Paul says: Be subject to government. This puts these verses on government squarely in the context of love for enemies. Furthermore, Paul returns to the theme of love for neighbour immediately after the final statement on respect for government. If one loves one's neighbour, one has fulfilled the whole law (13:8). And he concludes with the assertion that 'love does no wrong to a neighbour' (13:10).

The way this passage became a justification for war is most intriguing. Earlier commentators sometimes noticed that Paul frames his words on subjection to government with his strongest statement on nonretaliatory, nonviolent love. Therefore they argued that Paul inserted the section on government and the sword to make sure no one drew pacifist conclusions. Paul's words against retaliation and vengeance, they concluded, apply to the individual in personal relationships, not to the Christian in his public duties.[29]

The opposite conclusion is more likely. We saw in the last chapter that the command to imitate Christ and to love our enemies was the early Christian norm in every area of life. There is no adequate reason to think this passage is an exception.

Paul's basic purpose in 13:1–7 was to make sure that Christians in Rome exercised nonretaliatory love toward hostile government officials.[30] Paul probably had good reason for concern. A mere five years after Paul wrote this letter, Nero massacred many Christians in a horrible persecution (AD 64). Tension may very well have been building by the time of this letter.

Roman authorities probably viewed Christians as Jewish sectarians with dangerous, anarchistic, rebellious tendencies.[31] F. F. Bruce points out that 'Christianity started out with a tremendous handicap in the eyes of Roman law for the sufficient reason that its Founder had been convicted and executed by the sentence of a Roman magistrate.'[32] Jesus had died on a Roman cross for the alleged crime of political rebellion against Rome. That was the one and only record of Jesus known to Roman law. From both the book of Acts and the Roman historian Tacitus, it is clear that opponents could easily discredit Christians in the eyes of Roman officials merely by alluding to this 'revolutionary' beginning.[33] Nor did it help the Christian cause in Roman eyes that riots frequently accompanied Paul's missionary journeys. In fact, it is likely that the Romans expelled all Jews from Rome about AD 49 because of rioting that occurred when Christians introduced their faith into the Jewish community there.[34]

One other factor probably caused suspicion. The long-standing Zealot summons to arms was heating up. C. H. Dodd says that 'Jewish national feeling was running high at this time when things were brewing up to the crisis of AD 66.'[35] Only seven years after this letter, the Jewish rebellion began. Many Jewish Christians throughout the Empire would have shared some of the negative Jewish feelings about Rome. In this connection it is important to realise that for the first generation Roman officials considered Christians to be some variety of Judaism.[36] Rome had reasons for suspicion.

In this tense, dangerous setting, Paul wants to make sure the Roman Christians do nothing to provoke governmental opposition. How does he do it? By urging Christians to apply Jesus' nonretaliatory, overflowing love for enemies in their relationships with the state. In Romans 12:14 –13:10 Paul tells Christians how to respond to outsiders, including the government.[37] One should respond with love to enemies who curse, persecute and give occasion for vengeance. Thus this entire section is one unit with the overarching theme of responding to those outside the church with nonretaliatory love.

Taken together 12:19 and 13:4 provide clear evidence that Paul does not intend that Christians participate in the violent sword of the state. In 12:19, Paul forbids Christians to have any part in retaliatory vengeance: 'Beloved, never *avenge* yourselves, but leave it to the *wrath* of God.' Using *exactly* the same words, Paul says in 13:4 that the state acts as an avenger to execute God's wrath on the wicked: 'He does not bear the sword in vain; he is the servant of God to execute [*avenge*] his *wrath* on the wrongdoer.' If these two verses were in different books, the meaning would be less obvious. But Paul uses exactly the same words within the sustained reasoning of one passage.[38] Does not Paul mean to say that whatever justification there may be for the state to use the sword, Christians dare not participate in the retaliatory avenging of God's wrath against evil? The Evangelical scholar F. F. Bruce concludes with reference to verse 4: 'The state thus is charged with a function which has been *explicitly forbidden* to the Christian (xii. 17a, 19).'[39]

Nothing we have said implies or requires the conclusion that Christians should not participate in police activity. Even now most police work is nonviolent. If we devoted as much research and resources to exploring nonlethal ways of restraining and overcoming armed criminals as we now invest in lethal weapons, the police could protect society without these weapons.[40]

We might add that it is not necessary to conclude from Romans 13:4 that God *orders* the state to execute retributive punishment with a violent sword. Certainly God wills and ordains the state and its restraint of evil, but that does not mean he approves of all its deeds.[41] Throughout the Scriptures we find that God uses wicked governments and unjustified actions to restrain evil, advance his purposes and punish the wicked. Isaiah 45:1 even goes so far as to call the pagan Cyrus 'God's anointed' – the word for Messiah! That is even stronger than Paul's word *servant*. Although God used Assyria to punish Israel, Isaiah 10:12–19 makes clear that God would punish Assyria for the wicked, cruel ways in which it conquered other nations. According to Jesus, Pilate's authority came from God (Jn 19:11), but that hardly meant that God approved of Pilate's violent, unjust use of authority in ordering the death penalty for his only Son.[42]

In his providential control of the universe and in the moral order he establishes in history, God often uses both unjust, misguided actions and good, wise ones to accomplish his will. Thus he also uses the violent sword of the state to punish criminals. The state can be God's servant to restrain evil even when the state does so – as did Assyria – in ways that God does not explicitly order or endorse.

For our purposes two other things are important. First, Romans 13:1–7 says nothing about war. Verses 2–6 show that Paul is talking, not about the governmental function of waging war, but rather that of policing society. The question of whether or not the government ought to wage war is not the subject of discussion. Rather, it is the government's police role of punishing those who disturb society with wrongdoing. Even the word for 'sword' (*machaira*) used in verse 4 underlines this point. The *machaira* was a long dagger, not a long sword used in battle.[43] The *machaira* would be the equivalent of a policeman's pistol rather than a soldier's M-21 rifle.[44]

Second, Romans 13:1–7 in no way commands unconditional obedience to the state. We could have assumed that simply from the early Christian insistence that when government commands things contrary to God's will, Christians must disobey government in order to remain faithful to God. Since Paul says the state does things Christians dare not do, he must have assumed that Christians would disobey if ordered to do those things. That certainly is what the Christians of the first centuries thought. Further, however, this text itself provides evidence of this view. The verb 'be subject' is *not* the verb 'to obey.' In fact there were three perfectly good Greek verbs meaning obey, but Paul used none of them.[45] One can respect and be subject to government even when one disobeys out of obedience to God's higher law.

'*Buy a sword!*' In Luke 22:35–38, Jesus seems to command his disciples to buy swords:

And he said to them, 'When I sent you out with no purse or bag or sandals, did you lack anything?' They said, 'Nothing.' He said to them, 'But now, let him who has a purse take it, and likewise a bag. And let him who has no sword sell his mantle and buy one. For I tell you that this scripture must be fulfilled in me, "And he was reckoned with transgressors"; for what is written about me has its fulfilment.' And they said, 'Look, Lord, here are two swords.' And he said to them, 'It is enough.'

This obscure text has long puzzled biblical scholars. What did Jesus mean?

In his defence of war, Boettner argues that Jesus was urging all the disciples to go and buy weapons. They would soon be travelling on far-flung missionary journeys into dangerous areas with little police protection. Therefore they would need swords. Since Jesus approves of the sword, warfare is permitted.[46]

Such a view, however, is extremely unlikely for many reasons. First, verse 37 itself explicitly says that Jesus' words about the sword are connected with his death, not some future missionary journey. Second, Jesus then quotes Isaiah 53:12. If anything is clear in Isaiah 53, it is that the Suffering Servant is a peaceful, nonviolent figure. If Jesus referred to Isaiah 53 to explain his statement about the sword, he could hardly have intended to recommend that the disciples all arm themselves. Third, when Peter did use the sword at Gethsemane, Jesus sharply condemned him with a general condemnation against using the sword.[47] Fourth, Jesus explicitly told Pilate his disciples did not fight (Jn 18:36). Fifth, if Jesus did intend to speak literally, then it was surely naively absurd to say that two swords were sufficient. Jesus was not so ignorant of what it would have taken to defend themselves with violent weapons. Finally, to interpret this passage as a serious summons to buy weapons is to suggest that Jesus suddenly reversed his previous teaching. That is unlikely. The standard principle of interpretation is to explain obscure texts such as this one in the light of other, clearer passages.

What then did Jesus mean? Most commentators reject the view that Jesus was speaking literally.[48] It is more likely, in keeping with his love for powerful metaphors, that Jesus intended to refer in a figurative, symbolic way to the extremely perilous times that lay just ahead. Earlier, when Jesus had sent them out on their preaching mission, all had been easy (Mt 10:5–42). Now terrible trouble awaits them. Along with many other scholars, Leon Morris concludes that Jesus used figurative language to underline the coming difficulties: 'It is Jesus' graphic way of bringing it home that the disciples face a situation of grave peril.'[49]

But the disciples misunderstood. Taking his words literally, they produce two swords. In frustration Jesus ends the conversation. Morris explains: 'Jesus' response, "it is enough," means not, "Two will be sufficient," but rather, "Enough of this kind of talk!" It is a way of dismissing a subject in which the disciples were hopelessly astray.'[50]

We must conclude that Luke 22:35–38 does not support the use of lethal weapons. Jesus spoke figuratively, not literally. At Caesarea Philippi, Peter had angrily rejected Jesus' view of a suffering Messiah patterned after Isaiah 53. Here and in the garden he still could not fathom Jesus' revolutionary rejection of the way of the sword.

The cleansing of the Temple.   All four Gospels report that Jesus marched into the Temple and overturned the tables of the moneychangers and cattle salesmen, sending the startled merchants and cattle rushing madly out of the holy place. Whether Jesus cleansed the temple once or twice is not important to our point. John 2:15, though, mentions that he used a whip. Richard McSorley reports that he once heard this text used as the text for a sermon supporting the United States' military involvement in Vietnam.[51] Does this text justify war?[52]

There is no evidence that Jesus used violence of any sort beyond the psychological power of moral authority. The priests in charge of the Temple had a police force at their command. A Roman garrison was stationed nearby. If Jesus had physically attacked people, the police would have arrested him promptly.

Careful exegesis of the passage confirms this. The word

translated 'drive out' does not necessarily connote violence of any sort. For example, in Matthew 9:38, it is used to refer to God's sending out of labourers into the harvest. The text of John 2:15 shows that Jesus used the whip only on the animals.[53] Commentators agree that Jesus' cleansing of the temple was a symbolic messianic act. Certainly it involved vigorous direct confrontation with evil, even to the point of civil disobedience. But no one, not even an animal, was killed.

Rather than endorsing nationalistic violence, the text points to the New Testament's transcendence of all self-serving nationalism. From other sources, scholars tell us, it is clear that the merchants had set up their businesses in the Court of the Gentiles.[54] Since this was the only place in the Temple where Gentiles could come to pray and worship, this act of mercantile greed had perhaps banished the Gentiles from the Temple. Jesus denounced this ethnocentric selfishness: 'Is it not written, "My house shall be called a house of prayer *for all the nations*"?' (Mk 11:17).

Soldiers in the New Testament. The centurion who came to ask Jesus to heal his servant expressed so much faith that Jesus praised him highly: 'Truly, I say to you, not even in Israel have I found such faith' (Mt 8:10). Peter's first Gentile convert was the centurion Cornelius (Acts 10). In neither case is there any indication in the text that Jesus or Peter ordered these two Roman officers to leave the army. From the time of Augustine, Christians have con-cluded that the absence of any clear condemnation means that Jesus and the New Testament do not condemn the 'calling' of the soldier.[55]

How valid is this argument? Like all arguments from silence, it is weak. There is, to be sure, no evidence of condemnation. On the other hand, there is also no evi-dence that Jesus and Peter did not go on to teach both centurions that they ought to leave the Roman army. Many more things must have happened in both cases beyond what the text includes. The centurions' military occupation is not the theme of either passage. Speculation either way about something on which the text tells us nothing is surely dangerous.

It is quite clear in Jesus' encounter with the centurion that it is the centurion's faith, not his profession, which Jesus praises. 'Not even in Israel have I found such *faith.*'

In the same chapter of Luke, Jesus praised the prostitute who washed his feet (Lk 7:36–50). The text records no specific word of rebuke for the woman's profession. Nor is there any specific condemnation of the thief on the cross to whom Jesus promised Paradise (Lk 23:39–43).[56] But no one would argue that Jesus condoned prostitution or robbery. Elsewhere he condemned both just as elsewhere he condemned violence. To build a case for war on silence is to build on sand.[57]

Wars and rumours of wars.   Jesus predicted 'wars and rumours of wars,' and then added: 'But the end is not yet' (Mt 24:6; Mk 13:7; Lk 21:9). The text does not actually say that wars will persist until the Lord's return. But we have no doubt that they will. Does that harsh reality mean, as some have argued, that Christians dare not oppose war and work for peace?[58] Jesus also predicted terrible persecution and martyrdom for his disciples. Children, he said, would betray parents, and brothers would betray brothers (Lk 21:16–17). No one supposes that Christians should not oppose these awful evils with their prayers and actions. The same is true of war.

Until Christ returns, selfish persons and communities will unjustly impose their will on others. That does not mean that it is impossible or contrary to Jesus' prediction to abolish nuclear weapons or even other particularly lethal instruments of war. But it does mean that societal violence will persist until the shalom of Jesus' new kingdom comes in its fullness. Until then we should obey Jesus' and Paul's command to work and pray for peace.

Militaristic symbolism.   Paul refers to soldiers' armour to describe the 'weapons' of the Christian life (Eph 6:10 –17). He also calls on Timothy to suffer as a 'good soldier of

Jesus Christ' (2 Tim 2:3). Boettner argues that these militaristic metaphors justify war:

> It is hardly conceivable that the scriptures should present
> the Christian life under a symbolism having to do so
> distinctly with soldiering and warfare and at the same
> time repudiate the reality for which it stands as always
> and everywhere wrong. We cannot imagine the different
> aspects of the Christian life being set forth through a
> symbolism borrowed from the liquor traffic or the vice
> racket.[59]

As a matter of fact, Paul draws an analogy between being
drunk with wine and being filled with the Spirit (Eph 5:18).
Likewise Jesus drew an analogy between himself and a thief
in the night (Mt 24:43) and between God and an unjust
judge (Lk 18:1–8). No one would suppose, however, that
he was recommending nocturnal thievery or judicial corruption. To attempt to justify war on the basis of military
metaphors is to ignore the rules of literary interpretation.

Pacifism and Liberalism

Perhaps the most common theological criticism of Christian pacifism is that its foundations lie in theological
liberalism.[60] Pacifists, it is charged, reduce Jesus to a mere
human teacher of ethics. They deny the atonement, interpreting the cross only as an example to imitate. They reject
the Old Testament. Adopting a naively optimistic view of
human nature derived from the Renaissance and Enlight-
enment, they ignore human sinfulness. As a consequence
they suppose that people can easily establish the kingdom
of God on earth 'through such things as social legislation,
education and disarmament conferences.'[61] Reinhold
Niebuhr, of course, is the theologian who has most powerfully denounced this liberal view of human nature.[62] How
valid are these charges?

That a major portion of modern pacifists have belonged
to a liberal theological tradition is indisputable. It is easy to

cite instances of pacifists like William Ellery Channing naively claiming that the world is progressing year by year, closer and closer to blissful shalom.[63] On the other hand, we cannot forget that the church with the longest commitment to pacifism – the Mennonite Community – stands firmly within the centre of historic Christian orthodoxy. Historically, pacifists have come from many different theological traditions.

Is there, however, any *necessary* connection between rejection of war and theological liberalism? Absolutely not. In the preceding chapters we have argued that it is historic Christian orthodoxy which provides the only adequate foundation for Christian nonviolence.

It is precisely because Jesus was more than a great teacher, it is precisely because he was truly God incarnate, that we dare not brush aside his clear, explicit call to nonviolent love for enemies. It is the One whom the church confesses to be true God as well as true man who summons us to reject war. Therefore, it simply will not do to admit, as does Reinhold Niebuhr, that Jesus taught a clear uncompromising ethic of total opposition to violence, and then claim that Christians should set aside this 'impossible ideal.'[64] We dare not confess his lordship and deity with our lips and then deny it with our actions.

Nor do pacifists necessarily deny the atonement. In fact we have discovered that the New Testament grounds its call to nonviolence precisely in Christ's substitutionary atonement. The God-man took the deserved penalty of our sin upon himself at the cross. Because God loves even his enemies, so must we. The cross no less represents a substitutionary atonement because it also serves as a revelatory example. In fact, it is an example because it is first of all vicarious atonement.

Further, pacifists need not, in fact dare not, reject the Old Testament. The Old and New Testaments together are God's authoritative revelation. Christ's teaching and work are not the abolition of the Old Testament but rather its fulfilment.

Nor is there any more substance to the charge that we assume a naive, optimistic view of human nature. Since the Fall, persons have had terrible, egocentric selfishness at the core of their being. We do not suppose that sinful humanity, by daily diligence and educational endeavour, can succeed in faithfully applying Jesus' call to love enemies.

But Reinhold Niebuhr's classic essay has the title, 'Why the *Christian Church* Is Not Pacifist.' He is – or at least ought to be – talking about Jesus' new Spirit-filled, messianic community. With the early Christians, we believe that the new age has truly broken into this old order. We believe Jesus' new messianic community can, by the power of the Holy Spirit, begin to incarnate now the radical norms of Jesus' new kingdom. We do not believe in education and disarmament conferences, although both have value. We believe in the transforming power of the Holy Spirit.

In Niebuhr's thought, the church is a weak, pale reflection of the Spirit-filled New Testament community of transformed believers; the kingdom is entirely transcendent and future; and the Holy Spirit is almost nonexistent.[65] Does this not smack of liberalism? In his classic work, *Moral Man and Immoral Society*, Niebuhr argues that individuals are less selfish, wicked and immoral than social groups.[66] Therefore, he does not believe that any social groups, even the church, can practise in society as a whole Jesus' ethic of love for the enemy. But that is to deny both the practice and teaching of the first Christians. In the power of the Holy Spirit, they demonstrated a costly love both within and outside the church. The world could only utter in amazement, 'Behold how they love one another.' In the Spirit's power, it is possible to apply Jesus' ethic in the home and the marketplace, the church and the public arena. Again and again, the apostle Paul and the other apostles taught that Christians could and should live in the Spirit, not in the flesh. Why? Because the new age had begun. God has delivered Christians from the dominion of the old age and 'transferred us to the kingdom of his beloved Son' (Col 1:13). In the power of the Holy Spirit, the down payment and guarantee of the kingdom's presence, Christians can live lives that are dramatically different from their surrounding immoral societies.

In his classic essay, Niebuhr also operates with an inadequate concept of grace:

> Grace is conceived as 'justification,' as *pardon rather* than power, as the forgiveness of God, which is vouchsafed to man despite the fact he never achieves the full measure of Christ. . . . In this doctrine of forgiveness and justification, Christianity measures the full seriousness of sin as a permanent factor in human history.[67]

This appears dangerously close to an excuse for Christians to continue in sin that grace may abound. Certainly Christians in this life never attain earthly perfection. But they do, if Paul is not entirely mistaken, experience radical renewal by the power of the Holy Spirit. Therefore they should and can live according to the values of the new age.

Paul never argued that because sin still lingers in the Christian, it is therefore acceptable to fornicate, lie and steal. Why then would anyone argue that the awful persistence of sin even in Christians justifies our ignoring the New Testament's call to love our enemies? Certainly that is difficult. Certainly we will often fail. But surely we should not excuse or justify that sinful failure. Rather, with Paul we should repeat the glorious promise that in Christ all things are indeed possible.

That does not mean that non-Christians can do nothing good. Sin has not totally destroyed the image of God in persons. God's common grace is at work in all people. Because of that, it has been possible for non-Christians and Christians to work together to correct social injustice, abolish slavery and create democratic societies. Enlightened self-interest, undergirded by God's common grace, can accomplish significant good in history. In due time many non-Christians may be able to see that reversing the course of the nuclear arms race is in the interest of all people. Our hope, however, does not rest with non-Christians. People of good will cannot usher in the kingdom through disarmament campaigns. Sin, war and rumours of war will persist until Christ brings the fullness of the kingdom at his return. As we remember this important aspect of the truth, however, we cannot forget that Jesus' gospel was the good news that his kingdom had *already begun*. That is the basis of Christian hope and optimism.

Our hope rests with those who have been born again by the power of the risen Lord and therefore now yield their whole selves to the Holy Spirit. Christians know that the Nazarene teacher of love for enemies was God incarnate. Christians know that the incredible example of love revealed at the cross was God himself suffering in the place of his enemies. Christians know that even though sin continues to rampage through society, the new messianic age of shalom has already begun. Therefore Christians believe that in the power of the Holy Spirit, Jesus' new messianic community can begin even now to love its enemies, to reject retaliation against persecutors and to overcome evil by embracing a costly cross.

SECTION III

What to Do: Concrete Steps towards Peace

In the last section we argued that both the major Christian traditions on the problem of war – just war and pacifist – lead to a common conclusion in the nuclear age. Today all Christians must say no to the possession and use of nuclear weapons. But words are not enough. What can we do?

In the chapters that follow, we will look at how Christians can be peacemakers. We begin in chapter nine by asking what the individual *Christian can do for peace. Then chapter ten describes how* local congregations *can become peacemaking communities. Chapter eleven shows how Christians can reach beyond the congregation to witness for peace in* social and political structures, *and chapter twelve takes up the question of how Christians can work for* disarmament.

'*Nuclear war is inevitable, says the pessimist;*
Nuclear war is impossible, says the optimist;
Nuclear war is inevitable unless we make it
impossible, says the realist.'

Sidney J. Harris[1]

*Here are ten practical, specific things you can do right
now for peace:*
   1. Pray *for peace wherever you note the lack of
it – in your own spirit, in your relationships with
others, in the world.*
   2. Subscribe *to a magazine that discusses world
peace from a Christian point of view. Read it
regularly and act on its suggestions. (Appendix B lists
such magazines.)*
   3. Wear a button *with a peace slogan or put a
bumper sticker on your car. (Many of the peace
groups listed in appendix A distribute these.)*
   4. Join *a national peace organisation. (See
appendix A.)*
   5. Buy a book *with photos of the atomic
destruction of Hiroshima and Nagasaki and put it in a
prominent place in your home.*[2]
   6. Buy some stationery *with a peace motif.*[3]
   7. Encourage young people *to pray, think, read
and decide on a stance toward the armed forces.*
   8. Support Christian education *on peace,
disarmament and the arms race.*
   9. Write *a letter to the editor of your local
newspaper expressing your concern for peace.*
   10. Become politically active *for peace. Write to
your elected representatives and vote for candidates
who work for disarmament.*

The authors

The Christian Peacemaker

'Tell me the weight of a snowflake,' a coal-mouse [American tit-mouse or 'chickadee'] asked a wild dove.

'Nothing more than nothing,' was the answer.

'In that case, I must tell you a marvellous story,' the coal-mouse said. 'I sat on the branch of a Fir, close to its trunk, when it began to snow, not heavily, not in a raging blizzard, no, just like in a dream, without any violence. Since I didn't have anything better to do, I counted the snowflakes settling on the twigs and needles of my branch. Their number was exactly 3,741,952. When the next snowflake dropped onto the branch – nothing more than nothing, as you say – the branch broke off.'

Having said that, the coal-mouse flew away.

The dove, since Noah's time an authority on the matter, thought about the story for a while and finally said to herself: 'Perhaps there is only one person's voice lacking for peace to come about in the world.'[4]

John R. W. Stott calls Christians to be peacemakers: 'We need to hear again the words of Jesus: "Blessed are the peacemakers, for they shall be called God's children." Peacemaking is a divine activity, and we can claim to be authentic children of God only if we seek to do what our heavenly Father is doing.'[5] How can we follow Christ as peacemakers in the 1980s and '90s?

A 1980 poll taken in California showed that an astounding eighty-four per cent of those responding believed that nuclear war would come and that they personally would not survive it.[6] People feel immobilised. If you talk to them about nuclear war, you hear comments like: 'I feel impending doom.' 'It's so painful, I can't even think about it.' 'I've never been so confused before.' 'I can't make any difference; it's all up to the politicians.' 'It seems wrong. It makes me angry. But what can one person do?'

Christians get discouraged too. Many church leaders feel too ill-informed to speak out, or their concerns and interests are elsewhere. Most Christians who think at all about nuclear weapons still accept them, believing that somehow they can deter war.

Is there hope? Yes. Because of Easter. Sin, evil and hell did their worst at the cross, but God prevailed on Easter morning. The risen Lord Jesus is alive and well on planet Earth, waiting to enter and transform all who open their lives to him. He wants to continue the healing, loving and peacemaking he began at Bethlehem. He still wants to breathe his peace into us, just as he did with the first disciples. 'Peace I leave with you; my peace I give to you' (Jn 14:27). As he cried because Jerusalem did not know 'the things that make for peace' (Lk 19:42), so today he sorrows over the world's blind bumbling toward destruction. He yearns to empower and guide those who seek to make peace (Mt 5:9). There is also hope in the fact that God is the Lord of history. The One who has all power in heaven and earth is concerned about impending nuclear war, much more concerned than we are. He does not want us to destroy the earth that he created with such love.

There is hope for us in history. Recall, for example, the nineteenth-century movement to abolish slavery. At first, nearly all people, Christian and non-Christian, accepted slavery as a fact of life. People even justified slavery by quoting from the Bible. The individuals who spoke out against it were a tiny, frustrated minority.

Then something happened. Christians from many church backgrounds began to see that slavery was an appalling evil. Ministers began to preach that obedience to Christ required working to eliminate the whole institution of slavery. In the great Spirit-led revivals of Charles G. Finney, commitment to Christ came to be seen as leading the new convert inevitably into the abolitionist movement. Finney, who has been called the father of modern evangelism, even went so far as to refuse communion to slaveholders.[7] At first the movement against slavery faced almost insuperable odds and total apathy. Yet it grew and became a powerful, society-transforming force. Whole denominations abandoned slavery years before the cataclysm of the American Civil War. Today we wonder how anyone – especially Christians – could ever have condoned slavery.

In the early 1980s we see the beginnings of what may become a similar, dynamic movement of God's Spirit within American and Western European churches. A recent headline in the *New York Times* read, 'Churches Turning to Arms Race as Top Social Issue for the 1980's.'[8] *Newsweek* magazine reported that 'the disarmament movement is starting up again in the United States. . . . Its strength lies chiefly in the scientific and medical community and in the churches.'[9] At their November 1981 meeting the US Roman Catholic Bishops committed themselves to mobilising US Catholics against the nuclear arms race. And *Sojourners* magazine, which follows the Christian peace movement carefully, stated in a recent article: 'In a time when the nations are courting political and military disaster, there are signs of hope in the church. With increasing frequency, the call to peace is being heard from pulpits, seminary classrooms, and Christian publications. In many places, Christians are reaching a crucial turning point. They see the nuclear threat as having everything to do with their faith in Jesus Christ.'[10]

Just as nineteenth-century Christians came to see the incompatibility of Christian faith and slavery, so twentieth-century Christians are awakening to the enormous danger of nuclear war. Just as for many nineteenth-century Christians conversion came to involve rejecting slavery, so today conversion is coming to include a turning away from nuclear weapons. In this chapter we will examine what actions individual Christians can take to work for peace.

Pray

If the transforming power of Jesus' peacemaking Spirit is to flow more fully in our lives, we must fall on our knees. This is where the individual Christian's search to be a peacemaker begins. We cannot create shalom. Peace is the gift of Jesus Christ. 'My peace I give to you' (Jn 14:27), he promised. Peace begins in prayer. What we 'spend' in peacemaking must be based on the 'income' we receive in contemplation. We need to say with St Francis of Assisi, 'Lord, make me an instrument of *your* peace.'

We need to pray for ourselves, confessing our sin and all the darkness within us that blocks Christ's peace. We need to pray for the church, that it can become radiant with the Spirit's peace. We need to pray for our enemies, personal and national. We need to pray to God for the strength and wisdom to serve him in the paths of peace. We need to praise and thank God for being the God of peace. We need daily to rediscover Jesus as our abiding friend, to be purified by his goodness, challenged by his lordship, upheld by his love, grounded in his peace. We need to open our lives so that God can do his peacemaking work through us.

As we grow closer to God in prayer, one of the marvellous and unexpected things that happens is that we find a new love of life awakened in ourselves. Seeing the world more through God's eyes, we become more attuned to the beauty of the natural wonders he created, from the vastness of the stars to the symmetry of a leaf. Our love for the creation grows as we sense the Love who watches the sparrow fall, as we come to know the Lover who loved so much that he sent his Son to redeem humanity.

As we grow in love for God's precious creation, we will desire more deeply that it not be destroyed. We will become guardians of life and opponents of all that threatens and shows contempt for life. Our peacemaking will be rooted in faith, hope and love, not in fear and despair.

As we come to know more deeply the Christian reality of 'conversing with God,' we will come in contact with the Spirit who longs for peace far more deeply than we do and who knows what makes for peace. Walking and talking with Jesus, we will receive guidance in the choices we must make to reorder our lives for peacemaking. We will also gain greater insight into the steps which Christians working together can take for peace.

Knowing the God of peace through prayer will give us inspiration and zeal for peacemaking, wisdom and guidance in action, and endurance and tenacity for the long struggle.

Reconciled Relationships

Another thing that every Christian can do for peace is to determine to take a more forgiving, loving, peace-building attitude in relations with others. In our global concern for preventing international conflict, we must not forget this more immediate and personal responsibility. 'So far as it depends on you,' said St Paul, 'live peaceably with all' (Rom 12:18). If we are to be peacemakers in the Spirit of Christ, we need to apply this to *all* our relationships – with friends, coworkers, family members, strangers and people who antagonise and upset us.

The presence and teaching of Jesus enables us more fully to meet the incredibly difficult responsibility of loving our enemies. The authors confess that we find it very hard to love people who attack us and talk behind our backs. We have all encountered people with whom we have a hard time getting along. It is easy to love those who love us, but hard to love those whose personalities or opinions run contrary to our own. But if we cannot learn to love these potential 'enemies,' how can we ever respond to Jesus' call to love the fierce antagonists who threaten our national life?

One approach we have found helpful is to take quite literally Jesus' injunction to 'love your enemies and pray for those who persecute you' (Mt 5:44). We admit that when certain people antagonise us, we carry them with us in resentful thoughts. Often when they come to mind, we feel a burst of anger. We picture them looking cross. We replay the conflicts that set off our angry response. We even imagine a vengeful scene in which we make some cutting remark that puts us 'one up' on our disputants.

To pray for such persons means turning this antagonistic mental image into prayer. When an antagonist comes to mind, we try immediately to start praying for him or her to know God's love more deeply, and for us both to experience healing and reconciliation. We allow ourselves to form a mental picture of the person surrounded by God's love and light. We imagine walking together into the presence of Jesus and listening to his reconciling Word. Praying in this way tends to dissolve resentment and open new avenues for reconciliation. Peacemaking in our personal relationships can be a daily challenge which is as important as our work for international peace.

Our Families

We can also be peacemakers in our families. The family is the first school in which children learn what makes for peace. Yet when parents come to understand the imminent danger of nuclear destruction, they are sometimes tempted to rush into frenetic activity. They dash from committee meetings to conferences and demonstrations, neglecting the job of peacemaking that lies right at their doorstep. Ironically, children can be sacrificed, husband-wife relationships can suffer, family community can be harmed – all in the name of an outside call to 'peacemaking.'

As a father, Dick Taylor has struggled with this problem. While living in a low-income, multi-racial section of Philadelphia, Dick and his family learned about what it means to be a peacemaking family. Dick's ten-year-old-daughter Debby was attending the local state school. One afternoon she came home complaining that an older girl had been picking on her. The initial antagonism had grown into shouting matches on the way home. The larger girl would push Debby off the pavement and once she nearly ended up in the path of a car. Early mornings on the way to school were the worst times. The girl would shout at Debby and threaten her.

That evening after Debby had told them about the problem, Dick and his wife, Phyllis, invited some friends who had long experience in the peace movement to drop in to help them find a solution. After supper they spread out some large pieces of paper on the living-room floor. With Debby they tried to imagine and write down a wide range of possible responses.

'I could try to beat her up,' Debby said, 'but I'd probably get clobbered.'

'Try to beat her up' went down on the list. In fifteen minutes of discussion the group had brainstormed more than a dozen possibilities: 'go to school by a different route'; 'walk in a group'; 'get a ride'; and so on. Dick mentioned the biblical idea of agape. He suggested that Debby show good will toward the girl. Debby at first said she couldn't, but Dick wrote 'good will' on the list anyway.

Debby left the meeting thoughtfully, carrying the list. The next afternoon she came home all excited. On the way to school, the girl had shouted from across the street, 'Debby, you're wearing the most ugly dress I've ever seen!'

Debby called back, 'Thanks for telling me. I like to go to school looking my best.'

The girl retorted, 'Your shoes and socks don't even match!'

Debby said, 'I really appreciate your opinion. I like to know how my friends think I look. Maybe I'll go home and change.' Obviously taken aback and curious about this change in Debby's attitude, the girl crossed the street and struck up a normal conversation. By the time they arrived at school, they had begun to build a friendship which lasted as long as they knew each other.

This is just one example of what family peacemaking is all about. *Parenting for Peace and Justice* by Kathleen and

James McGinnis (see appendix A-3) draws on the experiences of three dozen Protestant and Catholic families who contributed to the book. It is chock-full of ideas, games, discussion starters and other resources for building family unity around peace and justice concerns. In addition, the McGinnises have organised the National Parenting for Peace and Justice Network (see appendix B-2).

Stephanie Judson is a Quaker teacher with long experience in doing workshops with students, parents and teachers. Her book, *A Manual for Nonviolence and Children* (see appendix A-3), gives a wealth of ideas, games and techniques for developing nonviolent attitudes and behaviour in children, especially those of pre-school and elementary ages. And Lorne Peachy (a Mennonite) has written a practical guide for parents who seek to build peacemaking lifestyles in the home and community. *How to Teach Peace to Children* is also listed in the appendix.

Learn

If we are to speak and act intelligently for peace, we must become better informed about nuclear war and how Christians can respond to its threat. Appendix A lists books that will deepen your understanding.

In addition to reading books, one of the best ways to become informed – and to keep up to date – is to subscribe to a magazine or newsletter that deals with peace and international issues. These are also listed in appendix A.

As you pick up ideas from books and magazines, you can talk them over in your family, at your job and at church. Discussion will help clarify your own thinking and will get others thinking too. Most people's opinions are formed largely in discussions with friends and relatives. Debating the issues is a responsibility for everyone in a democracy.

Act

As the concern for peace has deepened in the churches, Christians have set up both denominational and interdenominational organisations to work for the prevention of war.

Many denominations now have their own peace fellowships which draw together clergy and laity in study and action. Other peace organisations bring together Christians from many different denominational backgrounds (see appendix B).

Most groups may be joined by paying a small membership fee. Through newsletters, invitations to conferences and other resources, they will keep you abreast of current developments and put you in touch with peacemakers across the country and even in other lands. By working with others, you will multiply your own impact. By contributing financially, you will be supporting groups which, over the years, have developed expertise in peace education and action. They will help you not only to understand the issues better, but also to know how and when to act. Many of these national organisations have local chapters. In communities where there are no such chapters, Christians may form their own local groups.

Christian Peacemaking and the Armed Forces

Military professionals are in general dedicated and conscientious people who are doing the job society has assigned them. In time of war their job is to win. In peacetime it is natural for them to believe that national interests are best secured by strengthening military capabilities.

If our conclusions in section II are correct, Christians from both the just war and nonviolence traditions will oppose present military activity and plans. From a just war standpoint, Christians must, we have argued, reject the possession and use of nuclear weapons. For those espousing nonviolence, all military training and violent military defence is rejected. National defence is to be provided by means that are consistent with the love ethic of Jesus Christ. (In section IV we will discuss the subject of 'transarmament'.)

Direct support for the military comes from three main sources. First, the willingness of people to enter the armed forces, to prepare to use nuclear weapons, and to fight and

kill in time of war. Second, the willingness of people to
work in civilian jobs related to defence; for example, as
civilian employees of the Ministry of Defence, as workers
in private defence industry, or as scientists and technicians
in military research and development. Third, the willingness of citizens to pay taxes which support the military
budget.

If people became *un*willing to provide any *one* of these
sources of support, the military would not be able to
function, at least in its present form. Some alternative to
nuclear deterrence and military defence would have to be
found. If people substantially *lessened* their support in any
of these three areas, this would send a strong signal to our
leaders that we were disaffected with military solutions and
were demanding greater initiatives toward peace. We will
explore how to decrease support for military defence by:
(1) becoming a 'conscientious objector' to some or all forms
of military service; (2) refusing to work in military-related
jobs; and (3) refusing to pay 'war taxes.'

Conscientious Objection

Since July 1980, young men in the States on turning eighteen have been required to register with the US Selective
Service System by going to a local post office and filling in
a card. If Congress later approves a return to the military
draft (and many authorities believe that *will* happen[11])
these young men may be called to report for induction into
the armed forces. In the meantime, the military has increased its efforts to recruit volunteers through television
advertisements, programmes on school and college cam-
puses and so on. (The recruiters talk about 'serving your
country' and 'getting trained for a good job'; they do not
talk about learning to shoot other human beings or learning
to drop nuclear bombs on cities.)

If you are already in the armed forces or are thinking of
volunteering, you need to pray and think about what you
believe Christ asks of you. We encourage you to consider
conscientious objection carefully. A 'CO' is a person who,

for reasons of conscience, refuses to enter the armed forces to be trained to kill. He or she may be an 'absolute' CO, who refuses to participate in *any* war, or a 'selective' CO, who refuses to participate in a *particular* war regarded as unjust. Many churches recognise both the 'absolute' and the 'selective' CO positions as valid for Christians.

Information on the CO position is available from the peace groups listed in appendix B. Many of them have excellent books, leaflets, films and other materials telling why people have become CO's. They also explain the legal steps to achieve CO status.

Unfortunately, many Christians have never heard about conscientious objection. Even fewer realise that a person who is already in the Army, Navy, Air Force, Coast Guard or Marines can receive an honourable discharge and leave as a conscientious objector.

Some young people in the States feel so deeply about not supporting the military that they refuse to register under Selective Service laws, even though they realise that this may bring a jail sentence or other legal penalties.[12] Selective Service Director Thomas Turnage reports that about twenty-three per cent of the men born in 1963 who were supposed to register under current law failed to do so. These 300,000 nonregistrants are the largest number of violators in one year since the Selective Service began keeping records. Selective Service reports that since the current law was enacted some 800,000 eligible men have failed to register.[13] (In a later report of March 1982, Turnage estimated that the number of nonregistrates had dropped to 535,000.)

In the States, during the Vietnam War about a quarter of a million potential recruits failed to register. Even though the law provided fairly severe penalties, few were ever prosecuted. Less than one per cent of those who did not register ever went to jail, and of those most were released within a year. Many received probation and were given civilian work under court direction. There is, however, no way to predict what sentences might be given in the future.

One of the best ways to think through the CO position is to talk it over with someone from a special counselling agency set up for this purpose, such as the Central Board for Conscientious Objectors in London (listed in appendix B).

Renouncing Military Jobs

The difficult decisions are not avoided by civilians. If it is wrong to possess and use nuclear weapons, is it not also wrong to design or build them? If all war is wrong, is it not likewise wrong to help prepare weapons of war? Yet literally millions work in defence plants, do scientific research funded by military contracts, or work as civilian employees in the Ministry of Defence. If you are one of these, you will want to reflect on the relationship between your job and Christ's call to peacemaking. Christians working or doing research in the military area have to ask difficult questions. What is my work going *toward*? Is making weapons that harm and kill the best way to use the gifts God has given me? Is this the only kind of work I can do? How does my work relate to Christ's call to take up my cross and follow him? What would be the effect of my leaving my job?

We cannot tell you what position to take. But we urge you to ask these questions seriously and then ask God what he wants you to do. It may be that you will have to leave a well-paid, military-related job. You may be forced to make painful sacrifices. If so, other Christian peacemakers should help you find meaningful employment outside the military arena.

War Tax Resistance

A small[14] but growing minority of Christians are coming to believe that it is just as wrong to *pay* for war through the tax system as it is to train for it or to work in a military job. In England, the Peace Tax Campaign has been set up with the following aim:

To establish the statutory right whereby all who object to paying for war or military preparations on the grounds of conscience or profound conviction shall have that part of their tax payments, which is equivalent to their compulsory contribution to military expenditure, paid into a Peace Fund and used exclusively for non-military peacemaking purposes.[15]

In the summer of 1981 Roman Catholic Archbishop Raymond G. Hunthausen of Seattle declared that it is morally permissible for Christians to withhold the portion of their income tax used for the military. In fact, in early 1982 he announced that he intends to protest against the drift toward war by refusing to pay a portion of his Federal income tax. He stated: 'Form 1040 is the place where the Pentagon enters all of our lives, and asks our unthinking cooperation with the idol of nuclear destruction. I think the teaching of Jesus tells us to render to a nuclear armed Caesar what that Caesar deserves – tax resistance.'[16]

One of the authors is actively considering some form of tax resistance. The other has practised a limited form of tax resistance since 1966 by refusing to pay the Federal phone tax (a special tax which was levied to help finance the Vietnam War).[17] He and his wife also withhold thirty-four per cent of their taxes, since approximately one third of the Federal budget goes to finance current military expenditures. They send a letter to the Internal Revenue Service stating their objections to using tax monies to buy the weapons of mass killing.

Both authors have been challenged by the proponents of war tax resistance. Because we have not yet made up our minds on all aspects of war tax resistance, we think that the best service we can render to you is to share the arguments for and against tax refusal.

Before going further we need to face the fact that most forms of war tax resistance are illegal in the US and elsewhere.[18] Because of this some Christians reject it immediately, believing they should always obey the law. We deeply respect the law as the foundation of order and justice in a democracy. Laws should never be defied easily or flippantly. We try to obey them scrupulously. We believe, however, that conditions may arise in which it is right, after careful reflection and prayer, to disobey a human law in order to do what God requires. As the apostle Peter said, 'We must obey God rather than men' (Acts 5:29). In such cases, we believe that the person who conscientiously breaks a law should do so openly with a willingness to take the penalty that the law inflicts. Such steps show respect for the concept of law even while violating a particular law.

Space does not permit a detailed exposition of the case for Christian civil disobedience. In any case, this has been treated at length elsewhere.[19] But it should be pointed out that both Scripture and history give numerous illustrations of conscientious violations of particular laws which prevented people from doing God's will. The book of Esther presents two instances of people who, because of faithfulness to God, violated the king's laws. The Jewish people, in fact, were saved by acts of courageous lawbreaking (cf. Esther 3:2, 8; 4:10–11, 16). The early church defied the authorities who ordered them not to preach the gospel. And members of the early church were often persecuted and jailed for refusing to obey Roman laws which violated their consciences.

No one blamed those Germans who violated Hitler's anti-Semitic laws and saved Jews. Most of us would applaud American abolitionists who broke the Fugitive Slave Law of 1850 and refused to hand over escaping slaves to their pursuers. History has many renowned advocates of civil disobedience. It seems to us, then, that it is valid for Christians to break laws which either require them to do something wrong or prevent them from doing something right.

The Case against War Tax Resistance

Many Christians believe that it would be wrong to violate the tax law by refusing to pay income taxes. They put forward several arguments.

First, there is the problem of *moral ambiguity*. If our tax money went directly to the military, then it would be accurate to call it a war tax. For a Christian to pay such a tax would be to pray for peace while paying for war, as some tax resisters contend.[20] But in actual fact, our tax money is split between military and civilian purposes. Our taxes go into a large general fund. Out of this fund, payments are indeed made to the military. But payments are also made to beneficial government programmes (for example, aid to education, help for the poor) and for expenditures to maintain the basic structures of democratic government. The question is not, therefore, whether to pay 'war taxes.' The question is whether or not to pay *general* taxes, some of which go to military programmes and some of which are spent to keep democratic society alive and well.[21]

Tax refusers are caught in moral ambiguity no matter how they act. If, in objecting to their taxes being used to support the military, they pay *no taxes at all*, then they do not support the beneficial things the government does. They are not shouldering a basic obligation of citizenship, which is to share financially in the support of government. Their action points toward anarchism. If, on the other hand, they withhold a *portion* of their tax (perhaps based on the percentage of the budget that goes to military preparations), then the portion that they *do* pay goes into that big general fund, part of which gets parcelled out to finance defence. They still pay for war.

Because it is impossible to act with moral clarity and consistency through tax refusal, some Christians claim this is not a stance that Christians should take.

Another argument used against war tax resistance points out that *compromise is unavoidable*. We live in a society which, like all societies, is a mixture of good and evil. We cannot entirely escape the system and its evils. Even tax refusers put their savings in banks, which may turn around and invest in defence industries or buy government bonds. To buy petrol at a local station is to give money to a corporation which itself pays taxes and which may bribe governments overseas or engage in other unjust practices. War tax resistance, some say, is an attempt to obtain a moral purity which is not achievable in this life. Moral justification comes through the blood of Jesus Christ, not through our efforts to be pure.

A third argument says that war tax refusal is *a dangerous precedent*. Immanuel Kant's categorical imperative states that we should only act on that maxim which could at the same time become a universal law. Do tax refusers really want *everyone* to refuse to pay taxes *every* time they disagree strongly with some government policy? Do we pay taxes only to a government that supports everything we believe in? Would tax resisters advise racists to practise tax refusal because they do not like the government to enforce civil rights laws? Should the vast pro-life movement refuse to pay taxes because members abhor government-funded clinics which practise abortion? What would society be like if everyone refused to pay a portion of their tax every time they disagreed with some government policy?

A minimal commitment required of citizens who live in a democracy is that they contribute part of their financial resources to a common pool which is used to support that society. There will always be things we disagree with in government. That is the nature of living in a heterogeneous society.

Fourth, there is *scriptural evidence* to support paying taxes. When asked about paying taxes, Jesus said, 'Render to Caesar the things that are Caesar's, and to God the things that are God's' (Mk 12:17). When tax collectors asked Peter if Jesus paid the half-shekel tax, he answered yes (Mt 17:24–25).[22] There is no solid evidence that Jesus was a tax refuser.

Furthermore, Paul urged the church at Rome to pay 'taxes to whom taxes are due, revenue to whom revenue is due' (Rom 13:7). Since the passage seems to echo Jesus' 'render to Caesar' words, it is quite possible Paul believed Jesus intended to command the payment of Roman taxes. The early church did not start a tax resistance movement against Rome. According to historian Cecil John Cadoux, early Christians practised 'prompt and regular payment of all taxes which the state demanded . . . [believing that] if Christ paid these dues when he was not strictly liable to do so, how much more ought we to pay them!'[23] These taxes helped to finance the militaristic, imperialistic Roman Empire, which not only carried on brutal wars, but also persecuted Christians. If tax refusal was part of Jesus' intention for his followers, why did he not say so clearly?

Fifth, there is a *pragmatic argument* against tax refusal. One of the ironies of it is that the government often gets the money anyway – with interest and penalties added. When a person refuses to pay part of the tax due, the government follows a collection process, using various means to get the money owed. When taxes are not paid promptly, the government adds interest payments. When taxes are withheld illegally, the government can add fines on top of the amount owed. Thus, refusers may end up paying considerably *more* to the government than they would have if they had simply paid the tax in the first place.

Some tax refusers argue that the government spends more in collecting back taxes than they receive. However, it is doubtful that there is a net loss to the military. The military budget will not be lowered because of expenses elsewhere.

Other people point out the *impracticality* of tax resistance. Fighting the tax men can take a great deal of time. They can take tax refusers to court. They can take property and sell it to pay off back taxes. Legal fees, court battles and appeals can be extremely costly and time-consuming.[24] Is fighting the system really the best way for peacemakers to spend their time?

In addition, some say that war tax resistance lacks *effec-*

tiveness. Protest actions should communicate a clear message to the public. War tax resistance is not an action which meets this criterion. The broader public will accuse tax resisters (with some justification) of reneging on a fundamental obligation of citizenship and shifting the tax burden to others. The main issue of ending the arms race will get lost in endless debate about the validity of tax resistance.

Also, the effectiveness of tax resistance depends on its becoming such a large movement that the government will have to respond. However, if tax resistance grows, the government will crack down harder with heavier fines and longer prison sentences. Would the tactic be worth the effort? There are many other methods of peace education and action. Why choose a method which is ambiguous and ultimately impossible, when we can act clearly and unambiguously by other means? Instead of tax resistance, some say, peacemakers should campaign for 'peace candidates' for Congress or Parliament, demonstrate nonviolently at nuclear weapons plants, or work for a 'freeze' on the nuclear arms race.

These are the arguments of those who stand against war tax resistance. But there are also points in favour of it.

The Case for War Tax Resistance

Some Christians take the position that it is wrong voluntarily to pay all our income taxes when a large percentage goes to the military. They support their conclusions with a number of arguments. First, they say, war tax resistance is *a morally right stand*. They agree that there are other important avenues of peacemaking besides tax resistance. (Many tax refusers are at the forefront of peace education and action movements.) They also agree that it is impossible, given a sinful society, to act with complete moral purity or consistency. However, this does not absolve us of the obligation to try to bring our actions into the closest possible harmony with God's will. The Lord expects us to 'do that which is right in his eyes' (15:26).

Is it right to pay for war? In the States, over half the
Federal budget now goes to pay for past, present and future
wars. By 1986, if President Reagan's policies stand, about
sixty-five per cent of the controllable Federal budget (that
is, monies not tied up in trust funds like Social Security) will
go to the military. How can Christian peacemakers pay
their Federal taxes when the money they hand over is used
to construct atom bombs? Is this not like helping Hitler
finance his concentration camps and crematoria? As
Donald Kaufman says, 'To finance and pay for an activity is
to participate in it.'[25] How can we refuse our warm bodies
to the military while handing over our cold cash? Are we in
effect saying, 'I won't kill my neighbour, but I'll pay
someone else to do it'?

Nothing, say proponents of tax resistance, could be
clearer than the moral connection between taxes and war.
It costs money to build nuclear bombs and other weapons.
The money comes from our taxes. And at budget-cutting
time, it is usually the social programmes for the poor and
hungry that get cut while military finances increase to
astronomical proportions. In the past, government's main
requirement for making war was soldiers. In today's highly
technological world, the primary tool of war is money. The
conscription of money has become more important than
the conscription of men.

The question of *voluntary* action is crucial. Although it is
true that the government may eventually collect the taxes
with interest and penalties, there is a big difference between *willingly* paying taxes and being *forced* to do so. In
the first case, I give my willing assent. I support the evil
without even a word of protest. In the second case, I
remove at least my voluntary consent. I will resist the evil
rather than acquiesce in it. Is this not better, say tax
resisters, than letting the hideous business of collecting
billions for nuclear war go on unchallenged?

Second, although it is true that tax resisters are not free
from moral compromise, theirs is a *better compromise*. The
willing taxpayer helps finance the good things that the

government does, but also willingly finances potential
genocide. He or she wants to support the beneficial programmes of government, but must at the same time support
a war machine which is poised to destroy humanity. He or
she financially supports 'a hospital that butchers two and
heals one.'[26] Is not this compromise far worse than the tax
refuser's compromise? If we face a choice of evils, should
we not choose 'the lesser evil'?

Third, tax resisters insist that theirs is *not a dangerous
precedent*. Tax resisters are not advocating anarchy. They
respect the law. They are breaking the law only because of
the monstrosity of paying for the nuclear arms race. They
act openly and are willing to take the penalty. Therefore,
they are showing that they believe in the system of laws
in the west, even though they cannot support a particular
one.

Also, many war tax resisters advocate legislation such as
the World Peace Tax Fund Bill, which would enable people
to designate a percentage of their income tax (equal to the
military portion of the budget) to government programmes
aimed at peace and human betterment.[27] Therefore, while
protesting against what they regard as an evil law, they are
working hard for a *system* of law that they can in good
conscience obey.

Tax resisters also feel they have *a scriptural mandate* on
their side. The Bible asks believers neither to *pay* all taxes
nor to *refuse* all taxes. When Jesus said, 'Render to Caesar
the things that are Caesar's, and to God the things that are
God's' (Mk 12:17), he gave priority to the second obligation. Obeying God's will comes first. In our time, one of the
most important things we owe to God is to contribute to
peace rather than nuclear holocaust. If there is no evidence
that Jesus refused to pay Roman taxes, there is also no
evidence that he ever paid them! The tax referred to in
Matthew 17:24–27 was the Jewish temple tax, instituted in
Exodus 30:13 (see chapter eight). It went to support the
temple and had nothing to do with killing or war. If Jesus
lived today, would he pay for atom bombs?

Paul told Christians to pay 'taxes to whom taxes are due' (Rom 13:7). But if taken in the context of Paul's teachings, this statement probably does not mean that Paul believed in paying taxes to *any* government, regardless of the evil it did. Paul also urged Christians to be subject to government. But he and the other early Christians disobeyed the government when it commanded things contrary to God's will – such as to stop preaching the gospel. Taxes are not 'due' when they are used to promote evil. As New Testament scholar Willard Swartley argues, Jesus' and Paul's words about taxes must be seen in context: 'Can financial support of the arms race be harmonised with "owe no one anything except to love one another" (Romans 13:8) or "overcome evil with good" (Romans 12:21)? Or, as we discriminate over what belongs to God, do we say, "No, these taxes we cannot pay, because they violate our Christian being as God's people and his ethic of love for all people, even those considered enemies"?'[28]

Fifth, war tax refusers see great *potential and practicality* in their method of resistance. Even while the number of tax refusers is small, they can have an impact. Each refusal sparks interest in friends, work associates and so on. Sometimes it can provide a public forum to talk about peace. It can make people pause and think. If tax resistance were to grow into a mass movement, it would create a national debate about war and peace. The government would find it increasingly difficult to ignore the cry for peace. If it grew large enough, it could even affect the military's financial ability to function. It could throw a monkey wrench into the war machine.[29]

Part of the practicality of tax resistance is that it is a simple tactic available to just about everyone. It answers the question, But what can I do? I'm only one person. The reply is: You can stop paying taxes for war. For example, one woman wrote to the American Conscience and Military Tax Campaign: 'I used to think I couldn't do anything about [the arms race]. Now I think I have to. I can't be a conscientious objector because I'm a woman and can't be

drafted. But I can be a conscientious objector on paying
war taxes. From now on I will withhold the portion of my
payment which would be used for defence spending and
send it to Mother Teresa of Calcutta.[30] This also shows
how war tax resistance can be practical in another way.
Many tax resisters take the money they do not send to the
government and donate it or loan it to 'alternative funds' to
promote peace education and to meet the needs of the
poor. (There are at least nineteen 'alternative funds'
nationwide in the States. The Roxbury War Tax Scholarship Fund, for example, receives refusers' taxes and puts
them into education for disadvantaged children in a Boston
ghetto.)

Finally, war tax refusal is *a clear moral statement*. Tax
resistance is *un*ambiguous from the point of view of the
public and the government. No one doubts that the war tax
resister is trying to say in the strongest way that he or she
rejects war and will not voluntarily pay for its weapons. It is
a strong symbolic statement which reaches the public,
making people think about war and peace. It is a moral
stand which will be respected.

It is true that war tax resistance involves risks. But
risks should not be a deciding factor if it is right. We are
called to the way of the cross. We cannot back down because of inconveniene or the threat of fines or imprisonment.

These are the arguments of those who support tax resistance. But what should *you* do? You have heard both sides.
If you feel God is calling you to some form of war tax
resistance, we urge you to get in contact with a group that
can give you good advice. There is not just one, but several
methods of tax resistance. You should understand the
possible costs of the various kinds. If you choose a method
which is likely to lead to legal problems and a possible court
case, it will be helpful to know groups who can provide legal
assistance (see appendix B-2).

Because there are so many pros and cons, all of us as
Christians must respect, love and continue to think about

these issues and dialogue with those who disagree with us. Above all, we must seek the will of God in prayer on this important question.

'It is impossible for Christians to maintain a credible witness for peace unless the church is itself seen to be a community of peace.'

John R. W. Stott[1]

10

The Church as a Peacemaking Community

Individual decision and action are crucial to Christian peacemaking. But we cannot and should not work alone. Alone we are almost powerless. The biblical story is one of God's gathering a new, redeemed people. The corporate life of Israel and the church was to manifest God's purposes for the world. Jesus' new community is to be a visible demonstration of his coming kingdom. As salt, light and leaven, Christians also transform society. But this is possible only if the message and the reality of peace have begun to take deep root in our local congregations.

As John R. W. Stott has said: 'If charity begins at home, so does reconciliation. We need to obey the teaching of Jesus *first* to be reconciled to our brother and *then* to come and offer our worship (Mt 5:23–24). We need to forgive our enemies, mend our broken relationships, ensure that our homes are havens of love, joy, and peace, and banish from our church all malice, anger and bitterness.'[2] Christians have a hopeful word of peace for our dangerous world. But if we have not allowed the Holy Spirit to heal the dividing walls in our churches, we will not be heard.

This does not mean that local congregations must be perfect examples of peace and harmony before they can undertake significant action for peace. Even the early church had its inner tensions, disagreements and conflicts.[3] But it *does* mean that we must open ourselves again and again to the peace and reconciliation the Spirit wants to give every congregation. It means that we must dare to follow the steps toward reconciliation which Jesus gives in Matthew 5:23 and 18:15–17. It means that we cry and confess when we fail. It means that we resolve anew to offer Christ's costly, self-sacrificial love to the most difficult members of our fellowship. As the apostle Paul said to the church at Rome, 'Let us then pursue what makes for peace and for mutual upbuilding' (Rom 14:19). This is crucial. As Mernie King of the Sojourners' community said recently, 'The Church has no greater peace to give to the world than the quality of peace it experiences in its own fellowship.'[4]

As our congregations start with painful, halting steps toward a greater openness to the Spirit's shalom, what further steps of peacemaking can the church pursue?

A Peace Mission Group

Every Christian has the task and the joyful opportunity to work for peace. But some members feel a more *specific* call to give major time to the task of peacemaking, both within the congregation and in the world at large.

A 'peace mission group' is one excellent way for the local congregation to offer these persons support while at the same time deepening its own peace ministry. In Washington, DC, the Sojourners community financially supports several members who work full time in a peace ministry. In New York, Riverside Church's Disarmament Programme has two full-time staff. The Deer Park Baptist Church (a Southern Baptist congregation in Louisville, Kentucky) has established a World Peacemakers group which publishes *The Baptist Peacemaker*. This journal reaches some twenty thousand subscribers in the United States and twelve foreign countries.

The Scottish Episcopal Church has initiated a Project to promote discussion of the whole defence issue among its members. With the full backing of the Church Council, three full-time staff work on an individual, national and international level to encourage open and positive debate. They have produced a very helpful and informative Peace

Pack: *Peace Making in a Nuclear Age* (see appendix D). In addition, a Scottish Churches Peace Team has recently been formed to promote activities and conferences, and to set up ecumenical projects.

What would happen if even half of the Christian congregations in the United States and Western Europe had a person or mission group devoted to the task of peacemaking? Would this not enormously enliven the Church's peacemaking ability? Might not local churches become the building blocks of a new and powerful peace movement rooted in the power of the gospel? If this vision of the local church's ministry appeals to you, you could begin by inviting members of your local church to consider forming a peace group. Get your pastor behind you and be sure to draw in any member of the congregation who is interested in working for peace.

Here are some of the things such a peace team could do in the local congregation:

1) *Pray*. Worship and pray together regularly for peace in the lives of individuals, in the congregation, in the neighbourhood, the country and the world. Help the church to include peace in its worship life through sermons and prayers for governments, for enemies, and for peace and justice in the world.

2) *Build fellowship*. Your peace group can become a caring community where members share ideas, prayers and meals. Keep things personal. Help the group feel closely knit. Meet in a comfortable place like a living-room or church lounge. Share meals.

3) *Study*. Put information behind your prayers and seek answers to questions such as:

How could a nuclear war start?
What would be the consequences of such a war?
How many nuclear warheads might hit our area in a nuclear conflict?
How do we feel about dropping bombs on Soviet Chris-

tians, who make up twenty-seven per cent of the Soviet
population?
Ought Christians to participate in preparations for nu-
clear war?
How can nuclear war be prevented?
What actions can Christians take for peace?

Take a fresh look at the biblical view of peace, perhaps
using another book or study guide to assist you. Reflect
theologically on the role of the church in preventing nuclear
war. Examine the traditional Christian stances toward war,
such as the just war theory, pacifism, and so on. Read up on
the proposals that thoughtful people are making to reduce
the risk of war. Study and discuss books on peace and
disarmament. Encourage church members to subscribe to
magazines which explore peace issues from a Christian
point of view (see appendix A-5).

But don't get bogged down in the 'paralysis of analysis.'
You do not have to be an expert to speak and act for peace.
There are many more peace resources than your group can
ever exhaust. Try to get a basic understanding and some
key facts. Then move into action.

4) *Educate*. Become a resource group in your congregation for the best information on peace issues. Help members to strengthen their identity as informed and effective
peacemakers. Set up a literature table where church members can find the best books on peace or put up a bulletin
board with leaflets, posters and announcements about
peace.

Several groups have produced excellent films and slide
shows on nuclear war and disarmament (see appendix C).
Invite interested church members to an evening meeting
with a film or an outside speaker on peacemaking. Good
speakers can be located through existing peace organisations or by contacting denominations or universities. Organise forums and Bible-based study groups on peacemaking.
Encourage the use of peace-oriented curricula in Sunday-
school classes for adults and children (see appendix D).

Send your pastor material on peace for use in sermons, classes and fellowship groups. Encourage your minister to take special courses or go to conferences on peace.

5) *Join a network*. Keep in touch with Christian peace-makers nationwide. Join one of the strong and active national peace organisations, such as Christian CND (see appendix B).

6) *Seek unity*. After a period of education, you might approach your congregation and ask every member to commit a set period of time to prayer and study about the issue of nuclear deterrence and Christian faith.[5] The goal would be to explore whether God is calling the whole congregation to take a stand against the nuclear arms race. The following Peacemaker's Pledge is similar to one composed by a group of Christians in DeKalb, Illinois. You could see if everyone in your church would be willing to take such a pledge.

PEACEMAKER'S PLEDGE

Reflecting on the signs of the times:

☐ growing world tensions,

☐ the unparalleled danger of nuclear holocaust,

☐ the waste of billions of pounds annually on the arms race, money that could be used to fund human needs,

☐ the injustices that condemn millions of people to a life of poverty,

☐ the hopelessness and powerlessness experienced by many people, and recognising God's call to me to respond freely and personally, I make the following pledge:

1. I pledge myself to the peacemaking proclaimed by Jesus Christ, who calls me to truthfulness, compassion and reconciliation.

2. I will respect and promote the human rights of all persons as children of God, whose image and likeness they reflect.

3. I recognise that as a member of the global community I have a responsibility to promote the well-being of the

entire planet as a home for present and future generations.

4. I will labour with others toward the goal of a more just world order where basic human needs for food, shelter, health care, education and work are met.

5. I promise to simplify my lifestyle to express solidarity with those whose basic human needs have not been met – persons who are poor, oppressed and powerless.

6. I will promote global peace by joining a local Christian group of peacemakers who seek peace through personal and group prayer, reflection, education and nonviolent action.

7. I support the search for and use of creative alternatives to violence in providing security and in resolving conflicts between individuals, groups and nations.

8. I believe that the construction and possession of nuclear weapons is immoral; I commit myself to work for nuclear disarmament and promise not to earn my living by employment related to building or maintaining a nuclear weapons system.

9. I support all who, for reasons of conscience, refuse to bear arms or who seek to divert taxes from works of war to works of peace.

10. I rely on the power of the Holy Spirit to help me grow in my commitment as a peacemaker and to strengthen me with peace, joy, love, hope and courage.

You will have to decide whether such an approach is appropriate for your church.

7) *Support members in job changes.* A quarter of all the world's scientists and technologists are involved in weapons research and development.[6] Many individuals are involved in defence-related industries, in government agencies related to the forces. Others are in the armed forces. Many may be members of churches. Yet Christian discipleship should make unthinkable any support for those industries and institutions that perfect the instruments of nuclear holocaust. As the concern for peace grows in your church,

these people may begin to question whether their jobs conflict with Christ's call to a ministry of reconciliation. Some may come to believe that they can no longer continue in their jobs. The choice they confront is extremely difficult. It involves hard moral issues as well as serious questions of financial security. Be sensitive and supportive. Help them to work through the pros and cons. Be ready to help financially. Most importantly, if they decide to leave their current job, give them practical help in finding other work.

A Christian study group in a Dayton, Ohio, Baptist church helped one of its members who was a military officer by profession to leave his $25,000-a-year job with the Strategic Air Command and find work teaching mathematics in a local university.[7] Perhaps your peace group can give this kind of practical help.

Young people may be struggling with the question of whether a Christian can serve Christ in the forces. Help them to think through the issues. Provide them with books and other literature that explain the options of conscientious objection. Help them to get the counselling they may need to understand the legal, practical and moral ramifications of refusing military service. But make it clear that you will stand behind them *in whatever position they take*. That kind of support is essential for peacemaking within the congregation.

If a young man decides against going into the forces, perhaps your church could set up a system through which he can register this decision so that, if the draft is reinstated, there will be evidence to show that the young person has been thinking about being a CO for some time and is not just using it as an excuse to get out of the army.

8) *Support members making lifestyle changes.* As further study leads members of your church to deepen their understanding of global issues, the question of the relationship between peace and justice will inevitably emerge. People will ask whether there can be peace in a world so dangerously divided between rich and poor. They will question

whether the roots of war are not often found in greed. 'What causes wars, and what causes fightings among you?' asks the author of the book of James. 'You desire and do not have; so you kill. And you covet and cannot obtain; so you fight and wage war' (Jas 4:1–2).

Be prepared to help people break the habit of covetousness. Help them to experience the fulfilment that can come by reducing wants rather than increasing possessions. Study some of the recent books by Christians that show how to simplify life and work for justice.[8]

9) *Free people for peacemaking.* As you talk to members of your church about peace, you may find one or more people who feel especially called to work for peace, but who are not able to act on their call because of job or family obligations. Perhaps your congregation could support them by contributing to financial needs or providing some baby-sitting for a full-time parent. If the person is young and just starting out, your church might 'adopt a peaceworker' – find a family who will provide free room and board to enable him or her to give a year or two of full-time service to peacemaking. In 1979, for example, the Grantham Brethren in Christ Church, which is on the campus of Messiah College in Pennsylvania, raised $2,000 to provide room, board and expenses so that a Messiah student could work full time with the World Peace Tax Fund in Washington.

Beyond the Local Church

For many decades, the historic peace churches in the States have devoted major efforts to working for peace at the denominational level as well as through the local church. These denominations have appointed full-time staff who prepare materials on peace education, organise conferences, do research, participate in nonviolent vigils and otherwise work for peace through their denominational structures. In recent years other denominations have begun to support peace efforts with financial backing and staff.

At the British Methodist Conference of July 1981 in

Norwich, wholehearted support was given to the World Disarmament Campaign, and a call issued to the Methodist people to further the Campaign's objectives.

The Baptist Union Assembly of 1979 stated: 'We call on all governments of the world to stop production of, and trading in, the weapons of war, conventional and nuclear.'

The Quakers Yearly Meeting Epistle of 1979 stated: 'We abhor the existence of nuclear weapons and urge all Friends to work for their abolition.'[9]

What is happening in your own church on the national level? Does it have staff to help local churches become better informed about peace and justice? Has your denomination ever gone on record with a statement about war and biblical faith? Is your church body producing materials which can be used in local churches for peace education? Does your church magazine carry articles on issues like disarmament, the military budget, the effects of nuclear war, the biblical teaching on war and peace?

One way to work for peace is to encourage your denomination or diocese to make peace a priority. You might begin by asking to set up a peace literature display at an annual regional meeting. You can then invite interested people to small discussion groups where they can discuss their concerns, look at audio-visual materials, and hear a good speaker. Out of this might come proposals for a public statement on peace, the arms race and the Christian responsibility to help prevent nuclear war. Proposing such a resolution promotes serious thinking since everyone must vote.

Higher Education
Some Christian colleges and universities in the States support the military and defence industry. They permit campus ROTC programmes,[10] welcome military recruiters, have military speakers at chapels and convocations, or invest college funds in top defence industries.

Other Christian colleges, however, do not support such on-campus military activities, but have courses on peace, nonviolence and disarmament. At few have gone even further, instituting majors in peace studies.[11] At the Earlham School of Religion, for example, students working toward a masters degree can specialise in peace and justice studies. Students working for a Master of Ministry degree are *required* to take at least one course in peace and justice.

An organisation called the Consortium on Peace Research, Education, and Development (commonly known as COPRED and located at the Centre for Peaceful Change at Kent State University) has over three hundred members. It works to introduce peace studies into college curricula. More than twenty institutions around the USA have peace studies programmes and these are listed in appendix B-3.

In the UK, St John's Theological College, Nottingham has become affiliated to the Campaign for Nuclear Disarmament after a motion was passed by the Junior Common Room in 1981. They now have representation at the CND Conference, enabling them to participate in the discussions.

The School of Peace Studies at the University of Bradford is one of very few departments in the world offering full undergraduate and higher degree courses in Peace Studies together with opportunities for higher degrees by research. At the time of writing, it has nine full-time members of staff and over a hundred students.[12] In 1980, the school commenced publication of a series of Peace Studies Papers, intended to be of use to those engaged in peace research and peace action (see appendix B).

There are some things you can do to promote peacemaking in higher education. First, you could suggest ways to introduce courses on peacemaking into the college curriculum and explore the possibility of setting up a peace studies department. Perhaps students could have fieldwork placements with organisations working for peace.

Second, you could encourage faculty and students to become affiliated to a national peace organisation, such as CND. Or you could make the faculty aware of peace-oriented organisations in their fields. Doctors can join the

Medical Campaign Against Nuclear Weapons (MCANW); scientists can join Scientists Against Nuclear Arms (SANA); teachers can join Teachers for Peace (see appendix B-2).

Third, you could encourage regular events on campus dealing with the nuclear arms race and peace.[13]

Finally, you could urge the school library to purchase books, periodicals and audio-visual resources on peace.

Perhaps it is time for our theological colleges and universities to train our future leaders in the things that make for peace so that when they graduate they will be prepared to give prophetic leadership to their congregations and to society.

The deepest form of Christian peacemaking arises out of a prayerful body of believers striving to be reconciled. Out of this body peace ministries may grow. This will not happen quickly or easily in many cases. In some churches perhaps a vision for peace will never arise. Individuals in these churches who are concerned for peace will have to find support and interest among Christians outside their local congregations. This can be frustrating and lonely. But it is never hopeless.

As the Spirit of Christ moves in local congregations through the prophetic witness of local peacemakers, we believe that hearts will be stirred. As the Christian community through prayer, study, discussion and action deepens its understanding of peacemaking and its commitment to the Prince of Peace, we expect that it will begin to throw off the shackles which have hindered its witness in the past. A new revival may be born in the church, similar to the nineteenth-century revival which energised the movement for the abolition of slavery. A new abolition movement, in fact, may come into being – a widespread Christian movement for the abolition of nuclear weapons.

'I have come to see that we must not only talk about peace but we must work in whatever ways are open to us for the cause of world peace. . . . The issue of peace is not a political issue. It is a moral and spiritual issue. It demands the attention of every Christian.'

Billy Graham[1]

'Our future upon this planet, exposed as it is to nuclear annihilation, depends upon one single factor: humanity must make a moral about-face. At the present moment of history, there must be a general mobilisation of all men and women of goodwill.'

Pope John Paul II[2]

11

The Christian Witness for Peace in Society

Christ's peace and love are not meant to be grasped by Christians as our exclusive possession. Jesus taught us to pray, 'God's will be done on earth, as it is in heaven.' We know God's will is peace on earth. We must be witnesses for peace in the world. Jim Wallis writes that the church is to be 'a community created by conversion and offered for the sake of the world. . . . We are a people drawn into relationship to the Lord for the sake of God's purposes in history.'[3]

How can we do that? Each member of a local church must discern how God wants him or her to witness in the larger society. In the pages that follow we outline some of the crucial issues that face a Christian peace witness in today's world and some of the main methods Christians are using to work for peace. We are not suggesting that every individual or congregation should be involved in all of these. Rather we are describing a broad range of possibilities so that people can choose for themselves.

Evangelism

Evangelism should be a central way that Christians witness for peace in the larger society. But that will happen only if we see that biblical evangelism means preaching Christ as Lord as well as Saviour.[4] How often in our evangelism have we called unbelievers to faith, but failed to call believers to obedience? (See Rom 1:5.) Have we sometimes forgotten that Jesus' call is not just to baptise, but also to 'make disciples'? Have we sometimes neglected verse 20 of Matthew 28, where Jesus instructs us to teach people to '*observe* all that I have *commanded* you'?

The gospel we share with others is 'the gospel of peace' (Eph 6:15). It should call believers to obedience, to a new conversion where they place their security in 'the God of love and peace' (2 Cor 13:11) rather than in weapons of mass destruction.

Many local churches engage in evangelistic campaigns whose specific goal is to reach as many unbelievers as possible with the gospel. Sometimes there are door-to-door campaigns which emphasise one-by-one communication. Sometimes churches set aside a block of time for an outside evangelist to lead a series of revival meetings. In other cases, churches support campaigns sponsored by national groups like the Billy Graham Evangelistic Association.

Carl Henry once suggested a striking image of how a large evangelistic rally could become a vehicle for peace and social justice concerns.[5] Imagine a large hall packed with people listening to an evangelist's inspiring call to faith in Christ. Imagine the evangelist asking unbelievers to come forward to commit their lives to Jesus. But imagine the evangelist *also* saying, 'I know that many of you here tonight have already asked Jesus into your lives. I know that you are already active in local churches. I want to ask you to rededicate yourselves to Jesus, to winning the lost, and to a life of discipleship. At the back of this hall we have set up booths with literature from many Christian organisations that are working for justice. Jesus wants us to live out our faith in service. So why don't you tonight deepen your commitment by joining and working with one of these agencies? Some are devoted to jobs for the unemployed, others to working with drug addicts; some are working against race discrimination; some are ministering to the poor and needy or meeting other important needs. There must be one that you can help.'

Most evangelistic campaigns, as Carl Henry points out,

attract committed Christians as well as people who have never known a personal relationship with Christ. Why not design evangelistic campaigns so that believers have a chance to deepen their faith in the Prince of Peace and their involvement in practical witness? As non-Christians experience peace with God through the Cross for the first time, others will learn more about being God's peacemakers in the world.

If your church is planning a local evangelistic programme, you might suggest that the speakers emphasise Jesus' call to peacemaking. You might set up displays in the meeting hall to provide literature on local and national peace groups. You could have people available to answer questions and to sign up interested people as members of peacemaking groups.

Public Education

'Christian peacemakers,' says John R. W. Stott, 'must promote more public debate.'[6] A major focus of public education should be on the nature of nuclear war itself. Christians can help people in their town or city begin asking questions like: 'How could a nuclear war start? What would be the consequences? What would be the effects of an attack on my city or town? Can I support policies of mass nuclear destruction?' As more and more people in our country face questions like these, God may raise up a new movement to speak and act against the drift toward nuclear war. Three proven ways to do effective public education are by (1) organising a local conference on peace, (2) organising a peace visitation team, and (3) circulating a petition.

1. *Local conference on peace:* Four years ago, Riverside Church in New York City held a conference entitled, 'How to Reverse the Arms Race.' Rather than inviting just its own members, Riverside opened its doors to other Christians from New York and other parts of the country. So many people attended that the conference has become an annual event, involving worship, speakers, films and work-

shops on topics such as 'Influencing the Mass Media,' 'Developing Peace Education Activities' and 'Evaluating Current Disarmament Proposals.' Inspired by their experience at Riverside, hundreds of other churches in the States have followed up by organising similar conferences in their own cities and towns.

Perhaps your church could hold a similar meeting and draw in participants from other congregations. The inspiration of good speakers and films and the stimulation of well-led discussions can be a powerful means of education. They can create fellowship across congregational lines and a spirit of common mission in the work of building peace.

2. *Peace visitation team:* Whereas a local conference calls people *together*, a peace visitation team goes *out* to community groups and organisations with a peace message. In Philadelphia, the Jubilee Fellowship Church chose Peace Sunday as an opportunity to discuss the arms race with fellow Christians. They contacted local pastors and asked if they could make presentations during the worship service (see figure 5), at a Bible study, during Sunday school and so on. Jubilee sent one or two of its members to every church that responded favourably. They took good films and boxes of literature on peace. In some churches they gave the sermon; in others they led an adult class.

This kind of outreach is particularly valuable. It not only gets a message out to others, but also encourages your own team to think through and articulate what they believe.

Local service clubs, professional groups and community organisations, such as the Rotary Club and Lions, are often looking for guest speakers on timely topics. You can also contact local schools, colleges and universities. See about speaking or showing a film at a class or assembly. In Tallahassee, Florida, the local peace council helped the public schools organise a contest in which children contributed art, writing and drama around the theme Creating a Peaceful World. Local libraries may be willing to carry more books on peace and the nuclear arms race. Your team could supply them with the literature and help set up an

5 min.	Welcome by pastor.
30 min.	Show film (see appendix C)
10 min.	Sermon: "There Was a Time When Only God Could End the World."
10 min.	Readings by preselected members of the congregation of passages on nuclear war.
20 min.	Break into small groups to discuss what Christians can do to help prevent nuclear war.
10 min.	Small groups report, discuss what the groups said, make plans for future meetings.
5 min.	Inspirational song or hymn.
5 min.	Benediction and call for those who wish to remain and make more detailed plans

Figure 5. Suggested Programme for a Worship Service on Nuclear War.
From Nuclear War Prevention Kit *(Washington, D.C.: Center for Defense Information, 600 Maryland Ave. SW, Washington, D.C. 20023).*

exhibition with photos, posters and books on nuclear war.

Let your creativity guide you. In Amityville, New York, members of the Simpson United Methodist Church designed a puppet show called 'Puppets for Peace.' They combine the puppets with a peace information booth and travel to fairs and conferences. Maybe you could design something just as innovative.

3. *Peace petition:* A simple method of outreach that requires very little time and effort is to print up a peace petition and take it from door to door, asking for signatures. Following is the wording of the International Peace Petition. It was drawn up by a Presbyterian minister and a labour leader to be presented with hundreds of thousands of signatures to national leaders at the time of the 1982 United Nations Special Session on Disarmament.

To Presidents Ronald Reagan and Leonid Brezhnev:

We, the undersigned, call upon the United States and the Soviet Union to end the arms race which threatens all with annihilation. As a first step, we ask you jointly to terminate immediately all research, development, testing, manufacture, and deployment of nuclear bombs and missiles; and that you progressively, but quickly, destroy present stockpiles.

The Mass Media

If we want to stimulate broad public debate about the danger of nuclear war and the need for a change in public policy, one of the best ways is to get a message into the newspaper, on radio or television. If we do, hundreds of thousands – even millions – of people will see it. Here are some ways to go about that.

Letters to the Editor: Readership surveys show that the 'letters to the editor' section of a newspaper is among the best-read features. When a letter of yours appears on the editorial page, you probably have the largest audience you will ever address, including government employees. Your letter can thus have political as well as public educational impact.

Here are some suggestions for writing effective letters to the editors:[7]

1. Choose a timely topic that you feel strongly about,

e.g., 'Why aren't our leaders doing more to prevent nuclear war?'

2. If possible, use a typewriter and double-space the lines. If you have no typewriter, write plainly and neatly with ink on one side of the paper.

3. Express your thoughts clearly and concisely. The best letter is of no more than two hundred and fifty words, although editors will take longer ones with sufficient reader interest.

4. Write about only one topic per letter. Use simple words, short sentences and short paragraphs. But do not hesitate to use a relevant personal experience to illustrate your point.

5. Bring moral judgments to bear on the issue, but do not call names. Use rational arguments, not emotional language, to make your point.

6. Always sign your name and give your address and telephone number. Editors rarely, if ever, publish anonymous letters.

7. Do not get discouraged if your letter is not printed. Try again. If one letter in ten is accepted, you've reached an audience large enough to make your effort worthwhile. But your score will probably be better than that and improve as you gain experience.

Getting the media to cover local events: Is your peace group circulating a petition in the neighbourhood? Does your church have a local peace conference planned? Is a group of Christians going to talk to their local MP? All of these are newsworthy events. As you plan them, be sure you assign someone to write press releases or phone the radio, TV and newspapers. You may be surprised at how eager local reporters are to interview church members and find out how they became motivated to try to end the arms race. Talk to the religious editor of the local newspaper. There's a story for them in your church's peace activities. And most radio stations carry public service announcements that can advertise your events.[8] Your announcement should begin with an idea to catch people's attention –

perhaps a question or a surprising statistic. Then describe the event briefly and give the time, date and location.

Influencing the media: Does someone in your church work for a local newspaper, radio or television station? Perhaps he or she would be willing to get material on peace into the newspaper columns, on to the editorial page, or into the broadcast programming. Approach the programme director of your local TV station and see if he or she will broadcast a film on war and peace.

Is a visiting expert on disarmament coming to your locality? See about getting him or her on a local radio interview show. Is one of your interested church members unable to leave the house? He or she can perform a valuable service by phoning radio talk shows and sharing an opinion on war and peace issues.

Keep up your press contacts. The more regularly you inform them of newsworthy activities, the more likely they will be to carry them.

Christian broadcasters: Over the past decade, Christians have hit the airwaves in a big way; but Christian producers will not know that Christians want programmes about nuclear issues unless Christians contact them. Write a letter expressing this concern to some of the Christian programmes. Ask them to have on the air people who can speak knowledgeably about the threat of nuclear war.

Political Action

Senator Mark Hatfield says that the greatest debate in the history of the world will take place in Congress in the 1980s. The question will be, should we continue the arms race? If we are to pull back from the brink of nuclear war, peacemaking must become a far deeper commitment than it is at present among those who make the laws, vote on military budgets and set policy for arms control negotiations. Here are some suggestions on how to influence that debate and how to work for peace through the political system.

Write to your MPs and government officials. Many people ask, Does it make any difference whether I write or not? The answer is yes. Local public opinion strongly influences those who have a say in government.

'Those who sit down and write letters make their votes count more times,' said President John F. Kennedy in an August 1963 comment to editors of national women's magazines. '. . . Nothing is more effective than a letter that reflects both an understanding of the question involved and a sincere expression of a personal viewpoint based on that understanding.'[9]

Members of Parliament know that their jobs depend on local support.

When writing to government officials, use the same guidelines that you use for letters to the editor. Don't wait to compose the perfect letter. One congressman in the States commented that he gives much less attention to fancy form letters than to a sincere letter written by a concerned individual who gives personal illustrations. Be sure to put your name and address on the letter, and consider asking for a personal meeting. Perhaps you could take others with you and encourage serious discussion on the nuclear issue.

Put together a delegation of people who are deeply concerned about the escalating worldwide arms race. Familiarise yourself with your MP's voting record and views. Decide which person in your delegation will speak to emphasise which points.

At the meeting, make your presentation and then ask your MP how he or she is working to prevent nuclear war. Ask for specifics. Try to get commitments. Make it clear that you want to be represented in Parliament by someone who is making every effort to reverse the course of the arms race and build world peace.[10]

Direct contact with a government office by telephone is a good idea if you want to register your opinion quickly and strongly. If tens of thousands of Christians regularly contacted the government with their yearning to end the arms race, the administration would have to take notice. You might begin a letter with: What moral justification is there for our country to threaten death to hundreds of millions of men, women and children who have never hurt us in any way?

Participate in election campaigns. With nuclear war looming so close, we cannot afford a government that belligerently raises world tensions or acts as if atomic war were a good option. Everyone should participate in election campaigns and give support to candidates who are serious in their quest for peace. Some of us will just be able to vote for such candidates. Others will be able to give such candidates financial support or help with the campaign.

Here are some questions you can use to evaluate the candidate's stand on nuclear proliferation and war:

☐ Do they recognise the horror of atomic conflict and the impossibility of winning a nuclear war?

☐ Do they speak out about the danger of nuclear war and the urgent necessity of preventing it?

☐ In their international views, do they express an attitude of peacemaking and reconciliation or one of threat and belligerence?

☐ Do they work for arms control, arms reduction and disarmament?

☐ Have they developed a plan to enable the country to shift from military to civilian production without undue disruption and hardship?

☐ Do they seek to remove the cause of war by supporting programmes which help the poor to earn a living and create peaceful avenues for them to achieve a better life?

☐ Do they have a reputation for seeking peaceful solutions in situations of international tension? Do they advocate nonviolent methods of solving international conflict?

☐ Are they open to exploring nonmilitary ways of defending the country?

Support peace lobbies. When Christians in the States became deeply concerned about the problem of world hunger, they came together to create the lobbying organisation Bread for the World. Through letter-writing, prayer, visits to Congress and other citizens' action they have educated Congress and the public about the scandal of hunger here and abroad.

As the concern for world peace deepens among Christians, similar interdenominational lobbies focused on peace will develop. You can help by encouraging and supporting peace-lobbying through any avenues open to you.[11]

Political action by Christians is crucial if the world is to draw back from the nuclear abyss, yet involvement in politics can have a corrupting influence. The only answer is to stay close to the Lord Jesus in prayer, Bible study and Christian fellowship. We are invited by the Master to be in the world, but not of it. 'I do not pray that thou shouldst take them out of the world, but that thou shouldst keep them from the evil one' (Jn 17:15). We must not allow ourselves to be shaped by the world's corrupt patterns and values, but rather by the Spirit and ethic of Christ.

Nonviolent Direct Action
Sometimes the standard political steps of voting, lobbying and working for candidates are insufficient to achieve important goals.

Mass nonviolent action such as demonstrating has been an effective means of raising issues, provoking public debate and, ultimately, changing the political climate and passing needed laws. Perhaps it is not surprising, therefore, that many Christian peacemakers feel called to witness against nuclear war through various kinds of nonviolent action.

☐ A mother from Burlington, Vermont, stood outside the gate of the Electric Boat Company and handed out leaflets to employees working on the Trident submarine.

☐ Christians in Detroit walked solemnly on Good Friday in a 'stations of the cross' procession, stopping to remember the passion of Jesus at sites connected with the arms race.

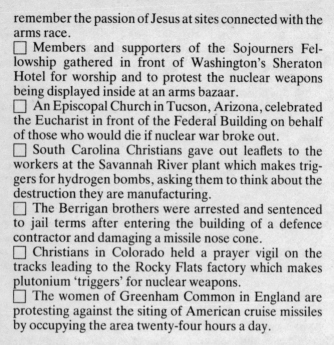

☐ Members and supporters of the Sojourners Fellowship gathered in front of Washington's Sheraton Hotel for worship and to protest the nuclear weapons being displayed inside at an arms bazaar.

☐ An Episcopal Church in Tucson, Arizona, celebrated the Eucharist in front of the Federal Building on behalf of those who would die if nuclear war broke out.

☐ South Carolina Christians gave out leaflets to the workers at the Savannah River plant which makes triggers for hydrogen bombs, asking them to think about the destruction they are manufacturing.

☐ The Berrigan brothers were arrested and sentenced to jail terms after entering the building of a defence contractor and damaging a missile nose cone.

☐ Christians in Colorado held a prayer vigil on the tracks leading to the Rocky Flats factory which makes plutonium 'triggers' for nuclear weapons.

☐ The women of Greenham Common in England are protesting against the siting of American cruise missiles by occupying the area twenty-four hours a day.

Nonviolent direct action can be as simple and as small as one individual praying quietly for peace in front of a local military installation. It can be as large and complex as thousands of people marching through the streets of the nation's capital. Your church's peace ministry could establish a prayerful presence for peace in your local community. You could form a nonviolent action group made up of people who feel called to such action. They could read up on nonviolent action (appendix A-3 lists a few of the many good books on the subject)[12] and seek advice about prayerful and truly nonviolent action.

The group could find a local defence contractor who makes components for nuclear weapons. In preparation for action, they could make posters, such as: It's a Sin to Build a Nuclear Weapon; Stop the Arms Race; and Nuclear

Weapons Betray Christ. They would get some large photos of the destruction of Hiroshima and Nagasaki and make them into posters. Then they would pick a time when members could go to the plant and when employees are leaving or arriving at work.

When everything was set, the group would gather at the plant, holding their posters and distributing leaflets to workers. They would pray aloud and read Scripture or hold a silent vigil. They would ask workers if they realise how destructive nuclear weapons are. They might even volunteer to help workers find other jobs. They would listen sympathetically to workers' problems and explain why, as Christians, they were concerned to end the arms race.

What would it be like if thousands of defence contractors across the country had this prayerful, nonviolent presence in front of their doors? Might it help people wake up to the fact that these nuclear facilities are like Auschwitz and Dachau? Might it help build the growing social movement which will be necessary if the world's governments are to take peace seriously? Millions of people still place their faith in the bomb. 'We need nuclear weapons for our security,' they say. By worshipping God at nuclear installations, we both call people to reject this false security, and we invite them to turn to Christ, our only true security.

*'I'm glad to hear President Reagan talk about Salt III.
I hope the Soviet response will be positive. But I wish
they would start discussing Salt X, and that means the
start of the destruction of all nuclear weapons and all
biochemical weapons, and all weapons that can
destroy civilisation overnight.'*

Billy Graham[1]

*'It is sobering to remember that modern history offers
no example of the cultivation by rival powers of
armed force on a massive scale which did not in the
end lead to an outbreak of hostilities. . . . You are
mortal men. You are capable of error. You have no
right to hold in your hands – there is no one wise
enough and strong enough to hold in his
hands – destructive powers sufficient to put an end to
civilised life on a great portion of our planet. No one
should wish to hold such powers. Thrust them from
you. The risks you might thereby assume are not
greater – could not be greater – than those which you
are now incurring for us all.'*

**George F. Kennan, former US Ambassador to the
Soviet Union**[2]

12

Disarming the Powers

When the atom bombs devastated Hiroshima and Nagasaki in August 1945, governments around the world realised that their long-standing conceptions of war and peace had been fundamentally changed. Humans now possessed the ability to create nuclear bombs. Other nations soon would develop nuclear weapons. Any war fought with atomic weapons would remove all meaning from the word *victory*. All antagonists would suffer defeat by the very weapons they had created.

Deep apprehension gripped people as the truth of potential nuclear annihilation sank in. The prevention of war became an urgent necessity. When the United Nations came into being on 24 October 1945, its charter stated that its purpose was 'to save succeeding generations from the scourge of war.' The very first, unanimously adopted UN resolution was to establish the Atomic Energy Commission (later named the Disarmament Commission). Its major task was to work 'for the elimination from national armaments of atomic weapons and of all other major weapons adaptable to mass destruction.'[3]

Dashed Hopes
Every American president since the founding of the UN has warned of the danger of the arms race and has reiterated the need to reverse the weapons build-up.[4] Subsequent history, however, has seen almost total frustration of these laudable goals. In spite of over six thousand arms

control and disarmament negotiation sessions since 1945, the nations have not been able to agree to destroy even a single nuclear weapon. Rather than achieving 'the elimination . . . of atomic weapons,' these weapons have spread to the USSR, China, Great Britain, France and India. Since 1945 the six nuclear powers have exploded well over a thousand nuclear devices in atmospheric and underground tests. Other countries are well on their way to joining the 'nuclear club.' Soon it will no longer be what nuclear physicist Robert Oppenheimer called 'two scorpions in one bottle,' but dozens of scorpions in one bottle.

In 1945 there was only one nuclear power with the capacity to destroy two cities. Now, four decades later, the combined nuclear arsenals of the superpowers can kill *everyone in the world several times over*. The number of nuclear weapons has grown to over fifty thousand, counting both tactical and strategic warheads in American and Soviet arsenals. In the United States about three new nuclear bombs are made every day. During the 1980s, the Reagan administration plans to add fifteen thousand new warheads to the US inventory.[5] The USSR is expected to do much the same.

This enormous expansion is only part of a more general arms build-up which has taken place since 1945. Governments have spent more than $6 trillion for armaments since World War II.[6] (If a person spent $1 million a day for 365 days every year, it would take over 16,000 years to spend $6 trillion.) Global arms spending now devours $550 billion per year. That amounts to about a thousand dollars per year spent on arms for every starving person in the world today. In dollar equivalent terms, $550 billion exceeds the total annual income of that half (two billion) of the world's people who live in the poorest countries. 'Since 1948,' says disarmament expert Robert C. Johansen, 'world military expenditures in real terms have increased at an average annual rate of 4.5%.'[7]

Such an enormous expenditure for weapons means that vast amounts of resources, skills and capital are not available to meet human needs. As President Dwight D. Eisenhower said: 'Every gun that is made, every warship launched, every rocket fired, signifies, in the final sense, a theft from those who hunger and are not fed, those who are cold and not clothed.'[8] One Trident submarine costs as much as a year's schooling for sixteen million children in poor countries.[9] To pour billions into weapons is to take away billions that could be spent to help the world's five hundred million starving people grow their own food, to provide teachers for the half of the world's children who cannot attend school, to provide homes and medicines for the half of the world's people who lack adequate shelter and health care.

And of course the weapons are used. Over a hundred non-nuclear wars have been fought since 1945 in places such as the Middle East, Korea, Vietnam, Africa and Afghanistan. The eighty different nations involved have killed more people than died in all of World War II.[10] And, as we noted in chapter three, the chances of one of those 'conventional' wars developing into a nuclear war are very high.

How does this forty-year history look from a Christian point of view? Why have the world's noble intentions toward peace been undercut so consistently? Certainly human failure to achieve peace comes as no surprise to Christians. Christians are acutely aware of the egotism, enmity and sin which, since the Fall and Cain's killing of Abel, have set human beings in violent conflict with each other.

Satan, our great Enemy who 'prowls around like a roaring lion, seeking some one to devour' (1 Pet 5:8), uses human enmity to achieve his purposes. His goal is to separate us from God's love, to turn our abilities into hurting one another and eventually to destroy the human race. 'He was a murderer from the beginning,' says Jesus (Jn 8:44). Imagine Satan's satisfaction as he sees the world tottering on the brink of nuclear mass murder.

Let us lay to rest once and for all the notion that God

desires the destruction of the Earth. War, as Pope John Paul II said in Hiroshima on 25 February 1981, is a 'man-made calamity.' Or, as Billy Graham said so well:

> God is not interested in destruction, but in redemption. Christ came to seek and to save that which is lost. He came to reverse the effects of the fall. . . . I cannot see any way in which nuclear war could be branded as being God's will. Such warfare, if it ever happens, will come because of the greed and pride and covetousness of the human heart. But God's will is to establish his kingdom, in which Christ is Lord.[11]

If nuclear war comes and life as we know it is destroyed, it will be a triumph for Satan, not for the Creator.

Where, then, should Christians stand? On God's side, not on Satan's! 'Resist him!' said Peter (1 Pet 5:9). God calls us to counter the Satanic powers that would draw our world fully into the 'dominion of darkness' (Col 1:13). God's will is that his children live in peace. To follow God's will we must call on the nations, as Pope Paul VI said, to 'Let the arms fall from your hands.'[12]

Practical Implications

How can we translate this concern into practical work for disarmament? Both Christian and secular thinkers propose a wide range of responses to the challenge of the arms race. We will outline eight of these. We believe, however, that only four of the responses are viable for Christians and that only the last two are wise.

1. *'Nuke 'em.'* One response, thankfully advocated by only a small number, says, 'Find a pretext and go to war.' The USSR or Cuba or Libya is the source of most of the world's evils, according to this militant view. We should build toward a military advantage and then strike. We hope we have shown convincingly that such a response would play into Satan's hands. It would violate Christ's teachings

and could easily bring about the destruction of all life on earth.

2. *'We're number one.'* This response to the arms race says that we should strive for military superiority and use it for political advantage. This response also fails on moral and practical grounds. Morally because it threatens God's children with genocide; practically because it could so easily lead to nuclear war.

3. *Mutually assured destruction* (MAD). A third answer says that we should maintain deterrence through a balance of terror. In chapter four we explored the inadequacies of this view for Christians.

4. *'Better red than dead.'* The fourth answer says we should surrender. Advocates of this position make survival the main goal. Their answer does not take into account the Christian mandate to resist evil and oppression – in this case the need to stand firm against the evils that Communist domination would bring. To give in to the rule of Communist totalitarianism would be a triumph for Satan, though not such a victory as he would achieve through the nuclear destruction of all life on earth.

5. *'No nukes.'* The fifth response says, 'Adopt nuclear pacifism.' This stance would renounce nuclear weapons as an immoral and totally unacceptable means of warfare. Nuclear pacifism is a significant step forward in that it renounces the most lethal weapons of war. It is a first step in the right direction. But we believe this stance does not go far enough because it does not reject conventional weapons, which can also kill massively, as they did in the firebombing of Dresden in World War II. This stance deals with the threat of nuclear war, but not with the problem of war in general.

6. *Unilateral disarmament.* This sixth response proposes disarmament. Its advocates hope that this step would so reduce tensions and fear in the world that others, and notably the USSR, would follow suit. Or, if this is too optimistic, they hope that God would honour a rejection of nuclear weapons and use divine power to lead the world

toward justice and peace. 'Trust in God, not in bombs.'[13]

This answer, it seems to us, is acceptable but unwise. Its inadequacy stems from its failure to take sufficient account of Soviet arms and Soviet intentions. And it forces Christians to surrender to tyranny and oppression rather than resist evil as we are told to do.

The wisest and most realistic responses are, we believe, seven and eight.

7. Transarmament. A policy of transarmament calls for the United States and the countries of W. Europe to transform their present military systems into nonmilitary defence systems. The nations would dismantle their current nuclear and conventional weapons and substitute a defence and deterrence system called civilian-based defence (CBD). Any aggression from outside would be met by vigorous, albeit nonmilitary, defence. We describe transarmament at length in section four. We believe it is a viable response because it rejects the mass killing of modern war, gives a practical strategy for countering evil, and uses tactics which are in harmony with the ethics of Jesus.

8. Multilateral disarmament. Multilateral disarmament is the other viable option for Christians. Multilateral means 'many-sided.' Multilateral disarmament contrasts with unilateral disarmament, in which one nation acts alone and renounces its arms. In multilateral disarmament, two or more nations reach agreement to mutually reduce their weapons. Most such agreements include some procedure to verify the arms reductions so that each side is reasonably sure the other is not cheating.

At the most radical level, advocates of multilateral disarmament propose that nations agree to reduce their arms to the point at which they only have sufficient weapons to enable their internal police forces to function. It means 'arms reductions to the lowest level possible without making local law enforcement impossible.'[14] This idealistic view of multilateral disarmament calls upon nations to arrive at mutual agreements that outlaw all military weapons, both nuclear and conventional. Disputes between nations would be resolved through mediation and other nonviolent means, rather than through armed clashes. The only groups holding weapons would be local police forces maintaining domestic order and protecting citizens' security.[15] Reliable verification would assure that no nation was rebuilding its war-making capacity. War would no longer be possible because nations would no longer have the necessary weapons.

This broad vision is certainly not achievable in the short run. Given human sinfulness, it is doubtful that it is achievable in human history.

At a more limited level, however, multilateral disarmament means mutual agreements by nations to turn toward peace by beginning the process of *reducing* the weapons of war. It refers to nations agreeing to cut back on their weapons rather than constantly increasing them. It can also involve agreements by nations not to *introduce* weapons into an area where they have not yet been placed. (An example is the Antarctica Treaty.) It can also mean nations agreeing not to *manufacture or deploy* weapons that they have the capacity to produce. (In the ABM Treaty, signed by the United States and the Soviet Union, both sides agreed not to set up a system of antiballistic defence rockets.) Or it can simply mean nations agreeing that they will try to work together to reduce the *risk* of war, thus removing some of the incentive for engaging in an arms race. (An example is the 1973 Agreement on the Prevention of Nuclear War.)

Multilateral disarmament is a viable policy for Christians to advocate. The more successfully and extensively it is implemented, the more it would both prevent war and remove the threat of armed expansion by aggressive nations. It is also appealing from a Christian point of view because the step-by-step dismantling of the world's costly military machines could release enormous resources and thousands of skilled people to attack world problems such as hunger, illiteracy and sickness.

Difficulties

Christians who work for disarmament must have a realistic view of the formidable barriers which so far have undercut the efforts toward disarmament. This is not to argue that disarmament is impossible. It is simply to recognise that it is one of the most challenging and difficult tasks in the world.

Why has disarmament been so hard to achieve? One reason is human enmity. Even small steps toward disarmament require a willingness to negotiate with one's antagonists. This is very hard to achieve when human combativeness, fear and suspicion are at epidemic levels. The human inclination to reject love and to follow Cain's murderous ways allows Satan to use us to accomplish his destructive purpose.

Another reason is that disarmament negotiations have been couched in highly technical language. Ordinary people find it hard to understand what is going on when politicians and disarmament negotiators bandy about terms like 'strategic asymmetry,' 'parity,' 'national technical means' and 'window of vulnerability.' People around the world come to feel that disarmament is just too technical for the layperson to understand. The reaction is to leave it to the experts. But this means that the only pressure put on the experts is from well-funded lobbies and interest groups that wish to keep the arms race in high gear. Little pressure is felt from the public, which is especially tragic since so many support disarmament.[16] (Contacts with Soviet citizens also indicate strong support for disarmament and a deep yearning for peace, based in no small part on the fact that they lost twenty million people in World War II.)

Another reason disarmament is difficult is due to the pressure from these interest groups. The military of every country, of course, has an enormous stake in armaments. Military leaders are trained to win. All their past experiences tell them that the side with the most capable armed forces supplied with the biggest, the best and the most weapons is the side that wins. They are suspicious of any suggestion that the size or capability of armies or weapons should be reduced. Furthermore, their jobs and prestige depend on a stable or expanding military budget. It is not surprising, therefore, that generals and admirals in the United States, the Soviet Union and elsewhere nearly always lobby against disarmament.

Linked with this is the *industrial* side of what President Eisenhower called 'the military-industrial complex.'[17] This consists of giant corporations which make high profits out of arms sales, unions protecting jobs for workers in defence industries, and university professors who depend on research grants from the Ministry of Defence. They each represent potent and well-financed vested interests which can be counted on to oppose arms reductions.

These powerful interests can appeal to anxieties in the population at large. People feel insecure in a world of competing ideologies and aggressive nations. They look to weapons as a means of protecting their way of life and warding off attack. Thus, although they long for peace and usually support disarmament negotiations, they can also easily be convinced to support higher military outlays when they are told that a hostile nation is gaining military superiority.

Politicians are ambivalent about disarmament. They want to represent their constituents' yearning for peace, but they also see no alternative to having weapons to defend their nations against Communist aggression. (Soviet leaders say the same thing about capitalist imperialism.) Cutting back on weapons may seem a sign of weakness or a loss of national prestige. It may also mean losing defence contracts that promise jobs for the districts they represent.

Another barrier to disarmament is what is technically termed *asymmetry of perception*. This means that, in any potential or actual disarmament talks, each side 'perceives' the other differently. There is no objective standard to tell if nations are 'even' or if one side is 'ahead' of the other in the arms race. Each tends to feel that the *other* is ahead, and that its own side must race harder to keep up. It is extremely difficult to agree on the actual balance of forces between nations. Does the fact that we have more nuclear warheads give *us* the lead? Or does the fact that their warheads are bigger and their rockets more powerful give *them* the lead? How do we weigh ambiguous factors like the reliability of each side's allies, differences in geography, access to oceans and so on? Lacking common values and a common information base, each side tends to see the other as especially threatening and as needing to make the larger disarmament concessions.

Fear also enters in. Neither side trusts the other. Each lives in fear of a disarmament treaty that would give its antagonist a decisive military advantage. Each fears that its competitor may secretly develop new weapons to give it a breakthrough to superiority. Each, therefore, wants to err on the safe side. Each truly believes that things would be better if *its* side were a little ahead.

The problem of 'cheating' is another factor complicating the disarmament process. Many politicians and citizens doubt the possibility of verifying whether countries are actually living up to their disarmament agreements. The Soviet Union generally has resisted the idea of disarmament inspectors setting foot on Soviet soil.[18] The problem of on-site inspection has been ameliorated by the development of highly competent means of verification (especially sophisticated photo reconnaissance by satellites) which do not require first-hand observation. Doubt remains on both sides, however, that any verification system can prevent a major violation.

Experts fear that the verification problem will become even more acute as the United States and the USSR deploy the cruise missile, which was described in chapter three. Whereas submarines, bombers and ICBMs are large enough to be spotted by reconnaissance satellites, the twenty-foot-long, nuclear-armed cruise missiles are small enough to be hidden in the basement of a house or on a small ship. Arms control experts say it will be difficult, if not impossible, to verify whether the United States or

USSR is manufacturing or deploying cruise missiles.[19]

A barrier to the dream of general and complete disarmament stems from the need for effective disarmament to involve *all* nations. The United States and the USSR would not give up all their military weapons in a world where Germany, France and China kept theirs. The nations of the world would not agree to mutual disarmament if Libya, for example, opted out. Yet to achieve mutual disarmament agreements from the 163 nations of the world would be an incredibly difficult if not impossible job. It would have to take into account the relative strength and weakness of dozens of armies, to say nothing of dealing with the vested interests and prestige needs of dozens of national leaders.

Is Disarmament Possible?

These are staggering obstacles to effective disarmament. Recounting them makes it easy to understand why a dedicated disarmament expert like Alva Myrdal concludes that the six thousand arms control and disarmament negotiations have been little more than a game played by superpowers.[20]

From a Christian point of view, however, these immense obstructions should come as no surprise. The stakes are incredibly high. On the one side is God the Father, setting before us 'life and death, blessing and curse,' and saying to his children: 'Choose life, that you and your descendants may live' (Deut 30:19). On the other side is Satan, the murderer, the deceiver, the father of lies, saying to us: 'Choose death, cling to your weapons; love is foolish; take the way of Cain' (cf. 1 Jn 3:10). The challenge to Christians is not to be immobilised by the obstacles Satan puts in the path of peace, but to mobilise our deepest prayer, our most intelligent thought, and our most determined action.

The nations involved in the arms race, especially the United States and the USSR, are like cars speeding along a road that ends at the edge of a cliff. Our job is to help them put on the brakes, to get them to stop before they plunge over the edge. Then we must encourage them to turn around and start going in the opposite direction.

Even very small, beginning steps are vitally important. Just to have nations sit down at the bargaining table for dialogue and negotiation reduces international tensions and the threat of war. To talk is infinitely better than to fight. When nations sign an actual disarmament treaty, even a minor one, a ray of hope is sent to a world desperately afraid of war. When agreements are kept, they build trust and the confidence that further steps are possible. They enhance global stability, and they release resources which can be used to alleviate human suffering and meet human needs.

We can be encouraged by the fact that, in spite of all the impediments, nations *have* been able to arrive at and to keep disarmament agreements.

The treaties described here have prevented the introduction of nuclear weapons into some areas of the globe, such as Antarctica and Latin America, and from some environments, such as the sea bed and outer space. They have eliminated the above-ground testing of nuclear weapons, which until 1963 had been poisoning the earth's atmosphere with radioactivity. They have enabled the superpowers to eliminate or curtail costly and threatening weapons systems, such as the antiballistic missile. They have built lines of communication between the superpowers in an effort to make accidental war less likely. They have built up a body of international law around arms control and disarmament. And, most importantly, they have provided a forum for the nations to, in Winston Churchill's words, 'jaw, jaw, jaw, rather than war, war, war.'[21]

Some Successful Arms Treaties in Force Today[22]

1817   *Rush-Bagot Agreement:* Limits the number and tonnage of US and British warships on the Great Lakes and Lake Champlain. Maintained for over a hundred and sixty years. Longest disarmament agreement in history.

1925   *Poison Gas and Bacteriological Warfare Treaty:* Prohibits use of poison and other gases and bacteriological weapons in warfare.

1959   *Antarctic Treaty:* A 'nonarmament' treaty in which the signers (nineteen nations, including the United States and the USSR) agree not to place any weapons, including nuclear weapons, in the enormous area of the South Pole. All parties can freely inspect one another's installations.

1963   *Hot-Line Agreement:* A direct communications link between Washington and Moscow so that at times of international crisis leaders can talk directly and avoid misunderstandings that might lead to nuclear war.

1963   *Partial Test Ban Treaty:* Bans nuclear explosions in the atmosphere, in ðuter space and under water. Signed by the United States, the USSR and 103 other nations, but not France and China. Has helped end radioactive contamination of the environment due to above-ground nuclear weapons tests.

1967   *Outer Space Treaty:* Prohibits nations from sending nuclear weapons or other weapons of mass destruction into orbit around the earth. Agrees not to place military bases on the moon or other celestial bodies and not to test weapons there.

1967   *Treaty Prohibiting Nuclear Weapons in Latin America:* The twenty-five nations signing agree not to produce, acquire, test or use nuclear weapons. When and if it is fully ratified and entered into force, it will make Latin America a nuclear-weapons-free zone.

1968   *Nuclear Non-Proliferation Treaty:* The more than one hundred non-nuclear nations signing agree not to possess or to try to obtain nuclear weapons. The nuclear powers (including the United States and the

USSR) agree to help the non-nuclear states in several ways and to work for nuclear disarmament.

1971   *Sea-Bed Treaty:* Prohibits nuclear weapons on the bottom of the ocean. Signed by almost a hundred nations, including the United States and the USSR.

1971   *Nuclear Accidents Agreement:* The United States and the USSR agree to several safeguards against accidents involving nuclear weapons.

1972   *Anti-Ballistic Missile Treaty:* The United States and the USSR agree to severely limit the number of ABMs. The agreement to forgo the ABMs has saved both sides billions of dollars.[23]

1972   *SALT I Agreement to Limit Strategic Nuclear Weapons:* The United States and the USSR agree to freeze at existing levels the numbers of their ICBMs. SALT stands for 'Strategic Arms Limitations Talks.'

1973   *Agreement on the Prevention of Nuclear War:* The United States and the USSR agree to try to remove the danger of nuclear war, to practise restraint in their mutual relations, and to pursue policies directed toward stability and peace. In the event of a nuclear confrontation, they commit themselves to try to avoid the risk of war.

1974   *Threshold Test Ban Treaty:* The United States and the USSR agree to keep the size of their nuclear weapons tests below 150 kilotons. (The US Senate has not yet ratified the treaty, but both countries have declared they will abide by the limit.)

1974   *Biological Weapons Convention:* Prohibits the development, production and stockpiling of biological weapons.

1976   *Peaceful Nuclear Explosions Treaty:* The United States and the USSR agree to limit these explosions to under 150 kilotons. (The US Senate has not yet ratified this treaty, but the policy of both countries is to abide by the limits.)

One of the encouraging things about this list of agreements

is the fact that Christians had a hand in achieving some of
them. Dr Herman Will, who has for years been a Washington peace lobbyist for the United Methodist Church, says
that church people helped get the Partial Test Ban Treaty
ratified by Congress. 'One Senator reported that a col-
league had told him that so many ministers were running
around the state of Iowa talking about love and brother-
hood and radioactive fallout that he had to vote for the
treaty.'[24]

It is true that the agreements so far have not reversed the
arms race. They have not led to the destruction of the
nuclear arsenals. But antagonistic nations *have* been able to
sit down and hammer out meaningful, verifiable treaties.
Some brakes have been applied in the mad race toward the
cliff. This gives hope that the disarmament process can be
deepened and extended. Perhaps the brakes can be slam-
med on harder. Perhaps the speeding cars can be slowed,
stopped and even turned around.

The Problem of Cheating

One of the most encouraging results of the arms control and
disarmament negotiations so far is the discovery that agreements *can* be verified. Many people do not realise this.
They say, 'But you can't trust the Russians. What's the use
of signing a paper agreement with them? They'll cheat on
agreements, lie about their violations and gain a military
advantage.' The point, however, is not that we need to trust
the Russians, but that we need ways to *verify* agreements to
make sure they do not break them secretly. The treaties
referred to above have a number of kinds of built-in
verification systems. The Antarctic Treaty, which de-
nuclearises and demilitarises the vast South Pole region,
allows each side to make both aerial and on-site inspections. Each side can thus make sure that the other side is not
cheating. In the words of the treaty, each inspector has
'complete freedom of access at any time to any or all areas
of Antarctica.'[25] American on-site inspections of Soviet
facilities have never found any armaments or military

activities. 'The observed activities at each station,' says a US government report, 'were in compliance with the provisions and spirit of the Antarctic Treaty.'[26]

Another fascinating method of verification is called *national technical means* of inspection. This includes the highly sophisticated radar, reconnaissance satellites, heat sensors and electronic receivers which the United States uses to monitor the SALT I Treaty and Soviet armaments in general. A pamphlet published by a group of American scientists describes their capabilities:

From 100 miles up, American reconnaissance satellites look straight down at every inch of Soviet territory. 'Search and find' cameras photograph strips of land a thousand miles wide, develop the film on board, and radio the pictures down. On command from ground controllers, 'close look' cameras zoom in on anything suspicious, snap ultra-detailed photos, and send film capsules parachuting back to earth.

'A satellite circulating the world in 90 minutes will pick up more information in a day than the espionage service could pick up in years,' writes retired Air Force Col E. Asa Bates. . . . Incredible as it sounds, these orbiting cameras can currently spot objects or features as small as one foot in length or smaller.

That level of detail allows Pentagon and CIA photo-interpreters to locate, identify, and count the Soviet's nuclear forces precisely. Missile silos, launch control systems, airbases, bombers on the ground, naval bases, and submarines in port are all visible. Factories, submarine construction yards, highways and railroads stand in clear view. There is little chance that the Soviets could build, transport and deploy weapons in excess of SALT ceilings without detection by the United States.[27]

The pamphlet goes on to describe the other equipment used by the United States. They have 'multispectral scanners' that can penetrate camouflage. They have 'image enhancement' mechanisms to highlight suspicious objects. They have amazing, over-the-horizon radars that can observe and evaluate missile launches and line-of-sight radar so sophisticated that it can spot an object the size of a basketball two thousand miles away.

If American observers see something suspicious, they report it to the SALT Standing Consultative Committee, a special group of Soviet and American experts that meet in Geneva. The United States has brought eight suspicious activities before the committee, the Soviet Union five. In each case, both sides were able to show they were not violating the SALT agreement. The Soviet officials responded to questions 'by either halting activities of concern or demonstrating their legality. The United States did likewise.'[28]

Not only can it be seen whether or not the Soviet government is cheating, but the Soviet officials also *know* they are being watched (and vice versa). It is not to their advantage to cheat when there is such a high likelihood of being caught and held up to the world's ridicule. Most arms control experts agree that, while the Soviet leaders are extremely hard bargainers, once a treaty on weapons control is agreed to, they stick to its provisions.

Military Expenditure and the Economy

Another encouraging factor which favours arms control and disarmament is the growing realisation that military expenditures can be damaging to the economy. In the past, people believed that a high military budget was important to keep the economy running. Indeed, military spending seems to have been a factor in the improvement of the US economy of the 1930s. But that does not mean that military spending is a *necessary* factor in a healthy economy. In fact, a look at the economies of post-World War II Japan and West Germany suggest otherwise.

A number of studies have been written which show that a high military budget may be more harmful than helpful to the economy.[29] A shift to greater civilian production could reduce inflation, help to modernise our industry, create jobs and provide funds to meet our people's needs. Here are some of the facts these studies reveal:

1) Military expenditure contributes to inflation. 'More money chasing fewer goods and services' is a classic definition of inflation. Military spending increases income (salaries to defence workers and so on) without increasing the supply of consumable goods (you cannot eat a battleship).[30] Furthermore, the constant cost overruns of military production (weapons costing far more than their original estimates) increase the price of scarce resources and give new impetus to inflation.

2) Military expenditures divert capital and technology from the civilian sector. Since World War II, the Defence Department in the United States has been the single largest user of capital and technology. Over a third of the country's scientific and engineering talent is in the defence sector and half of all Federal research and development funds are invested there. Countries with relatively low military budgets (for example, Japan) tend to invest their capital and skills in civilian industry, thus keeping it efficient and competitive. The United States, on the other hand, has a very modern military establishment but an increasingly antiquated industrial base. It builds 'smart' missiles, but not efficient, low-cost trains. It is falling further and further behind other countries in international competition in non-military products and technology while becoming increasingly dependent on foreign arms sales. Foreign producers of nonmilitary goods (such as cars and cameras) are capturing large chunks of the American market.

3) Greater military spending may increase unemployment. According to the US Bureau of Labour Statistics, military spending creates fewer jobs per billion dollars spent than any other sector except the space programme.[31] A billion dollars spent in civilian industry creates fourteen thousand more jobs than a billion dollars spent in military industry. This is because military-related jobs are more capital-intensive than labour-intensive. (That means it takes a small number of highly trained, highly paid workers using sophisticated machinery to produce weapons.)

4) Military spending diverts resources from human needs. As long as military budgets increase beyond the inflation rate, all other sectors of the economy must compete for money that is scarcer and scarcer. This means less money to provide housing, health, transport, education and nutrition. That hurts everyone, but especially the poor. Money directed toward social programmes and transport, on the other hand, creates more jobs and provides goods and services for those who need them.

Given these optimistic studies, how can Christians encourage the shift from a war-oriented to a civilian economy? What disarmament steps should we support? What steps will put the brakes on the arms race and start to turn it around?

The 'Nuclear Freeze' Campaign

The most promising current proposal is the call for a mutual 'freeze' of nuclear weapons by the United States and the USSR. The call is being put forward by church and peace groups around the world. The proposal is simple and profound at the same time. It says that the way to stop the arms race is to stop. It asks the United States and the Soviet Union to stop all further testing, production and deployment of nuclear weapons and of the missiles and aircraft designed to carry them.

The Soviet Union, for example, would stop deploying their SS-18 heavy rockets and other ICBMs. They would stop building the SS-20 rocket, which has threatened Western Europe, and stop manufacturing the rocket-carrying Typhoon submarine. They would not develop a new heavy bomber or more cruise missiles. They would not add new nuclear warheads to their stockpile or increase the number of warheads in their existing missiles. They would stop developing the rockets which have inspired speculation that a Soviet attack could knock out American land-based missiles.

The United States would also halt any further growth in its nuclear arsenal. It would not develop the MX missile nor any more Trident submarines. Plans for the B-1 bomber or new cruise missiles would be scrapped. The production lines that now manufacture three new nuclear bombs every day would be shut down.

Senator Mark Hatfield (Republican Senator for Oregon) was one of the first national US leaders to speak out for a freeze. During the 1979 SALT II debate, he proposed that the United States and the USSR call a nuclear moratorium. He said, 'I consider a bilateral moratorium on nuclear weapons deployment and testing to be the single most crucial issue facing mankind today.'[32]

The American magazine *Christianity Today* editorially endorsed Senator Hatfield's plan, urging Christians to support a 'complete freeze on the development, testing and deployment of strategic missile systems by both the Soviet Union and the United States.'[33] In the same magazine, the Rev. John R. W. Stott also urged such a freeze as part of his 'Call for Christian Peacemakers.'[34] Now numerous other Christian leaders, churches and peace groups are campaigning for it, and scientists from forty nations are supporting it.[35]

The freeze idea has enormous advantages as a disarmament proposal. The arms race between the West and the Soviet Union has proceeded in an upward spiral. We build a missile, and they build a missile to counter it. They increase their military spending; we increase ours. The freeze stops this spiral. It hits the brakes. It gets both sides to stop. It starts to reduce the enormous tensions between the superpowers and therefore reduces the risk of war.

A freeze could be verified, since it would stop the development and deployment of the hard-to-verify cruise missiles. It would be a hopeful first step and could be the basis for further negotiations to reduce arms. Implementation of a US/Soviet freeze also should make it easier to persuade other countries to freeze or abandon their own nuclear development programmes.

There are some indications that the USSR would accept a freeze proposal. It would be to their advantage, since it would stop the US and Western European nuclear build-up, which the Soviets find just as threatening as we do theirs. It would enable them to put more money into their ailing civilian economy rather than into another round of arms increases. Over the past five years, Soviet officials have made several proposals along the lines of a mutual freeze.[36]

The US government could initiate the freeze by sounding out Soviet officials and then making some moves to show sincerity. If the Soviet response was at all favourable, negotiators would start to work out details. The freeze could begin informally even before the treaty was signed.[37] Once a treaty was signed, the two sides could start new negotiations to reduce nuclear and other weapons. Having hit the brakes and stopped the race before plunging over the cliff, they could pursue steps to turn around and back away from the precipice.

Already church and peace groups across the USA are working hard on a nuclear freeze campaign. They have collected hundreds of thousands of signatures on petitions, handed out leaflets, organised meetings, sponsored radio and TV spots, placed ads in newspapers, and sent letters to both President Reagan and Chairman Brezhnev.

The results have been very heartening. In November 1980, fifty-nine per cent of the voters passed a ballot resolution in western Massachusetts supporting the freeze. Later analysis of the vote showed that supporters came from across the political spectrum.[38] In the summer of 1981, the state legislatures of New York, Oregon and Massachusetts passed similar resolutions. In October 1981, Governor Brendan Byrne of New Jersey proclaimed October 25–31 'Mutual Nuclear Arms Freeze Week.' In March 1982, sixteen Vermont town meetings voted to support the freeze. A great many religious groups (for example, the national board of the YWCA and several Catholic orders) have gone on record in support of the freeze. Tens of thousands of individuals and dozens of local groups around the country are involved in the campaign.

The goal is to build popular support to persuade Congress and the administration to propose the idea of a freeze to the Soviets. Once the freeze is achieved, peacemakers would continue to press the United States and Soviet Union and other countries in Western Europe for new agreements to *reverse* the arms race.

But the freeze is not the only important issue. Many other public policy issues may arise. Will the SALT process be revived? Will a proposal for START – Strategic Arms *Reduction* Talks – gain support? What about George Kennan's proposal for a mutual fifty per cent cut in the nuclear arsenals?[39] Will governments consider treaties to cut back conventional arms?[40] Being on the mailing list of a Christian peace organisation that specialises in disarmament will keep you in touch with national movements of Christians working for peace.

Christians are called to be part of the force which halts the arms race and beckons the nations back from the nuclear abyss. To respond, we must participate in citizen movements that cry for peace so loudly that the world's leaders cannot ignore us. There must be a 'new abolitionist movement' which says no to the arms race as forcefully as the old abolitionists said no to slavery.

As Billy Graham said, nuclear war, if it happens, will not be God's fault. It will happen because of human greed and pride and covetousness. In the same way, nuclear war can be prevented if enough concerned people pray and act and insist that the nations respond to God's imperative: 'Choose life, that you and your descendants may live' (Deut 30:19).

SECTION IV

Biblical Faith and National Defence

How do we apply the perspective of the preceding chapters to Western defence? Our answer is given in five steps.

1. Our main concern as Christians should be to follow Jesus in obedient faith rather than to defend our country or any other nation.

2. It is, however, legitimate to have an effective system of defence to protect a nation's cherished values and institutions against outside aggression.

3. People see military weapons as the main element in such a defence. They are unlikely to give up the weapons of war unless they see an alternative means of defence that seems both practical and moral.

4. It is possible to safeguard Western freedom, independence and democracy by nonmilitary means.

5. Therefore, Christians should support a nonmilitary defence system.

We realise that this conclusion will seem startling and perhaps far-fetched. Nonmilitary defence? Absurd! Unrealistic! But, in fact, it is current 'wisdom' and policy that are absurd. We urge readers to hear us out. In the face of nuclear holocaust and Jesus' rejection of lethal violence, God calls us in very new directions.

In this section we will look at nonmilitary defence and how it works. Chapter thirteen will examine historical cases of nonmilitary defence. Then we will look into the nature of nonmilitary defence and, in chapter fifteen, provide a scenario of how one nation, the United States, might substitute nonmilitary defence for its current reliance on nuclear weapons.

'Nonviolence does not mean meek submission to the will of the evil-doer, but it means putting one's whole soul against the will of the tyrant.'

Mahatma Gandhi[1]

13

Is Nonmilitary Defence Possible?

In Section II we stated our belief that participation in nuclear war – and in war itself – is contrary to God's will. Christians must not participate in war, support it or contribute to preparations for it. To live in obedient faith means no longer to rely upon war. Not only must we not *use* the weapons of violence against others; we must not even threaten to use them. If the act of war is against God's will, then threats and preparations are also.

But what if this attitude toward war and weapons were taken seriously by more than a small minority? What would it mean for military defence? What would it mean for nuclear deterrence? What if all Christians renounced war and military preparations? Obviously, no nation could maintain its military forces in a high state of readiness if, say, half its people opposed and voted against military preparedness.

Anxiety about Military Weakness
Most Westerners (including most Christians) would react with deep anxiety to the prospect of the West being radically weakened. 'Wouldn't the Russians march in, take over and destroy everything we hold dear? Without our military power, we would have to surrender.' The Christian who believes that Jesus forbids violence seems to be on the horns of a dilemma. On the one hand, obedient faith calls for a renunciation of war. On the other hand, winning large numbers of people to that faith would undercut the nation's

military posture, possibly opening us to Soviet attack and the destruction of our way of life.

Some seek a way out of this dilemma by minimising the Soviet threat. Prominent church leaders have argued that fear of Russian intentions is an 'irrational prejudice built by Western propaganda' and that 'we have to convince the public we're not seriously threatened.'[2] Studies have been published which argue that Soviet ideology and military power either do not really threaten the West or are much less of a threat than is usually imagined.[3]

We agree that Soviet citizens are not devils. We should not see them as the embodiment of all the evil in the world. Sin and evil come from many sources. They exist in all people and nations, including our own. This is why we must beware of extreme nationalism, which makes the state an idol. However much we love our country, we must recognise the evils and injustices committed in its name. We must also recognise that many of the wars in modern history have resulted from excessive idolatrous nationalism. Christians committed to God first, rather than 'my country right or wrong,' must develop a global outlook.

We cannot agree, however, that the Soviet threat is nonexistent, or that it can be safely ignored.

Threat is defined by Webster as 'an expression of an intention to inflict evil, injury, or damage on another.'[4] By this definition, the Soviets *do* threaten us. At the most basic level, we are threatened physically by the Soviet nuclear weapons, which could unleash incredible 'evil, injury, or damage' on the West. Just as they are threatened by our rockets, so we are threatened by theirs.

Another level of threat is ideological. Soviet Communism remains a major competing philosophy, challenging much of what Westerners hold dear. Its totalitarianism is at odds with our idea of democracy. Its atheism contradicts our religious beliefs. The suppression and brutalisation of dissidents in the USSR and its satellites shows how little the Soviet government values freedom of thought, assembly and expression. The universalism of Communist philosophy requires that its adherents seek to spread it throughout the world,[5]

The Soviet Communists have clearly demonstrated their willingness to use military force and subversion to achieve their ends.[6] The enormous Soviet military build-up of the last decade, Soviet military intervention in Hungary, Czechoslovakia and Afghanistan, the presence of Soviet or Cuban troops or military advisers in Angola, Mozambique, Ethiopia, Libya and South Yemen, and Soviet attempts to spread the Communist system elsewhere all show that the Soviet threat is not simply an 'irrational prejudice built by Western propaganda.'

Because of the reality of the Soviet threat, we believe that if America's defence were abandoned unilaterally and nothing put in its place, the United States would face the danger of Soviet invasion. This also applies to other Western nations.

Even if it could be proved that there is no Soviet threat, Christians know that 'wars and rumours of wars' will persist and that 'nation will rise against nation' until Christ returns (Mt 24:6–7). Political science joins biblical faith in a realistic analysis of the world. Powerful nations regularly impose their will on others.[7] History gives countless examples of one state attempting to extend its power and influence by invading another.

If Soviet Communism were not in the picture, a new Nazism or some other form of expansionist totalitarianism might arise to threaten the integrity and independence of surrounding nations. Tyranny and despotism are far from dead. Some means of response to the oppression they bring has been and will be necessary.

Military Defence and Its Alternatives

When peaceful mechanisms fail, nations have felt it necessary to rely on military means to protect their independence and sovereignty. If the alternative is either to fight or to submit to outside rule, economic exploitation or extermination, most people see no alternative to war. In spite of all its brutalities, war has provided people with a means to fight the forces that they believed to threaten their national integrity, liberty and way of life.[8]

Given this reality, how should Christians respond? Defence with modern weaponry is morally unacceptable, but Christians have an obligation to resist evil, to 'seek justice, correct oppression; defend the fatherless, plead for the widow' (Is 1:17). If a tyrannical regime invaded the United States or Western Europe, we would be obliged to try to correct the oppression it would bring.

A way out of this dilemma could be found in a defence system which does not rely on military weapons, yet which gives hope of protecting liberties and life. If such a means were available, it could serve as a *substitute*, an alternative, to military defence and war.

The need for an alternative is crucial. People cling to military weapons partly because they believe that they are the only deterrent against aggression. But we believe that there is a method of defence which meets the high call of Jesus to 'love your enemies, and pray for those who persecute you' (Mt 5:44). We believe nonmilitary defence is feasible.

Even to pose the question of a nonmilitary means of defence sounds startling to most people. We have been taught that defence *means* military defence. A nonmilitary defence sounds like a contradiction in terms. It may look like an invitation to surrender.

But there are scholars, military experts, theologians and peace advocates who believe nonmilitary defence is a genuinely viable option.[9] Several European countries (Sweden, Norway, Denmark, the Netherlands) have taken an interest in these ideas, have studied them and, in at least one case, have run army 'exercises' based on nonviolent defence.[10] In December 1980, for example, the Swedish government authorised its Minister of Defence to set up a special government body to prepare a plan for nonmilitary defence as part of Sweden's overall defence strategy.

Just as surprising, perhaps, is the interest in and even support for nonmilitary defence that has come from military officers and institutions. For example, Dr Gene Sharp, an American proponent of nonmilitary defence, has lectured at the US Army War College in Carlisle, Pennsylvania. Sharp published a large scholarly book entitled *The Politics of Nonviolent Action*, which contained many examples of nonmilitary defence. The volume received reviews in a number of American military periodicals:

[A] landmark study, certain to become a classic. . . . A coolly reasoned, well-documented case for nonviolence as a practical alternative to domestic violence and war which demands the most serious consideration. (Richard Burns, *Naval War College Review*, July/Aug. 1974.)

This volume makes a great deal of sense. (Col Donald F. Bletz, US Army War College, *Military Review*, Apr. 1974.)

An important work . . . deserving of most serious study. (Col Malham M. Wakin, professor, US Air Force Academy, *Air Force Magazine*, Nov. 1974.)

In Europe, General André de Bollardière, who served with the French army in Vietnam and Algeria and is one of France's most highly decorated generals, has strongly advocated nonviolent defence as a replacement for France's armed defence.[11] Captain Sir Basil Liddell Hart, military editor of the *Encyclopedia Britannica* and widely acknowledged as the foremost military writer of our time, wrote of this form of defence: 'Probably the more that governments come to realise their incapacity for effective military defence, the more they will begin to take nonviolent civilian defence seriously.'[12] A retired British officer, Commander Sir Stephen King-Hall, wrote two books which advocate nonmilitary strategies as the best means of defending Britain against foreign aggression (see appendix A-4).

Hungary's War without Weapons[13]

Nonmilitary defence can perhaps best be illustrated by reference to historical cases in which it has been used to counter outside aggression or tyranny. One relatively unknown story is that of Hungary's successful nonmilitary resistance against Austrian rule. This case, which took place from 1859–67, is especially significant for Christians because of the important role of Protestant churches in the resistance.

At various times in its history, Hungary was an independent kingdom with its own constitution and parliament (called the 'Diet'). During the late 1700s and early 1800s, however, it was ruled by Austria, its powerful neighbour to the west. Austria throttled the development of Hungarian industry in favour of its own. Hungary's economy stagnated. The Austrian government often ruled by decree, suspending the Hungarian constitution and ignoring or suppressing its Diet. Austria's King Joseph II even ordered that the German language rather than Hungarian be spoken in government, the courts and all schools above the primary level.

In 1849 a Hungarian military revolt was crushed by Austrian troops aided by an army from the Russian Czar. Austria made savage reprisals against the Hungarians and put the country under martial law, ruling it directly from Vienna. The Diet was suppressed, the constitution repealed, and the country divided into districts run by Austrian military officers.

Since leaders of both the Lutheran and the Reformed churches had supported the armed Hungarian freedom movement, many of their pastors and bishops were imprisoned and their autonomous church organisations dissolved. Austrian officers listened in on all church meetings. Militarily defeated, Hungary seemed to have no alternative but to submit to Austrian rule.

The spark of a nonmilitary revolt was lit by Ferencz Deák, a highly respected Hungarian lawyer and jurist. When the Austrian Minister of Justice tried to confer with him in 1850, Deák refused, saying that the Hungarian constitution must first be restored. Deák's letter of refusal was published widely. In it he urged his countrymen neither to recognise Austrian rule nor to seek to repel it by force. In later statements he continually warned against violence. But he pleaded for absolute resistance to any 'transfer to a foreign assembly sitting in the capital of a foreign country the right to make law for ourselves and our children.'[14]

The Protestant church spearheaded the resistance. When Austrians tried to prevent church councils from meeting, they met in full force. In one case, five hundred church leaders shouted to an Austrian official, who had troops stationed outside the building: 'We shall hold the meeting; we will not disperse.'[15]

When the Austrians demanded that a decree be read from every pulpit, every minister refused. Many were arrested as a result. Police broke up church meetings only to find that huge crowds would gather wherever a church leader spoke in defiance of Austrian law. To show solidarity with arrested church leaders, students dressed in black held silent demonstrations. In court, the leaders rejected any legal defence, saying they were acting in accord with their constitutional rights. Those not imprisoned carried on with church affairs as if Austrian decrees did not exist.[16]

When Austria tried to tighten its control, Ferencz Deák contended, 'We can hold our own against armed force. If suffering be necessary, suffer with dignity.'[17] The Austrians ordered the Diet and local county governments to be dissolved. Hungarian officials refused and continued to meet until Austrian troops forced them out of their chambers at gunpoint. They held protest marches, met informally under other auspices, and continued their work. In 1861 Hungary refused both Austria's levy for Hungarian troops and its demand that Hungary send representatives to Austria's parliament.

When Austrian tax collectors tried to collect taxes from Hungarians, they refused to pay, saying that they were 'illegal persons.' When police seized the tax refusers'

goods, the Austrians could not find any Hungarian auctioneers to sell them to pay the defaulted taxes. When
Austrian auctioneers were brought in, no Hungarians
would bid on the property. Hungarians also boycotted
Austrian goods and ostracised Austrian troops billeted in
Hungarian homes. These and similar tactics led the London
Times to editorialise: 'Passive resistance can be so organised as to become more troublesome than armed
rebellion.'[18]

After almost two decades of struggle, Austria found
itself derided in the foreign press and threatened by war
with Prussia. Hungarian nationalism and pride, meanwhile, flourished. Finally, in December 1866, Austria
agreed to reopen the Hungarian Diet and in 1867 to restore
its constitution. Thus Hungary, through nonmilitary
means, resisted outside tyranny, won complete internal
independence and equal partnership with Austria, restored
its own government and constitution, and prevented the
destruction of its churches' autonomy.

Examples like this always raise the question of what
would have happened if the Austrian government had been
more brutal. What if it had been headed by Hitler and its
army run like the Nazi SS? Perhaps things would have gone
as they did in Nazi-occupied Norway.

Norway Confronts Nazism[19]

Hitler's armies conquered Norway in June 1940 after two
months of armed resistance. Beginning in September, the
Nazi occupiers began to destroy Norway's long-standing
democratic institutions, establish Nazism and turn Norway
into a province of Germany.

Nazi decrees disbanded Norway's parliament, outlawed
all but fascist political parties and installed Vidkun Quisling, a Norwegian fascist, as the head of state. Quisling
abolished the constitution and all elections. All government offices were filled from above. The new government
was backed by the Hird, a military police unit modelled
along the lines of the German storm-troopers. Resisters

were to be arrested, tortured and shipped to concentration camps.

Quisling's goal was to transform Norway into a fascist 'corporative state,' as Mussolini had done in Italy. He selected the country's teachers, the moulders of the minds of youth, as his first recruits for the new order. During late 1940 and early 1941, Quisling issued a series of decrees: his portrait must be hung in all schools; the curriculum must be revised along fascist lines; and teachers must give students a sympathetic view of the fascist regime. He also ordered students to join a fascist youth movement and teachers to join a union headed by the Hird.

The teachers refused. They agreed on common guidelines: do not obey government orders which conflict with conscience; do not teach Nazi propaganda; do not cooperate with fascist organisations. Resistance leaders met in Oslo and issued a declaration, which they distributed widely. It said that Quisling's orders went against conscience and should not therefore be obeyed.

Within weeks twelve thousand of Norway's fourteen thousand teachers had signed the declaration and refused to join the new union. Massive numbers of students refused to join the youth movement. Over two hundred thousand parents and all of Norway's Lutheran bishops wrote letters of protest to Quisling. When the few fascist teachers attempted to hold classes, students refused to attend.

In exasperation, the government closed the schools in February 1941. Teachers responded by holding classes in their own homes. Thirteen hundred teachers were arrested and sent to Gestapo-run concentration camps in Norway's frigid north. Quisling went personally to the famous Stabekk school near Oslo to order arrests. On the following day, teachers who had been absent went to the prison and demanded to be incarcerated along with their colleagues.

The arrested teachers held firm. In the concentration camp they were put on starvation rations and forced to do 'torture gymnastics' in the snow. Yet only thirty-two teachers gave in. On April 25 the schools reopened. The remaining teachers still refused to join the fascist union. They read a statement to their students which said: 'The teacher's vocation is not only to give children knowledge; teachers must also teach their pupils to believe in and uphold truth and justice. Therefore, teachers cannot, without betraying their calling, teach anything that violates their conscience. . . . That, I promise you, I shall not do.'[20]

The Gestapo spread a rumour that if the teachers did not give in their arrested colleagues would be killed. After a tremendous struggle of conscience, the teachers decided to continue the resistance. In response, Quisling sent the arrested teachers to a concentration camp farther north, above the Arctic Circle, where they had to do forced labour along with Russian prisoners of war. As the trainloads of teachers passed through the mountains, children stood at the stations and sang patriotic songs to encourage them. Five hundred teachers were shipped north on a vessel designed for ninety-six passengers. Two teachers died in the freezing camps.

Quisling believed that these harsh measures would intimidate the teachers, but they refused to back down. Their courage inspired the nation. Finally, in November 1942 Quisling released the arrested teachers, who returned home to triumphal processions. Quisling showed his exasperation in an enraged speech to teachers at the Stabekk school in which he said: 'You teachers have destroyed everything for me.'

When Quisling gave up with the teachers, he turned elsewhere to implement the corporative state. These efforts also failed due to nonmilitary resistance. Norwegians published illegal newspapers and distributed thousands of leaflets to protest against the occupation. Labour unions struck and sabotaged machinery, in spite of imprisonments and executions of labour leaders. Citizens wore paper-clips on their lapels to signify, 'Keep together.' They never spoke to German soldiers or sat beside them on buses, but treated them as if they did not exist. When the Nazis tried to round up Norwegian Jews, over half were successfully hidden or smuggled to neutral Sweden.

The Norwegian Evangelical Lutheran Church, a state church embracing ninety-seven per cent of the population, also led in non-military resistance. Its leaders gave sermons and issued pastoral letters protesting against the terrorism of the Hird, encroachments on Norwegian democracy and attempts to teach fascism in the schools.

When Quisling tried to recruit pastors into a 'Christian Unity Movement,' only twenty of Norway's one thousand ministers joined – and these were then boycotted by most of their congregations.

In early 1942 the government ordered that the 11 a.m. service at Norway's Nidaros Cathedral be given by a fascist clergyman. The cathedral's rector, who normally led the liturgy, announced that he would lead worship at 2 p.m. Only a handful of people came to the morning service, but thousands to the afternoon one. After the police closed the doors, several thousand people lined up outside in below-zero cold and sang 'A Mighty Fortress Is Our God.'

The government fired the rector the next day. In response, all the bishops resigned their posts in the state church, while affirming their intention to continue pastoring their people. They published a declaration stating:

> To continue administrative cooperation with a state that uses force against the Church would be to break faith with the Holy of Holies. As the time came for Luther, so it has come for us to follow our convictions and to uphold the righteousness of the Church as opposed to the injustice of the State. . . . God Himself stands opposed to tyranny through the power of His Word and His Spirit. Woe unto us if we here do not obey God rather than man.[21]

When Roman Catholic Bishop Mangers issued a supporting statement, he was summoned to Gestapo headquarters, threatened, and ordered to withdraw his signature. 'You can take my head, but not my signature' was his firm reply.[22]

In April 1942 ninety-three per cent of Norway's Lutheran clergy followed their bishops' lead and resigned from the fascist-run state church. Quisling tried to get round this by making himself head of the church and appointing his followers as pastors. But parishioners boycotted the services and followed their former pastors.

Eivind Berggrav, bishop of Oslo and titular head of the Norwegian church, spoke out so strongly against the government that they forbade him to preach. He replied: 'If you want to keep me from going to church, you will have to use force.'[23] Quisling responded by first imprisoning him, then putting him under house arrest. The bishop later said of the struggle against Nazism: 'We were called to battle for the Gospel, to protect right and justice. Here God's cause and the country's cause were one.'[24]

Bishop Berggrav was guarded by twelve special police under orders to permit no visitors. But his loving and forthright manner so won over his captors that soon he was exchanging visits with Resistance leaders and writing manifestoes. One guard even made a police uniform to fit the bishop so that he could travel in disguise to Oslo.

Finally, in April 1945, his guards helped him escape. The bishop, concerned that the men would be shot for assisting him, tied them up with British parachute cords, thus giving the impression that a team of paratroopers had overpowered the guards and freed him.

Quisling gave up his efforts to control the Norwegian church. Hitler himself finally ordered Quisling to give up the whole plan for a corporative state. This resistance to Nazism was remarkable since there was no advance preparation or training for it. Although violent resistance (such as sabotage) occurred, Quisling's efforts to establish the corporative state were defeated primarily by non-military means. While the Nazi regime in Norway was probably less harsh than in other occupied countries (the Nazis had expected Norwegians, as true Aryans and Nordics, to adopt Nazi philosophies), resisters were still imprisoned, tortured and sent to death camps.

Nonmilitary resistance did not free Norway from Nazism. Full liberation came with the Allied military victory over Germany. Yet Norway's struggle stands as an example of how nonmilitary means can withstand severe repression and battle a tyrannous government into a stalemate.

Resisting Hitler's Final Solution

Undoubtedly the most vicious aspect of Hitler's tyranny was his attempt to exterminate Europe's Jewish population. Neither Allied armies nor nonviolent resistance were able to prevent Hitler's mass murder of six million Jews, a crime unprecedented in world history. Nonviolent resistance was practised by only a tiny minority of the people overrun by the Nazis. But this small effort shows that nonmilitary means can play a powerful role in undercutting the plans even of a Hitler.

The Jews who resisted the Nazis sometimes used violent methods. Poorly armed Jewish men, women and children defended the Warsaw ghetto for a month against German troops backed by armoured cars and artillery. But the Jewish community also used a variety of nonmilitary tactics against the Nazi onslaught, saving thousands of their people from destruction. Jewish youth groups, for example, secured false papers for escaping Jews and smuggled them across borders into Spain and Switzerland. Jews in some countries marched in street demonstrations to protest against anti-Semitic laws. Others refused Nazi orders to register as Jews or to move into ghettos. Some would not put on the yellow Star of David which the Nazis ordered them to wear to distinguish them from the rest of the population. In many Jewish ghettos, rabbis, teachers and youth groups published underground newspapers and organised secret schools and prayer services, even though these were punishable by death. Jews reached out to non-Jewish friends, appealing for help and support.

Tragically, most non-Jews turned a deaf ear to this cry for

aid, and so millions of God's people went to the gas chambers and crematoria. A small but significant group of non-Jews, however, engaged in effective nonmilitary resistance against anti-Semitism.

In Nazi-occupied Denmark, the population as a whole used nonviolent methods to thwart Hitler's extermination scheme. A Jewish historian of the period wrote: 'From old King Christian to the lowliest fishermen, the entire Danish people resisted the destruction of its Jews and succeeded in saving most of them.'[25]

Unlike other European countries, Denmark passed no anti-Jewish legislation, did not expropriate Jewish property and did not expel Jews from government jobs. In September 1943, however, Hitler decided that Danish Jews must be shipped to concentration camps. Tipped off by a sympathetic German shipping attaché that mass arrests of Jews would begin in two weeks, the Danes systematically transported seven thousand of them across the Øresund Sound and through the German blockade into neutral Sweden. As one writer noted: 'The saving of Danish Jews was a complete success for resistance by nonviolent means. When the Germans came to arrest the Jews, they were met not by gunfire but by empty houses. Practically the whole Jewish population of Denmark had been warned in advance that arrests would be made. The Jews left their homes, were hidden in hospitals and churches and by friends, until the boats could take them across the Sound to Sweden.'[26] Ninety-three per cent of Denmark's Jewish population made it to Sweden. Only 477 Danish Jews fell into Nazi hands. Most of these survived the war, despite internment in Theresienstadt concentration camp, because of continual intervention on their behalf by Danish officials and the king. Adolf Eichmann, head of the Nazi office for extermination of Jews, admitted that 'the action against the Jews of Denmark has been a failure.'[27]

Finland also refused to give up its Jews, even though it was allied with Germany. Heinrich Himmler, Hitler's chief of security police (the SS), went to the country demanding that the Jews be deported. He threatened to cut off the Finnish food supply if no action was taken. In one conversation, Finnish Foreign Minister Rolf Whitting said in response to Himmler's demands: 'Finland is a decent nation. We would rather perish together with the Jews. We will not surrender the Jews!'[28] Out of two thousand Finnish Jews, only four were ever deported to concentration camps.

Because Scandinavia had a relatively small Jewish population, the Nazis probably were not so ruthless there as elsewhere. But significant nonmilitary resistance took place outside Scandinavia and saved hundreds of thousands of Jewish lives. The Dutch, for example, used mostly nonviolent means to respond to a brutal anti-Jewish campaign. Christian leaders issued pastoral letters. People gathered in large protest demonstrations and strikes. Jews were hidden in homes, given false documents and smuggled out of the country. The famous *Diary of Anne Frank* tells the story of one Jewish family hidden by the Dutch. Corrie ten Boom's *The Hiding Place* recounts the sufferings of a Christian family who hid Jews. The Nazis deported some twenty thousand Dutch Christians to concentration camps along with one hundred and five thousand Dutch Jews. But the resistance helped to save forty-five thousand Jews.

France had a prewar Jewish population of about two hundred and seventy thousand. Whereas its collaborationist Vichy government enacted vicious anti-Jewish laws and assisted in the deportation of thousands of Jews, other French citizens resisted.

Christians were among those who spoke and acted against the Nazi terror. The Archbishop of Toulouse, for example, said publicly: 'The Jews are our brethren. They belong to mankind. No Christian dare forget that.'[29] Protestants and Catholics organised a group called Christian Friendship to place Jewish children in Christian institutions, promising not to convert them.

The Protestant pastor André Trocmé, a strong pacifist, helped make his whole town of Le Chambon in southern France a centre for hiding Jews and smuggling them into

Switzerland. When an official of the Vichy government came to inspect a school that Trocmé had organised, thirty students handed him a letter stating, 'We have learned that in Paris Jews are herded into the stadium and then deported. After that, all trace of them is lost. This, in our Christian eyes, is unbearable. Even though such may be the law in northern France, we will not obey it if applied here in southern France. No matter what the government orders, we will hide Jews.'[30]

Later on, when the citizens of Le Chambon had helped many Jews escape to Switzerland, the Gestapo threatened to level the town in retaliation. The local German commandant, impressed by the honest and loving demeanour of the townspeople, refused to allow it, saying, 'I do not understand these people. But I have talked with them and I know that they do not hate us. . . . You shall not do this thing.'[31]

In other parts of France clandestine organisations were set up to hide Jews and provide them with false identity papers. When Jews were forced to wear the yellow Star of David, many non-Jews did the same. About seventy-five per cent of French Jews escaped the Nazi grasp, although approximately eighty thousand died.

In Italy, an ally of Germany, Jews suffered under harsh fascist legislation which excluded them from the civil service and limited property ownership. But many Italians refused to cooperate with the Nazi programme. The non-military resistance they offered, combined with Jewish measures (including fleeing and going into hiding) saved over eighty per cent of Italy's fifty-seven thousand Jews.

The Bulgarian government, also a German ally, at first passed strict anti-Jewish legislation. Later, however, both Jews and non-Jews resisted all collaboration with the Nazi programme. The Jews themselves organised large street demonstrations to protest at their mistreatment. When it was decreed that Jews wear the yellow star, most refused. Those who did wear the star received such open sympathy from the rest of the population that, according to the Nazi counterintelligence chief, 'they actually are proud of their sign.'[32] In October 1942 the Bulgarian government took the extraordinary step of halting production of the badges by cutting off electricity to the factory manufacturing them.[33]

When under strong Nazi pressure the government issued an order to expel Jews from the capital, Sofia, citizens gathered at the railway station to try to prevent their departure. Large crowds then carried their protest to the front of the king's palace.

The Jews who were sent to the countryside were treated sympathetically by the peasants. Their dispersal into rural areas made it even harder for them to be rounded up for deportation. Meanwhile, Bulgarian unions, town meetings and professional groups sent floods of letters and telegrams to the king and parliament protesting against all anti-Jewish measures.

The top Christian leader of Sofia, Metropolitan Stephan of the Bulgarian Orthodox Church, not only spoke out against persecution of the Jews, but also hid the chief rabbi of Sofia in his own home. The metropolitan told King Boris that persecution of the Jews would put the ruler's soul in mortal danger. Bulgarian clergy accepted large numbers of Jewish converts to Christianity, making clear to them that this was a trick to escape the Nazis and that they could renounce their vows later. Bishop Kiril told the king that if deportations were attempted he would lead a campaign of civil disobedience against them, 'including personally lying down on the railroad tracks before the deportation trains.'[34] Due to these and other nonmilitary forms of resistance, none of Bulgaria's fifty thousand Jews was deported or killed.[35]

Most non-Jews in Europe failed to speak or act against Hitler's genocide out of fear, personal anti-Semitism or apathy. Those who did resist paid a heavy price. Tens of thousands were jailed, tortured, gassed in concentration camps, shot, or hanged in public squares.[36] Yet their heroic actions saved thousands of Jewish lives. They refute the notion that only military means are effective in defending people and their values against the very worst form of outside tyranny.[37]

If nonmilitary means could undercut the final solution, Hitler's most Satanic scheme, then we must ask if such means could not also do effective battle against other totalitarian systems.

Gandhi's Battle with Britain

Far from Europe, another example of successful nonmilitary resistance occurred in India. It is the well-known story of Gandhi's movement to free India from British rule. In three decades of nonviolent struggle, Gandhi's mass action campaign uprooted a powerful British imperial system that had ruled India for over two hundred years. In spite of its overwhelming military forces and a determined effort to stay in control, British rule in India ended with the latter's complete independence on 15 August 1947.

It is sometimes alleged that the British were relatively easy to overthrow because they were decent, civilised people with highly developed consciences who were not given to brutality, repression and depravity.

Certainly the British were not Nazis. But we dare not forget the ruthless methods they employed to colonise India and to put down rebellions, such as the Sepoy rebellion of 1857–58. They machine-gunned unarmed Indians in the Amritsar massacre of 1919 and used torture and other forms of repression in their struggle against the Mau Mau in Kenya and against the revolutionaries of colonial Malaya. They also did not hesitate to kill civilians on a massive scale in bombing attacks on German cities during World War II.

This is not to deny the decent, humane side of British character. But we should not overlook the fact that, historically, Britain has been willing to use brutal methods against opponents who threatened her imperial interests or national liberties.

Struggle in Africa

A less well-known story of nonmilitary resistance to outside invasion took place in Ghana. Great Britain invaded Ghana and defeated its peoples in 1873–74. In 1901 the country became a British colony ruled by a British governor directly responsible to the Colonial Office in London.

Agitation against colonial rule grew over the years. In 1949 Kwame Nkrumah, a US-educated native of Ghana, organised the popular Convention People's Party (CPP), which demanded immediate independence and self-government. When Britain failed to respond, Nkrumah started a well-organised campaign of non-cooperation based on Gandhi's philosophy of nonviolence. He instructed the nation: 'There shall be no looting or burning of houses or rioting or damage or disturbances of any sort. Nonviolence is our creed.'[38]

The CPP's basic tactic was a twenty-day general strike which crippled transportation and shut down the economy. The British responded by jailing Nkrumah and other leaders. However, the CPP won so much respect through its nonviolent tactics that it quickly became Ghana's most powerful political force. On 6 March 1957 it won self-government for Ghana and complete independence from British rule.

Germany Fights Back without Arms[39]

Whereas Ghana's nonmilitary campaign against the British was entirely successful, Germany's nonmilitary resistance to an invasion by France and Belgium in 1923 was only partly effective. It did demonstrate, however, how nonviolent struggle against a militarily powerful invader can achieve significant objectives.

France and Belgium invaded the Ruhr section of Germany on 11 January 1923 because Germany was behind in the reparations imposed on it after World War I. The invaders' goal was to split off the Ruhr area, with its rich coal mines, and put it under French control. Since the defeat in World War I had severely reduced Germany's defence potential, military resistance was impossible. The Germans had to choose between submission and some form of nonmilitary defence.

The government in Berlin told all state, provincial and local authorities not to obey any directives issued by the occupiers. They were to follow only the orders of German officials. They appealed to the inhabitants of the Ruhr: 'Remain steadfast in suffering and in faith, be firm, be calm, be sensible. Have trust in our just cause, and face the invaders with dignity until the day dawns when justice and freedom are restored.'[40]

When French and Belgian troops marched into Essen, a major Ruhr city, they occupied empty factories, mines and government offices. Windows were curtained; shops were closed. The city seemed deserted. Everyone had gone on strike.

The occupiers ordered the coal-mine owners to deliver coal to France and Belgium. The owners refused and were put on trial outside Essen. Thousands of protesters gathered outside the courtroom. Others sent telegrams of protest and delegations objecting to the proceedings. The owners received heavy fines, but their return to Essen became a triumphal procession cheered by large crowds.

In the nonmilitary defence which followed, a large number of creative tactics were used. Civil servants refused to obey orders. When they were arrested, others took their places and continued to work as before. Police quit their jobs rather than salute French officers. Stores and restaurants refused to serve foreign troops. Trolleys stopped dead when soldiers boarded them. When the military entered factories, sirens blared and workers crowded into the yard to demonstrate against the occupation. Newspapers refused to obey censorship rules. When they were shut down by force, they published under a new name. Railway workers stopped the rail system rather than follow orders. When the French and Belgians finally got some trolleys rolling, Germans refused to ride them. Only four hundred workers out of one hundred and seventy thousand previous rail employees agreed to work under the new administration.

Unfortunately, much of the resistance was carried on in a spirit of hatred generated by the past World War. Violent sabotage was mixed in with nonviolent tactics. In one case, for example, Germans blew up a railway bridge, killing ten Belgian soldiers and wounding forty. This gave the occupiers a pretext for clamping down harder than they might otherwise have done.

Also, the nonmilitary resistance was almost totally lacking in preparation and organisation. It was an ad hoc tactic, based on Germany's inability to defend itself militarily. Therefore, it lacked the staying power that a better prepared movement, like Gandhi's, exhibited.

In response to the German defiance, the occupation authorities declared a state of siege and passed innumerable decrees to control key areas of life. Mine owners received enormous fines and long prison sentences. Government officials were exiled to other parts of Germany. Strikers were whipped and clubbed. Troops shot and killed over one hundred people.

The disruption of life in the Ruhr brought great economic hardships, including severe inflation, unemployment and food shortages. In September 1923 the Berlin government agreed unconditionally to stop its resistance and to accept a new schedule of payments. France and Belgium, however, also agreed to withdraw troops. The final settlement was somewhat more favourable to Germany than the one the French had originally demanded. Although Germany had to give up its nonviolent struggle, the French and Belgians failed in their attempt to control the Ruhr.

Our historical examples so far have focused on nonmilitary resistance to invasion, to colonialism, or to the policies of foreign occupiers. Invasion and occupation, however, are not the only circumstances in which unarmed people have overcome a determined and militarily strong opposition. Examples of such resistance are far too numerous to mention here. Dr Gene Sharp in *The Politics of Nonviolent*

Action describes literally hundreds of nonmilitary campaigns – from before the time of Christ to the present – which won victories over powerful oppressors. Even though the majority of the cases he cites do not involve defence against invasion, we can learn lessons about the possibility of nonmilitary defence from them, since they show how people without military weapons can contend successfully against well-armed opponents. We shall mention only two cases of the many that could be cited: in Latin America and the United States.

El Salvador in the 1940s

Because military clashes in the tiny Central American country of El Salvador have been much in the news, it is important to realise that its people once overthrew a Salvadorean dictator by totally *non*-military means. We mention the Salvador case because a repressive dictatorship, even though homegrown, can violate a people's rights just as surely as an outside invader.

General Maximiliano Hernández Martínez came to power in December 1931 through an army coup d'état. In 1932 he put down a peasant insurrection by killing, according to some estimates, as many as thirty thousand people.[41] He then centralised all power, put military officers in control of the government, abolished labour unions, and forbade publication of 'wilful criticism of officials and public employees.'[42] The constitution limited his term of office. But when the term expired, he forced through legal changes that allowed him to continue to rule.

In 1944 objections to his autocratic government boiled over into armed revolt. Martínez squashed the revolt, executing fourteen people and torturing others. In response, a group of university students conceived the idea of a general strike. Martínez could be brought down peacefully, they reasoned, if everyone would simply stop working, thus bringing political and economic life to a grinding halt.

The students spread the idea through leaflets and secret meetings. During the next two weeks, doctors left their posts at hospitals; lawyers abandoned the courts; engineers resigned government jobs; teachers and students left their classes; shopkeepers closed their doors; the Salvadorean railways suspended operations.

When the police fired on a group without warning and killed a seventeen-year-old boy, thousands of Salvadoreans poured into the streets in protest. At the large funeral procession which followed, students set up a peace-keeping force to help calm public anger. In one case they prevented irate citizens from lynching the army chief of staff.

At first Martínez was adamant. When a delegation of doctors presented him with a declaration calling for reforms, he took out a match and burned the document in front of them. He threatened shopkeepers with loss of licences, fired doctors at the government hospital, charged on the radio that the strike was a Nazi plot, and sent armed police to workers' homes to order them back to their jobs. Finally, however, faced with massive popular unrest, low morale among his soldiers and threats of resignation from his cabinet, the dictator resigned. In exile in Guatemala, he made the following statement: 'In the first few days of April, I defeated the seditionaries with arms, but recently they provoked a strike. Then I no longer wanted to fight. Against whom was I going to fire? Against children and against youths who did not completely realise what they were doing? Women also were enlisted in the movement, and in this way I no longer had an objective at which to fire.'[43]

Latin America is thought of as the continent of violent revolution, but El Salvador's experience with nonmilitary revolution is not unique. Nonviolent general strikes have overthrown at least seven Latin American dictators, including: Carlos Ibáñez del Campo of Chile (1931), Gerardo Machado of Cuba (1933), Jorge Ubico of Guatemala (1944), Elie Lescot of Haiti (1946), Arnulfo Arias of Panama (1951), Paul Magloire of Haiti (1956), and Gustavo Rojas Pinilla of Colombia (1957).

Black Americans Defend Their Human Rights

Perhaps the example of effective nonviolent resistance best known to us is that of the Civil Rights Movement. America's Civil Rights Movement is not, of course, an example of citizens defeating an invader. But the story of Black Americans' nonviolent effort to overcome discrimination and gain rights that had been denied them for centuries – an effort carried on in the face of lynchings, beatings, jailings, bombings and assassinations – shows again the power of nonviolent struggle against oppression.

Since readers are probably familiar with this movement, we will not recount its story here. But we want to point out that an important element was the commitment to love the enemy – to show good will toward those in opposition. Understandably, civil rights protesters were not always able to maintain this commitment. In the heat of struggle, confronted with so much hatred, they sometimes struck back in rioting or isolated acts of violence. But all in all, the Civil Rights Movement, under Dr Martin Luther King, Jr, maintained a firm nonviolent discipline. Attacked by ferocious police dogs, soaked with fire hoses, beaten with axe handles, vilified by screaming mobs, the protesters most often responded with remarkable courage, patience and turning of the other cheek.

Whites who supported this mostly Black movement were continually amazed at how Black people could show good will toward their opponents, even in the face of incredible provocation. A White woman from Philadelphia who joined a freedom rally in a Black church in Williamston, North Carolina, noted that the heads of many Black participants were bandaged. White segregationists had beaten them viciously during earlier attempts to integrate the town's public amenities. Yet as they filed out of the church toward a furious White crowd determined to prevent any integration, she was astounded to hear Black marchers praying quietly, 'Lord Jesus, help us to love our enemies; Lord Jesus, help us to love our enemies.'[44]

When Dr Martin Luther King Jr's house was bombed on

30 January 1956 he urged the angry Blacks who gathered on the front yard to put away their weapons, to practise nonviolence and to 'love our white brothers no matter what they do to us.'[45] King's philosophy is best summed up in the words that appeared often in his sermons and writings: 'Returning hate for hate multiplies hate, adding deeper darkness to a night already devoid of stars. Darkness cannot drive out darkness; only light can do that. Hate cannot drive out hate; only love can do that.'[46]

Primitive Christianity and Roman Occupation

King's words reflect a spirit found much earlier in Christianity – the spirit of the primitive church as it confronted a hostile pagan world. We often forget that Christianity sprang up in a region occupied by a foreign invader that used brutal military power to enforce its will. As we saw in chapter six, it was in occupied territory that Jesus instructed his disciples to love their enemies and turn the other cheek.[47]

The church of the first three centuries had plenty of opportunity to practise these teachings. Prior to the conversion of the Emperor Constantine, Roman Caesars mounted ten major persecutions against the fledgling church. The Emperor Nero, for example, had Christians torn to pieces by dogs and set afire to illuminate his ghastly circuses. When Christians refused to obey the Emperor Decius's decree that all citizens sacrifice to the gods, many were imprisoned or executed. Emperor Valerian in AD 257 punished by death any Christians attending church. He also ordered bishops, priests and deacons to be executed. Diocletian in AD 303 ordered the destruction of church buildings and used torture to try to force Christians to deny their faith.

Wholesale slaughter of Christians was not unknown. In one case, 'a Christian town was surrounded by soldiers and burned, together with its inhabitants.'[48] In addition to official governmental oppression, Christians also faced persecution by irate members of pagan society.

Early Christians, therefore, had to respond to the tyranny and oppression of foreign rulers. What did they do? Like the resisters of our earlier examples, the primitive Christians engaged in active struggle against what they saw as evil. When Rome passed decrees which violated Christian conscience, church members responded with protest and noncooperation. Cecil John Cadoux reports:

> One Christian tore down the first edict of persecution posted up by Diocletianus; another fearlessly seized the governor's hand as he was in the act of sacrificing and exhorted him to abandon his error; another strode forward in open court and rebuked the judge for his ruthless sentences. A Christian woman, dragged to the altar and commanded to sacrifice upon it, kicked it over. . . .
>
> The faithful Christian always met the demand for sacrifice to the heathen gods or for an oath to the genius of the Emperor with a firm and unqualified refusal, whatever penalty he [or she] might thereby incur. . . .
>
> It seems not to have been uncommon for Christians attending trials of their co-religionists to protest boldly in open court against the condemnation of innocent men [and women], and by thus disclosing their own faith to draw the death sentence upon themselves also. . . .
>
> Christians condemned in the persecution to undergo a boxing contest [in the gladiatorial games] went on a hunger strike and refused to submit themselves to the necessary training.[49]

While some Christians broke under persecution and fled or renounced their faith, the official stance of the church was to refuse any step which required a Christian to violate his or her beliefs. Christian leaders poured forth a torrent of protest, defiance and censure against the persecutors and their decrees. But they did it without violence and with a willingness to endure suffering. As St Chrysostom, a church leader of the fourth century, said: 'What then, ought we not to resist an evil? Indeed we ought; but not by retaliation. Christ hath commanded us to give up ourselves to suffering wrongfully, for thus we shall prevail over evil. For one fire is not quenched by another fire, but fire by water.'[50]

This nonviolent stance of the primitive church, as we saw in chapter five, was so strong that no Christian writer up until the time of Constantine condoned Christian participation in warfare. The church leader Origen (AD 185–254) made a typical statement when he said, 'We Christians no longer take up sword against nation, nor do we learn to make war anymore, having become children of peace for the sake of Jesus, who is our leader.'[51] Tertullian, the great apologist, wrote that Christians were numerous enough to successfully resist the Caesars by force of arms, but that they would rather be killed than kill.[52]

The early Christians, however, went beyond simply not killing their enemies. They sought to pray for their enemies and to love them. Aristeides says of the Christians: 'They appeal to those who wrong them and make them friendly to themselves; they are eager to do good to their enemies; they are mild and conciliatory.' 'They are reviled and bless,' says the friend of Diognetus, 'they are insolently treated, and they are respectful.' Justinus says, 'We pray for our enemies and try to persuade those who hate us unjustly.'[53] The church leader Justinian exhorted Christians with the questios: 'If you love merely those that love you, what do you that is *new*?' Tertullian told them that love of enemies is 'the principal precept' of Christian life.[54]

The minds of the early Christians were immersed in scriptural passages enjoining love for enemies and forbidding retaliation and vengeance. In fact, they used the Sermon on the Mount as the basic text to instruct new converts in the faith.[55] Thus, when St Cyprian confronted his persecutors, he could say in all honesty: 'None of us offers resistance when he is seized, or avenges himself for your unjust violence, although our people are numerous and plentiful. . . . It is not lawful for us to hate, and so we

please God more when we render no requital for injury.
. . . We repay your hatred with kindness.'[56]

The Christians of the first centuries of the church saw this
mild and conciliatory attitude, not just as something commanded by Christ, but as a power that would reach into
their enemies' souls, confront them with God's love and
open them to repentance and faith. It was in this belief
that the church leader Ignatius instructed the church at
Ephesus:

> And on behalf of the rest of men, pray unceasingly. For
> there is in them a hope of repentance, that they may
> attain to God. Allow them, therefore, to become disci-
> ples even through your works. Towards their anger [be]
> ye gentle; towards their boasting [be] meek; against their
> railing [oppose] ye your prayers; against their error [be]
> ye steadfast in faith; against their savagery [be] ye mild.
> . . . Let us be found their brothers in forbearance; and let
> us be eager to be imitators of the Lord.[57]

Christianity began as the faith of a tiny minority whose
founder was executed by a repressive state. It was treated
with contempt by pagan philosophers, disdained by its
surrounding culture, persecuted by the powerful caesars
who eventually tried to stamp it out entirely. However, as
church historian Kenneth Scott Latourette has said, 'In
what must have seemed an unequal contest between naked,
ruthless force and unarmed, passive resistance, it was not
the imperial government but Christianity which emerged
victor.'[58] Christianity not only defeated its pagan and Roman persecutors, but eventually won the professed allegiance of much of the Empire's population and even of the
state.

Of course, much more than nonviolent resistance and
love of enemies was involved here. More central to winning
the Empire was Christian preaching of the gospel message
and the reliance of early Christians on the power of the
Holy Spirit.

But it is just as clear that the gospel would not have been

heard if it had not been embodied in people who, within the limits of human fallibility and sin, were living it out. Jesus became real to the pagan world not only because pagans heard the gospel, but also because they met disciples. They saw a company of people whose lives had been transformed by the Holy Spirit, who were trying to follow Jesus, and who, like their Lord, stood up against evil with sacrificial love. The gospel of the cross became real because non-Christians saw Christians bearing their own crosses in a myriad of confrontations with evil.[59] The early church overcame Roman tyranny by loving nonviolence.

Implications for Nonmilitary Defence

At the outset of this discussion we asked whether there is a means of defending a nation and its people which avoids both passive submission to tyranny and the dangers and immorality of modern war. Could we design a nonmilitary defence system which could defend democracy and give people the security they formerly sought in armaments? Could such a system meet Jesus' high call to love all people, even enemies?

If the goal of national defence is to preserve a people's values and institutions, to maintain national sovereignty and to prevent tyranny from imposing its will on a nation, then the examples we have described must be extremely thought-provoking. All used nonmilitary means to battle against tyranny and to preserve a valued way of life.

Of course none of these historical examples prove that nonmilitary means can be substituted for military ones in the defence of a nation. But they show that people *have* thwarted tyranny and defended their most precious values without violence or military weaponry. They show that invaders and occupiers *have* been defeated nonviolently. They point to a power to resist evil which does not rely on the ability to kill and injure.

The historical examples are all the more remarkable when we consider their very primitive and unrefined nature as compared with military defence. Usually nonmilitary

movements have not used any advance preparation or
training. This suggests that a more carefully thought-out
and prepared nonmilitary defence could produce even
more powerful results.

Dr Kenneth Boulding, a social scientist, expounds what
he calls Boulding's First Law: 'What exists is possible.'[60]
Nonmilitary defence exists. In the next chapter we will
describe how its theory and methods might be applied to
the defence of a nation.

'Modern man is travelling along a road called hate, in a journey that will bring us to destruction and damnation. Far from being the pious injunction of a Utopian dreamer, the command to love one's enemy is an absolute necessity for our survival. Love even for enemies is the key to the solution of the problem of our world. Jesus is not an impractical idealist; he is the practical realist.'

Dr Martin Luther King, Jr[1]

14

How Nonmilitary Defence Works

Nonmilitary defence might be defined as systematic, organised, active, nonviolent resistance against a power which is regarded as evil, unjust or contrary to a particular way of life. Its purpose is to protect a nation's freedom and sovereignty and to thwart the goals of an invading enemy. The first and most important characteristic of nonmilitary defence is that it is *active*. It is not a passive, sit-on-your-hands approach, as terms such as *passive resistance* or *nonviolence* might indicate. It is neither weak nor cowardly. It requires both physical and moral courage. This is why the active term *defence* is appropriate.

Yet this is not a defence which uses standard military training and procedures. It is defence as practised by the entire (or almost entire) population of a country. Hence the expression *civilian-based defence* (CBD) has become widely used in writings on this subject.[2]

Civilian-based defence encompasses a number of general features. One is that CBD is grounded in *noncooperation*. The population refuses to cooperate with orders, laws or policies that appear to be evil or unjust. Citizens strike, mount boycotts, refuse to pay taxes. They deny a usurper's sovereignty. They say no to joining his[3] organisations. They accept arrest, exile or even death rather than assent to tyranny or oppression.

CBD is also *nonviolent*. Rather than replying to the opponent's violence in kind, the defenders suffer under it, seeking simultaneously to limit it, make it ineffective and end it. In this rejection of violence, CBD is most unlike military defence. But in the expectation of suffering, it is similar. Both CBD and military defence assume that victory demands sacrifice and that people may be injured or die in battle. Both require courage and willingness to take risks. Neither can easily abide what Tom Paine, the American patriot, called 'the summer soldier and the sunshine patriot,' for both agree with him that 'tyranny, like hell, is not easily conquered.'

Sometimes another important ingredient is found in CBD – the expression of *good will* toward opponents. We believe that this aspect of CBD is even more crucial than some have thought. Good will can profoundly deepen the effectiveness of resistance, as Bishop Berggrav of Norway discovered when his loving persuasion turned his jailers into helpers.

In this chapter we want to look at the features of CBD and why unarmed resistance movements have been effective against some heavily armed invaders and dictators. Why haven't the latter, with all their ability to cause suffering and death, simply overwhelmed the resisters and forced them to submit? What about the theory that power derives from violence and victory goes to the side with more and better guns?[4]

The Power of Mass Involvement

The ability of CBD to generate significant power stems from its five unique features. The first is the involvement of large numbers of people.[5] In ordinary warfare the actual fighting is done by military units made up of a small percentage of the nation's total population. If civilians are involved in the fighting it is as casualties or refugees. When one side is defeated, the war ends. The enemy can march in and take over a demoralised nation. If resistance continues, it is by an underground organisation which, again, makes up only a small percentage of the population.

In CBD enemy occupation is considered the *beginning*, not the end of the battle. The distribution of enemy soldiers and functionaries throughout the country is seen not as defeat, but as 'the initial stage of a longer struggle at close range.'[6] The whole population resists. The invading troops meet not a beaten and prostrate nation, but a trained and prepared citizenry whose 'combat strength' has not yet been tested and who are ready to engage in protracted struggle to preserve their way of life. Gene Sharp makes clear how this action works:

> [CBD] can be actively applied by men and women, old and young, city dwellers and rural people, factory workers, intellectuals and farmers, educated and uneducated, able-bodied and the physically weak. Virtually no one in the population need be excluded. This makes possible a much higher number of actual combatants than in any other technique. . . . This will not only increase the strength of the grievance group, but this large and diverse popular participation is also likely to cause especially severe problems for the opponent. There will be many more people against whom he must act. . . . Application of his usual control measures and repression against the old, women, the young, handicapped, etc. – the very groups usually excluded from active combat – is likely to provoke reactions which weaken his power position and strengthen that of the nonviolent group.[7]

The Power of Resistance and Noncooperation

Active resistance and noncooperation are the second and third features of CBD. In ordinary warfare once a nation is conquered the defeated population grudgingly and despairingly goes along with the new rulers. They generally obey the new regime and accept its leaders because they assume that the military strength of the invaders *requires* obedience.

For example, most of the French population cooperated with the German government after the French army was defeated in World War II. Economic life went on much as before. The collaborationist government of Marshal Pétain kept the bureaucracy running smoothly. Bands played in the parks. French police helped the Gestapo track down and arrest French resisters. Some French actors even went to Germany and made films. The moderately successful resistance to deportation of French Jews, which we described in chapter twelve, was a resistance to an *aspect* of the German occupation, not to the occupation itself.

In CBD, however, enemy occupation signals the start of massive resistance. The population does not accept the equation: guns = power. In truth the enemy's power lies in the fear and obedience elicited by his guns. So the people refuse to give in to that fear. They determine not to obey. They realise that their consent to be ruled is voluntary.

This noncooperation takes many forms. People commit acts of *omission* by refusing to do things that the enemy commands. (The Hungarians refused to pay Austrian taxes; the Norwegian bishops resigned from the Nazi-controlled state church.) The people commit acts of *commission* by doing things the enemy forbids. (The Danes hid Jews and transported them safely to Sweden.) Through a thousand acts they defy the enemy, dramatise public disapproval of the occupation and maintain allegiance to their own way of life.

Even when the enemy punishes citizens with prison, exile, torture and death, they remain firm. They will *never* do the enemy's will. This defiance is extremely disruptive to the conqueror. Power to govern rests on a significant degree of willing cooperation by the governed. In the words of Lt Col Alun Gwynne Jones, who served with the British army in Burma, Palestine, East Africa, Malaya and Cyprus, 'Whether one has invaded the country to use the railway lines that run through it, to use its granaries to feed one's troops, or to use its industrial potential for a further development of one's political aims, it is always vital to have the cooperation of that country.'[8] An invader's power, therefore, is dependent on sources outside his own military and bureaucracy. It depends to an important degree on the consent of those who are ruled.

To consolidate his rule, the invader requires people to perform a multitude of political, economic and social functions. He requires the skills of a myriad of local administrators and technicians. He needs people to submit to the ideology of his new order, just as Quisling needed the Norwegian teachers to implement his corporate state. He cannot arrest or replace at a stroke the millions of people who make a society work.

In CBD the population refuses this necessary acquiescence. They make it impossible for the occupier to consolidate his rule. They continually undercut the power on which his rule is based. In doing so, they necessarily build their own countervailing power. The enemy may find that, instead of winning an easy victory, he has fallen into a political ambush.

The Power of Nonviolence

The fourth feature of CBD is its refusal to use violence and the willingness of its practitioners to suffer rather than to inflict suffering. In ordinary warfare, a contest's outcome hinges on which side can cause the most injury and death to the other. 'The most effective way of imposing one's will has always been to make the opponent suffer until he gives in or to kill him if he persists in his obstinacy.'[9] As in the simplest fight between two children, when one side says uncle, the other side wins.

At first glance, the refusal of violence seems to give an enormous advantage to the side holding military weapons. Paradoxically, however, this apparent powerlessness can become a form of power. As we saw in the last chapter, El Salvador's General Martínez took only two days to crush an armed revolt against his dictatorship in April 1944. But when faced with unarmed strikers in May, he lost the will to fight – 'Against whom was I going to fire? Against children and against youths . . . ?'[10] The general's experience is only one of hundreds that could be cited in which well-armed soldiers or police refused to fire on nonviolent crowds. The reasons for this are many.

The preservation of any society requires at least a minimum respect for human life. No society can function if citizens are free to kill for whim or personal advantage. The prohibition of murder is so basic a rule that some minimal inhibition against killing is part of every society.

The kill-or-be-killed atmosphere of war or violent social conflict provides the stimulus to overcome this inhibition. People are often taught that the enemy is not human and does not deserve to live. (The Nazis were not taught to kill Jewish mothers, fathers and children, but 'Jewish vermin.') The willingness to kill also increases when people believe that an opponent hates them and wants to kill them. And a soldier in the battlefield with his comrades falling and shells exploding around him realises that he will die if he does not shoot first.

But what if the soldier confronts an opponent who has no weapons and who gives every sign of not hating him? What if he meets unarmed men, women and children who insist that he behave fairly? What if they do not run in fear, but stand up to his violence with their own suffering?[11] What if they act in a way that elevates human dignity?

In such circumstances, a kind of 'moral jujitsu'[12] often occurs. The soldier is thrown off balance. Not meeting the counterviolence he had been trained to expect, not finding his life threatened, not seeing comrades being wounded or killed, the soldier may find it extremely hard to justify violence. It does not seem brave or manly to kill defenceless people. He may develop respect or even sympathy for resisters who are willing to suffer for their beliefs. He begins to doubt the propaganda about the enemy population.

Soldiers, therefore, may find continued repression distasteful. They may start to talk sympathetically to other soldiers about the resistance. They may object to the meaningless brutality they are being ordered to perform. They may become confused, disillusioned and resentful.

They may carry out orders unenthusiastically, inefficiently or not at all.

In some cases, the normal chain reaction of violence producing violence may break completely. The soldier may become unreliable, hostile and mutinous. He may shoot into the air, or even disobey orders and refuse to fire, rather than to kill people who do not harm him and who may even seem to have a just cause.

Of course, refusing to meet violence with violence does not always bring positive results. History holds many examples of soldiers or police killing unarmed people. Less known, however, are the many historical cases where soldiers refused to shoot unarmed civilians, even though they were punished or even executed for their disobedience. During the 1917 Russian revolution, for example, peaceful demonstrators talked to soldiers and tried to win them over. The Volynsky regiment was one of several which at first shot at the demonstrators, but then mutinied and refused to fire.[13] These mutinies undercut the Czar's power and were crucial to the revolution.

At the time of India's struggle against the British, 'a group of soldiers were court-martialled in the frontier province after they had refused to fire on a mass meeting of Gandhi's followers.'[14] In another dramatic case, one of hundreds that could be cited from this conflict, a follower of Gandhi was hit again and again by police until blood flowed from his face, and he fell to the ground. An observer reported: 'With a grin he stood up to receive some more. The police sergeant drew back to strike a final blow. Then he dropped his arms to his side, and said to a nearby newspaper reporter: "It's no use. . . . You can't hit a bugger when he stands up to you like that." '[15]

In more recent times, during the Soviet invasion of Czechoslovakia in 1968, Czechs stood without weapons in front of Soviet tanks and even climbed onto the turrets and argued with the soldiers. One Soviet tank captain responded: 'I am afraid that you are right about a number of things. [The invasion] is a terrible tragedy.'[16] Disobeying orders was so widespread among the soldiers that Soviet commanders had to rotate the invasion troops to prevent them from becoming convinced by the Czech arguments.

The same kind of disobedience occurred among Soviet and Polish troops commanded to put down the predominantly nonviolent uprising in East Germany in 1953. Seventeen Soviet soldiers were subsequently shot for refusing to obey orders.[17]

During the Hungarian revolt of October 1956, nonviolent demonstrators talked to Soviet tank crews. They asked them bluntly why the tanks were firing on peaceful protesters. They explained why they wanted to expel Stalinists from the Hungarian government. In one case, the crew of a Soviet tank said they were convinced of the justice of the Hungarian cause. They asked the demonstrators to go with them to explain what they wanted. The tank, decorated with Hungarian flags and with demonstrators hanging on the sides, then proceeded to the parliament building.[18]

When the British military writer Captain Basil Liddell Hart interrogated German generals after World War II, he found that even these highly indoctrinated men had difficulty with the nonviolent resistance they had encountered:

> Their evidence also showed the effectiveness of nonviolent resistance as practised in Denmark, Holland, and Norway – and, to some extent, in France and Belgium. Even clearer was their inability to cope with it. They were experts in violence, and had been trained to deal with opponents who used that method. But other forms of resistance baffled them – and all the more in proportion as the methods were subtle and concealed. It was a relief to them when resistance became violent.[19]

There is ample historical evidence, then, that nonviolence can have a 'moral jujitsu' effect on soldiers and police. Another important effect of nonviolence is its impact on bystanders. Often courageous suffering will arouse sympathy and lend crucial support to the resisters' cause. Thus the Gandhian movement in India won support from the British population and made it more difficult for the colonial government to repress the freedom movement. Similarly, the nonviolent response of Black civil rights protesters in the United States won sympathy from the broader American population. The political pressure of this larger group helped to pass the major civil rights legislation sought by the Black movement.

The nonviolent response of the early church to persecution also brought sympathy and support from third parties. In the words of the church historian Cadoux:

> The endurance of suffering [by the Christians] aroused the sympathy, as well as the astonishment, of the onlookers. Some were moved to pity and grief; others admired and congratulated. At the prayers of Polycarpus in the face of death, many were amazed and repented that they had come to witness his martyrdom. When Thecla was led to the stake and exposed to the beasts, the governor, so it was said, wept, and the women and children protested and invoked the penalty of destruction on themselves and their city. When Agathonice leaped on to the pyre, the bystanders exclaimed: 'What a dreadful judgement! What unjust orders!' . . . That martyrdoms were the means of winning over many to Christianity there can be no doubt. The Apostles proudly ask non-Christians to observe that the more the Christians are persecuted, the more their numbers increase.[20]

If civilian resistance can in this way build respect and sympathy while baffling the invader's leaders, reducing morale and causing soldiers to mutiny, it will undercut the aggressor's power and add to its own.[21]

The Power of Good Will
In ordinary warfare, contempt for and hatred of the enemy are the fuels that drive the military machine. The enemy is

the 'Hun,' the 'Jap,' the 'Gook.' Any meaningful attempt to do good to the enemy is condemned as collaboration or treason.

In CBD, on the other hand, the resisters act on the premise that 'the answer to profound hatred is profound love.'[22] This is the fifth characteristic of CBD as we define it.[23] In the practice of CBD, resisters condemn evil aggression but try to show concern for evil-doers as persons.[24] Not only do they not harm enemy soldiers, but they also surprise the enemy with acts of consideration and kindness.

In those nonviolent movements deeply inspired by the life and teachings of Jesus, the resisters go even further. They try to see beneath the surface of an enemy to find the person of inestimable worth who is made in God's image, who is loved by the Father and whom Jesus died to save.[27] They seek to speak to their antagonists, to be vulnerable, even to be ready to heal their enemy's wounds. They take seriously the apostle Paul's call to bless when cursed (1 Cor 4:12) and thus to overcome evil with good (Rom 12:21). They take whatever opportunity presents itself to speak to the enemy about the gospel and its saving power.[28]

If they are attacked, they try to practise, as did Martin Luther King, Jr, 'the necessity, over and over again, of forgiving those who inflict evil and injury upon us.'[29] If they are imprisoned, they try to accept it without bitterness, remembering the cloud of Christian witnesses who have been imprisoned before them. If they face death, they hope to die like Stephen (Acts 7:60), praying that God will forgive their enemies. Knowing that only Christ himself can give the power to love as he taught, they 'pray at all times in the Spirit' (Eph 6:18) for that union with the Lord which enables one to love even in the face of hatred.

An African family in Kenya exemplified this spirit to an extraordinary degree. The Mau Mau (a terrorist group) had tried to force Pastor Samuel Muhoro and his wife, Sara, to take an oath to kill Europeans. Though cut and stabbed by the terrorists' knives, the couple stood fast. 'We saw Jesus standing by our side. Our bodies were badly beaten and blood was flowing like water, but he was with us. He gave us words of love to speak to our persecutors, who said they didn't know we were "that type of God people," and asked for our prayers.'[30]

Where does this immense faith in the power of love and good will come from? The world thinks of love as weak. Love of enemies is unrealistic at best and traitorous at worst. Christians, however, know that love has immense power. Genuine love, according to the New Testament, is of the very essence of God, 'for God is love' (1 Jn 4:8). It is the astonishing character of God's love for his sinful 'enemies' that overcomes their hostility (1 Jn 4:9–11). In Christian thought, therefore, love is the most powerful force in the universe. As Dr Lewis Smedes of Fuller Theological Seminary has written in his book on 1 Corinthians 13:

> Everything rests on the power of love. . . . Love holds all things together, carries them along, keeps them moving, sustains them. Love is the amazing power that makes the world go around and human history move ahead. Love is the power that sustains the universe itself; it is the invisible foundation of all the structures of life. . . . It is the energy that catalyses all other sources of energy. . . . Agapaic love, therefore, is the central, dominant, and ultimately irresistible power of the universe. Love is more powerful than evil.[31]

Agape is the Greek word which the Bible uses to describe the love of God. It is outgoing, creative good will to every creature, every person. It is a love which makes the 'sun rise on the evil and on the good, and sends rain on the just and on the unjust' (Mt 5:45). It is a love which reaches out to enemies and friends alike. According to Christian faith, it is seen most clearly in the cross of Christ, where the Son of God accepted the worst his enemies could do and responded with love and forgiveness. In the 'weakness' of the cross, as Louis Smedes says, 'infinite power was set loose in the world. . . . Ultimate kindness is ultimate power.'[32]

Jesus calls Christians to take up their own cross of suffering love.[33] When this cross bearing leads Christians to love those who persecute them, then they imitate Christ. When we love with cross-bearing love, 'God abides in us and his love is perfected in us' (1 Jn 4:12). When we commit ourselves to agape love, we experience the miracle of 'God himself working in us.'[34]

Agape love has seldom if ever been expressed in all its fullness in mass movements against tyrants or invaders. What would be the result if it were? If it is hard for a soldier to shoot unarmed demonstrators, it would be even more difficult for him to fire on people who are praying for him, protecting him and forgiving him. Indeed, like the German commandant of Le Chambon, he might find himself protecting the very people his superiors ordered him to suppress.[35]

When in the power of the Holy Spirit, Christian resisters apply Christ's love for enemies, the most powerful force in the universe is at work. It is not surprising, then, that the expression of such love can have enormous impact on the enemy. Love compels him to question the rightness of what he is doing. Love softens his heart. Love touches his conscience. Love awakens in him a longing for reconciliation with his neighbour and with God.[36]

This process may not be evident on the surface. At some level within the opponent, however, God is using agape love to arouse in the enemy that 'hope of repentance' about which Ignatius wrote in his letter to the Ephesian church.

Even if the resister is not acting out of a Christian context, evidence exists that the expression of caring, outgoing love has significant power to produce positive results. Dr Pitirim Sorokin, a well-known sociologist who before his death did extensive research on altruistic love, concluded: 'Evidence of the power of love is supplied by innumerable facts showing that unselfish love is at least as "contagious" as hate and that love influences human behaviour as tangibly as hate does. . . . The main rule that love begets love and begets it as frequently as hate generates hate is clear from the data. . . . The rule of love begetting love has been well confirmed.'[37]

The opponent, however, is not the only one who is influenced by the power of agape love. The resister also experiences its power. For example, when the Black civil rights marchers of Williamston prayed, 'Lord, help us to love our enemies,' they received strength to walk with courage into a raging, club-wielding mob. Sharing Christ's sufferings, they came to 'know him and the power of his resurrection' (Phil 3:10). They discovered the reality behind the words of Paul: 'We are afflicted in every way, but not crushed; perplexed, but not driven to despair; persecuted, but not forsaken; struck down, but not destroyed; always carrying in the body the death of Jesus, so that the life of Jesus may also be manifested in our bodies' (2 Cor 4:8–10).

Dom Helder Câmara has been called a contemporary Brazilian apostle of nonviolence. His house has been machine-gunned and his life threatened innumerable times. He has described movingly the power that can come to those who follow Jesus' way of cross-bearing love:

> Very often I am questioned about living here all alone, especially during the night, opening the door myself to all the callers. It would be so easy to be killed they say.
>
> My reply is always the same, 'But I do not live by myself.'
>
> 'Ah, yes . . . so there is someone else here?'
>
> 'But certainly. There are three persons – the Father, the Son, and the Holy Spirit. See! How I am protected!'[38]

The mighty power of God is present in those who engage in loving resistance to aggression. For Christians God provides inner resources to stand up to oppression with patience, confidence, boldness and endurance.[39] This is an armour (Eph 6:11) which ultimately gives more protection than missiles or guns.[40]

In summary, then, the power of CBD is based on its

potential to thwart an aggressor's plans. CBD uses a large portion of the population in widespread resistance, thus frustrating the opponent by giving him innumerable targets against which to act. It can undercut a crucial aspect of the opponent's power by causing disobedience and mutiny among soldiers and police. It can cause dissension in the invader's ranks, making it harder to carry out consistently repressive policies. It can arouse sympathy and support from third parties within and outside the invaded country. And CBD can bring into the struggle the awesome force of agape love, with its God-given ability both to strengthen the resister and to convert the enemy.

Christians and Civilian-based Defence

We have assumed that non-Christians, as well as Christians, would participate in CBD. But we believe Christians would play a special role. Our basic assumption has been that national defence through nuclear weapons is totally incompatible with Christian faith. We hope that we have shown through our historical examples and our description of CBD that there is no conflict between the gospel and CBD. Joining a movement based on the five characteristics of CBD (large-scale participation, resistance to evil, non-cooperation with injustice, refusal to kill, and good will toward opponents) would enable Christians to implement the New Testament's call to be peacemakers, to love their enemies and to overcome evil with good. CBD, therefore, is a form of national defence in which Christians can join with integrity.

Moreover, Christians can give vitally needed leadership in CBD. In the past, Christians often have been at the forefront of movements which sought to defend people and values by nonmilitary means. In many of the historical cases we cited, Christians took extremely important roles. Therefore, we would expect that, if America and Western Europe were to choose a nonmilitary defence system, Christians would make an enormously crucial contribution. In the description of a CBD system for the United States which follows, we have assumed that Christians are not only participants, but also active leaders.

The style and motive of Christian participants, however, will be different from that of persons whose goal is only to preserve their nation against national enemies. Christians have concerns which go far beyond the desire to 'provide for the common defence.'[41] They belong to Christ and are first and foremost citizens of his kingdom (Mt 6:33). The flag is not their object of ultimate allegiance. They can struggle with non-Christians to resist the invader's evil designs and to uphold freedom and justice. Yet they know that their ultimate battle is not 'against flesh and blood, but against the principalities, against the powers, . . . against the spiritual hosts of wickedness in the heavenly places' (Eph 6:12). And they know also what many superpatriots do not know. There are evils and injustices in the United States and Western Europe, as well as in any enemy. God, with his winnowing fork, will be at work to correct all injustice.

In addition, Christians' attitudes toward opponents are different from those of non-Christians. Christians see enemies as persons whom Christ has commanded us to love, as precious individuals whom the gospel may bring to salvation.

Finally, as we have noted, Christians can draw upon resources unknown to non-Christians. To those who are in Christ Jesus, the Spirit provides gifts of endurance, patience, courage, steadfastness, boldness, confidence and strength. Gifted with these resources and this perspective, Christians can join other citizens and make a unique contribution to the nonmilitary battle against tyranny.

'We have grasped the mystery of the atom and rejected the Sermon on the Mount.'
General Omar Bradley, US Army Chief of Staff[1]

'Today the choice is no longer between violence and nonviolence. It is either nonviolence or nonexistence.'
Dr Martin Luther King, Jr[2]

15

Defending a Nation by Nonmilitary Means

If a nation adopted a civilian-based defence system, what would it look like? We cannot give a detailed description any more than a military tactician can say exactly how military defence would unfold in all its details. Different circumstances – the nature of the attack, the goals of the attacker – call for different responses. But we can describe some overall principles and some possible tactics to give an idea of how CBD would look. The nation featured in the scenario which follows is the USA, although the principles can of course be applied to other nations.

The following assumes that, after intense debate over a number of years, the country elected a president and a Congress committed to CBD. Such a decision seems almost unthinkable at present, but as more and more people come to see the severe dangers of the present policy, openness to an alternative will increase.

If as a nation the USA decided to adopt CBD, it would not abandon all attempts to foster multilateral disarmament. But it would publicly announce its intention to disarm regardless of the response of others. It would embark on a massive national programme of CBD. It would train every citizen to take his or her place in the defence of American freedom and independence. Although certain people would receive specialised training to perform special tasks, every citizen would have a part to play in resisting tyranny, defending American democracy and repulsing the invader. During the several-year process of preparation for CBD, America would get rid of all nuclear and conventional weapons.

We believe that such an action could very likely result in a Soviet invasion. Invasion, to be sure, is not inevitable. It would depend on a number of factors, such as the Soviet's assessment of the gains and losses to be expected from invasion, whether or not Western Europe also adopted CBD, and how the Soviets would view China's response to their invasion of North America. Nor are the Soviets the only possible invaders. Given the topsy-turvy nature of international relations, the Chinese might become again the kind of threat they were thought to be to the United States in the 1950s.

In the following description, however, we have assumed that the Soviet Union is the invader.

If invaded, Americans would respond nonviolently. Two basic principles would underlie the stance of every American resisting aggression:

1. The invader's orders are illegitimate and are not to be obeyed. Our allegiance is to our own constitutional system and to our God. We will follow our own consciences and the laws passed by our democratically elected representatives. We will not follow the decrees of foreign despots who would alter our way of life without our consent. We will die rather than surrender.

2. The invader's troops and functionaries are children of God made in his image. Therefore, we will not harm them, but will seek to show them good will. We will use every opportunity to convince them to give up their oppression.

The initial invasion might be met by a 'nonviolent blitzkrieg' – an all-out demonstration of our will to resist. A general work stoppage would be called. Masses of people would quietly fill the streets and go to the docks, airports and other areas where enemy soldiers would be landing.

The enemy's jumbo jets would disgorge heavily armed combat infantry, tanks and armoured cars. Parachute commandos would move quickly toward key points. Seaborne troops would spread out through coastal cities and towns. Behind them would come administrative staff with supplies to support further operations.

The landing would be peaceful. No American artillery would fire; no jets would strafe. Instead of American soldiers crouching behind tanks and pointing guns at them, the invaders would see tens of thousands of unarmed people carrying signs with messages in the invader's language: Go Home! We Won't Harm You; Don't Shoot – We Are Your Brothers and Sisters; Your Life Is Precious; You Are a Child of God.

Like the Czechs, Hungarians and East Germans during the Russian invasion of those countries, Americans would climb up on tanks and try to talk to soldiers: 'Why have you come? Why are you invading a peaceful nation that is not threatening you?' Loudspeakers would explain that the troops are welcome as tourists but will be opposed as invaders.

Demonstrators would hand out leaflets in the invaders' language, countering the propaganda they had been fed about the reasons for the invasion. The leaflet would explain that the invaders would not be harmed, but that Americans would suffer and die rather than give up their democratic way of life. Each demonstrator would also carry a bilingual pamphlet giving a nonviolent code of discipline such as the following:

OUR COMMITMENT AS FREE PEOPLE
1. We will stand up for our democratic way of life. We will act as free men and women.
2. We will not cooperate with the invasion. We will not obey the invader's orders, decrees or laws, even if the penalty is death.
3. We will not harm the invaders. We will try to convince them that they are wrong. We will protect them from

harm, and try to show them good will, even at the risk of our own lives.˙

If members of the crowd were not able to keep discipline and started to threaten the soldiers, special US Peace-keeping Teams would move in nonviolently to restrain the persons who were losing control. If injuries occurred, the invaders would find that American medical teams were as ready to help them as they were to help the demonstrators.

Determined Noncollaboration

After the initial period of work stoppage and mass demonstrations, people would return to work. They would, however, meet the invaders at every point with staunch noncooperation. Police would refuse to locate or arrest resisters or to follow any other orders. Journalists and editors would refuse to obey censorship rules or to publish enemy propaganda. If shut down, newspapers would appear under new names or would be published by secret presses.[3] Clandestine radios and TV would broadcast from hidden transmitters, as they did in Czechoslovakia during the 1968 Soviet invasion.[4] Information about the attack and resistance would also be beamed overseas to the invaders' home country and to other countries.

Workers and managers in industry would follow their former rules and procedures. No one would join new labour organisations set up by the invaders or attend their meetings. If enemy troops invaded a factory or mine, workers would either stage a sit-down strike and refuse to leave or would abandon the plant entirely, leaving enemy troops to try to run it on their own. Strikes, delays, and the disappearance of indispensable experts and spare parts would paralyse industry put under the invader's management.

Rather than striking or abandoning the plant, however, most workers would continue in their jobs without collaborating with the enemy, the technique used by German workers against the Franco-Belgian invasion of the Ruhr.[5]

All orders from the invader would be ignored. If a supervisor were arrested or removed from the plant, the next person in line would take over and direct operations as before. A person ordered at gunpoint to obey might try 'schweikism,' a practice derived from the Czech novel *The Good Soldier Schweik* by Jaroslav Hašek. Private Schweik repeatedly fouled up his orders because he 'misunderstood' them or was 'too incompetent' to carry them out. This procedure was used by the Czechs against the Soviet invaders in 1968.[6] If the invaders forcibly closed an entire plant, workers would stand outside with signs saying, 'We Want to Work.'

Enemy troops arriving at a city hall would be received courteously by the mayor, but told that he would not surrender any of his previous authority. If the mayor were then arrested or removed, the next in rank would succeed him or her, and so on, down the line of succession. City governments would not enact the invader's laws. City departments would continue functioning until enemy orders were given, when they would ignore them or cease work altogether. If pressure was removed, they would immediately go back to work in the old manner.

Similar noncooperation with the invader's rule would be practised in all areas of American life. Private and professional groups would not recognise or participate in new organisations set up by the invader.[7] Taxpayers would refuse to pay any taxes levied by the invader, as they did in Hungary. As in occupied Norway, teachers would refuse to teach enemy propaganda and would instead teach students to resist. Buses would stop when troops boarded them. Trains would not carry their material. Builders would refuse to put up barracks. Postal and telegraph workers would not transmit enemy messages. Workers in garages and petrol stations would serve the civilian population only. The invader would have to confiscate food supplies, since no one would voluntarily provide them.

Citizens would pour into the streets rather than obey curfew laws. As in Hungary under Austrian occupation, churches would become centres of defiance and rallying points for resistance.[8] Any attempt to suppress religious freedom or to limit any expression of freedom of speech or assembly would produce illegal meetings all over the country. The invaders would be looked upon as unauthorised persons with no right to give orders. Requests by the invader for information would be politely denied. The only information given would be about the advantages of freedom.

Everywhere in the country, acts of protest would symbolise the determination of Americans to maintain their independence. Old 'Don't Tread On Me' buttons from the American revolution might appear on every lapel. Or, as in the Norwegian resistance, people could fasten paper-clips to their lapels, symbolising 'hang together.' Bells would toll. Sirens would wail. Tens of thousands of marchers dressed in black would join funeral processions for resisters killed in the struggle. Popular singers would broadcast new songs extolling the resistance. American flags would fly everywhere.

Because all Americans had received an orientation in effective nonviolent resistance, they would be prepared to carry out protest and noncooperation.[9] Radio appeals, sermons, pamphlets and personal example would reinforce what people learned. If nonviolent discipline broke down and an enemy soldier were injured or killed, the local government might call for a fast to express regret and to seek deeper dedication to nonviolence.

Assertive Good Will

In addition to refusing to harm the enemy, Americans would seek to reach them on a personal level. They would treat the invaders both as children of God and as potential recruits for the democratic way of life.[10] Whenever possible, resisters would speak to the enemy about their way of life and why they are committed to its defence. They would look for opportunities to show unexpected acts of kindness, thus setting in motion the mechanism of 'moral jujitsu.'

Invaders would be treated like alcoholics – people whose habit merits disapproval, but who as individuals merit respect.[11]

Citizens would invite soldiers to union halls, civic clubs and other public places and show them friendly hospitality. Christians would invite the enemy to church and would speak to them about the gospel's liberating power. Remembering Jesus' call to pray for persecutors, churches might stay open day and night. Christians would follow Paul's instructions: 'If your enemy is hungry, feed him; if he is thirsty, give him drink' (Rom 12:20).

Under the pressure of invasion, many churches would experience a rebirth of Christian community. Like the early church under Roman persecution, Christians would find new ways of caring, sharing and laying down their lives for one another.[12] 'See how these Christians love one another!' would again be the amazed response of onlookers. As in apostolic times, this mutual love would be the most persuasive witness to the enemy, the most irresistible missionary expression. The invading enemy would not only hear the gospel message, but see it embedded in loving, worshipping, singing, praising, healing communities – communities that had the courage to stand up for their convictions, and that expressed a love which spilled over, even to the persecuting enemy.

Problems for the Invader

This kind of widespread resistance would cause mammoth problems for the invader. Every American city, town and village would be a battleground. As units of the invader's army moved from one area to another, trying to compel obedience, they would be constantly confronted with transportation problems. Uncooperative train engineers and flight controllers would halt or delay the movement of troops and supplies. If buses, trains or planes were commandeered, the invaders would find that key equipment was 'lost' and that needed fuel had 'spilled.'

More difficult would be actual control. Americans would

refuse to work under anyone but other Americans. At each stage of the enemy advance, enough troops would have to be left behind to hold a gun at the head of each worker or to try to run the local factories, mines and transportation systems by themselves. Enemy personnel would be spread thinly throughout the country.[13] This would create enormous difficulties of supply, communication and coordination. The invader's inability to concentrate his forces would make effective pressure harder to exert on the recalcitrant population. His own troops also would be more subject to the ideas of the resisters. If troops or technicians were pulled out of one area because needed elsewhere, American workers would immediately restore the pre-invasion economy at the rear of the invading force.

The immensity of the control problem can be seen more clearly when we remember that the total number of Soviet armed forces is 3,658,000 regulars, 5,000,000 reserves, and 460,000 paramilitary troops.[14] A large percentage are busy controlling restive satellite nations, patrolling uneasy borders and meeting internal security needs. Even if a significant portion of these troops could be released for a US invasion and new troops added through mobilisation, economic control of the United States would still require subduing 70 million management and blue-collar workers and 4 million farmers.

If these millions of Americans could not be forced to work under Soviet control, it would be impossible to replace them with Soviet technicians. As Commander Sir Stephen King-Hall has commented: 'A modern society . . . cannot possibly be operated by a horde of non-English-speaking foreigners.'[15]

If the invader's objective was political rather than economic control, he would have to arrest and replace – or somehow master – over 13 million federal, state and local government employees.

Even ideological indoctrination would be extremely difficult. If the invader tried to force his views through schools or the mass media, he would be faced with Norwegian-style opposition from nearly 3 million teachers, 60 million students, and a half-million radio, TV and newspaper workers.

But perhaps the biggest problem facing the invader would be from his own troops. Totalitarian governments, like the USSR, go to great lengths to prevent their citizens from experiencing a freer way of life. Usually only the most loyal people are permitted to visit the West. (Even then, defections are fairly common.) The Berlin Wall is only one example of the Soviet rulers' fears of the 'bacteria of democracy.' Apparently they believe that, if too many of their people are exposed to this dangerous disease called freedom, an epidemic of liberty might spread to the home country and sicken the totalitarian state. Already, thousands of Soviet and satellite citizens, infected with the bacteria of freedom, have fled to countries where the search for truth is not crushed by rigid political dogma and one-party control. Captain Sir Basil Liddell Hart says that the real reason the USSR did not overrun Europe after World War II was that Soviet leaders did not want their troops mixing with the people of the West.[16]

A US invasion would require that huge numbers of Soviet citizens enter a culture where free thought, inquiry, speech and assembly are prized above all else. Freedom is catching. How would the invaders prevent their personnel from becoming infected?

The startling contradiction between what enemy soldiers had been told and the real situation in the United States would immediately prompt doubts and questions. These would be compounded by the resisters' commitment to nonviolence and good will. Troops would have to repress unarmed men, women and children who not only pose no threat, but who protect them, pray for them, and show them personal friendship. How long would soldiers be able to continue repression when the only response was sacrificial love? How would they respond to Christians whose only desire was to share with them the gospel message? Would they remain loyal and disciplined, or would they begin to disobey orders and mutiny, as troops have done in the past?

Finally, though these problems might have little effect on the Soviet Union, the invading government might face unrest at home and lack of support for the invasion. In the Franco-Belgian invasion of the Ruhr discussed in chapter thirteen, French soldiers home on furlough told friends and family that the Germans were entirely different from what they had been taught to believe. Also other independent countries of the world might protest against their actions. In 1956 the United Nations took collective nonmilitary action against the Anglo-French Suez expedition.

In anticipation of these many problems, a potential aggressor might even decide not to invade. A decision to attack is based on the desire to achieve some objective. Military and political leaders must decide that a proposed invasion has a reasonable chance of success. They must calculate that the operation will bring gains that outweigh the human and material costs of military engagement. What if these leaders foresee that invasion may bring many negative results – increased dissent and disruption at home, opposition and diplomatic losses abroad, rebellion in satellite nations, disaffection and mutiny in their own invading army, and the inability to achieve meaningful control of the invaded country? Might they decide that the potential risks outweigh the advantages?

Considerations such as these have convinced several students of CBD that a carefully worked-out system of nonmilitary defence could provide the deterrence which is now a major goal of US defence policy.[17]

It is quite likely, of course, that an enemy would perceive CBD as a less potent means of deterrence than nuclear retaliation. Even so, CBD is vastly preferable to nuclear deterrence, both morally and pragmatically. Morally because nuclear deterrence relies upon a willingness to commit mass murder; pragmatically because any failure of nuclear deterrence means unimaginable chaos and worldwide destruction. Any failure of CBD to deter an enemy would lead to a conflict of vastly less violence and with a hope of meaningful resolution.

This does not mean there would be no suffering in CBD. Invasion would bring repression, torture and martyrdom. Although historically nonviolent struggles against oppression have brought many fewer casualties than violent resistance, it is possible that hundreds of thousands, perhaps even millions, might die. But nuclear war would kill vastly more people. And it would make followers of Christ commit genocide. If human life is of inestimable value to God and if we are called to cherish it, then avoiding death and murder on this scale is a divine imperative.

In nuclear strategy, the breakdown of deterrence means the end of any meaningful defence, the annihilation of hundreds of millions of people, and the possible end of civilisation. In CBD the breakdown of deterrence means the initiation of the real defence of a country and its values through the nonmilitary struggle of its citizenry.

Response to Repression

If CBD fails as a deterrent, and an aggressor invades, it is highly likely that the invading army would try to threaten, terrify and coerce the populace into submission. Among the possible methods of repression are levying of fines, denial of food and other supplies, spying, infiltration, use of provocateurs, enforcement of curfews, establishment of prohibited zones, censorship, imprisonment in jails and concentration camps, deportations, hostage taking, torture, random brutality, terrorism, executions, mass reprisals, and extermination of whole groups. Repression may be implemented by regular troops or by special forces or secret police. It may be supplemented by propaganda and by rewards to anyone who cooperates.

Repression should come as no surprise to practitioners of CBD. Again CBD is analogous to military defence. Military strategists realise that victory comes only with great sacrifice, pain, and death. (Over 16 million people died in battles during World War II; the conflict brought some 40 million casualties in all.) Although nonmilitary defence would cause many fewer deaths than military engagement, CBD also requires painful sacrifice to achieve its goals. One cannot buy freedom cheaply by either military or nonmilitary means.

The suffering could be awful. Children would helplessly watch their parents go to prison. Torture would create cowed collaborators. Families would lose sons and daughters. Fear would tempt resisters to give up the struggle.

But all of this and more has happened in past wars, whereas the agony of nuclear war would dwarf the pain of all previous wars. Is suffering in violent warfare more attractive than suffering in nonviolent resistance? 'It is remarkable how many people,' says Gene Sharp, 'who accept as natural millions of dead and wounded in a military war find the dangers of execution and suffering in civilian defence a decisive disadvantage. This is especially puzzling when there is evidence that casualty rates in nonviolent struggles are vastly smaller than in regular warfare.'[18]

The beginning of harsh repression should never mean the end of CBD. Just as defeat in conventional war is certain if soldiers run away or surrender when fired upon, so CBD will collapse if its practitioners crumble under repression. Gene Sharp says, 'The shortest way to end brutalities is to demonstrate that they do not help to achieve the opponent's objectives.'[19] The invader must be confronted by people who have determined *never* to do his will, regardless of the consequences.

We need only recall the witness of the early church to remember that faith-filled people can withstand and overcome even extreme forms of repression. And as our other historical cases have illustrated, even ordinary human beings have an amazing capacity, when gripped by some overriding ideal, to resist and overcome repression. Specific methods of response to specific forms of repression are treated extensively in the literature on nonviolence and CBD,[20] so we need not repeat them here.

In the face of harsh repression, Christians will be helped by the biblical perspective on persecution. Jesus told his followers to expect persecution, but he also assured them that they would receive the Father's help to withstand it. 'If they persecuted me, they will persecute you' (Jn 15:20; cf. Mt 10:16–39; 24:9). 'Blessed are those who are persecuted for righteousness' sake, for theirs is the kingdom of heaven' (Mt 5:10; cf. Lk 21:12–19).

The New Testament is filled with exhortations to Christians to be willing to suffer and even die for the sake of truth, righteousness and the gospel. It is no less filled with reassurance that the suffering will not be in vain and that God will strengthen and protect his children in the midst of it.[21] The apostle Paul was persecuted very often during his missionary work. Even so, Paul could write that when suffering is so severe that one feels like a sheep being led to slaughter, Christians can know overwhelming victory through the love of God in Christ (Rom 8:35–39). Christians down through the ages have known God's grace under repression and martyrdom. One recent example is the testimony of Adolfo Pérez Esquivel, an Argentine Christian who won the 1980 Nobel Peace Prize for his nonviolent leadership in the battle for human rights in Latin America. After spending fifteen months in an Argentine prison and undergoing torture, Esquivel wrote:

Prison was a very hard experience for me, but also very rich. . . . For me, prayer was important. Meditation. Feeling the permanent presence of God. . . . It was a difficult but rich experience to understand the meaning of the Gospel and its nonviolent power, especially under torture. To see and discover how these persons who were torturing us are also brothers. . . . We are very weak and very small, and we have to ask God to help us. It's not easy, what Christ said in the Gospel, that you must renounce yourself to follow him. We know that this is very painful, but also that there is one stronger than ourselves. One must place oneself in the hands of Christ, and say with Paul, 'It is not me, but Christ who works in me.'[22]

Filled with the love of Christ, Christians would have a unique contribution to make in withstanding and overcoming repression. Christians could exhibit the very love of God through the Holy Spirit (Rom 5:5). They could literally put into practice Jesus' summons, 'Pray for those who persecute you.' For example, Christians might learn this simple prayer in the invader's language. 'God be with you,' or 'God bless you.' Thus, invaders would hear these prayers wherever they would go. As they broke into factories and homes to try to impose their will, they would see all around them a population praying that God would touch them, that they would see the evil of their ways and turn from them, that they would come to know Christ as personal Lord and Saviour.

How long could an ordinary soldier keep shooting people when through his gun sights he sees them looking at him calmly and lovingly, praying that he be surrounded by God's light and love?

Atomic Repression?

One of the questions often asked about CBD is, If our nuclear guard were dropped, what would prevent the USSR from blowing up some of our cities with A-bombs – or threatening to do so? Wouldn't we have to give up any resistance under such a threat?

We doubt that any aggressor, including the USSR, would use nuclear weapons against an unarmed and peaceful United States. There are a number of reasons to believe this. First, there is the danger of *increasing* the resistance movement. The Gestapo did not kill the Norwegian teachers, even though they had the physical power to do so. They realised that this martyrdom might only deepen Norwegian resistance. Similarly, neither the USSR nor Poland's Communist Party killed Cardinal Wyszynski, even though for three decades he was a painful thorn in their side. His murder would have caused even greater problems in Poland and around the world. The anticipation of negative consequences is a powerful restraining force, even for despots.

Second, if the USSR were the potential attacker, it would mean their killing, wounding and sickening hundreds of thousands of workers. These are the very people that Communist ideology tells them to rescue from 'the chains of capitalism.' Wouldn't it make more sense to invade the country and convince the workers that the invaders are their liberators?

Moreover, why would they slaughter people unnecessarily when they could march into the country with conventional forces and not face any military resistance? The USSR did not bomb Hungarian or Czech cities during the Warsaw Pact invasion of those countries.

Fourth, the Soviet Union might face condemnation both at home and abroad for a nuclear attack on an unarmed nation.[23] Admittedly, in a totalitarian state protest at home might be fairly small, but world opinion might be broadly negative. The United States justified the use of atomic bombs on Japan with the argument that we were at war. Japan had attacked Pearl Harbour, had killed tens of thousands of men, and would kill thousands more if we attempted an invasion. On the other hand, the United States did not use nuclear weapons against North Vietnam because of the difficulty of justifying such an attack to Americans at home and allies abroad.

Finally, if the United States adopted CBD, the entire element of physical threat would disappear from US-Soviet relations. As Jerome Frank, a noted psychologist, has written in his study of nonviolent national defence: 'The danger of nuclear attack seems very small, because the main incentive – fear of a pre-emptive attack by the United States – would be gone. It is pointless to destroy another country unless it is perceived as a threat to one's own existence.'[24]

When military threats and intimidation escalate, as in the current arms race, the other side feels justified in 'upping the ante' and preparing to use equal or greater violence in response. Nations escalate violence or the threat of violence to counter the opponent's threat. CBD sets in motion the opposite process. With the military threat removed from the United States, it would be hard for an adversary to justify massive military threats.[25]

If a nuclear attack *were* threatened against a United States defended by CBD, we might try a 'strategic surrender' – reducing noncooperation to a minimum, but with plans for escalated resistance at a later date.[26] Another approach would be an apparent capitulation, but using schweikism and other forms of low-level resistance as the main form of struggle.

Or we might just stand up to the threat. When Himmler said to Finland's foreign minister, 'The Finns will have to choose between hunger and delivering up their Jews,' Whitting replied, 'Finland is a decent nation. We would rather perish together with the Jews. We will not surrender the Jews!'[27]

Some things are worth dying for. The founders of our republic proclaimed, 'Give me liberty, or give me death.' And the early church did not give in to Rome when Roman troops slaughtered everyone in a Christian town. We can imagine America's leaders saying to the aggressor: 'You can create scorched earth and dead cities, but you cannot make us give in to tyranny. You can kill the innocent, but their blood will cry out against you, and God will hear. We will not kill you, but we will not give in. Give us liberty, or give us death.' Such a refusal to be cowed might call the enemy's bluff. What would be the use in killing every living thing in a nation so committed to liberty? And where would the aggressor be – in his own eyes and the eyes of the world – after such a genocidal act?

We face risks whether we keep or renounce our nuclear weapons. Our choice is whether to take a risk *with* Jesus or *against* him. For a Christian it is better to be crucified oneself than to crucify others. As A. J. Muste once said, the question is 'not whether defeat can always be avoided, but whether it can be such a "defeat" as Jesus suffered on Calvary.'[28]

Defence through CBD can by no means offer an assured promise of victory. In this respect, CBD is no different from military defence. In a military conflict, a strong opponent will overcome a weak one. So too in CBD. The outcome will depend on which adversary ends up having the greatest amount of physical, economic, political, psychological, social and spiritual power. This, of course, is not a reason for rejecting CBD, but rather for preparing for it in such a way that it will be as effective as possible.

Even though no absolute promise of winning can be given, there is a possibility that CBD would bring victory over an invader. After much suffering, the invader might withdraw. America's freedom and independence would be restored. How might this happen?

An effective campaign of CBD would confront the aggressor with the enormous problems we have described earlier – disaffection among troops, dissent at home and abroad, failure to crush resistance, and the inability to achieve meaningful control over a defiant and noncooperating US population.

Stymied by such difficulties, the invader might seek a way to extricate himself. He might enter into negotiations with American leaders to seek a face-saving solution to help him justify his withdrawal. On the other hand, various circumstances might *force* him to withdraw without any negotiations. For example, nonmilitary revolts against his rule (inspired by the dramatic resistance in the US) might explode in satellite nations, forcing him to pull out his troops for more urgent duty nearer to his own borders. Or, opposition forces within his own country might overthrow the invading regime and call the troops home, giving as their reasons the failure of the invasion, the increased difficulties at home, and the diplomatic and economic pressures from other countries. Or, such a sea of uncertainty, rebellion, disintegration and mutiny might arise among his own troops and personnel as to make it clear that any attempt to push them further would only lead to total disaster. Lastly, the much-feared 'epidemic of freedom' might break out and spread so widely among the invading forces that they would desert on a large scale, making further operations impossible.

Another scenario is also possible. Soviet totalitarianism might be able to conquer the United States and then go on to impose its rule throughout much or all of the world. As the Romans did, they would rule directly in some places and indirectly through collaborating governments in others. Such a prospect is horrifying to contemplate. It would mean widespread repression. Democratic institutions might largely disappear for years into the future.

We believe, however, that even the worst possible outcome is preferable to an American decision to go down the nuclear road that leads to mass murder by the hundreds of millions. And, if history is any clue, totalitarianism would eventually weaken. Enormous progress toward greater freedom can be (and has been) made in the space of a century or less. Yet a major nuclear war could easily set civilisation back not just a hundred, but thousands of years.

Transarmament

Advocates of civilian-based defence are not proposing unilateral disarmament. Instead, they are advocating a *shift* from one method of defence to another, from military defence to nonmilitary. A country that adopts CBD arms itself with a new kind of weaponry. To emphasise this point, many writers on the subject use the term *transarmament* to describe the process of transforming the US defence system. The country would not be giving up defence, but changing over to 'a new defence capability that provides deterrence and defence without conventional and nuclear military power.'[29]

The switch from military to nonmilitary defence would, of course, begin with public debate and congressional investigations into the feasibility and structure of nonmilitary defence.[30] Election campaigns might focus on the nuclear issue and alternatives to nuclear defence.

If the decision were made to transform our defence establishment, private and governmental training centres to teach the theory and methods of CBD to specialists and leaders might be set up. (In 1978 a US Congressional commission began studying the feasibility of a federally funded National Peace Academy. In October 1981 the commission recommended establishment of the academy to Congress and the president.[31]) The private and governmental agencies needed to carry out CBD (such as a Department of Civilian-Based Defence) would have to be created, along with a plan for the necessary economic readjustment that would come with the conversion from military to nonmilitary defence.

We would also need a foreign policy of nonviolence to encourage other nations to adopt CBD and dismantle their nuclear and conventional weaponry. Since our military weapons would no longer be available to protect vulnerable allies, we would help all our allies to adopt civilian-based defence also. We could set up an alliance of states that would mutually adopt CBD and negotiate mutual assistance pacts to replace current military treaties.[32] An International Nonmilitary Defence Force could be set up to help counter aggression anywhere in the world.[33]

Military personnel and weapons industry workers would have to be retrained for civilian or CBD jobs. Some former military personnel might be used to set up an international disaster rescue team which would use military equipment and technicians to render aid wherever floods, earthquakes or other disasters struck. The money, technology and skilled workers which were formerly used by the military could instead be used to modernise industry, find a cure for cancer, solve energy problems, improve conditions for the poor, provide adequate nutrition for the hungry and generally raise the standard of living at home and abroad.

Earlier we tried to be realistic and to discuss the worst-possible scenarios. Surely it is equally appropriate to sketch a best-possible scenario. A transarmament programme by the United States would be a marked act of courage in a world edging toward nuclear annihilation. It would reduce the international tension and anxiety that comes from superpower threats and nuclear brinkmanship. It would reduce, and potentially eliminate, the spread of nuclear weapons to other countries. It would pressure the Soviet Union to give up its own nuclear weapons, since the main rationale for holding them – defence against the US nuclear threat – would disappear.

Enormous human and material energy could be freed to tackle world problems like illiteracy, slums and disease. Military production would no longer gobble up the world's nonrenewable resources. Military projects would no longer destroy the world's fragile ecosystem. Military expenditure would no longer imbalance national budgets and cause inflation. The size of government could be reduced, since many defence responsibilities could be shifted away from military and civilian bureaucracies and given to independent civilian institutions. America could see a rebirth of freedom as all its citizens trained themselves in freedom's defence. And Americans would be freed from the morally intolerable position of having to defend themselves by means that required mass murder. In a thousand ways a nonmilitary defence programme would benefit the nation and similarly any other nation.

Yet even if by God's special grace every piece of this optimistic scenario occurred, we would not have a world of peace and shalom. Human effort will never usher in the consummated kingdom. Sin, selfishness, hate and greed would remain. Wars and rumours of war would continue, as Jesus said they would (Mt 24:6). To be sure, Jesus' statement in no way makes nuclear disarmament unbiblical. To claim that would be to indulge in the most arbitrary kind of eisegesis, reading one's own ideas into the biblical text. Worldwide nuclear disarmament, or even fairly widespread adoption of CBD by many nations, is not at all incompatible with Jesus' warning. But even if nuclear weapons were banished from the earth and many nations adopted CBD, there would still be national competition, rivalry among nations, and selfish, violent attempts to dominate others. Wars and rumours of wars will cease only when our Lord returns. Until he does, however, he calls his disciples to be peacemakers, persistently and patiently striving to reduce the pain and suffering of human selfishness.

Someone once said that it is not that Christianity has been tried and has failed, but that it has never been tried. With nuclear holocaust looming so near, might this be the time to try a new means of defence which does not rely on turning cities into crematoria?

Working towards Civilian-Based Defence

Those who see the need for CBD can begin now to work for it. We can talk to people about it. We can encourage colleges and universities to do research on it. We can urge it upon government officials. We can vote for candidates for political office who show sincere interest in it. We can form groups that are using nonviolent means to attack existing social injustices and thus gain the practical experience needed to form nonmilitary defence groups. We can use nonviolent demonstrations to oppose specific military programmes, while educating the public about a better means of defending the country. Most of all, we can deepen our commitment to that life of prayer, Bible study and Christian fellowship that will give us the wisdom and strength we need to see clearly the way ahead.

Not every Christian, however, should put all his or her efforts into developing CBD. CBD is still a very new and, to most people, a startling idea. It involves a reversal of most defence thinking of the past. Public understanding will take time to develop. Political change and the adoption of a CBD policy by Western nations will take even longer. In the meantime, we believe it is vital to press ahead with the kinds of peacemaking steps we outlined in section III.

Peacemaking, however, is incredibly costly. Jesus followed his blessing on peacemakers with an immediate blessing on those who are persecuted for righteousness' sake. Peacemaking and cross bearing were inextricably linked in his life. The following statement underlines the costly character of peacemaking:

> We have assumed the name of peacemakers, but we have been, by and large, unwilling to pay any significant price. And because we want the peace with half a heart and half a life and will, the war, of course, continues, because the waging of war, by its nature, is total – but the waging of peace, by our own cowardice, is partial. So a whole will and a whole heart and a whole national life bent toward war prevail over the (mere desire for) peace. In every national war since the founding of the republic we have taken for granted that war shall exact the most rigorous cost, and that the cost shall be paid with cheerful heart. We take it for granted that in wartime families will be separated for long periods, that men will be imprisoned, wounded, driven insane, killed on foreign shores. In favour of such wars, we declare a moratorium on every normal human hope – for marriage, for community, for friendship, for moral conduct toward strangers and the innocent. We are instructed that deprivation and discipline, private grief and public obedience are to be our lot. And we obey. And we bear with it – because bear we must – because war is war, and good war or bad, we are stuck with it and its cost.

But what of the price of peace? I think of the good, decent, peace-loving people I have known by the thousands, and I wonder. How many of them are so afflicted with the wasting disease of normalcy that, even as they declare for peace, their hands reach out with an instinctive spasm in the direction of their loved ones, in the direction of their comforts, their home, their security, their income, their future, their plans – that five-year plan of studies, that ten-year plan of professional status, that twenty-year plan of family growth and unity, that fifty-year plan of decent life and honourable natural demise. 'Of course, let us have the peace,' we cry, 'but at the same time let us have normalcy, let us lose nothing, let our lives stand intact, let us know neither prison nor ill repute nor disruption of ties.' And because we must encompass this and protect that, and because at all costs – at all costs – our hopes must march on schedule, and because it is unheard-of that in the name of peace a sword should fall, disjoining that fine and cunning web that our lives have woven, because it is unheard-of that good men should suffer injustice or families be sundered or good repute be lost – because of this we cry peace and cry peace, and there is no peace. There is no peace because the making of peace is at least as costly as the making of war – at least as exigent, at least as disruptive, at least as liable to bring disgrace and prison and death in its wake.[34]

The thought of standing vulnerable before an enemy's nuclear bombs is terrifying. Yet we are vulnerable *now*, even with all our nuclear weapons poised to destroy. If through miscalculation or madness, the Soviet Union launched their ICBMs at our cities, our most advanced technology could not snatch the missiles from the air and prevent them from decimating our people. *There is no military defence in the nuclear age*. All that we can do is to launch our rockets in retaliation. All that we can do is slit a hundred million enemy throats a few seconds after they have slit ours.

Having nuclear weapons or not having them – both postures involve awesome risk. We face a dark chasm of uncertainty and risk never known before. Obedient faith in Jesus Christ is the only bridge over the chasm. Never in the history of the planet has there been a more desperate need for Jesus' way of costly love for enemies. Jesus taught us to love, not to hate; to heal, not to kill; to pray for our persecutors, not to destroy them. Does he want us now to prepare ourselves massively to kill or massively to love our enemies?

Afterword

The authors of this book do not claim to have all the answers. We have simply tried to share some implications of our belief that Jesus Christ does not want his followers to turn the cities of the world into crematoria. We hope, indeed, we beg and plead that all Christians will join in the search for better answers.

We confess that heavy foreboding has slowly settled upon us in the months that we have worked on this book. We have not abandoned hope, but it comes harder now. As we talk with our teenagers about their future, we experience a deep sadness. We find it difficult to brush aside a terrible sense that they may never experience the joy of fishing and canoeing with their children. We agree with what Admiral Hyman G. Rickover said in his farewell speech in February 1982: 'The US-Soviet arms race is so wildly out of control that instead of increasing our capacity to defend ourselves we are more likely to wipe out the human race in nuclear war. . . . I think probably we will destroy ourselves,' he warned.

Rickover is right. Doom awaits us unless the people of the world turn back from the zealot path toward death. Is that possible? We believe it is. But our hope is rooted in God, not people.

At the worst of times in the past, God has broken into human history with a mighty demonstration of his transforming power. The great revivals of the eighteenth and nineteenth centuries created movements that changed British and American history. Surely it is not naive to pray and believe that God will do the same in the late twentieth century.

The Teacher from Nazareth is the risen Sovereign of history. From the mountains of the universe he still pleads with us to love our enemies and follow him in the path of peacemaking. He promises that the same divine power that raised him from the dead is now available to all who believe in him. In the power of the resurrection, it is possible for Christians today to turn our militaristic world upside down. In the power of the Holy Spirit, it is possible for Christians today to tug our trembling planet back from the nuclear abyss.

We dream of a new movement of biblical Christians who choose peace. We dream of a mighty revival blowing through the church, converting sinners and revitalising believers. We dream of a peace movement that immerses its strategising, marching and lobbying in intercessory prayer and radical dependence on the Holy Spirit. We dream of a new abolitionist movement against nuclear war that sweeps through the church, not just in North America and Western Europe, but also in Eastern Europe and the Soviet Union. We dream of a movement that knows that the cross comes before the resurrection, a movement that dares to suffer for the sake of peace. A resounding *no* to nuclear weapons will be costly for Christians behind the Iron Curtain. It will also be costly for Christians here. We dream of a biblical movement of Spirit-filled Christians ready to challenge their government's militaristic madness even if it involves a cross.

The next two decades are the most dangerous in the history of the planet. Many people have already succumbed to despair. But Christians need not, must not, give in to paralysing hopelessness. We know that the risen Lord Jesus has not abandoned the task of peacemaking. Neither should we.

The Lord of history summons the people of the world to a most momentous choice: 'I call heaven and earth to witness against you this day, that I have set before you life and death, blessing and curse; therefore choose life, that you and your descendants may live' (Deut 30:19). One way or the other, this generation will decide the nuclear question. Will we persist in our frantic clutching for security through weapons of global suicide? Or will we allow the risen Lord Jesus to show us the things that make for peace?

Appendix A

Bibliography

We have not attempted to list every book written on the subject of nuclear war. Rather, our bibliography focuses on those written from a Christian perspective or those which contain especially important facts or perspectives. The list is divided into five categories: facts about nuclear war, biblical-theological perspectives (general, biblical studies, just war tradition and nonviolence tradition), practical steps towards peace, nonviolence and non-military defence, and periodicals.

1. Facts about Nuclear War

Aldridge, Robert C. *The Counterforce Syndrome: A Guide to U.S. Nuclear Weapons and Strategic Doctrine*. Washington, DC: Transnational Institute, 1978.

Arkin, William. *IPS Research Guide to Current Military and Strategic Affairs*. Washington, DC: Institute for Policy Studies, 1981.

Barnet, Richard J. *The Giants: Russia and America*. New York: Simon and Schuster, 1977.

——————. *The Roots of War*. Baltimore: Penguin Books, Inc., 1973.

Beres, Louis René. *Apocalypse: Nuclear Catastrophe in World Politics*. Chicago: Univ. of Chicago Press, 1982.

Calder, Nigel. *Nuclear Nightmares: An Investigation into Possible Wars*. New York: Penguin, 1982.

Campbell, Duncan. *War Plan UK – the Truth about Civil Defence in Britain*. London: Burnett Books, 1982.

Donovan, Col. James. *U.S. Military Force 1980: An Evaluation*. Washington, DC: Centre for Defence Information, 1981.

The Effects of Nuclear War. Washington, DC: US Arms Control and Disarmament Agency, 1979.

Freedman, Lawrence. *Britain and Nuclear Weapons*. London: Macmillan, 1980.

Glasstone, Samuel, and Dolan, Philip J., eds. *The Effects of*

Nuclear Weapons. Washington, DC: US Department of Defence and US Department of Energy, 1977.

Goldwater, Barry, and Hart, Gary. *Recent False Alerts from the Nation's Missile Attack Warning System*. Report to the Committee on Armed Services, US Senate. Washington, DC: Government Printing Office, 1980.

Greene, Owen. *London after the Bomb: What a Nuclear Attack Really Means*. London: Oxford University Press.

Ground Zero. *Nuclear War: What's in It for You?* New York: Pocket Books, 1982.

Hershey, John. *Hiroshima*. New York: Bantam, 1956.

Hiroshima-Nagasaki: A Pictorial Record of the Atomic Destruction. Tokyo: Hiroshima-Nagasaki Publishing Committee, 1978.

Is America Becoming Number 2? Current Trends in the U.S.-Soviet Military Balance. Washington, DC: Committee on the Present Danger, 1978.

Joyce, James Avery. *The War Machine*. London: Hamlyn, 1981.

Katz, Arthur M. *Life after Nuclear War*. Cambridge, Mass: Ballinger, 1982.

Lens, Sidney. *The Day before Doomsday: An Anatomy of the Nuclear Arms Race*. Boston: Beacon Press, 1978.

——————. *The Bomb*. New York: Dutton, 1982.

Long-Term Worldwide Effects of Multiple Nuclear Weapons Detonations. Washington, DC: National Academy of Sciences, 1975.

The Military Balance. London: International Institute for Strategic Studies, 1979.

Myrdal, Alva. *The Game of Disarmament: How the United States and Russia Run the Arms Race*. Nottingham: Spokesmen Books.

Neild, Robert. *How to make your mind up about the Bomb*. London: Deutsch, 1981.

Physicians for Social Responsibility. *The Final Epidemic: The Medical Consequences of Nuclear Weapons and Nuclear War*. Chicago: Educational Foundation for Nuclear Science, 1981.

Rogers, Dr Paul. *As Lambs to the Slaughter*. London: Arrow, 1981.

Schell, Jonathan. *The Fate of the Earth*. New York: Knopf, 1982.

Sivard, Ruth L. *World Military and Social Expenditures*. Leesburg, Va: WMSE Publications, 1981.

Stockholm International Peace Research Institute. *Nuclear*

Radiation in Warfare. London: Taylor and Travis, 1981.

Thompson, E. P., and Smith, Dan (eds). *Protest and Survive*. London: Penguin, 1980.

Tucker, Anthony, and Gleisner, John. *Crucible of Despair: the Effects of Nuclear War*. London: Menard Press, 1982.

US, Congress, Office of Technology Assessment. *The Effects of Nuclear War*. London: Croom Helm, 1980.

US, Congress, Senate, Committee on Banking, Housing and Urban Affairs. *Economic and Social Consequences of Nuclear Attacks on the United States*. Washington, DC: Government Printing Office, 1979.

Zuckerman, Solly. *Nuclear Illusion and Reality*. London: Collins, 1982.

2. Biblical-Theological Perspectives

a. General

Aukerman, Dale. *Darkening Valley: A Biblical Perspective on Nuclear War*. New York: Seabury, 1981.

Bainton, Roland H. *Christian Attitudes toward War and Peace: A Historical Survey and Critical Re-evaluation*. New York: Abingdon Press, 1960.

Boettner, Loraine. *The Christian Attitude toward War*. Grand Rapids, Mich: Eerdmans, 1940.

Church of England Working Party. *The Church and the Bomb*. London: Hodder and Stoughton, 1982.

Clouse, Robert, ed. *War: Four Christian Views*. Downers Grove, Ill: InterVarsity Press, 1981.

Ellul, Jacques. *Violence: Reflections from a Christian Perspective*. Oxford: Mowbray, 1978.

Gardiner, Robert W. *The Cool Arm of Destruction: Modern Weapons and Moral Insensitivity*. Philadelphia: Westminster Press, 1974.

Grannis, Christopher, Laffin, Arthur, and Schade, Elin. *The Risk of the Cross: Christian Discipleship in the Nuclear Age*. New York: Seabury, 1981.

Greet, Dr Kenneth. *The Big Sin*. London: Marshall, Morgan & Scott, 1982.

Gremillion, Joseph, ed. *The Gospel of Peace and Justice: Catholic Social Teaching since Pope John*. Maryknoll, NY: Orbis, 1976.

Guinan, Edward. *Peace and Nonviolence*. New York: Paulist, 1973.

Hamilton, Michael P., ed. *To Avoid Catastrophe: A Study in Future Nuclear Weapons Policy*. Grand Rapids, Mich: Eerdmans, 1977.

Holmes, Arthur F., ed. *War and Christian Ethics*. Grand Rapids, Mich: Baker, 1975.

Kirk, J. Andrew. *Theology Encounters Revolution*. Leicester: InterVarsity Press, 1980.

Long, Edward LeRoy, Jr. *War and Conscience in America*. Philadelphia: Westminster Press, 1968.

Merton, Thomas, ed. *Breakthrough to Peace: Twelve Views on the Threat of Thermonuclear Extermination*. New York: New Directions, 1962.

Milford, T. R. *Christian Decision in the Nuclear Age*. Philadelphia: Fortress Press, 1967.

Osterle, William H., and Donaghy, John, eds. *Peace Theology and the Arms Race: Readings on Arms and Disarmament*. N.p.: College Theology Society, 1980.

Rankin, William W. *The Nuclear Arms Race: Countdown to Disaster: A Study in Christian Ethics*. Cincinnati: Forward Movement Pub., 1981.

Rockman, Jane, ed. *Peace in Search of Makers: Riverside Church Reverse the Arms Race Convocation*. Valley Forge, Pa: Judson Press, 1979.

Russett, Bruce M. 'Short of Nuclear Madness.' *Worldview*, April 1972, pp. 31–37.

Shannon, Thomas A. *War or Peace? The Search for New Answers*. Maryknoll, NY: Orbis, 1980.

Wallis, Jim. *Call to Conversion*. New York: Harper & Row, 1981.

b. Biblical Studies

Brueggemann, Walter. *Living toward a Vision: Biblical Reflections on Shalom*. Philadelphia: United Church Press, 1976.

Cassidy, Richard J. *Jesus, Politics and Society: A Study of Luke's Gospel*. Maryknoll, NY: Orbis, 1978.

Craigie, Peter C. *The Problem of War in the Old Testament*. Grand Rapids, Mich: Eerdmans, 1978.

Cullmann, Oscar. *The State in the New Testament*. Rev. ed. London: SCM Press, 1963.

Eller, Vernard. *War and Peace: From Genesis to Revelation*. Scottdale, Pa: Herald Press, 1980.

Furnish, Victor P. *The Love Command in the New Testament*. New York: Abingdon, 1972.

Hengel, Martin. *Victory over Violence*. Translated by David E. Green. London: SPCK, 1975.

Lasserre, Jean. *War and the Gospel*. Translated by Oliver Coburn. Scottdale, Pa: Herald Press, 1962.

Lind, Millard C. *Yahweh Is a Warrior: The Theology of Warfare in Ancient Israel*. Scottdale, Pa: Herald Press, 1980.

Macgregor, G. H. C. *The New Testament Basis of Pacifism and the Relevance of an Impossible Ideal*. New York: Fellowship Publications, 1960.

Morris, Leon. *The Cross in the New Testament*. Exeter: Paternoster Press, 1976.

Piper, John. *'Love Your Enemies': Jesus' Love Command in the Synoptic Gospels and in the Early Christian Paraenesis*. Cambridge: Cambridge Univ. Press, 1979.

Zimmerli, W., and Jeremias, J. *The Servant of God*. Studies in Biblical Theology, No. 20. Naperville, Ill.: Alec R. Allenson, 1957.

c. Just War Tradition

Bennett, John C., ed. *Nuclear Weapons and the Conflict of Conscience*. New York: Scribner's, 1962.

Childress, James F. 'Just War Theories: The Bases, Interrelations, Priorities, and Functions of Their Criteria.' *Theological Studies*, 39 (Sept. 1978): 427–45.

Drinan, Robert F. *Vietnam and Armageddon: Peace, War and the Christian Conscience*. New York: Sheed and Ward, 1970.

Finn, James, ed. *A Conflict of Loyalties: The Case for Selective Conscientious Objection*. New York: Pegasus, 1968.

—————. *Peace, the Churches, and the Bomb*. New York: Council on Religion and International Affairs, 1965.

Ford, Harold P., and Winters, Francis Y., ed. *Ethics and Nuclear Strategy*. Maryknoll, NY: Orbis, 1977.

Gessert, Robert A., and Hehir, J. Bryan. *The New Nuclear Debate*. New York: Council on Religion and International Affairs, 1976.

Hehir, J. Bryan. 'The Catholic Church and the Arms Race.' *Worldview*, July–Aug. 1978, pp. 13–18.

Johnson, James T. *Ideology, Reason, and the Limitations of War: Religious and Secular Concepts, 1200–1740*. Princeton, NJ: Princeton Univ. Press, 1975.

—————. *The Just War Tradition and the Restraint of War:*

A Moral and Historical Inquiry. Princeton, NJ: Princeton Univ. Press, 1981.

Lawler, Justus George. *Nuclear War: the Ethic, the Rhetoric, the Reality: A Catholic Assessment.* Westminster, Md: Newman Press, 1965.

Niebuhr, Reinhold. *Christianity and Power Politics.* New York: Scribner's, 1946

————————. *An Interpretation of Christian Ethics.* New York: Harper, 1935.

O'Brien, William V. *Nuclear War, Deterrence and Morality.* New York: Newman Press, 1967.

Ramsey, Paul. *The Just War: Force and Political Responsibility.* New York: Scribner's, 1968.

————————. 'A Political Ethics Context for Strategic Thinking.' In *Strategic Thinking and Its Moral Implication,* edited by Morton Kaplan. Chicago: Univ. of Chicago Centre for Policy Study, 1973, pp. 101–47.

————————. *War and the Christian Conscience: How Shall Modern War Be Conducted Justly.* Durham, NC: Duke Univ. Press, 1961.

Rohr, John A. *Prophets without Honor: Public Policy and the Selective Conscientious Objector.* Nashville, Tenn: Abingdon, 1971.

Stein, Walter, ed. *Nuclear Weapons and Christian Conscience.* London: Merlin Press, 1961.

Tucker, Robert W. *The Just War: A Study of Contemporary American Doctrine.* London: Greenwood Press, 1979.

Walters, LeRoy Brandt. 'Five Classic Just War Theories: A Study in the Thought of Thomas Aquinas, Vitoria, Suárez, Gentili, and Grotius.' PhD dissertation, Yale Univ., 1971.

Walzer, Michael. *Just and Unjust Wars: A Moral Argument with Historical Illustrations.* London: Penguin, 1980.

d. Nonviolence Tradition

Berrigan, Daniel. *Uncommon Prayer.* New York: Seabury, 1978.

Berrigan, Philip. *Of Beasts and Other Beastly Images: Essays under the Bomb.* Portland, Oreg.: Sunburst Press, 1978.

Brock, Peter. *Pacifism in the United States: From the Colonial Era to the First World War.* Princeton, NJ: Princeton Univ. Press, 1968.

Clark, Robert E. D. *Does the Bible Teach Pacifism?* New Malden, Surrey: Fellowship of Reconciliation, 1976.

Douglass, James. *The Non-Violent Cross: A Theology of Revolution and Peace*. New York: Macmillan, 1969.

Durnbaugh, Donald F., ed. *On Earth Peace: Discussions on War/Peace Issues between Friends, Mennonites, Brethren and European Churches 1935–1975*. Elgin, Ill: Brethren Press, 1978.

Ferguson, John. *The Politics of Love: The New Testament and Non-Violent Revolution*. Cambridge: James Clarke and Co., n.d., 1973.

Hornus, Jean-Michel. *It Is Not Lawful for Me to Fight: Early Christian Attitudes toward War, Violence, and the State*. Translated by Alan Kreider and Oliver Coburn. Scottdale, Pa: Herald Press, 1980.

Hostetter, Paul, ed. *Perfect Love and War: A Dialogue on Christian Holiness and the Issues of War and Peace*. Nappanee, Ind: Evangel Press, 1974.

McSorley, Richard. *New Testament Basis of Peacemaking*. Washington, DC: Centre for Peace Studies, Georgetown University, 1979.

Merton, Thomas. *Faith and Violence*. Notre Dame, Ind: University of Notre Dame Press, 1968.

Raven, Charles E. *The Theological Basis of Christian Pacifism*. New York: Fellowship Publications, 1951.

Rutenber, Culbert G. *The Dagger and the Cross: An Examination of Christian Pacifism*. New York: Fellowship Publications, 1950.

Schrag, Martin H., and Stoner, John K. *The Ministry of Reconciliation*. Nappanee, Ind: Evangel Press, 1973.

Shelly, Maynard. *New Call for Peacemakers: A New Call to Peacemaking Study Guide*. Newton, Kans: Faith and Life Press, 1979.

Sider, Ronald J. *Christ and Violence*. Tring, Herts: Lion, 1980.

Trocmé, André. *Jesus and the Nonviolent Revolution*. Translated by Michael H. Shank and Marlin E. Miller. Scottdale, Pa: Herald Press, 1973.

Yoder, John Howard. *Karl Barth and the Problem of War*. New York: Abingdon Press, 1970.

——————. *Nevertheless: The Varieties of Religious Pacifism*. Scottdale, Pa: Herald Press, 1971.

——————. *The Politics of Jesus*. Grand Rapids, Mich: Eerdmans, 1972.

————————. 'What Would You Do If . . . ?' *Journal of Religious Ethics*, 1974, pp. 81–105.

Zahn, Gordon C. *An Alternative to War*. New York: Council on Religion and International Affairs, 1963.

————————. *War, Conscience and Dissent*. New York: Hawthorn Books, 1967.

3. Practical Steps toward Peace

Advice for Conscientious Objectors in the Armed Forces. Philadelphia: Central Committee for Conscientious Objectors, 1980.

Anderson, Marion. *The Impact of Military Spending on the Machinists' Union*. Washington, DC: International Association of Machinists, 1979.

Arms Control and Disarmament Agreements: Texts and History of Negotiations. Washington, DC: US Arms Control and Disarmament Agency, 1977.

Berrigan, Daniel. *No Bars to Manhood*. Garden City, NY: Doubleday, 1970.

The Boston Study Group. *The Price of Defense: A New Strategy for Military Spending*, New York: Times Books, 1979.

Caldicott, Helen. *Nuclear Madness: What You Can Do*. London: Bantam Books, 1981.

Corson-Finnerty, Adam. *World Citizen: Action for Global Justice*. Maryknoll, NY: Orbis, 1982.

Disarmament Action Guide. Washington, DC: Coalition for a New Foreign and Military Policy, 1981.

Geyer, Alan. *The Idea of Disarmament: Rethinking the Unthinkable*. Elgin, Ill: Brethren Press, 1982.

Grannis, Christopher J., Laffin, Arthur, and Schade, Elin. *The Risk of the Cross: Christian Discipleship in the Nuclear Age*. New York: Seabury, 1981.

Handbook for Conscientious Objectors. Philadelphia: Central Committee for Conscientious Objectors, n.d.

Jack, Homer. *Disarmament Workbook*. New York: World Conference on Religion and Peace, 1978.

Johansen, Robert C. *The Disarmament Process: Where to Begin*. New York: Institute for World Order, 1977.

————————. *Toward a Dependable Peace*. New York: Institute for World Order, 1978.

Joyce, James Avery. *The War Machine: The Case against the Arms Race*. New York: Quartet Books, 1981.

Judson, Stephanie. *A Manual for Nonviolence for Children*. Philadelphia: Friends Peace Committee, n.d.

Kaufman, Donald D. *The Tax Dilemma: Praying for Peace, Paying for War*. Scottdale, Pa: Herald Press, 1978.

Keyes, Ken, Jr. *The Hundredth Monkey*. St Mary, Ky: Vision Books, 1982.

Kincade, William H., and Porro, Jeffrey D., eds. *Negotiating Security: An Arms Control Reader*. Washington, DC: Carnegie Endowment for International Peace, 1980.

Kownacki, Mary Lou, ed. *A Race to Nowhere: An Arms Race Primer for Catholics*. Chicago: Pax Christi, 1980.

Kraybill, Donald. *Facing Nuclear War: A Plea for Christian Witness*. Scottdale, Pa: Herald Press, 1982.

Lall, B. G. *Prosperity without Guns: The Economic Impact of Reductions in Defense Spending*. New York: Institute for World Order, 1977.

Levicoff, Steve. *Building Bridges: The Prolife Movement and the Peace Movement*. Eagleville, Pa: Toviah Press, 1982.

A Matter of Faith: A Study Guide for Churches on the Nuclear Arms Race. Washington, DC: Sojourners Peace Ministry, 1981.

McGinnis, James, and McGinnis, Kathleen. *Parenting for Peace and Justice*. Maryknoll, NY: Orbis, 1981. Five 60-minute cassettes are also available for use with the book.

McSorley, Richard. *Kill? For Peace?* Washington, DC: Centre for Peace Studies, 1977.

Melman, Seymour, ed. *Defense Economy: Conversion of Industries and Occupations to Civilian Needs*. New York: Praeger Publications, 1970.

Nuclear War Prevention Kit. Washington, DC: Centre for Defence Information, 1981.

Peachey, Lorne. *How to Teach Peace to Children*. Scottdale, Pa: Herald Press, 1981.

Ravenal, Earl C. *Toward World Security: A Program for Disarmament*. Washington, DC: Institute for Policy Studies, 1978.

Rockman, Jane, ed. *Peace in Search of Makers*. Valley Forge, Pa: Judson Press, 1979.

Wallis, Jim, ed. *Waging Peace: A Handbook in the Struggle to Abolish Nuclear Weapons*. San Francisco: Harper & Row, 1982.

4. Nonviolence and Nonmilitary Defence

American Friends Service Committee. *In Place of War: An Inquiry into Nonviolent National Defense.* New York: Grossman, 1967.

Bondurant, Joan V. *Conquest of Violence: The Gandhian Philosophy of Conflict.* Princeton, NJ: Princeton Univ. Press, 1958.

Boserup, Anders, and Mack, Andrew. *War without Weapons: Nonviolence in National Defense.* New York: Shocken Books, 1974.

Cooney, Robert, and Michalowski, Helen. *The Power of the People.* Culver City, Calif: Peace Press, 1977.

Fischer, Louis. *The Life of Mahatma Gandhi.* London: Mentor (New American Library), 1965.

Friedman, Philip. *Their Brothers' Keepers.* New York: Crown Publishers, 1957.

Gandhi, Mohandas K. *An Autobiography or the Story of My Experiments with Truth.* London: Housemans, 1972.

——————. *Nonviolent Resistance.* London: Housemans, 1972.

Gregg, Richard B. *The Power of Nonviolence.* Cambridge: J. Clarke, 1960.

Hallie, Philip. *Lest Innocent Blood Be Shed: The Story of the Village of Le Chambon and How Goodness Happened There.* London: Michael Joseph, 1979.

Hinshaw, Cecil E. *Nonviolent Resistance: A Nation's Way to Peace.* Wallingford, Pa: Pendle Hill Pamphlet, 1956.

Horsburgh, H. J. N. *Nonviolence and Aggression: A Study of Gandhi's Moral Equivalent of War.* London: Oxford Univ. Press, 1968. See esp. chap. 5.

Hunter, Allan A. *Christians in the Arena.* Nyack, NY: Fellowship Publications, 1958.

——————. *Courage in Both Hands.* New York: Ballantine, 1962.

King, Coretta Scott. *My Life with Martin Luther King.* New York: Holt, Rinehart and Winston, 1969.

King, Martin Luther. *Strength to Love.* London: Collins, 1969.

——————. *Stride toward Freedom.* New York: Harper & Row, 1958.

——————. *Where Do We Go from Here? Chaos or Community?* New York: Harper & Row, 1966.

——————. *Why We Can't Wait*. London: Mentor (New American Library), 1963.

King-Hall, Commander Sir Stephen. *Defense in the Nuclear Age*. Nyack, NY: Fellowship Publications, 1959.

——————. *Power Politics in the Nuclear Age: A Policy for Britain*. London: Gollancz, 1962.

Lynd, Staughton, ed. *Non-Violence in America: A Documentary History*. New York: Bobbs-Merrill, 1966.

Lyttle, Bradford. *National Defense through Nonviolent Resistance*. Chicago: Shanti-Sena Pub., 1958.

Mahadevan, T. K., Roberts, Adam, and Sharp, Gene, eds. *Civilian Defense: An Introduction*. New Delhi: Gandhi Peace Foundation, 1967.

Miller, William Robert. *Nonviolence: A Christian Interpretation*. New York: Shocken Books, 1972. See esp. chap. 6.

Pratt, Colin. *Non-Violent Defense*. Nottingham: Shaftesbury Project, n.d.

Roberts, Adam, ed. *Civilian Resistance as a National Defense: Nonviolent Action against Aggression*. Harrisburgh, Pa: Stackpole Books, 1967.

Sakamoto, Yoshikazu, and Saxe-Fernades, J., eds. *Strategic Doctrines and their Alternatives*. Paris: UNESCO, forthcoming. See chap. by Gene Sharp.

Seifert, Harvey. *Conquest by Suffering*, Philadelphia: Westminster Press, 1965.

Sharp, Gene. *Exploring Nonviolent Alternatives*. Boston: Porter Sargent, 1970.

——————. *Gandhi as a Political Strategist*. Boston: Porter Sargent, 1979.

——————. *Making the Abolition of War a Realistic Goal*. New York: Institute for World Order, 1980.

——————. *The Politics of Nonviolent Action*. Boston: Porter Sargent, 1973.

——————. *Social Power and Political Freedom*. Boston: Porter Sargent, 1980.

Shridharani, Krishnalal. *War without Violence: A Study of Gandhi's Method and Its Accomplishments*. New York: Harcourt Brace, 1939.

Sibley, Mulford Q., ed. *The Quiet Battle: Writings on the Theory and Practice of Non-Violent Resistance*. Garden City, NY: Doubleday, Anchor Books, 1963.

Taylor, Richard K. *Blockade: Guide to Nonviolent Intervention*. Maryknoll, NY: Orbis, 1977.

5. Periodicals

The Baptist Peacemaker. Deer Park Baptist Church, 1733 Bardstown Rd, Louisville, KY 40205. Sixteen-page quarterly goes to 20,000 subscribers in the United States and abroad.

Bulletin of Atomic Scientists. 1020–24 E. 58th St, Chicago, IL 60637. Written in lay language by scientists concerned to prevent nuclear war.

The Catholic Worker. 36 E. First St, New York, NY 10003. Catholic perspective on peace, justice and the poor.

Christianity and Crisis. 537 W. 121st St, New York, NY 10027. Incisive comment on world issues.

Christianity Today. 465 Gundersen Dr., Carol Stream, IL 60187. The major evangelical fortnightly. Deals with a wide range of issues, including peace.

The Defense Monitor. Centre for Defence Information, 600 Maryland Ave SW, Washington, DC 20024. Headed by a retired admiral and other military officers. Excellent research. Deep concern to prevent nuclear war. Watchdog on military spending and operations.

Disarmament Times. Room 7B, 777 United Nations Plaza, New York, NY 10017. Published by experts close to the disarmament negotiations at the United Nations and elsewhere in the world.

END Bulletin. 6 Endsleigh St, London WC1. Quarterly.

FCNL Newsletter. Friends Committee on National Legislation, 245 2nd St NE, Washington, DC 20002. Widely acclaimed newsletter of a Quaker lobby.

Fellowship. Fellowship of Reconcilation, PO Box 271, Nyack, NY 10960. Relates peace action to religious faith.

Just Peace. Blackfriars Hall, Southampton Rd, London, NW5. Produced by Pax Christi.

National Catholic Reporter. PO Box 281, Kansas City, MO 64141. Newspaper format. Catholic perspective on national and world issues, including peace.

The Other Side. 300 W. Apsley St, Philadelphia, PA 19144. Applies biblical faith to current issues of peace and justice.

The Pacifist. 6 Endsleigh St, London WC1. Peace Pledge Union Monthly.

Peace Education Newsletter. 9 Coombe Rd, New Malden, Surrey. Produced by the Fellowship of Reconciliation.

Peace News, 8 Elm Ave, Nottingham. Fortnightly, promotes pacifism and non-violent revolution.

SANE World. SANE, 514 C St NE, Washington, DC 20002. Published by SANE, a major US peace group.

Sanity. 11 Goodwin St, London N4 3HQ. Monthly magazine of CND.

Sojourners. 1309 L St NW, Washington, DC 20005. A rigorously biblical approach to the deepest issues of our time, including world peace.

WIN. 326 Livingston St, Brooklyn, NY 11217. Focuses on nonviolent approaches to peace and justice issues, including a monthly column on war tax resistance.

Appendix B

Organisations Working for Peace

This listing is not exhaustive, but gives most of the major peace organisations in the United States and some elsewhere. Not listed are the scores of local peace groups which do important work in parishes, congregations, neighbourhoods, cities and so on.

All of the groups listed are working for peace, but their orientations may be either pacifist or nonpacifist. We list the organisations without evaluation; listing them does not imply approval of everything they do.

Specifically Christian and denominational groups are listed in the first section. The second section includes secular groups and groups which cover a broad spectrum of religious orientation. The third section lists the various colleges and universities offering peace studies programmes. In England, Bradford University offers undergraduate and higher degree courses in peace studies.

1. Christian Peace Organisations

American Friends Service Committee. 1501 Cherry St, Philadelphia, PA 19102. National Quaker organisation with many regional offices across the United States. Offices provide speakers, printed material and audio-visuals on disarmament, militarism, effects of nuclear attacks, nonviolent action for peace, peace education. Long experience working for peace from pacifist point of view. Thirty-five peace education offices.

Anglican Pacifist Fellowship. St Mary's Church House, Bayswater Road, Oxford OX3 9EY. The Fellowship is especially concerned with persuading fellow-Churchmen that pacifism is inherent in the Faith which they profess.

Atlantic Life Community/Jonah House. 1933 Park Ave, Baltimore, MD 21217. Ecumenical peace community out of which Daniel and Philip Berrigan, Elizabeth McAlister and others have worked. Uses nonviolent action to oppose nuclear arms race.

Baptist Peace Fellowship. Contact: Larry Pullen, Peace Concerns, National Ministries, American Baptist Churches, Valley Forge, PA 19481. An association of Baptists who have made a common commitment to live nonviolently and to work for world peace. Publishes a newsletter; sponsors workshops.

Brethren in Christ Commission on Peace and Social Concerns. 728 Fulton St, Akron, PA 17501. The official agency of a denomination which belongs to the National Association of Evangelicals.

Brethren Peace Fellowship. Contact: Charles Boyer, On Earth Peace, Church of the Brethren, 1451 Dundee Ave, Elgin, IL 60120.

Catholic Peace Fellowship. Tom Cornell, National Secretary, 12 Bay View Terr., Newburgh, NY 12550. Staff: Bill Ofenlock, 339 Lafayette St, New York, NY 10012. Approaches peace and disarmament questions from perspective of New Testament and Catholic teachings.

Centre for Peace Studies. 2 O'Hara, Georgetown Univ., Washington, DC 20057. Provides peace education resources from point of view of teachings of Christ and the gospel. Books, slide shows, posters, pamphlets, tapes, films.

Christian CND. 11 Goodwin St, London, N4 3HQ. A specialist section of CND concerned with work in the churches.

Christian Movement for Peace. Stowford House, Bayswater Rd, Oxford.

Church of God Peace Fellowship. Maurice Caldwell, Chairperson, Missions Board, Church of God, 1303 E. 5th St, Anderson, IN 46011.

The Churches' Centre for Theology and Public Policy. 4400 Massachusetts Ave NW, Washington, DC 20016. An ecumenical study centre to strengthen the vocations of Christians in the political order. Special studies on peace include: 'Public Opinion and Disarmament: Challenge to the Churches' and 'Arms Exports in Christian Perspective.'

Commission for International Justice and Peace. 38 Eccleston Sq., SW1. Roman Catholic peace organisation.

Disciples Peace Fellowship. Alton Beaver, President, 4415 6th St, Medford, OK 73759. Ian McCrae, Executive Secretary, PO Box 1986, 222 S. Downey, Indianapolis, IN 46206.

Episcopal Peace Fellowship. Rev. John Gessell, Chairperson, School of Theology, University of the South, Sewanee, TN 37375.

Evangelicals for Social Action. 25 Commerce SW, Grand Rapids, MI 49503. Biblical concern for justice and peace from evangelical Christian base. National membership organisation with local chapters. Produces newsletter, conferences, pamphlets. Holds workshops on stopping the nuclear arms race.

Friends Committee on National Legislation. 245 Second St NE, Washington, DC20002. Quaker lobby and information centre. Works to influence Congress and the administration on a broad range of peace and justice issues. Compiles voting records to show how Representatives vote on key issues. Publishes newsletter, pamphlets and other written material on disarmament and foreign policy issues.

Lutheran Peace Fellowship. Rev. John F. Backe, Coordinator, 168 W. 100th St, New York, NY 10025. Develops programmes for congregational and retreat use. Publishes a newsletter and other sources of information. Counsels individuals on questions of conscience. Stresses disarmament, nonviolence, peace education and lifestyle.

Mennonite Central Committee, Peace Section. 21 S. 12th St, Akron, PA 17501. The centre for education and coordination of peace witness for the various Mennonite bodies.

Network. 806 Rhode Island Ave NE, Washington, DC 20018. Catholic multi-issue social justice lobby. Publishes quarterly articles on disarmament and human rights, including Vatican statements on disarmament.

New Call to Peacemaking. PO Box 1245, Elkhart, IN 46515. A renewal movement within the historic peace churches (Mennonite, Brethren and Quaker).

Pacific Life Community. 631 Kiely Blvd, Santa Clara, CA 95051. Ecumenical Peace community committed to nonviolent action to reverse the arms race.

Pax Center. 345 E. 9th St, Erie, PA 16503. Maintains a centre that supplies books, audio-visuals, speakers, curriculum on nonviolence, peace, social justice. Works for nuclear disarmament. Sponsors Prolifers for Survival. Publishes newsletter: *Erie Christian Witness*.

Pax Christi. St Francis of Assisi Centre, Pottery Lane, London, W11. An international Roman Catholic peace organisation.

Prolifers for Survival. 252 E. 9th St, Erie, PA 16503. An anti-abortion group which also works to link the prolife and peace movements. See also Pax Centre.

Quaker Peace Fellowship. Contacts: Jack and Chris Payden-

Travers, 523 N. Broadway, Nyack, NY 10960. Lee Stern, 57 4th Ave, Nyack, NY 10960.

Quaker Peace and Service. Friends House, Euston Rd, London, NW1 2BJ. Has a selection of peace posters and literature, and also a Peace Caravan that tours the country visiting fairs etc.

Riverside Church Disarmament Programme. 490 Riverside Dr, New York, NY 10027. Provides speakers and materials for local disarmament education, especially for the religious community. Publishes Blue Book Series of sermons and speeches on peace. Also books, posters, audio-visual packets telling how to organise a Peace Sabbath.

Sojourners Peace Ministry. 1309 L Street NW, Washington, DC 20005. A ministry of the Christian community that publishes *Sojourners* magazine. Emphasises biblical perspective. Produces written materials and study guides for churches on nuclear arms race and Christian response. Organises nonviolent actions against nuclear idols.

Southern Baptist Convention, Christian Life Commission. 460 James Robertson Pkwy, Nashville, TN 37219. Staffed programme on peacemaking.

Southern Presbyterian Peace Fellowship. Genevieve Yancey, Chairperson, 1808 Stokes La, Nashville, TN 37215. Lilith Otey, Secretary-Treasurer and Editor, 726 Hartford Ave, Charlotte, NC 28209. Produces newsletter.

United Church of Christ Peace Advocacy Project. Dr Zelle Andrews, Director, 110 Maryland Ave NE, Washington, DC 20002. A staffed peace effort.

United Church Peace Fellowship. Contacts: Rev. T. A. Braun, 505 Orchard Dr, Carbondale, IL 62901. Dr Howard Schomer, 475 Riverside Dr, New York, NY 10027.

United Methodist Board of Church and Society, Department of Peace and World Order. Robert McClean, Director, Churches Centre for the United Nations, 777 UN Plaza, New York, NY 10017.

United Methodist Peace Fellowship. Dr John Swomley, 5123 Truman Rd, Kansas City, MO 64127.

United Presbyterian Peace Fellowship. John Connor, Chairperson, 101 NW 23rd, Corvallis, OR 97330. L. William Yolton, Executive Secretary, 216 Thurston, Rochester, NY 14619. Provides support for those seeking to live a nonviolent lifestyle and to advocate policies of peace.

United States Catholic Conference, Office of International Justice and Peace. 1312 Massachusetts Ave NW, Washington, DC 20005. Addresses the arms race in the context of Catholic teaching. Aids US Catholic Bishops in forming policy. Publishes special studies, e.g., 'The Arms Race: Illusion or Security.'

World Peacemakers. 2852 Ontario Rd NW, Washington, DC 20009. Arose out of the Church of the Saviour. Provides resources for local Christian peace groups that engage in individual peacemaking and political action. Publishes *Handbook for World Peacemaker Groups, World Peace Papers* and other materials. Holds training workshops, conferences.

2. Interreligious and Secular Peace Organisations

American Committee on East-West Accord. 227 Massachusetts Ave NW, Washington, DC 20002. Organisation of prominent Americans who support peace efforts through negotiation and detente.

American Security Council. 1101 17th St NW, Washington, DC 20005. Opposite point of view of this book. Works for strong military. Opposed SALT II arms control agreement. 'Peace through strength.'

Another Mother for Peace. 407 N. Maple St, Beverly Hills, CA 90210. Peace lobby begun during Vietnam War.

Anti-Nuclear Campaign. 9 Poland St, London W1V 3DG.

Armaments and Disarmament Information Unit. Mantell Building, University of Sussex. A small but active unit intended to provide information for anyone interested in armaments and disarmament. Produces a bi-monthly bulletin, especially useful for a detailed listing of papers and articles published in newspapers and general academic journals.

Arms Control and Disarmament Agency. Department of State, Washington, DC 20451. Official US government body doing research and publications on arms control and disarmament.

Arms Control and Disarmament Research Unit. Foreign and Commonwealth Office, London. Source of statements on British Government Policy. Publishes regular newsletters containing up-to-date articles.

Arms Control Association. 11 Dupont Circle NW, Washington, DC 20036. National nonpartisan organisation using conferences, seminars and newsletter (*Arms Control Today*) to promote arms control policies and programmes.

Business Executives Move for New National Priorities. 901 N.

Howard St, Baltimore, MD 21201. More than two thousand businessmen and women who oppose excessive military spending and work to transfer military monies to civilian programmes. Newsletter: *Newsnotes*.

Campaign against the Arms Trade. 5 Caledonian Rd, London, N1.

Campaign for Nuclear Disarmament. 11 Goodwin St, London N4. Membership growing fast and a significant trend in 1981 was its increasing support from trade unions and some political parties.

Carnegie Endowment for International Peace. 11 Dupont Circle NW, Washington, DC 20036. Promotes national and international conferences on disarmament and peace. Publishes books and articles. Does research on foreign policy issues.

Central Board for Conscientious Objectors. 6 Apollo Place, London SW10. Gives advice on the rights of those in the armed forces who claim to have a conscientious objection to military service.

Central Committee for Conscientious Objectors. 2208 South St, Philadelphia, PA 19146; and 1251 2nd Ave, San Francisco, CA 94122. Provides military and draft counselling and legal help. Produces written materials (such as *Handbook for C.O.'s*) and audio-visual materials (such as *Are You a Conscientious Objector: Resisting War in the '80s*) designed especially for secondary-school and college groups.

Centre for Defense Information. 303 Capital Gallery W., 600 Maryland Ave SW, Washington, DC 20024. A research organisation staffed in part by former military officers. Supports a strong defence, but opposes excessive military spending and advocates nuclear disarmament. Publishes newsletter (*The Defense Monitor*), special reports, the *Nuclear War Prevention Kit*, and a film called 'War without Winners.'

Centre for Defence Studies. University of Aberdeen. Involved in research and planning of defence issues at a national and international level. Runs an M.Litt degree course in Strategic Studies for postgraduates.

Centre for War/Peace Studies. 218 E. 18th St, New York, NY 10003. Publishes *Global Report* magazine. A research centre with the motto 'applied research toward a world of peace with justice.'

Centre on Law and Pacifism. PO Box 1584, Colorado Springs, CO 80901. Provides advice and materials for war tax resisters. Publishes a newsletter and a comprehensive guide entitled

People Pay for Peace. Write for information and prices. Chapters in over twenty-eight states.

Clergy and Laity Concerned. 198 Broadway, New York, NY 10038. An interfaith organisation with national staff and 40 chapters. Dedicated to religious and political action for peace and justice. Newsletter: *CALC Report*. Publishes *Worship and Action Resources for a Non-Nuclear Future*.

Coalition for a New Foreign and Military Policy. 120 Maryland Ave NE, Washington, DC 20002. Coalition of church and civic groups working for peace and justice. Regular mailings on disarmament, economic conversion, military budget. Focus on influencing government policy and legislation. Eight thousand grassroots members.

Committee on the Present Danger. 1028 Connecticut Ave NW, Washington, DC 20036. Major nonpartisan think-tank calling for American military superiority. Opposite point of view of this book.

Conscience and Military Tax Campaign. 44 Bellhaven Rd, Bellport, NY 11713. Encourages war tax resistance and advises resisters. Seeking signatures on a resolution by people who will begin war tax resistance as soon as 100,000 signatures are collected.

Consortium on Peace Research, Education, and Development (COPRED). Centre for Peaceful Change, Stopher Hall, Kent State University, Kent, OH 44242. Over 300 members. Works to promote peace studies in college curricula.

Council for a Livable World. 11 Beacon St, Boston, MA 02108. Legislative Office: 100 Maryland Ave NE, Washington, DC 20002. A public interest group. Raises funds for political candidates who work for arms control. Issues fact sheets, recommends alternative government policies.

Council on Economic Priorities. 84 5th Ave, New York, NY 10011. Produces regular data reporting the relation between defence spending and employment and how to convert military into civilian production.

Council on Religion and International Affairs. 170 E. 64th St, New York, NY 10021. Publishes *Worldview* magazine. Active seminar programme on peace and global issues.

Disarm Education Fund. 175 5th Ave, New York, NY. Produces printed and multi-media material on the impact of military spending and the arms race. Special focus on Congress and the mass media.

Educators for Social Responsibility. 25 Kennard Rd, Brookline, MA 02146. Organised to give peace education in colleges and secondary schools.

European Nuclear Disarmament. 227 Seven Sisters Rd, London N4. Developed partly as a response to the NATO decision to deploy cruise missiles and the Pershing II. Work is co-ordinated by a small group and contact maintained by quarterly END publication.

Federation of American Scientists. 307 Massachusetts Ave NE, Washington, DC 20002. Licensed lobby of seven thousand scientists and engineers concerned with the threat of nuclear weapons. Acts as a conscience to the scientific community. Publishes books and reports on arms control and disarmament.

Fellowship of Reconciliation. Box 271, Nyack, NY 10960 and 9 Coombe Rd, New Malden, Surrey, KT3 4QA. An interfaith organisation with chapters in twenty-eight countries. Members committed to nonviolence. Publishes *Fellowship* magazine. Produces books, audio-visuals, and other materials on peace, nonviolence, disarmament, and war taxes. Sells cards, notes and gifts with peace motifs.

The Fund for Peace. 121 Constitution Ave NE, Washington, DC 20002. Supports three research centres that do in-depth research on military matters. Sponsors the radio programme 'In the Public Interest.'

Global Education Associates. 552 Park Ave, East Orange, NY 07017. A network of people from fifty countries who work to create a more peaceful world order. Emphasises values of social and economic justice, peace, ecological balance and participation in decision making.

High Technology Professionals for Peace. 52 Walker St, Newtonville, MA 02106. Sponsors a nonprofit employment agency to help people find employment in non-defence work.

Hiroshima Peace Culture Foundation. 1–2 Nakajima-cho, Naka-ku, Hiroshima City 733, Japan. Major Japanese peace education centre. Maintains peace museum, library with thousands of volumes on bombing of Hiroshima. Newsletter: *Peace Culture*.

Hudson Institute. Quaker Ridge Rd, Croton-on-Hudson, NY 10520. A think-tank for studies on nuclear war. Generally takes positions opposite to those in this book, including the position that nuclear war can be limited and can be won.

IMPACT. 100 Maryland Ave NE, Washington, DC 20002. Grassroots network of individuals motivated by religious or moral convictions to influence US policy on issues including disarmament. Sends out action alerts and anlyses once a month.

Institute for Defense and Disarmament Studies. 251 Harvard St, Brookline, MA 02146. Does research and public education on the nature and purpose of US military forces. Their *American Peace Directory* describes 2,000 national and local American peace groups.

Institute for World Order. 777 UN Plaza, New York, NY 10017. Produces written and audio-visual materials on the arms race. Their World Order Models Project focuses on how to build a more peaceful world.

International Association of Machinists. 1300 Connecticut Ave NW, Washington, DC 20036. An international union which supports planned economic conversion to a less militarily oriented economy. Produced the study 'The Impact of Military Spending on the Machinists Union.'

International Institute for Strategic Studies. 23 Tavistock St, London WC2. IISS is the major applied research institute for strategic studies in Western Europe. Its orientation is strongly pro-NATO. It publishes a bi-monthly journal, *Survival*, and two important annual surveys: *Strategic Survey* and *Military Balance*. Its publications are regarded as reasonably authoritative but by no means infallible.

International Peace Academy. 777 UN Plaza, New York, NY 10017. Trains diplomats and government officials in peacekeeping and mediation techniques. Studies and evaluates UN peace-keeping efforts.

Jewish Peace Fellowship. PO Box 271, Nyack, NY 10960. Jewish clergy and laity focusing on nonviolent conflict resolution and promoting social justice.

Lawyers Against the Bomb. O. N. Davies, 2 Garden Court, Middle Temple, London EC4.

Medical Campaign Against Nuclear Weapons. c/o Claire Ryle, 23a Tenison Rd, Cambridge. Supplies speakers, film, cassette and slide material for use by other groups. The group is concerned with both the long-term and short-term effects of nuclear war.

Mid-Peninsula Conversion Project. 867 W. Dana St, Mountain View, CA 94041. Focuses on arms race, military budget and how to achieve economic conversion. Published research project *Creating Solar Jobs: Options for Military Workers and Communities*.

Mobilization for Survival. 48 Saint Marks Place, New York, NY

10003. A coalition of religious and secular groups emphasising education and action in peace and justice. Produces educational resource packets, newsletter, audio-visuals, buttons, T-shirts. Organises large nonviolent demonstrations.

Movement for a New Society. 4722 Baltimore Ave, Philadelphia, PA 19143. Grassroots network of people that train for and carry out projects based on active nonviolence.

National Action/Research on the Military-Industrial Complex. 1501 Cherry St, Philadelphia, PA 19102. Does research and provides reports and audio-visual resources on disarmament and the military.

National Council of Churches of Christ in the U.S.A. Subcommittee on Peace, Security and Disarmament. 475 Riverside Dr, New York, NY 10027. Brings together denominational representatives to consider Christian responses to current issues.

National Interreligious Service Board for Conscientious Objectors. 550 Washington Building, 15th and New York Ave NW, Washington, DC 20002. Service organisation sponsored by a broad coalition of religious groups to aid conscientious objectors, both those outside and those inside the military. Provides attorneys for those needing legal counsel.

National Nuclear Weapons Freeze Clearinghouse. 4144 Lindell Blvd, No. 201, St Louis, MO 63108.

National Parenting for Peace and Justice Network. 2913 Locust St, St Louis, MO 63103. Provides workshops, literature and other resources to help families integrate family life and social ministry. Members receive a Network newsletter and other mailings.

National Peace Academy Campaign. 1625 Eye St NW, Suite 125, Washington, DC 20006. A nonpartisan, public interest campaign to establish a Federal educational institution to promote peace.

Non-Governmental Organization Committee on Disarmament. Room 7D, 777 UN Plaza, New York, NY 10017. Publishes *Disarmament Times* newspaper and runs a Disarmament Information Centre, especially during special UN sessions on disarmament.

Nuclear Weapons Facilities Project. 1428 Lafayette St, Denver, CO 80218. Provides information and coordinates actions to convert nuclear weapons facilities into socially useful production. Produces organising packet, slideshow, studies.

Peace Pledge Union. 6 Endsleigh St, London WC1. Members pledge to renounce war and never support or sanction another.

The PPU is a British Section of the War Resisters' International.

Peace Science Society. Peace Science Unit, University of Pennsylvania, 3718 Locust Walk, Philadelphia, PA 19104. An association of peace teachers and researchers from around the world. Publishes *Journal of Peace Science*.

Peace Tax Campaign. 26 Thurlow Rd, Leicester, LE2 1YE. Campaigns for the right to refuse to pay defence/war taxes.

Peacemakers. PO Box 627, Garberville, CA 95440. An association of people who refuse to pay income tax to protest against the arms race. Publishes *The Peacemaker* newsletter and *Handbook on the Non-Payment of War Taxes*.

Physicians for Social Responsibility. PO Box 295, Cambridge, MA 02238. National membership organisation of over twelve thousand doctors, medical students and other health professionals. Produces studies and holds conferences to provide the medical community and the public with information on the dangers and medical effects of nuclear power and nuclear weapons. Newsletter, slide show, special reports. Chapters across the United States.

Promoting Enduring Peace. PO Box 103, Woodmont, CT 06460. A research service which sends out hundreds of reprints of articles on peace. Also sponsors seminars, international trips.

SANE. National office: 711 G St SE, Washington, DC 20003. National organisation mobilising grassroots support for American initiatives for peace and disarmament. Sponsor radio show: 'Consider the Alternatives.' Newsletter: *SANE World*.

School of Peace Studies. University of Bradford, Bradford BD7 1DP, West Yorkshire. It was established, with considerable Quaker support, in 1973 and runs undergraduate and postgraduate degree courses in peace studies. Has a series of Peace Studies Papers, covering many topics.

Scientists Against Nuclear Arms. c/o Christopher Meredith, 8 Medland, Woughton Park, Milton Keynes, MK6 3BH. An independent organisation of scientists, formed in response to the acute dangers of the continued escalation of nuclear armaments and the consequent risk of nuclear war. The term 'scientist' includes natural and social scientists, engineers and technologists.

Stockholm International Peace Research Institute. Bergsrama. S-17173, Sona, Sweden. Independent institute for research into problems of peace and conflict, especially those of disarmament and arms regulations.

Union of Concerned Scientists. 1348 Massachusetts Ave, Cambridge, MA 02238. Scientists, engineers and technologists campaigning for nuclear arms control. Arms control programme based at: 1725 I St NW, Suite 601, Washington, DC 20006.

United Nations Information Center. 2101 L St NW, Washington, DC 20037. Provides material on UN programmes, including studies on disarmament, and the periodical *Disarmament*.

War Resisters International. 55 Dawes St, London SE17 1EL. Exists to bring together pacifists, war resisters, conscientious objectors to military service and nonviolent activists from around the world.

War Resisters League. 330 Lafayette St, New York, NY 10012. National pacifist organisation opposed to armaments, conscription and war. Publishes a free newsletter, *WRL News*, and subscription magazine, *WIN*. Regional offices and local chapters. Publishes excellent organisers' manual and *Guide to War Tax Resistance*.

Women's International League for Peace and Freedom. 1213 Race St, Philadelphia, PA 19107. An international organisation stressing nonviolent solutions to domestic and international problems. Local chapters work on disarmament and related issues. Issues newsletter and other printed material.

Women's Strike for Peace. 145 S. 13th St, Philadelphia, PA 19107. Women working to ban nuclear testing, end the arms race and achieve disarmament. Local chapters.

World Conference on Religion and Peace. 777 UN Plaza, New York, NY 10017. Draws together religious leaders from many traditions and countries for common work for peace. Publishes a newsletter and disarmament workbook. Holds conferences.

World Disarmament Campaign. 21 Little Russell St, London WC1 4HF. Aims primarily at supporting United Nations initiatives for multilateral disarmament. Has many local affiliated groups and attracts support from members of all the major political parties. *Churches Liaison*: The Revd Will Elliott, 35 Station Rd, Harpenden, Herts.

World Federalists Association. 1011 Arlington Blvd, Suite W-119, Arlington, VA 22209. Educational organisation working to create global institutions with authority to deal with global problems, including one to oversee multilateral disarmament and settle international disputes. Chapters throughout the United States. Seeks to reform and revitalise the UN.

World Peace Tax Fund. 2111 Florida Ave NW, Washington, DC 20008. Lobbies for an alternative for people opposed to paying taxes to support the arms race. Provides materials on the issue, including a slide show.

World without War Council. 175 5th Ave, New York, NY 10010. Publishes comprehensive *World Disarmament Kit* and other materials.

3. Peace Studies Programmes

College and university peace research and education is coordinated by a federation of over ninety peace institutions (most of them located in schools of higher education) called the *Consortium of Peace Education, Research and Development* (COPRED). Centre for Peaceful Change, Stopher Hall, Kent State University, Kent, OH 44242.

Peace study programmes are available at many colleges and universities, including the following:

Antioch International. Yellow Springs, OH 45387. MA in peace studies.

Associated Mennonite Biblical Seminaries. Elkhart, IN 46417. MA in peace studies.

Bethel College. Newton, KS 67117. Bachelor degree in peace studies as part of an undergraduate double major.

Boston College. Chestnut Hill, MA 02167. Undergraduate associate degree.

Chapman College. Orange, CA 92666. Undergraduate minor with internship.

Colgate University. Hamilton, NY 13346. Bachelor degree.

Conrad Grebel College, University of Waterloo. Waterloo, Ontario, Canada.N2L 3G6. Undergraduate degree.

Cornell University. Ithaca, NY 14580. Graduate programme only.

Earlham College. Richmond, IN 47374. Certificate or major in peace studies.

Earlham School of Religion. Richmond, IN 47374. MA or MMin.

Garrett-Evangelical Peace and Justice Center. Evanston, IL 60201. MDiv, MTS, PhD (with Northwestern University).

Georgetown University. Washington, DC 20057. Undergraduate major.

Goddard College. Plainfield, VT 05667. Bachelor degree.

Goshen College. Goshen, IN 46526. Co-major bachelor degree.

Gustavus Adolphus College. St Peter, MN 56082. Informal programme of lectures.

Juniata College. Huntington, PA 16652. Bachelor degree.

Kent State University. Kent, OH 44242. Bachelor degree.

Manchester College. North Manchester, IN 46942. BA or BS.

Manhattan College. Bronx, NY 10471. Undergraduate and graduate programmes.

St Joseph's University. Edwardsville, IL 62026. Undergraduate minor.

Syracuse University. Syracuse, NY 13210. Bachelor and graduate-level degrees in conjunction with a social science PhD.

University of Akron. Akron, OH 44325. Undergraduate certificate or minor.

University of Colorado. Boulder, CO 80309. Undergraduate major or minor.

University of Denver. Denver, CO 80208. Academic programme without degree.

University of Missouri. Columbia, MO 65211. Bachelor degree.

University of Notre Dame. Notre Dame, IN 46556. Studies, no degree.

University of Pennsylvania. Philadelphia, PA 19174. Master and doctoral programmes.

University of Wisconsin. Madison, WI 53703. Bachelor degree.

Wayne State University. Detroit, MI 48202. Undergraduate co-major.

Wilmington College. Wilmington, OH 45177. Undergraduate major or minor.

Appendix C

Audio-Visual Materials

For a comprehensive guide to recent films on war and peace, see John Dowling's *War Peace Film Guide* (World without War Publications, 67 E Madison, Suite 1417, Chicago, IL 60603). This resource not only lists and describes almost three hundred films, it also gives suggestions on how to organise a film series, lead a discussion and so on.

The films and film strips listed below are available from their distributors or may be obtained through some local libraries or the local office of a national peace group. In addition, the following two organisations may have copies available for rental: American Friends Service Committee, 1501 Cherry St, Philadelphia, PA 19102 (215/241-7000); Audio-Visuals Library, Mennonite Central Committee, 21 S 12th St, Akron, PA 17501.

Some two hundred 'peace' films are available from Concord Films Council in England, 201 Felixstowe Rd, Ipswich, Suffolk, IP3 9BJ.

1. Films

Boom (11 min., 16 mm., colour) UN cartoon on nuclear war. Distributed by Concord Films Council, 201 Felixstowe Rd, Ipswich, Suffolk, IP3 9BJ.

The Day after Trinity: J. Robert Oppenheimer and the Atomic Bomb. (88 min., 16 mm.) Pyramid Films, PO Box 1048, Santa Monica, CA 90406. Received an Academy Award nomination for best documentary. Shows how scientists like Oppenheimer collaborated to make the bomb, then became troubled and, in some cases, worked for disarmament. Highlights ethical issues.

The Fence. (7 min., 16 mm., colour, animated) BFA Educational Media, 2211 Michigan Ave, Santa Monica, CA 90404. A man throws rubbish over the fence into his neighbour's yard. Retaliation follows, until house and yard are demolished. Shows development of violence and explores alternatives.

Gandhi. (27 min., 16 mm., b/w) CRM/McGraw-Hill Films, 110

15th St, Del Mar, CA 92014. Narrated by Walter Cronkite. Simply and lucidly explains the Indian independence movement and Gandhi's philosophy of nonviolent social change.

Ground Zero at Bangor. (28 min., 16 mm., colour) Religious Broadcasting Commission, 356 Post-Intelligencer Building, 521 Wall St, Seattle, WA 98121. Explores the emotional debate between advocates of disarmament and advocates of military superiority. Includes scenes from nonviolent protest at Bangor, Washington, Trident submarine base.

Hiroshima-Nagasaki, August 1945. (15 min., 16 mm., b/w) Concord Films Council, 201 Felixstowe Rd, Ipswich, Suffolk, IP3 9BJ. A highly realistic and therefore gruesome film of the bombing of Hiroshima and Nagasaki. Not for young children.

The Last Epidemic: Medical Consequences of Nuclear Weaponry and Nuclear War. (45 min., 16 mm., colour or 3/4 video cassette) Impact Productions, 135 Hughes Ave, Santa Cruz, CA 95062; or Resource Centre for Nonviolence, PO Box 2324, Santa Cruz, CA 95063. Prominent scientists, doctors and arms-control specialists describe the medical results of an atomic attack. Action scenes are interspersed.

The Magician. (13 min., b/w) Concord Films Council, 201 Felixstowe Rd, Ipswich, Suffolk, IP3 9BJ. Children are enticed by a magician to learn to shoot, first at targets, then. . . . A powerful story on the dynamics of war and violence.

Martin Luther King, Jr. (30 min., 16 mm., b/w) Time-Life Films, 100 Eisenhower Dr, Paramus, NJ 07652. Impressive and moving portrayal of King and his nonviolent struggle for justice.

Missiles of October. (155 min., 16 mm., colour) Learning Corporation of America, 1350 Avenue of the Americas, New York, NY 10019. Dramatisation of the Cuban missile crisis of October 1962.

Nonviolence: Mahatma Gandhi and Martin Luther King. (15 min., 16 mm., colour) Picture Films, 111 Eighth Ave, New York, NY 10011. Explores the parallels between the two leaders. Includes an interview with Gandhi, excerpts from King's speeches, action documentary of the Indian and Black movements.

Nuclear Countdown (28 min., 16 mm., colour) UN documentary on nuclear war. Distributed by Concord Films Council, 201 Felixstowe Rd, Ipswich, Suffolk, IP3 9BJ. For information about other UN films, write to United Nations Radio and Visual Services Division, New York, NY 10017.

One Thousand Cranes: The Children of Hiroshima. (24 min., 16 mm., b/w) MacMillan Films, 34 Macquesten Pky S, Mt Vernon, NY 10550. Sensitive film showing the efforts of Japanese children to dramatise the effects of the atomic bombing by folding paper cranes.

Paul Jacobs and the Nuclear Gang. (60 min., 16 mm., colour) Concord Films Council, 201 Felixstowe Rd, Ipswich, Suffolk, IP3 9BJ. Winner of Emmy award for best documentary. Shows effects of radiation on humans from the atomic-bomb tests of the 1950s, and the government response to GIs who participated.

Training for Nonviolence. (20 min., 16 mm., b/w) Concord Films Council, 201 Felixstowe Rd, Ipswich, Suffolk, IP3 9BJ. Shows the process used to maintain nonviolence during civil disobedience campaign at the Seabrook, New Hampshire nuclear power plant in 1977. Shows that nonviolence is the result of a lot of training, discussion and discipline.

The War Game. (49 min., 16 mm., b/w) Concord Films Council, 201 Felixstowe Rd, Ipswich, Suffolk, IP3 9BJ. Fictional but highly realistic depiction of a nuclear attack on England. Grimly powerful.

War without Winners. (27 min., 16 mm., colour) Concord Films Council, 201 Felixstowe Rd, Ipswich, Suffolk, IP3 9BJ. Highly professional film. Shows realities of nuclear age. Interviews ordinary citizens in the USA and the Soviet Union who express their fears and hopes.

The Weight. (60 min., 16 mm., colour) Tells the story of a conscientious objector. J. Ronald Byler, MBM/Media Ministries, PO Box 1252, Harrisonburg, VA 22801.

Who's in Charge Here? (15 min., 16 mm., colour). Operation Turning Point, 777 UN Plaza, New York, NY 10017. Narrated by Eli Wallach. Examines economic impact of US military spending on jobs, taxes, inflation. Interviews defence workers. Looks at alternatives.

2. Slide Shows and Filmstrips

Acceptable Risk? The Nuclear Age in the United States. (35 min. slide show or filmstrip with cassette/tape narration and study-action guide.) Concord Films Council, 201 Felixstowe Rd, Ipswich, Suffolk, IP3 9BJ. Examines the costs, problems and alternatives of both nuclear power and nuclear weapons.

Are You a Conscientious Objector? Resisting War in the '80s.

(17 min. colour slide show with tape narration) Central Committee for Conscientious Objectors, 2208 South St, Philadelphia, PA 19146. Introduces secondary-school and college-age people to the concepts of conscientious objection and war resistance. Especially appealing to teenagers.

A Call to Arms Control. (15 min. slide show with tape cassette) Operation Turning Point, 777 UN Plaza, New York, NY 10017. Good discussion-starter. Discussion guide included.

Christians and the Arms Race. (15 min. slide show or filmstrip with tape cassette) Riverside Church Disarmament Programme, 490 Riverside Dr, New York, NY 10027. Also from Mennonite Central Committee, Audio-Visuals Library. Old and New Testament bases for Peacemaking. Discussion guide included.

Every Heart Beats True: Christian Perspectives on the Military Service. (20 min. slide show with tape narration) Packard Manse Media Project, PO Box 450, Stoughton, MA 02072. Encourages high-school and college young people to consider conscientious objection. Reviews peace witness of early Christian, just war theory, present nature of military service.

Guns or Butter? Uncle Sam's Military Tapeworm. (30 min. slide show with tape narration) SANE, 318 Massachusetts Ave NE, Washington, DC 20002, or from Mennonite Central Committee, Audio-Visuals Library. Shows how growth of military spending drains resources needed for civilian economy at home and to meet needs abroad. Narrated by Paul Newman.

I Have Three Children of My Own. (20 min. slide show with tape narration) Packard Manse Media Project, PO Box 450, Stoughton, MA 02072. Dr Helen Caldicott gives an inspiring narration of the dangers of nuclear development.

John and Mary, MIRV and MARV: The Arms Race and the Human Race. (15 min. colour slide show with tape narration) Institute for World Order, 777 UN Plaza, New York, NY 10017. Urges the United States and the USSR to realise no-one can win the nuclear arms race. Leadership kit accompanies.

The Last Slide Show. (20 min. slide show with tape narration) Clergy and Laity Concerned, 198 Broadway, New York, NY 10038, and Packard Manse Media Project, PO Box 450, Stoughton, MA 02072. Hopeful and life-affirming presentation about the arms race. Ends on joyous note of people's ability to prevent nuclear war.

Nuclear Disaster. (slide show with cassette tape and transcript)

Centre for Peace Studies, 2 O'Gara, Georgetown University, Washington, DC 20057. Uses charts and Hiroshima photos to illustrate blast, firestorm and radiation effects of nuclear weapons.

Peace in Search of Makers. (30 min. slide show with tape narration) Riverside Church Disarmament Programme, 490 Riverside Dr, New York, NY 10027. Graphic history of the nuclear era from Hiroshima onward. Explores theological and biblical themes.

The Race Nobody Wins. (15 min. colour slide show or filmstrip with guide and tape narration) SANE, 318 Massachusetts Ave NE, Washington, DC 20002. Well-documented presentation of threat of nuclear war, costliness of international arms race. Narrated by Tony Randall.

Rocky Flats Slide Show. (25 min. slide show with script) American Friends Service Committee, Rocky Flats Project, 1432 Lafayette, Denver, CO 80218. Background on nuclear arms race and history of five-year campaign to close the Rocky Flats Nuclear Weapons Plant.

War to End All Wars. (22 min. slide show or filmstrip) The Shaftesbury Project, Audio-visuals, 8 Oxford St, Nottingham, NG1 5BH, or from Concord Films Council, 201 Felixstowe Rd, Ipswich, Suffolk, IP3 9BJ. A biblically based presentation by The Shaftesbury Project on Christian Involvement in Society. Explores just war theory and pacifism as Christian response to modern war.

Whose Budget Is It Anyway? (20 min. slide show or filmstrip) National Action/Research on the Military-Industrial Complex, 1501 Cherry St, Philadelphia, PA 19102. Shows how increased military spending undercuts needed programmes for education, the elderly and so on. Calls for citizen action to reshape the Federal budget to meet human needs.

Appendix D

Curriculum Materials for Local Congregations

Christian CND Resource Pack. Set of four information leaflets.
CND, 11 Goodwin St, London N4 3HQ.

Christian Perspectives on Nuclear Weapons, by Sydney D. Bailey.
A pamphlet produced by the Division of International Affairs
of the BCC, 2 Eaton Gate, London SW1.

Christians at the Crossroads. Recent church statements on war
and nuclear weapons. CND, 11 Goodwin St, London N4 3HQ.

David C. Cook Sunday-School Materials. These frequently include questions on peace and justice. David C. Cook Publishers, 850 N. Grove Ave, Elgin, IL 60120.

Disarming God's World. Six-session study programme with group
activities, worship aids, Bible studies and discussion ideas.
Order with leader's guide from Peacemaking Ministry, 165 W.
86th St, New York, NY 10024.

Educating for Peace and Justice. Geared especially for teachers.
Written by James and Kathleen McGinnis. Available from
Peace and Justice Institute, 2913 Locust St, St Louis, MO
63103.

Friendly Classroom for a Small Planet. Teachers' manual available from the Fellowship of Reconciliation, PO Box 271,
Nyack, NY 10960.

How to Teach Peace to Children. A paperback available from
Friends United Meeting, 101 Quaker Hill Dr, Richmond, IN
47374.

*A Matter of Faith: A Study Guide for Churches on the Nuclear
Arms Race*. Over thirty essays on the facts and faith issues
surrounding the nuclear arms race. Questions for thought and
discussion. Sojourners Peace Ministry, 1309 L St, NW,
Washington, DC 20005.

A New Call to Peacemakers. A ten-session study guide on the
roots of violence, God's plan for peace, and how God's people
can work for peace. Designed for secondary school students to

adults. Written by Maynard Shelly. Mennonite perspective. Available from Faith and Life Press, Newton, KS 67114.

Nuclear Mapping Kit. Gives instructions on how to determine the impact of a nuclear bomb exploding in your community. New Manhattan Project, American Friends Service Committee, 15 Rutherford Place, New York, NY 10003.

Nuclear War Prevention Kit. Describes effective ways for people to make their voices heard through letter writing, films, educational programmes and work with the mass media. Simple, practical, informative. Appropriate for adult church or action group. Centre for Defense Information, 303 Capitol Gallery W., 600 Maryland Ave SW, Washington, DC 20024.

Peace Making in a Nuclear Age. A Peace Pack intended to provide a stimulus to discussion and action, containing a comprehensive variety of material on the nuclear issue. The Scottish Episcopal Church, Bishop's House, Fairmont Rd, Perth, PH2 7AP, Scotland.

Blessed are the Peacemakers. Collection of sermons and articles. CND, 11 Goodwin St, London N4 3HQ.

Prayer for Peace. The prayer is available in a variety of formats, postcards, posters, stickers, music. The Caravan, 197 Piccadilly, London W1V 9LF.

Notes

Chapter 1: The First Hour

[1] *Sojourners* interview, Aug. 1979, p. 12.

[2] This description of the effects of a nuclear explosion on Moscow (and the US-USSR nuclear exchange described in chapter two) are taken from personal observations of Hiroshima and Nagasaki, discussions with survivors of the 1945 bombing of those cities, and the following written sources:

A Call from Hibakusha of Hiroshima and Nagasaki, Proceedings of the International Symposium on the Damage and After-Effects of the Atomic Bombing of Hiroshima and Nagasaki, July 21–Aug. 9, 1977.

Sidney D. Drell and Frank Von Hipple, 'Limited Nuclear War,' *Scientific American*, Nov. 1976, pp. 27ff.

Samuel Glasstone and Philip J. Dolan, eds., *The Effects of Nuclear Weapons* (Washington, DC: US Department of Defence and US Department of Energy, 1977).

John Hershey, *Hiroshima* (New York: Bantam, 1956).

Howard Hiatt, 'A Nuclear Attack on Washington,' statement before the US Senate Subcommittee on Health and Scientific Research, 19 June 1980, rpt in *Defense Monitor* 9, no. 6, pp. 6–8.

Hiroshima-Nagasaki: A Pictorial Record of the Atomic Destruction (Tokyo: Hiroshima-Nagasaki Pub., 1978).

Hiroshima Peace Memorial Museum, *The Outline of Atomic Bomb Damage in Hiroshima* (Hiroshima: Peace Memorial Museum, 1978).

Erwin Knoll and Theodore Postol. 'The Day the Bomb Went Off,' *The Progressive*, Oct. 1978, pp. 16ff.

Yoshiteru Kosakai, *A-Bomb: A City Tells Its Story* (Hiroshima: Hiroshima Peace Culture Centre, 1972).

Kevin N. Lewis, 'The Prompt and Delayed Effects of Nuclear War,' *Scientific American*, July 1979, pp. 35ff.

National Academy of Sciences, *Long-Term Worldwide Effects of Multiple Nuclear Weapons Detonations* (Washington, DC: National Academy of Sciences, 1975).

New Manhattan Project, *Nuclear Mapping Kit* (New York: American Friends Service Committee, 1979).

Physicians for Social Responsibility, *The Medical Consequences of Nuclear Weapons and Nuclear War* (Transcript of a conference held at the Harvard Science Centre, sponsored by Harvard Medical School and Tufts University School of Medicine, Feb. 1980).

Report from Nagasaki on the Damage and After-Effects of the Atomic Bombing (Nagasaki: Preparatory Committee for International Symposium on the Damage and After-Effects of Atomic Bombing of Hiroshima and Nagasaki) 1978.

Hitoshi Takayama, ed., *Hiroshima in Memoriam and Today* (Hiroshima: Toppan Printing, 1979).

US, Arms Control and Disarmament Agency, *The Effects of Nuclear War* (photocopied, Washington, DC, 1979).

US, Congress, Office of Technology Assessment, *The Effects of Nuclear War* (Washington, DC: Government Printing Office, 1979).

US, Congress, Senate, Committee on Banking, Housing and Urban Affairs, *Economic and Social Consequences of Nuclear Attacks on the United States* (Washington, DC: Government Printing Office, 1979).

[3]For a description of Soviet city defence see US, Library of Congress, Congressional Research Service, *United States and Soviet City Defense* (Washington, DC: Government Printing Office, 1976), pp. 13ff. Although Moscow has an antiballistic missile (ABM) system of sixty-four rockets designed to protect the city, 'US arms could easily saturate the single ABM site covering Moscow' and smash the city (p. 25). (The Soviet ABM system is permitted under the terms of the ABM treaty signed by both the United States and the USSR.)

[4]An Air Force missile crewman actually made a similar statement of commitment to Christ in an interview in the *Chicago Sun Times*, 14 Oct. 1979, p. 100. The article, which featured the role of women missile operators, was entitled, 'Female Hands Also at the Trigger of Powerful Nuclear Missiles.'

[5]For a description of Russian Baptists and other Christians in the USSR, see Christel Lane, *Christian Religion in the Soviet Union* (Albany: State University of New York Press, 1978), pp. 138ff. See also Walter Sawatsky, *Soviet Evangelicals since World War II* (Scottdale, Pa: Herald Press, 1981); John Lawrence, *Russians Observed* (Lincoln, Neb: University of Nebraska Press,

1969), pp. 61ff.; and Bart McDowell, *Journey across Russia: The Soviet Union Today* (Washington, DC: National Geographic Society, 1977), p. 184. A recent estimate of religion in the USSR puts the total number of religious believers (including 43 million Muslims and 3 million Jews) at some 115 million, about 45% of the country's population. See William G. Fletcher, *Soviet Believers: The Religious Sector of the Population* (Lawrence, Kans: Regents Press of Kansas, 1981); see also *Time*, 23 June 1980.

[6]Nothing in nature compares with the winds created by a nuclear explosion. A storm is classified as a hurricane when its winds top 74 mph. Catastrophic hurricane damage is caused by winds of 100–175 mph. The highest winds of the most violent hurricanes are under 250 mph. (See Ben Funk, 'Hurricane!' *National Geographic*, Sept. 1980, pp. 346ff.)

[7]The Kremlin, established in 1156, was originally built as a walled enclosure to hold Moscow's most important religious and public buildings. Moscow became the seat of the Eastern Orthodox faith in 1453. Under Ivan III and Tsar Ivan IV ('The Terrible') Moscow underwent a large-scale church building programme and became the artistic heart of Russia. Most of the Kremlin churches built in medieval times were preserved as artistic treasures by the Communists after they took power in 1917. See *New International Illustrated Encyclopedia of Art* (New York: Greystone Press, 1970), pp. 3790, 3794.

Chapter 2: The Awesome Destruction

[1]Remarks made in Strasbourg, 11 May 1979. Reprinted in a leaflet by the Campaign for Nuclear Disarmament, London, n.d.

[2]Richard McSorley, *Kill? For Peace?* (Washington, DC: Centre for Peace Studies, 1977), p. 5.

[3]Many studies have been done on the projected effects of nuclear war. No one can say with certainty exactly how many people would be killed or injured in such a war or what would be the exact effect. Some of the variables that have to be taken into account are the size of the attack, its timing (winter or summer, day or night), the targets hit, whether bombs explode in the air or on the earth's surface (the latter produce more radioactive fallout), warning times, and the effectiveness of defences. Some US Defence Department studies in the early 1970s outlined a rather optimistic estimate of casualties under a

nuclear attack. Congressional questioning prompted a new appraisal which was much less rosy, giving fatality figures four times as high as the earlier estimate. See US, Congress, Research Service, *United States and Soviet City Defense* (Washington, DC: Government Printing Office, 1976), pp. 20–23. See also Kevin N. Lewis, 'The Prompt and Delayed Effects of Nuclear War,' *Scientific American*, July 1979; and Sidney D. Drell and Frank Von Hipple, 'Limited Nuclear War,' *Scientific American*, Nov. 1976. All serious analysts conclude that all-out nuclear war would be far worse than any disaster humanity has ever experienced.

[4]The SS-N-8 carries a warhead with the explosive power of one megaton. A megaton is the amount of energy that would be released by the explosion of one million tons of TNT. The largest US warhead is nine megatons. Some Soviet warheads range up to twenty megatons. Since it is hard to envision a million tons, physicist Philip Morrison used the following illustration: Suppose the million tons of dynamite were to be delivered by freight train. The train would have to be as long as the state of Pennsylvania. The train would take more than six hours to pass a crossing. Yet that gigantic trainload of power would represent the power of a single submarine-loaded Polaris missile. (Cf., 'Scientists Preach Peace at MIT,' *Christian Century*, 15–22 Aug. 1979, p. 779.)

[5]ACDA, *The Effects of Nuclear War* (Washington, DC: Arms Control and Disarmament Agency, 1979), pp. 1–15.

[6]To comprehend what '1500 times' the Hiroshima bomb means, imagine a bomb the size of the Hiroshima bomb going off in Chicago. Now imagine another bomb of the same size hitting Chicago the next day, and every day of every year for *four years*. That is the amount of destructive power carried by just one rocket (SS-9) loaded with just one twenty-megaton warhead.

[7]Erwin Knoll and Theodore Postol, 'The Day the Bomb Went Off.' *The Progressive*, Oct. 1978, pp. 16ff.

[8]Estimate by Jack Geiger, quoted in *In These Times* 5, no. 29 (1–14 July 1981): 8.

[9]ACDA, *Effects of Nuclear War*, p. 16.

[10]This information from *London After the Bomb* is quoted in the *Christian Action Journal*, Winter 1982/3, which contains a Study Guide to the Anglican Report *The Church and the Bomb* (London: Hodder and Stoughton/CIO Publishing, 1982).

[11] Drell and Von Hipple, *Scientific American*, July 1979, p. 33.

[12] 'Special: SALT II,' National Broadcasting Company, 17 June 1979, p. 6.

[13] *Nuclear Weapons Storage and Deployment Sites* (Philadelphia: National Action and Research on the Military-Industrial Complex, 1980), p. 2.

[14] OTA, *Effects of Nuclear War*, pp. 63–80.

[15] The US death toll is higher because US refineries are nearer to large cities than are Soviet refineries. Also, Soviet missiles are larger and so cause more damage.

[16] OTA, *Effects of Nuclear War*, pp. 81–94.

[17] See Drell and Von Hipple, *Scientific American*, p. 33, for information on fallout patterns.

[18] When we think of disasters, we think of 'help from outside' (the Red Cross, etc.) pouring in to aid the survivors. Such outside aid arrived almost immediately in Hiroshima and Nagasaki. However, in full-scale atomic war, the 'outside' areas (the United States or its allies) would also be under attack and so would not be able to help a particular locale. With minor exceptions, each bombed area would be left to deal with the destruction on its own. See Dr H. Jack Geiger, 'The Illusion of "Survival,"' *Bulletin of Atomic Scientists* 37, no. 6 (June–July 1981): 16ff.

[19] US, Senate, Committee on Banking, Housing and Urban Affairs, *Economic and Social Consequences of Nuclear Attacks on the United States* (Washington, DC: Government Printing Office, 1979), p. 95.

[20] ACDA, *Effects of Nuclear War*, p. 23.

[21] Committee on Banking, *Economic and Social Consequences*, p. 20.

[22] John Hershey, *Hiroshima* (New York: Bantam Books, 1946), pp. 18, 33–34.

[23] Dr Howard Hiatt's undated statement is in the Centre for Defence Information's newsletter, *The Defense Monitor*, vol. 9, no. 6, 1980, p. 7.

[24] OTA, *Effects of Nuclear War*, p. 21.

[25] Kevin Lewis, *Scientific American*, p. 40.

[26] OTA, *Effects of Nuclear War*, p. 23.

[27] Ibid., p. 110.

[28] *To the UN: 1976: Hiroshima-Nagasaki* (booklet prepared by Mayors of Hiroshima and Nagasaki, n. p., p. 41). See also *A Call From Hibakusha of Hiroshima and Nagasaki*, Proceedings

of the International Symposium on the Damage and After-Effects of the Atomic Bombing of Hiroshima and Nagasaki, July 21–Aug. 8, 1977, pp. 62, 87.

[29] *To the UN*, p. 42. See also Dr Helen Caldicott, *Nuclear Madness: What You Can Do* (Brookline, Mass: Autumn Press, 1978), pp. 35–36.

[30] OTA, *Effects of Nuclear War*, p. 112.

[31] Ibid., p. 113. For a description of how genetic mutations are caused by radiation, see Dr Helen Caldicott, *Nuclear Madness*, pp. 31–32.

[32] *Long-Term Worldwide Effects of Multiple Nuclear Weapons Detonations* (Washington, DC: National Academy of Sciences, 1975), p. 16.

[33] Giff Johnson, 'Paradise Lost,' *Bulletin of Atomic Scientists*, Dec. 1980, p. 25.

[34] Dr Seymour Melman of Columbia University stated on 26 March 1980 that a nuclear warhead striking a large tank of waste nuclear material would create what experts call a 'beach.' The term is taken from the movie *On The Beach*, which describes the death in Australia of the last members of the human race through radioactivity from a nuclear war. According to Professor Melman, the radioactivity released from the nuclear waste 'would circle the hemisphere in such a large quantity that a burst in the northern part of the hemisphere would finally carry around the earth reaching Australia (where the movie was filmed) terminating life on the planet Earth.' Quoted in *The Corporate Examiner* (New York: Interfaith Centre for Corporate Responsibility, Oct. 1980), p. 38.

[35] ACDA, *Effects of Nuclear War*, p. 23.

[36] For a discussion of the problems of evacuation, see US, Congress, Congressional Research Service, *United States and Soviet City Defense* (Washington, DC: Government Printing Office, 1976), p. 17.

[37] ACDA, *Effects of Nuclear War*, p. 24. The worldwide impact would also be devastating, since other countries depend so heavily on the United States and Canada for grain. See *Long-Term World-Wide Effects*, p. 5 of letter of transmittal.

[38] For a detailed analysis of industrial impact, see Committee on Banking, *Economic and Social Consequences*.

[39] OTA, *Effects of Nuclear War*, p. 8.

[40] *Long-Term World-Wide Effects*, p. 6.

[41] ACDA, *Effects of Nuclear War*. The OTA study by the same

title, however, suggests that ozone depletion would not be this serious (p. 114). But Dr Kosta Tsipis, Professor of Physics at MIT says that even if only 'ten to twenty per cent of the Earth's ozone layer were depleted, all visual organisms – insects, birds, and mammals – would soon be blinded.' *Physicians for Social Responsibility Newsletter*, Dec. 1980, p. 3.

[42] *Long-Term World-Wide Effects*, p. 14, predicts 'an increase in skin cancer incidence of about 10%, with a range of uncertainty of perhaps three to thirty per cent.' This increase 'would be experienced at mid-latitudes for about forty years after the detonations.'

[43] Dr Henry Way Kendall, 'The Medical Consequences of Nuclear Weapons and Nuclear War,' speech at February 1980 conference of Physicians for Social Responsibility, p. 12.

[44] See, for example, Dr Ernest J. Sternglass, 'The Death of All Children,' *Esquire*, Sept. 1969. See also 'Pugwash 1980,' *Bulletin of Atomic Scientists*, Nov. 1980, p. 9. The article quotes the statement of an international group of scientists gathered at the Aug. 1980 Pugwash Conference on Science and World Affairs: 'A major nuclear war would mean the end of civilisation and could lead to the extinction of the human race.'

[45] Caldicott, *Nuclear Madness*, p. 82.

[46] Kendall, 'Medical Consequences,' p. 16.

[47] See Herman Kahn, *On Thermonuclear War* (Princeton, NJ: Princeton University Press, 1961).

[48] *Long-Term World-Wide Effects*, letter of transmittal, p. 2.

Chapter 3: Will Nuclear Weapons Be Used?

[1] Farewell Speech, 14 Jan. 1981.

[2] The word *strategic* refers either to long-range atomic weapons which can travel from one continent to another or to very powerful weapons designed to destroy an enemy's war-making potential. The United States, NATO, the USSR, the Warsaw Pact countries and China also have many short-range *tactical* atomic weapons, designed for battlefield use, which are not included in the calculations about the power of atomic weapons. The United States alone, for example, has about 22,000 tactical weapons, including nuclear artillery, nuclear land mines, anti-ICBM missiles, antisubmarine rockets. Even though they are designed for short-range use, many of these are more powerful than the Hiroshima bomb.

[3] The information on Soviet and American strategic forces (in-

cluding the estimated balance of forces for the early 1980s) is based on the following sources:

Arming for the '80's (Philadelphia: National Action and Research on the Military-Industrial Complex, 1980).

Thomas S. Burns, *The Secret War for the Ocean Depths* (New York: Rawson Associates Pub., 1978).

Is America Becoming Number 2? Current Trends in the U.S.-Soviet Military Balance (Washington, DC: Committee on the Present Danger, 1978).

Rear Admiral Gene R. LaRoque, 'Speech to United Nations,' *Defense Monitor*, July 1978.

The Military Balance (London: International Institute for Strategic Studies, 1979).

Paul H. Nitze Presentation before the Committee on Foreign Relations of the U.S. Senate, 12 July 1979.

US, Congress, House Committee on Foreign Affairs and Senate Foreign Relations Committee, *Fiscal Year 1981 Arms Control Impact Statements* (Washington, DC: Government Printing Office, 1980).

US, Congress, Office of Technology Assessment, *The Effects of Nuclear War* (Washington, DC: Government Printing Office, 1979), cf. appendix B, 'Strategic Forces Assumed.'

[4]The Soviet Union also has twenty-nine diesel-powered subs capable of launching ICBMs. In the autumn of 1980, the Soviet navy launched the first of its gigantic Typhoon subs. Typhoons are about forty feet longer and eleven thousand tons heavier than America's largest sub, the Trident. The Trident, launched in April 1979 and scheduled for patrol in 1982, carries twenty-four ICBMs, while the larger Typhoon carries twenty. See 'Soviets Launch World's Largest Sub,' *Philadelphia Inquirer*, 11 Nov. 1980, p. 3-A.

[5]John F. Kennedy, speech to the UN General Assembly, 25 Sept. 1961, reprinted in *Public Papers of the Presidents* 1, no. 387 (Washington, DC: Government Printing Office, 1961), p. 620.

[6]Robert F. Kennedy, *Thirteen Days: A Memoir of the Cuban Missile Crisis* (New York: W. W. Norton, 1969), p. 23. Cf. Elie Abel, *The Missiles of October: The Story of the Cuban Missile Crisis* (London: MacGibbon and Kee, 1969); Arthur M. Schlesinger, Jr, *Robert Kennedy and His Times* (Boston: Houghton Mifflin, 1978), esp. pp. 499–532.

[7]Kennedy, *Thirteen Days*, p. 93.

[8]Ibid., p. 106.

[9]Quoted in Schlesinger, *Robert Kennedy*, p. 529.

[10]Lloyd J. Dumas, 'Human Fallibility and Weapons,' *Bulletin of Atomic Scientists*, Nov. 1980, p. 16.

[11]*CBS Reports: The Defense of the United States, Part I: Ground Zero*, 14 June 1981, transcript, p. 13. See also Robert C. Aldridge, 'Just Who Can Push the Button? Not Solely Presidential,' *Philadelphia Inquirer*, 19 Aug. 1981, p. 15-A.

[12]*Time*, 3 Nov. 1961, pp. 23–24.

[13]Alva Myrdal, *The Game of Disarmament* (New York: Pantheon, 1976), p. 51.

[14]A three-day conference at Colorado's Aspen Institute attended by members of Congress and representatives of industry, the environment and academe, warned that 'a serious disruption in oil supplies from the Persian Gulf would disrupt mobility, close factories, and create an economic crisis comparable to the Great Depression. It would tear at the fabric of the Western alliance and could provoke dangerous confrontation with the Soviet Union.' Reported in the *Philadelphia Inquirer*, 4 July 1980, p. 8-A.

[15]Michael T. Klare, 'Is Exxon Worth Dying For?' *The Progressive*, July 1980, p. 19.

[16]'Pentagon Trumpets "Tripwire" A-Arms,' *Washington Post*, 8 Feb. 1980, p. A-1; and 'Using Our Nukes,' *Tulsa World*, 23 Feb. 1980, p. 29.

[17]*Philadelphia Inquirer*, 25 Nov. 1979, p. 3-L. See also *Philadelphia Inquirer*, 10 Nov. 1979, p. 1; and 11 Nov. 1979, p. 7-A.

[18]*Philadelphia Evening Bulletin*, 6 June 1980, p. 8-A.

[19]'Pentagon Reports New False Alarm,' *Philadelphia Inquirer*, 8 June 1980, p. 3-A.

[20]'What's Cheap, Tiny, and Very Alarming?' *New York Times*, 22 June 1980, p. 4-E.

[21]Senator Mark Hatfield (Republican Senator for Oregon) states flatly that 'Soviet [military] computers are inferior to our own.' 'The Age of Anxiety,' *Hatfield Backgrounder*, no. 193 (June 1981):9. The *Backgrounder* is a newsletter which focuses on issues pertinent to legislation. It is issued several times per year by Senator Hatfield's office.

An article in the *New York Times* (10 June 1980, p. A-16), entitled 'Brown Says False Alarm Cannot Activate Missiles,' outlined how a computer malfunction could lead to all-out nuclear conflict. The article pointed out three reasons why

Soviet officers would be tempted to launch their missiles if they received a signal of an apparent US attack: (1) The fact that Soviet computer and warning systems are less sophisticated than American systems means that Soviet officers will have less time for considered judgments and decisions; (2) Soviet military strategists are less reticent than those in the United States about using nuclear weapons; and (3) since about seventy-five per cent of the Soviet nuclear strike force is land-based and therefore more vulnerable than the more balanced land-sea-air forces of the United States, Soviet officers would want to get their missiles off the ground rather than risk having them destroyed in their silos.

22 *Philadelphia Inquirer*, 25 Nov. 1978, p. 3-L. Also, former Defence Secretary Harold Brown said in his 5 June 1980 news conference that computer malfunctions have happened in the past and 'they're going to continue.' Accidents also happen. A Department of Defence document published in Dec. 1980 said that there have been twenty-seven serious nuclear weapons accidents. One came very close to producing a nuclear explosion. It happened on 24 Jan. 1961. Two atom bombs accidentally fell out of a B-52 bomber flying over Goldsboro, North Carolina. One of the bombs was jolted so hard on impact that five of its six safety switches were released. 'Only one switch prevented the explosion of a 24-megaton bomb, 1,800 times more powerful than the one dropped on Hiroshima.' See 'Report Cites 27 Nuclear Accidents,' *Philadelphia Inquirer*, 22 Dec. 1980, p. 8-B.

23 *Philadelphia Inquirer*, 30 Oct. 1980, p. 3-A. See also Senators Gary Hart and Barry Goldwater, *Recent False Alerts from the Nation's Missile Attack Warning System* (Washington, DC: Government Printing Office, 1980), pp. 4, 13.

24 America's proposed MX missile, for example, is designed both to be accurate enough to destroy Soviet missiles in their silos and also mobile enough to elude Soviet attack.

25 Joint Committee Print, *Fiscal Year 1981 Arms Control Impact Statements*, p. 63. The Federation of American Scientists' *Public Interest Report* (Oct. 1980, p. 1) points out a further incentive to a nation to strike first: 'a nation that strikes first does so with its command structure, control mechanisms, and communications devices wholly intact, alerted and ready. Each and every telephone line, satellite and antenna is functioning and every relevant person is alive and well. By contrast, the

nation which seeks to launch a retaliatory attack may find its chain of command highly disrupted, its telephone lines dead, its satellites inoperative, its radio signals interfered with, and its communications officers out of action.' The advantage, therefore, goes to the attacker.

[26]See, for example, General Sir John Hackett, *The Third World War* (New York: Berkeley Books, 1980). The whole book assumes that World War III can be a limited war. See also Wade Greene, 'Rethinking the Unthinkable,' *New York Times Magazine*, 15 Mar. 1981, pp. 45ff.

[27]Quoted in *The Defense Monitor*, Feb. 1979, p. 6.

[28]Quoted in an undated pamphlet published by the Campaign for Nuclear Disarmament.

[29]'A Change of Heart: Billy Graham on the Nuclear Arms Race,' *Sojourners*, Aug. 1979, p. 12.

[30]Quoted in *Philadelphia Inquirer*, 6 Feb. 1982, p. 9-A.

Chapter 4: The Just War Tradition

[1]*Eternity*, June 1980, pp. 16–17.

[2]Michael Walzer, *Just and Unjust Wars: A Moral Argument with Historic Illustrations* (New York: Basic Books, 1977), p. 174.

[3]*Christianity Today*, 8 Feb. 1980, p. 45.

[4]'*Gaudium et Spes*,' para. 80, quoted in Joseph Gremillion, ed., *The Gospel of Peace and Justice: Catholic Social Teaching since Pope John* (Maryknoll: Orbis, 1976), p. 317.

[5]The standard work on the history of Christian thinking on this issue is still Roland H. Bainton, *Christian Attitudes toward War and Peace: A Historical Survey and Critical Re-evaluation* (New York: Abingdon Press, 1960). Arthur F. Holmes has edited a volume of the most significant Christian statements in *War and Christian Ethics* (Grand Rapids: Baker, 1975).

[6]It is important to note that the just war tradition is really a number of overlapping traditions. See, for instance, LeRoy B. Walters, Jr, 'Five Classic Just War Theories: A Study in the Thought of Thomas Aquinas, Vitoria, Suárez, Gentili and Grotius' (PhD diss. Yale University, 1971); Frederick H. Russell, *The Just War in the Middle Ages* (New York: Cambridge University Press, 1975). Among the most significant modern attempts to work in the just war tradition are Michael Walzer's *Just and Unjust Wars*; and the many works of Paul Ramsey, especially *War and The Christian Conscience: How Shall Modern War Be Conducted Justly?* (Durham: Duke University

Press, 1961) and his major collection of pamphlets and articles, *The Just War: Force and Political Responsibility* (New York: Scribners, 1968); and James T. Johnson, *The Just War Tradition and the Restraint of War: A Moral and Historical Inquiry* (Princeton: Princeton University Press, 1981).

[7]Edward L. Long, *War and Conscience in America* (Philadelphia: Westminster Press, 1968), pp. 22–33. See also R. B. Potter, *The Moral Logic of War* (Philadelphia: United Presbyterian Church, n.d.); James F. Childress, 'Just War Theories: The Bases, Interrelations, Priorities, and Functions of Their Criteria,' *Theological Studies* 39 (Sept. 1978): 427–45.

[8]Long, *War and Conscience*, p. 24.

[9]Ibid.

[10]Ibid., p. 27.

[11]Ibid.

[12]Ibid., p. 28.

[13]Ibid., p. 29.

[14]Justus George Lawler, 'The Council Must Speak,' in *Peace, The Churches and the Bomb*, ed. James Finn (New York: The Council on Religion and International Affairs, 1965), pp. 33–34.

[15]See J. Bryan Hehir, 'The Just War Ethic and Catholic Theology' in *War or Peace? The Search for New Answers*, ed. Thomas A. Shannon (Maryknoll: Orbis, 1980), p. 19.

[16]See Robert A. Gessert and J. Bryan Hehir, *The New Nuclear Debate* (New York: Council on Religion and International Affairs, 1976). See also n. 49 below.

[17]Quoted in Walter Stein, 'Would You Press the Button?' in *Peace, The Churches and the Bomb*, p. 21 (italics added).

[18]Quoted in Stein (italics added).

[19]'American policy for deterring conflict in Europe has not changed for over 20 years.' *Philadelphia Inquirer*, 22 Oct. 1981, p. 3-A.

[20]Quoted in Stein, 'Would You Press the Button?' p. 21 (italics added).

[21]Quoted in Bruce M. Russett, 'Short of Nuclear Madness,' *Worldview*, April 1972, p. 31 (italics added).

[22]See Paul Ramsey's continuing critique of this policy in 'The Background Music,' *Worldview*, Jan.–Feb. 1979, pp. 46–48.

[23]From his Einstein Peace Prize Address, in *Disarmament Times* 4 (June 1981):1.

[24]See chap. two.

[25]'Rumours of Wars,' *Eternity*, June 1980, pp. 16–17.

[26]See chap. two.

[27]*Philadelphia Inquirer*, 21 Jan. 1981.

[28]*Pacem in Terris*, quoted in Hehir, 'The Just War Ethic,' p. 20.

[29]See chap. two.

[30]'Calling for Peacemakers in a Nuclear Age, Part I,' *Christianity Today*, 8 Feb. 1980, p. 45.

[31]'*Gaudium et Spes*,' para. 80.

[32]Richard T. McSorley, 'The Gospel and the Just War,' in *Peace Theology and the Arms Race: Readings on Arms and Disarmament*, College Theology Society Sourcebook Series, vol. 1, ed. William H. Osterle and John Donaghy (mimeograph, 1980), p. 143.

[33]Hehir, 'The Just War Ethic,' p. 27.

[34]J. Bryan Hehir, 'The Catholic Church and the Arms Race,' *Worldview*, July–Aug. 1978, p. 15.

[35]Quoted in Gessert and Hehir, *New Nuclear Debate*, p. 62.

[36]Ramsey, *Just War*, p. 249; cf. also pp. 246ff. and Ramsey, *War and the Christian Conscience*, pp. 162–63.

[37]Frances X. Winters, 'The Nuclear Arms Race,' in *Ethics and Nuclear Strategy?* ed. Harold P. Ford and Francis S. Winters (Maryknoll: Orbis, 1977), p. 148.

[38]Ramsey, *War and the Christian Conscience*, p. 169.

[39]Ibid., p. 170. See also Walzer, *Just and Unjust Wars*, p. 275 and John C. Bennett, 'Moral Urgencies in the Nuclear Context,' in *Nuclear Weapons and the Conflict of Conscience*, ed. John C. Bennett (New York: Scribner's, 1962), p. 101.

[40]Harold P. Ford, 'Politics, Ethics and the Arms Race,' in Ford and Winters, *Ethics and Nuclear Strategy?* p. 44.

[41]'Human Nature and the Dominion of Fear,' in *Breakthrough to Peace*, ed. Thomas Merton (New York: New Directions, 1962), p. 168.

[42]*Eternity*, June 1980, p. 17.

[43]Approximately 5% of the population attends Sunday services on any given Sunday in Western Europe. Obviously no precise figures are available for the Soviet Union. According to the 1979 census, the population of the USSR was 262,436,000. In his book *Discretion and Valour*, Trevor Beeson says: 'No precise figures are available for the number of Orthodox Christians who now attend church . . . but informed observers usually estimate figures ranging between 25,000,000 and 30,000,000' (*Discretion and Valour: Religious Conditions in Russia and*

Eastern Europe [London: Fontana, 1974], p. 77). Thirty million would be one-half of the sixty million Orthodox Christians. There are also four million Eastern Orthodox Christians, four million Roman Catholics and three million Protestants. If half of these also attend, the total figure would be 30–35 million church attenders, i.e. 11.4% to 13.3% of the total population. For other literature on Christians in the USSR, see chap. one, n. 5.

It may even be that these figures are too conservative. In the recently published *World Christian Encyclopedia* (New York: Oxford Univ. Press, 1982), David B. Barrett says there are 97 million Christians in the USSR. (Cited in *Time*, 3 May 1982, p. 67.)

For an excellent analysis of evangelical Christians in Russia, see Walter Sawatsky, *Soviet Evangelicals since World War II* (Scottdale: Herald Press, 1981).

44'A Change of Heart,' *Sojourners*, Aug. 1979, p. 13.

45Herman Kahn, *On Thermonuclear War* (Princeton: Princeton University Press, 1960) and *Thinking about the Unthinkable* (New York: Horizon Press, 1962).

46Kahn, *Thinking about the Unthinkable*, p. 134.

47For a brief history of US policy, see Ford, 'Politics, Ethics, and the Arms Race,' p. 62; see also Gessert and Hehir, *New Nuclear Debate*.

48See chap. three.

49One should not exaggerate the change, because some US nuclear weapons have always been targeted on Soviet weapons. See Ford, 'Politics, Ethics and the Arms Race,' p. 63.

50Gessert and Hehir, *New Nuclear Debate*, p. 20.

51Walzer, *Just and Unjust War*, p. 275; Ford, 'Politics, Ethics, and the Arms Race,' p. 61.

52Ramsey, *Just War*, pp. 250–51.

53See especially his 'The Limits of Nuclear War' (1965) in *Just War*, pp. 211ff. and *War and the Christian Conscience*, pp. 159–60.

54Ramsey, *Just War*, pp. 236–43. Earlier attempts by nuclear pacifists to reject all nuclear weapons on the basis of proportionality and discrimination fail because technological developments have produced small, precisely targeted weapons that need not kill large numbers of noncombatants. See Hehir in Gessert and Hehir, *New Nuclear Debate*, pp. 49–50. Stein acknowledges this in 'Would You Press the Button?' p. 24.

[55]Ramsey now prefers the phrase *countercombatant warfare*. See his 'A Political Ethics Context for Strategic Thinking,' in *Strategic Thinking and Its Moral Implication*, ed. Morton Kaplan (Chicago: Univ. of Chicago Center for Policy Study, 1973), pp. 140–42.

[56]Ramsey, *Just War*, p. 154.

[57]Ibid., p. 234.

[58]Ibid., p. 154.

[59]Ibid., p. 213: 'So far public opinion in this country seems to ignore the difference between 25,000,000 dead as the probable result of all-out counter-force warfare and 215,000,000 dead as a result of all-out counter-city warfare.'

[60]Walzer, *Just and Unjust Wars*, p. 280: 'The danger of collateral damage is unlikely to work as a deterrent unless the damage expected is radically disproportionate to the end of the war.'

[61]Walter Stein, 'The Defence of the West,' in *Nuclear Weapons and Christian Conscience*, ed. Walter Stein (London: Merlin Press, 1961), pp. 28–29. See also his critique of Ramsey in 'The Limits of Nuclear War,' in *Peace, The Churches and the Bomb*, pp. 79–83.

[62]Walzer, *Just and Unjust Wars*, p. 280. At the same time, Walzer accepts the threat of massive countercity attack as an emergency measure (ibid., p. 283)! Ramsey rejects that.

[63]G. E. M. Anscombe, 'War and Murder,' in *Nuclear Weapons and Christian Conscience*, p. 57.

[64]Ramsey, *Just War*, p. 253 (his italics).

[65]Ibid., p. 254.

[66]Walzer, *Just and Unjust Wars*, p. 277.

[67]See chap. three, p. 57, n. 27.

[68]Winters, 'Nuclear Arms Race,' p. 145.

[69]Ibid.

[70]Arthur I. Waskow, *The Limits of Defense* (Garden City: Doubleday, 1962), p. 41.

[71]Gessert and Hehir, *New Nuclear Debate*, p. 49.

[72]See Robert W. Gardiner, *The Cool Arm of Destruction: Modern Weapons and Moral Insensitivity* (Philadelphia: Westminster, 1974), pp. 117–20; and Bennett, *Nuclear Weapons and the Conflict of Conscience*, p. 103.

[73]See Stein, 'The Limits of Nuclear War,' pp. 82–83.

[74]Ramsey, *Just War*, pp. 254–56. Subsequently, Ramsey re-

jected this third proposal for 'bluffing.' See his 'A Political Ethics Context,' p. 142.

[75] Stein, 'Would You Press the Button?' pp. 22–23.

[76] Gessert and Hehir, *New Nuclear Debate*, pp. 63–69.

[77] Alain C. Enthoven, '1963 Nuclear Strategy Revisited,' in *Ethics and Nuclear Strategy?* p. 78.

[78] Walzer, *Just and Unjust Wars*, pp. 279, 283.

[79] Quoted in Gessert and Hehir, *New Nuclear Debate*, p. 20.

[80] William V. O'Brien, 'Relevant Knowledge and Moral Issues,' in *Peace, The Churches and the Bomb*, p. 100. See too, a short summary of the pros and cons of deterrence in T. R. Milford, *Christian Decision in the Nuclear Age* (Philadelphia: Fortress Press, 1967), pp. 38–39.

[81] Stein, 'The Defense of the West,' p. 36.

[82] Hehir, 'The Catholic Church and the Arms Race,' p. 14.

[83] Ibid., pp. 15–16.

[84] Ramsey's phrase in *Just War*, p. 251.

[85] Hehir, 'The Just War Ethic,' p. 28.

[86] Hehir in Gessert and Hehir, *New Nuclear Debate*, p. 69.

[87] Ibid., p. 52.

[88] See Walzer, *Just and Unjust Wars*, p. 271.

[89] McNamara, Einstein Peace Prize Address, italics added.

[90] Gessert and Hehir, *New Nuclear Debate*, p. 53.

[91] Senators Gary Hart and Barry Goldwater, *Recent False Alerts from the Nation's Missile Attack Warning System* (Washington, DC: Government Printing Office, 1980), pp. 12–13.

[92] Lloyd J. Dumas, 'Human Fallibility and Weapons,' *The Bulletin of the Atomic Scientists*, 36 (Nov. 1980): 16.

[93] Ibid., p. 19.

[94] Gardiner, *Cool Arm of Destruction*, p. 40.

[95] Gessert and Hehir, *New Nuclear Debate*, p. 56.

[96] *Philadelphia Inquirer*, 4 Dec. 1981, pp. 1, 4.

[97] Quoted in Gardiner, *Cool Arm of Destruction*, p. 63.

[98] Bennett, *Nuclear Weapons and the Conflict of Conscience*, p. 103 (italics added).

[99] Pierce S. Corden, 'Ethics and Deterrence,' in *Ethics and Nuclear Strategy*, p. 179 (italics his). Walzer took a similar position; see *Just and Unjust Wars*.

[100] Printed in *Sojourners*, May 1978, along with the names of the signers.

[101] *Newsweek*, 11 Jan. 1982, pp. 70–71.

[102] *Christianity Today*, 8 Feb. 1980, p. 45. Ramsey, of course, is correct in rejecting the term 'nuclear pacifist' because these people come from the just war tradition. See his *War and Christian Conscience*, p. 154.

[103] 'Rev. Donn D. Moomaw, 'Peacemakers in a Nuclear Age,' an unpublished sermon at Bel Air Presbyterian Church, 19 Oct. 1980.

Chapter 5: Is the Just War Tradition Adequate?

[1] *Darkening Valley: A Biblical Perspective on Nuclear War* (New York: Seabury, 1981), p. 141.

[2] Quoted in G. H. C. Macgregor, *The New Testament Basis of Pacifism*, rev. ed. (New York: Fellowship Pub., 1960), p. 98.

[3] 'Gaudium et Spes,' para. 80.

[4] *Just and Unjust Wars*, p. 282.

[5] 'How The "Peace Bishops" Got That Way,' *The Washington Post*, 27 Dec. 1981, D:5–6.

[6] Perhaps this is only a vivid way of saying that the principles of the just war tradition lead to the conclusion that *nuclear* war could never be justified. In that case it is not very precise to say that nuclear weapons 'explode' or 'shatter' the just war tradition. Its principles continue to help distinguish just from unjust wars, and all nuclear war falls in the latter category. On the other hand, this language may suggest that the awfulness of nuclear weapons is prompting some to reject the central affirmation of the just war tradition – that war is sometimes justified.

[7] See chap. four, n. 43.

[8] The contemporary church desperately needs to recover the early church's sense that we are aliens and sojourners in all lands because our true citizenship is in the kingdom of heaven. See, for instance, Jean-Michel Hornus, *It Is Not Lawful for Me to Fight: Early Christian Attitudes toward War and Peace*, rev. ed., trans. Alan Kreider and Oliver Coburn (Scottdale: Herald Press, 1980), pp. 98–109.

[9] J. Andrew Kirk, *Theology Encounters Revolution* (Downers Grove: InterVarsity Press, 1980), p. 152.

[10] Gordon C. Zahn, 'The Case for Christian Dissent,' in *Breakthrough to Peace*, p. 120.

[11] Ibid., p. 121.

[12] Ibid., p. 128. In spite of the small confessing Church and

individuals like Bonhoeffer, German Protestants did little better. See, for example, the statements of support for Hitler made by a leading Protestant bishop. Quoted in Ulrich Duchrow, ed., *Lutheran Churches – Salt or Mirror of Society?* (Geneva: Lutheran World Foundation, 1977), p. 266.

[13] Cited in Culbert G. Rutenber, *The Dagger and the Cross* (New York: Fellowship Pub., 1950), p. 90.

[14] Quoted in Rutenber, p. 90.

[15] *An Interpretation of Christian Ethics* (New York: Harper, 1935), pp. 125–26.

[16] Kirk, *Theology Encounters Revolution*, p. 154.

[17] Robert E. D. Clark, *Does the Bible Teach Pacifism?* (New Malden: Fellowship of Reconciliation, 1976), p. 49.

[18] Rutenber, *Dagger and the Cross*, p. 46.

[19] Quoted in Macgregor, *New Testament Basis of Pacifism*, p. 95.

[20] Quoted in Macgregor, p. 96.

[21] See LeRoy B. Walters, 'Five Classic Just-War Theories' (unpublished PhD diss., Yale University, 1971), pp. 286, 330–38. Grotius (see pp. 337–38) placed somewhat more stress on the individual's obligation to refuse to fight if doubtful of the justice of the war. See also John A. Rohr, *Prophets Without Honor* (Nashville: Abingdon, 1971), pp. 109–12.

[22] Kirk, *Theology Encounters Revolution*, p. 151.

[23] See, for instance, Loraine Boettner, *The Christian Attitude toward War* (Grand Rapids: Eerdmans, 1940), pp. 69, 77. Zahn's article on German Catholics (see n. 11) cites a Catholic archbishop in 1935 who argued that the government must decide because the decision is too complex for individual Christians. Paul Ramsey points out the danger of private, individual judgment in *War and Christian Conscience*, p. 132. Rohr (*Prophets without Honor*, pp. 109–17) says that in the 'just war tradition, doubts are resolved in favor of the government' (p. 47) and argues that a person dare fight even if he knows the war is unjust if refusing to fight would involve a serious loss such as prison (p. 114).

[24] See, for example, J. Bryan Hehir, 'The Just War Ethic and Catholic Theology' in *War or Peace?* pp. 20ff.; and James Finn, ed., *A Conflict of Loyalties: The Case for Selective Conscientious Objection* (New York: Pegasus, 1968).

[25] Roland H. Bainton, *Christian Attitudes toward War and Peace: A Historical Survey and Critical Re-evaluation* (New York: Abingdon, 1960), p. 53. See also the more recent (1980) book

by Hornus (*It Is Not Lawful for Me to Fight*) which has useful and extensive footnotes and a large bibliography.

[26]Ramsey, *War and Christian Conscience*, p. xv.

[27]Ibid., p. xvi.

[28]Bainton, *Christian Attitudes*, p. 69. Hornus says seven (*It is not Lawful*, p. 119).

[29]Bainton, *Christian Attitudes*, p. 68.

[30]Ibid., pp. 68–69.

[31]Ibid., p. 79.

[32]Ibid.

[33]Ibid., p. 69.

[34]Ibid., p. 74.

[35]Ibid., p. 77.

[36]*On the Garland* 11. 2; quoted in Richard McSorley, *New Testament Basis of Peacemaking* (Washington, DC: Centre for Peace Studies, 1979), p. 78.

[37]*Against Celsus* 8. 73; 5. 33, quoted in *New Testament Basis for Peacemaking*, p. 75.

[38]*Dialogue with Trypho* 110; quoted in John Ferguson, *The Politics of Love: The New Testament and Non-Violent Revolution* (Cambridge: James Clarke, n.d.), p. 57. For further discussion of the early Christians' attitude toward war, see chap. twelve, pp. 33–38.

[39]See the quotations in Ferguson, pp. 57–62.

[40]*Church Dogmatics*, III/4 (Edinburgh: T. and T. Clark, 1961), p. 453; quoted in Aukerman, *Darkening Valley*, p. xvi.

[41]Ibid., p. 169.

Chapter 6: Jesus and Violence

[1]We prefer to use the word *nonviolence*, rather than *pacifism*, because pacifism suggests acquiescence in the face of evil whereas nonviolence connotes an active but loving confrontation of injustice and evil. For the former view, see Guy F. Hershberger, *War, Peace and Nonresistance* (Scottdale, Pa: Herald Press, 1953). See also John Howard Yoder, *Nevertheless: The Varieties of Religious Pacifism* (Scottdale, Pa: Herald Press, 1971) and Ronald J. Sider, *Christ and Violence* (Tring, Herts: Lion, 1980), chap. two.

[2]For example, Reinhold Niebuhr, 'Why The Christian Church Is Not Pacifist,' *Christianity and Power Politics* (New York: Scribner's, 1946), chap. one; and Loraine Boettner, *The Christ-*

ian Attitude toward War (Grand Rapids, Mich.: Eerdmans, 1940), pp. 82ff.

[3]See Gerhard von Rad's discussion under 'ιήνη in Gerhard Kittel and Gerhard Friedrich, eds, *Theological Dictionary of the New Testament* (hereafter cited as *TDNT*), 10 vols, trans. Geoffrey W. Bromiley (Grand Rapids, Mich.: Eerdmans, 1964 –1976), 2:402–6. See also Walter Brueggemann, *Living toward a Vision: Biblical Reflections on Shalom* (Philadelphia: United Church Press, 1976).

[4]*TDNT*, 2:405–6.

[5]See also Ps 85:10 where righteousness and peace kiss and Is 48:17–19; 60:15–22.

[6]Lk 2:14. Foerster says that this text means that the promise of eschatological peace is fulfilled in Jesus. Eschatological salvation is now present (*TDNT*, 2:413).

[7]Origen, *Contra Celsus*, 5.33 quoted in Richard McSorley, *New Testament Basis of Peacemaking* (Washington, DC: Centre for Peace Studies, Georgetown Univ., n.d.), p. 75; so too Justin Martyr quoted above in chap. 5, n. 39.

[8]The Gospels repeatedly summarise Jesus' preaching with this message that the kingdom of God became present in the person and work of Jesus (e.g., Mk 1:14–15; Mt 4:23; 24:14; Lk 4:43; 16:16).

[9]We are quite aware, of course, that many modern scholars have rejected the view that Jesus understood himself to be the Messiah. But we agree with Martin Hengel that the 'thesis of a totally unmessianic Jesus has led a major portion of German New Testament studies along a false trail.' *Victory over Violence* (London: SPCK, 1975), pp. 81, 112. See also the careful overview and the extensive citation of the literature in George Eldon Ladd, *Theology of the New Testament* (Guildford: Lutterworth, 1975).

[10]See the literature for the divergent views in Ladd, *Theology of the New Testament*, pp. 57–69.

[11]For this section, see ibid., pp. 65ff.

[12]Cf. Is 35:5–6; 42:7; 61:1.

[13]See also Lk 17:20–21 and Ladd's discussion in *Theology of the New Testament*, p. 68. Also, Ladd points out that the parable of the tares, leaven and mustard seed all suggest that the kingdom is present, albeit hidden (ibid., pp. 95–100).

[14]See Mt 25:31–46; 13:36–43; Lk 13:23–30.

[15]See C. F. D. Moule, ed., *The Significance of the Message of the*

Resurrection for Faith in Jesus Christ (London: SCM Press, 1968), p. 9.

[16]See Leonard Swidler, *Biblical Affirmations of Woman* (Philadelphia: Westminster Press, 1979), pp. 154–57.

[17]Mt 20:25–28; Mk 10:42–5; Lk 22:24–28. Notice that already here servanthood is grounded in the cross.

[18]See beyond these brief references, the more than four dozen passages from the Gospels in Ronald J. Sider, *Cry Justice: The Bible on Hunger and Poverty* (Downers Grove, Ill: Inter Varsity Press, 1980), and Sider, *Rich Christians in an Age of Hunger* (London: Hodder and Stoughton Ltd, 1978).

[19]See Robert Sloan's *The Acceptable Year of the Lord* (Austin, Text: Schola Press, 1977) and Donald W. Blosser, 'Jesus and the Jubilee' (unpublished PhD diss., Univ. of St Andrews, 1979).

[20]See Hengel, *Victory over Violence*, p. 80, who calls this act 'an exemplary demonstration against the misuse of the sanctuary to enrich the leading priestly families.'

[21]Ibid., p. 58. For the literature on the Zealots, see ibid., p. 22, n. 19, and the notes on pp. 55ff.

[22]Ibid., pp. 39–41.

[23]Palestinian Targum on Gen 49:10 quoted in ibid., p. 69.

[24]Ibid.

[25]In the following section, we depend largely on ibid., pp. 38ff. Beginning at this point in our text, we use, by permission from the publisher, some portions of chaps. one and two of Ronald J. Sider, *Christ and Violence* (Tring, Herts: Lion 1980).

[26]Hengel, *Victory over Violence*, p. 63.

[27]This Judas was not Jesus' disciple, Judas Iscariot. Jesus' disciple, however, may have been a Zealot. See Oscar Cullmann, *The State in the New Testament* (London: SCM, 1963), pp. 18ff.

[28]Ibid., pp. 55–56.

[29]Ibid., pp. 57–60.

[30]Ibid., p. 71.

[31]Mt 18:23–27; Lk 7:41–43; 15:3–7, 8–10, 11–32; 18:9–14; Mt 20:1–15. The quotation is from Hans Küng, *On Being a Christian*, trans. Edward Quinn (London: Collins, 1977).

[32]Ladd, *Theology of the New Testament*, p. 78.

[33]For the extensive debate about the meaning of the term 'Son of man' and Jesus' usage, see the literature cited in ibid., p. 145, and Ladd's discussion (pp. 146–58).

[34]Ibid., p. 78.

[35]See the discussion in John Piper, *'Love Your Enemies': Jesus' Love Command in the Synoptic Gospels in the Early Christian Paraenesis* (Cambridge: Cambridge Univ. Press, 1979), pp. 82–84.

[36]That is the assumption of Mt 18:23–35. So, Piper (ibid.) and Ladd, *Theology of the New Testament*, p. 78.

[37]There are explicit quotations (Mt 8:17, 12:17–21; Lk 22:37; Jn 12:38; Acts 8:32–33) and numerous allusions. See W. Zimmerli and J. Jeremias, *The Servant of God*, Studies in Biblical Theology, no. 20 (Naperville, Ill: Alec R. Allenson, 1957), pp. 88ff.

[38]Ibid., pp. 99ff.; So also Oscar Cullmann, *The Christology of the New Testament*, rev. ed., trans. Shirley C. Guthrie and Charles A. M. Hall (Philadelphia: Westminster Press, 1963), pp. 51 –82.

[39]Mk 8:31; 9:30–32; 10:32–34. See Zimmerli and Jeremias, *Servant of God*, pp. 100–101.

[40]Jeremias believes there is a reference to Is 53 (ibid., p. 102). 'In Mark 10:45, we have the word "minister" (which means "serve"), the phrase "for many" ("many" occurs four times in the Servant poem), and the substitutionary giving of life (which is the theme of Isaiah 53).' Leon Morris, *The Cross in the New Testament* (Exeter: Paternoster, 1976). So also Oscar Cullmann, C. E. B. Cranfield and others – noted in Ladd, *Theology of the New Testament*, p. 156.

[41]So Morris, *Cross in the New Testament*, pp. 52–53.

[42]So Jeremias, in Zimmerli and Jeremias, *Servant of God*, p. 104.

[43]For example, see C. E. B. Cranfield, *The Gospel According to Mark*, The Cambridge Greek New Testament Commentary (Cambridge: Cambridge Univ. Press, 1963), pp. 353–54.

[44]Foerster, *TDNT*, 2:413.

[45]Vincent Taylor, *The Gospel According to Mark* (London: Macmillan, 1952), p. 452.

[46]Culbert G. Rutenber, *The Dagger and the Cross* (New York: Fellowship Publications, 1950), p. 39. Mt 26:53–54 does go on to say that he will not call on legions of angels to protect him because he must die. But that in no way denies that the saying, 'All who take the sword will perish by the sword' is a saying with general implications beyond the particular setting.

[47]It is important to note one significant implication of this statement for Christians in the just war tradition. At the very least, Jesus means to forbid the use of violence to defend or extend his kingdom. Christians who defend war to protect Christians from

'godless Communism' need to ponder Jesus' clear prohibition of fighting to protect his kingdom and its members.

[48] So Rutenber, *Dagger and the Cross*, p. 39.

[49] For a careful analysis of this whole text and its relationship to Luke 6:27–36, see Piper, *Love Your Enemies*, pp. 50–60, especially his words against speculation. He rejects the view that only antitheses 1, 2 and 4 of Mt 5:38–48 go back to Jesus. Piper finds no reason for thinking that Jesus is not the source of it all (pp. 52–53). Generally, Piper considers Matthew original and Luke an adaptation (pp. 58–59).

[50] Hengel, *Victory over Violence*, p. 76.

[51] Piper, *Love Your Enemies*, pp. 21–48. See also W. F. Albright and C. S. Mann, *Matthew*, Anchor Bible (New York: Doubleday, 1971), p. 71 and Eduard Schweizer, *The Good News According to Matthew* (Atlanta: John Knox, 1975), p. 132: 'The principle, "love your neighbor" (Lev. 19:18), to be sure, was always interpreted so as to apply to fellow Israelites, not to others.'

[52] Piper, *Love Your Enemies*, p. 33. Some psalms, however, do speak of hating those who hate God.

[53] Schweizer, *Matthew*, p. 132; also Piper, *Love Your Enemies*, pp. 40–41.

[54] Quoted in John Stott, *Christian Counter-Culture* (Leicester: InterVarsity Press, 1978).

[55] Schweizer, *Matthew*, p. 194.

[56] Also, Lev 24:20; Deut 19:21; so Piper, *Love Your Enemies*, p. 89. Arthur Holmes's suggestion that Mt 5:39 means only that individuals are to be nonresistant and not take the law into their hands in private schemes of retributive justice is quite wrong. The *lex talionis* ('eye for an eye') refers not to private retaliation, but to a basic principle of the Mosaic legal system. See Arthur Holmes's contribution to *War: Four Christian Views*, ed. Robert G. Clouse (Downers Grove, Ill: InterVarsity Press, 1981), p. 71.

[57] Schweizer, *Matthew*, p. 130.

[58] Albright and Mann, *Matthew*, p. 69.

[59] Schweizer, *Matthew*, p. 130.

[60] See further Sider, *Christ and Violence*, chap. 2. Reinhold Niebuhr, of course, denounces this kind of attempt to distinguish between nonviolence and nonresistance and then justify nonviolent resistance on the authority of Jesus. See, for instance, his 'Why the Christian Church Is Not Pacifist,' *Christ-*

ianity and Power Politics (New York: Scribner's, 1946), p. 10. As the following discussion shows, we believe that Jesus calls not for total nonresistance in the face of evil, but rather costly love so governed by the needs of the neighbour that it does not retaliate, does not reciprocate evil for evil and persists with love regardless of the other's response. That kind of love is fully compatible with economic boycott, prophetic condemnation and political pressure, but it is not compatible with lethal violence. In the former cases, one can genuinely love the other person and call on him as a free person to repent and change, but it makes no sense to call a person to repentance as you put a bullet through his head.

Police activity, as currently performed, sometimes involves lethal violence. The long tradition of unarmed British police, however, demonstrates that unarmed police can be very effective. We would favour creative efforts to expand the many ways that police can use nonlethal coercion. In any case, police work is radically different from warfare; see especially John Howard Yoder, *Politics of Jesus* (Grand Rapids, Mich: Eerdmans, 1972), p. 206.

[61] Rutenber, *Dagger and the Cross*, p. 50.

[62] It is precisely this principle that enables one to determine, for example, when to suffer a costly economic loss that could be avoided by legal action and when to go to court *in the interests* of the careless debtor. (See briefly, Sider, *Christ and Violence*, p. 49). We do not agree with Tolstoy that Jesus' teaching requires the abolition of the judicial system.

[63] For further discussion of God's retribution and vengeance against evil, see chap. seven. Only God has the infinite wisdom needed to combine infinite justice and infinite mercy in such a way that retributive punishment is applied appropriately.

[64] See the discussion of Paul Althaus in *Two Kingdoms and One World: A Source Book in Christian Social Ethics*, ed. Karl H. Hertz (Minneapolis: Augsburg, 1976), pp. 176–79.

[65] See the concise summary of different Christian interpretations of the Sermon on the Mount in Carl F. H. Henry, *Christian Personal Ethics* (Grand Rapids, Mich: Eerdmans, 1957), pp. 278–326.

[66] See Stott, *Christian Counter-Culture*, pp. 108–13.

[67] See the many passages in Macgregor, *New Testament Basis of Pacifism*, p. 48.

[68] John Stott claims to reject pacifism, not because it is unrealistic,

but because it is unbiblical. In fact, however, he places a lot of weight on the 'unrealistic' character of the pacifists he cites (*Christian Counter-Culture*, pp. 108–10). The only biblical counterargument he cites is Romans 13, discussed below in Chap. seven.

[69] For a historical analysis of the doctrine of the two kingdoms, see Ulrich Duchrow, ed., *Lutheran Churches – Salt or Mirror of Society: Case Studies on the Theory and Practice of the Two Kingdoms Doctrine* (Geneva: Lutheran World Federation, 1977). For a more intensive treatment, see three volumes of sources edited by Duchrow and published in Germany from 1972–76. See also Hertz, *Two Kingdoms and One World*.

[70] Hertz, *Two Kingdoms and One World*, pp. 184–85.

[71] Piper, *Love Your Enemies*, p. 96 (Piper's italics). After Piper's superb exposition of Jesus' teaching, it is astonishing to have him undermine Jesus' whole argument (although, to be sure, it shows how very tempting it is to do that). Piper offers no textual support for this except the fact that Jesus did not intend to abolish the law (Mt 5:17). But that in no way proves his point.

[72] See Piper, ibid., p. 91. (This makes his undermining of Jesus' teaching even more astonishing.) This paragraph suggests what is true generally – New Testament ethics is eschatological ethics. It is based on the assumption that in the power of the new age, it is possible to live a life radically different from that of the fallen world.

Chapter 7: The Way of the Cross

[1] Jim Wallis, *Call to Conversion* (Tring, Herts: Lion, 1982).

[2] Notice the many political aspects of Jesus' trial: mockery as a king with a royal robe, a crown and sceptre: Pilate's inscription, 'King of the Jews.' See further André Trocmé, *Jesus and the Nonviolent Revolution*, trans. Michael H. Shank and Marlin E. Miller (Scottdale, Pa: Herald Press, 1973), p. 61.

[3] Jürgen Moltmann, *The Crucified God* (New York: Harper & Row, 1974), pp. 125, 132.

[4] For a discussion of our understanding of the nature and importance of the resurrection, see Ronald J. Sider, 'The Historian, The Miraculous and Post Newtonian Man,' *Scottish Journal of Theology*, 25 (1972): 309–19; Sider, 'The Pauline Conception of the Resurrection Body in I Corinthians 15:35–54,' *New Testament Studies*, 21 (1975): 428–39; Sider, 'St Paul's Understanding of the Nature and Significance of the Resurrection in I

Corinthians 15:1–19.' *Novum Testamentum*, 19 (1977): 1–18; Sider, 'Resurrection and Liberation,' in *The Recovery of Spirit in Higher Education*, ed. Robert Rankin (New York: Seabury, 1980), pp. 154–77.

[5]The imagery of the first fruits probably comes from the early Jewish harvest festival of the first fruits (Ex 23:16). Coming at the beginning of the harvest, it demonstrated that the full harvest was truly on the way. C. K. Barrett says the phrase refers to 'the first portion of the harvest, regarded both as a first instalment and as a pledge of the final delivery of the whole.' *Romans* (London: Adam and Charles Black, 1957), p. 167.

[6]So Wolfhart Pannenberg, *Jesus: God and Man*, trans. Lewis L. Wilkens and Duane A. Priebe (Philadelphia: Westminster Press, 1968), p. 67.

[7]Johannes Behm, ἀρραβών, in Gerhard Kittel and Gerhard Friedrich, eds, *Theological Dictionary of the New Testament* (*TDNT*), 10 vols, trans. Geoffrey W. Bromiley (Grand Rapids, Mich: Eerdmans, 1964–76), 1:475.

[8]Culbert Rutenber's insistence on this is important. See *The Dagger and the Cross* (New York: Fellowship Publications, 1950), pp. 50–55.

[9]In light of Jesus' emphasis on peacemaking, it is not surprising to find in the Gospels a process for peacemaking in the church – Mt 18:15–20. See Sider, 'Spare the Rod and Spoil the Church,' *Eternity*, Oct. 1976, pp. 18ff.

[10]G. H. C. Macgregor points out that the fact that Jesus grounds his love for enemies on the nature of God refutes those who dismiss it today as an interim ethic. *New Testament Basis of Pacifism* (New York: Fellowship Publications, 1960), pp. 34–50.

[11]Moltmann, *Crucified God*, p. 142. We would want to put somewhat differently what Moltmann describes as the 'revolution in the concept of God.'

[12]See the statement by A. M. Hunter, *The Work and Words of Jesus* (London: n.p., 1956), p. 100, quoted in Leon Morris, *The Cross in the New Testament* (Grand Rapids, Mich: Eerdmans, 1965), p. 406.

[13]Except perhaps Luke where the text is uncertain.

[14]As C. E. B. Cranfield says, 'As the Old Covenant had been ratified by the sprinkling of sacrificial blood (Exod. xxiv 6–8), so God's New Covenant with men is about to be established by Jesus' death.' *The Gospel According to Mark*, The Cambridge

Greek Testament Commentary (Cambridge: Cambridge Univ. Press, 1963), p. 427.

[15]Walter Grundman, δόκιμος, *TDNT*, 2:257.

[16]Morris, *Cross in the New Testament*, p. 370.

[17]Ibid., p. 410.

[18]Dale Brown calls it a heretical doctrine of the atonement. *Brethren and Pacifism* (Elgin, Ill: Brethren Press, 1970), p. 121.

[19]Rufus H. Jones, in *The Church, the Gospel and War* (New York: Harper, 1948), p. 5.

[20]Charles E. Raven, *The Theological Basis of Christian Pacifism* (New York: Fellowship Publications, 1951), p. 56. Also: 'If we agree that God uses other means [than suffering love] – as we do in respect of the Last Judgment if not of the Mosaic Law – to that extent we are Arians' (p. 65).

[21]For example, Mt 8:11–12; 13:30, 40–42; 25:41, 46; Lk 13:27–28. See also Rom 2:8; 12:19; Rev 20:9, 15.

[22]Cf. also Jesus: 'Will not God bring about justice for his chosen ones, who cry out to him day and night?' (Lk 18:7 NIV).

[23]So John Piper, *Love Your Enemies* (Cambridge: Cambridge Univ. Press, 1979), pp. 62–63.

Certainly the Lord will destroy and punish the wicked at the end of the age. Mt 24, and Mk 13, Lk 21 make this clear. But in none of these places is there any indication whatsoever that *Christians* take part in the violent overthrow of the wicked. It is God alone and his angelic armies that destroy the wicked. Christians, on the other hand, conquer by the blood of the Lamb, the word of their testimony and martyrdom (Rev 12:11). When Jesus Christ comes (19:11ff.) to conquer the wicked, he overcomes with the 'armies of heaven' (19:14), not people. And when Satan makes one last desperate attempt to destroy the saints (20:7–9), fire from heaven, not human swords, rescues them (20:9).

[24]Macgregor, *New Testament Basis of Pacifism*, p. 73.

[25]Thus Richard Mouw, *Politics and the Biblical Drama* (Grand Rapids, Mich: Eerdmans, 1976), pp. 112–16, is correct in arguing that Yoder is wrong in asserting that Christians must universally and consistently imitate the cross. But that does not in any way undercut Yoder's thesis that the cross is the norm for the Christian life. See John Howard Yoder, *Politics of Jesus* (Grand Rapids, Mich: Eerdmans, 1972).

[26]Loraine Boettner, *The Atonement* (Grand Rapids, Mich: Eerd-

mans, 1941), p. 32, quoted in Morris, *Cross in the New Testament*, p. 389 (our italics).

[27]Here the explicit command is to imitate God, but imitation of Christ is also implied. Piper points out that in the New Testament epistles, the usual call is to imitate Christ (*Love Your Enemies*, p. 62).

[28]Rom 15:33; 16:20; Phil 4:9; 1 Thess 5:23; 2 Thess 3:16; 2 Cor 13:11. Also Heb 13:20.

[29]The central passages are Rom 5:10–11; 2 Cor 5:17–21; Eph 2:11–17; and Col 1:19–22.

[30]Morris, *Cross in the New Testament*, p. 250. See his entire discussion on pp. 247–52, especially p. 251.

[31]Paul uses the word this way too in 1 Cor 7:11. See Friedrich Büchsel, καταλλάσσω, *TDNT*, 1:254–59.

[32]Ibid., p. 255. See entire discussion.

[33]It is important to see that reconciliation with other persons depends on prior reconciliation with God. See further Sider's comments in 'Evangelicalism and the Mennonite Tradition,' *Evangelicalism and Anabaptism*, ed. C. Norman Kraus (Scottdale, Pa: Herald Press, 1979), pp. 157–61.

[34]See 2 Cor 8–9 and Sider, *Rich Christians in an Age of Hunger*, pp. 103–10.

[35]In his study, Piper concludes that Jesus' command to love enemies was very influential in the early church. (*Love Your Enemies*, chaps. 1, 2, 4.)

Chapter 8: Some Critical Objections

[1]Charles E. Raven, although by no means a Marcionite, represents a similar tendency in his book, *War and the Christian* (London: SCM, 1938); see, for example, p. 51.

[2]See, for example, Jean-Michel Hornus, *It is Not Lawful For Me To Fight* (Scottdale, Pa: Herald Press, 1980), pp. 52ff. The fathers also justified the difference of viewpoint on the basis of the new covenant's superiority to the old.

[3]So Vernard Eller, *War and Peace from Genesis to Revelation* (Scottdale, Pa: Herald Press, 1981), pp. 58–59, 77–78. 'It simply is impossible to reconcile the savage, city-levelling Yahweh of Joshua with the God and Father of Jesus' (p. 58).

[4]So Millard C. Lind, *Yahweh Is a Warrior: The Theology of Warfare in Ancient Israel* (Scottdale, Pa: Herald Press, 1980).

[5]See John Gray, *A History of Jerusalem* (London: Robert Hale, 1969), pp. 236–37.

[6]Loraine Boettner, *The Christian Attitude toward War* (Grand Rapids, Mich.: Eerdmans, 1940), p. 22; see all of chap. three.

[7]So too many other texts; for example, Num 31:17; Deut 20:10–18; Josh 8:18, 23–25.

[8]See Lind's discussion in *Yahweh Is a Warrior*, pp. 104–5.

[9]Ibid. Lind has an excellent overview of the literature on pp. 24–31 and in his notes.

[10]Ibid., p. 23.

[11]E.g., 1 Sam 5–6 (Lind, p. 97); 2 Kings 18:13–19:36 (Lind, pp. 140–41). See Lind, pp. 46ff., for a discussion of the escape at the sea.

[12]Ibid., p. 171.

[13]For example, Is 2:6–8; 31:1; Hos 10:13–15. In Zech 9:9–15, in the vision of the peaceful Messiah, chariots and cavalry disappear.

[14]Richard McSorley, *New Testament Basis of Peacemaking* (Washington, DC: Centre for Peace Studies, Georgetown Univ., 1979), p. 61.

[15]Paul's concept of God's wrath has a double time frame. God's wrath operates within history as God allows the evil consequences of sinful choices to work themselves out. (That is the clear teaching of Rom 1:18–32). But there will also be a final day of wrath (Rom 2:4–8).

[16]*The Faith of a Moralist*, Series I (London: n.p., 1951), p. 183, quoted in Leon Morris, *The Cross in the New Testament* (Grand Rapids, Mich: Eerdmans, 1965), p. 386.

In chapter six we distinguished retributive punishment, which is proper only for God, from disciplinary punishment which is quite appropriate for Christians. A careful study of the New Testament words ἐκδικέω, ἐκδικος, ἐκδίκησις (translated as 'punishment' or 'vengeance') would support the view taken here that God rightly executes retributive punishment but Christians should not. In the Septuagint, these words often mean revenge and retribution whereas in ordinary Greek the terms normally refer simply to the judicial process of deciding a legal action (Gerhard Kittel and Gerhard Friedrich, eds., *Theological Dictionary of the New Testament* [*TDNT*], 10 vols, trans. Geoffrey W. Bromiley [Grand Rapids, Mich: Eerdmans, 1964–76], 2:442–46). Both usages appear in the New Testament. Lk 18:3, 5 and perhaps 2 Cor 7:11 (so Schrenk, *TDNT*, 2:446) refer to judicial action. 2 Cor 10:6 and 2 Cor 7:11 may refer to what we have called disciplinary punishment. Most of the time, however, the words are used to speak of God's retributive punishment of sin, usually at the final judgment (Lk 18:7, 8; 21:22; 2 Thess 1:8; Heb 10:30; Rev 6:10; 19:2). But Paul explicitly prohibits Christians from participating in that kind of punishment or vengeance (Rom 12:9; Schrenk says this passage 'does not mean "do not procure justice for yourselves" but "avenge not yourselves" for the divine judgment to which we yield replaces revenge'; *TDNT*, 2:444). Twice these words are used of the activity of government (Rom 13:4 and 1 Pet 2:14). As we will argue later, however, neither of these texts needs to be interpreted to mean that God *commands* government to execute retributive vengeance. Government's good task of restraining evil and protecting society could be performed with disciplinary punishment apart from retaliation and vengeance. See, for instance, the successful experiments in applying the principle of restitution in the case of various crimes. For information on the Victim-Offender Reconciliation Program and other innovative work in this area, write to Howard Zehr, Office of Criminal Justice, Mennonite Central Committee, 220 West High St, Elkhart, IN 46515.

[17] McSorley, *New Testament Basis of Peacemaking*, p. 69.

[18] For one recent view and extensive bibliography on this issue, see Daniel P. Fuller, *Gospel and Law: Contrast or Continuum?* (Grand Rapids, Mich: Eerdmans, 1980).

[19] See the many examples in John Piper, *Love Your Enemies* (Cambridge: Cambridge Univ. Press, 1979), p. 89.

[20] Jeremias says this passage is 'the key to the understanding of all Jesus' ethical demands.' Jeremias, *Jesus*, pp. 68–69, quoted in Piper, *Love Your Enemies*, p. 89.

[21] Eduard Schweizer, *The Good News According to Matthew* (Atlanta: John Knox, 1975), p. 108.

[22] Culbert G. Rutenber, *Dagger and the Cross* (New York: Fellowship Pub., 1950), p. 63.

[23] E.g., Rom 4:1ff.; Gal 3:6ff.; 3:11 (citing Hab 2:4).

[24] See Piper's discussion of the Old Testament citations in Rom 12:17–20 (*Love Your Enemies*, pp. 111–14) and 1 Pet 3:10–12 (Piper, pp. 122ff.).

[25] For example, Rom 13:8–10; see Piper, ibid., pp. 113–14.

[26] See, for example, Boettner, *Christian Attitude toward War*, p. 40.

[27] See Calvin's statement of this in his *Institutes*, IV, chap. 20, sect. 32.

[28]Rutenber, *Dagger and the Cross*, p. 30.

[29]See, for example, Sanday and Headlam, *Romans* (ICC), p. 366; quoted in G. H. C. Macgregor, *New Testament Basis of Pacifism* (Nyack, NY: Fellowship Pub., 1960), p. 86.

[30]Gottlob Schrenk says the government's role as avenger of divine judgment 'is here insisted upon in opposition to revolutionary tendencies in the Roman Church.' ἔκδικος, *TDNT*, 2:445.

[31]C. H. Dodd, *The Epistle to the Romans*, 'The Moffat New Testament Commentary' (London: Fontana Books, 1959), p. 209.

[32]F. F. Bruce, *The Epistle of Paul to the Romans*, Tyndale New Testament Commentaries (Grand Rapids, Mich: Eerdmans, 1963), p. 232.

[33]Ibid.

[34]Ibid., p. 14.

[35]Dodd, *Romans*, p. 208.

[36]Bruce, *Romans*, pp. 231–32.

[37]For the discussion on the division of 12:9ff., see Piper, *Love Your Enemies*, pp. 103 and 211, n. 13. Many scholars see v. 14 beginning a new section on 'outsiders.' Piper rightly notes that v. 12 includes a reference to outsiders. V. 15 (and perhaps 16) may refer to Christians. One likely explanation for the fact that the division is 'not at all strict' (Piper, p. 211, n. 13) is that (*pace* Piper) Paul believed that love for enemies applied in all situations, including relationships in the church and with the state. Hence he could move back and forth with no sense of inappropriateness. There is no textual basis for Piper's claim (pp. 131–32) that 12:14, 17–21 refers to the local neighbourhood, but not to the state. This arbitrary distinction, however, is the basis of his claim that love for enemies does not apply in the public arena. If, as we argue here, 12:14–13:10 is one unit, then Piper's claim (p. 132) that the call for enemy love never applies in areas where subjection is ordered is wrong here as elsewhere.

[38]John Howard Yoder, *Politics of Jesus* (Grand Rapids, Mich: Eerdmans, 1972), esp. pp. 199–200.

[39]Bruce, *Romans*, p. 238 (our italics). See too Dodd, *Romans*, pp. 210–11. Bruce, however, goes on to appeal to the idea of a dualistic ethic which allows the Christian as ruler to do what to the Christian as believer is forbidden (ibid.). We disagree.

[40]Two books that point in this direction are Dave Jackson, *Dial 911: Peaceful Christians and Urban Violence* (Scottdale, Pa:

Herald Press, 1981), and Howard Zehr, *The Christian as Victim* (Akron, Pa: Office of Criminal Justice, Mennonite Central Committee, 1982). See also Zehr's bibliography.

[41]See Yoder's and Aukerman's discussion of the meaning of 'institute' (Rom 13:1): Yoder, *Politics*, pp. 200–205; and Dale Aukerman, *Darkening Valley* (New York: Seabury, 1981), p. 95. Cf. also Gerhard Delling, τάσσω, *TDNT*, 8:27–31.

[42]In connection with this permissive will of God with reference to rulers, see Aukerman's discussion of Rev 13:5–7 (Aukerman, *Darkening Valley*, p. 95).

[43]W. Michaelis, μάχαιρα, *TDNT*, 4:524–27.

[44]Yoder, *Politics*, pp. 205–6. Again, we are not saying that this passage approves or commands this use of the sword by the government. We are merely pointing out that the passage speaks of police activity, not international conflict.

[45]See C. E. B. Cranfield, *A Commentary on Romans 12–13* (Edinburgh: Oliver and Boyd, 1965), pp. 69–71; and Sider, *Christ and Violence*.

[46]Boettner, *Christian Attitude toward War*, pp. 33–34.

[47]See Rutenber, *Dagger and the Cross*, p. 34, for a good brief discussion of this passage.

[48]For example, see John Martin Creed, *The Gospel According to St Luke* (London: Macmillan, 1950), p. 270; F. C. Burkitt, *The Gospel History and Its Transmission* (Edinburgh: T. and T. Clark, 1925), pp. 140ff.; G. B. Caird, *The Gospel of Saint Luke*, Pelican Gospel Commentaries (Baltimore: Penguin, 1963), pp. 240–41; and Leon Morris, *The Gospel According to St. Luke* (Grand Rapids, Mich: Eerdmans, 1974), p. 310. Caird says: 'The instruction to sell their coats and buy swords is an example of Jesus' fondness for violent metaphor (cf. Mt 23–24, Mk 10:25), but the disciples take it literally as pedants have continued to do ever since' (p. 241).

[49]Morris, *Luke*, p. 310.

[50]Ibid.

[51]McSorley, *NT Basis of Peacemaking*, p. 24.

[52]S. G. F. Brandon, *Jesus and the Zealots* (Manchester: Manchester Univ. Press, 1967), makes this text the basis of his thesis that Jesus used violence. See George R. Edward's decisive critique, *Jesus and the Politics of Violence* (New York: Harper & Row, 1972), and the brief, excellent discussion in Yoder, *Politics of Jesus*, pp. 48–53, and the literature cited there.

[53]See Yoder, *Politics of Jesus*, p. 51 (and the article in n. 38); and Macgregor, *NT Basis of Pacifism*, p. 17, n. 2.

[54]See Cranfield, *Mark*, p. 357; Morris, *Luke*, p. 282.

[55]See examples, including *The Westminster Confession*, chap. XXIII, in Macgregor, *NT Basis of Pacifism*, p. 18. Also Boettner, *Christian Attitude toward War*, p. 32.

[56]One might argue that in both these latter accounts the story as a whole contains a recognition of sin. But that is true likewise of the centurion in Acts who surely repented of sin. It remains the case that there is no specific word of condemnation of the woman's prostitution or the thief's robbery.

[57]We should also mention John the Baptist's words to soldiers in Lk 3:14. Mt 11:7–15, however, says explicitly that John the Baptist was the last of the prophets of the old covenant; therefore his views, if they do contradict those of Jesus, are not normative. It is not clear, however, what John did tell the soldiers. The KJV translates his advice as 'Do *violence* to no man.' See Rutenber, *Dagger and the Cross*, p. 36.

[58]See examples in Rutenber, *Dagger and the Cross*, p. 31.

[59]Boettner, *Christian Attitude toward War*, p. 83.

[60]We use the word *pacifism* in this section because that is the word most frequently used by those who offer the critique discussed here.

[61]Boettner, *Christian Attitude toward War*, p. 83.

[62]Reinhold Niebuhr has offered the most persistent, vigorous challenge to pacifists. See among other things, his 'Why The Christian Church Is Not Pacifist.' *Christianity and Power Politics* (New York: Scribner's, 1946), pp. 1–32; *An Interpretation of Christian Ethics* (New York: Harper, 1935). Also, Harry R. Davis and Robert C. Good, *Reinhold Niebuhr on Politics* (New York: Scribner's, 1960), pp. 131–63. For a good critique, see G. H. C. Macgregor's *The Relevance of an Impossible Ideal: An Answer to the Views of Reinhold Niebuhr* reprinted in *NT Basis of Pacifism*, pp. 113–60; and John H. Yoder, *Reinhold Niebuhr and Christian Pacifism* (Washington, DC: The Church Peace Mission, n.d.).

[63]See this and another example in Rutenber, *Dagger and the Cross*, pp. 109, 22.

[64]See, for instance, the clear statement of this in 'Why the Christian Church Is Not Pacifist,' p. 8.

[65]See the development of this critique in Macgregor, *NT Basis of Pacifism*, pp. 135–36, 140.

[66] Reinhold Niebuhr, *Moral Man and Immoral Society* (New York: Scribner's, 1932).

[67] Niebuhr, 'Why the Christian Church Is Not Pacifist,' p. 3. We are quite aware that Niebuhr, in the sentence just before the one quoted, recognises grace as 'the power of righteousness which heals the contradiction within our hearts.' But Niebuhr does not maintain Paul's balance of these two aspects of grace. Later (pp. 18ff.), Niebuhr asks whether Gal 2:20 means primarily justification or renewal. He says it means both, but then he proceeds to emphasise only the former. A recent scholarly study of Paul's doctrine of *dikaiosunē* makes it quite clear that for Paul grace means both forgiveness and Spirit-empowered renewal in equal measure. J. A. Ziesler, *The Meaning of Righteousness in Paul: A Linguistic and Theological Enquiry* (Cambridge: Cambridge Univ. Press, 1972). This balanced doctrine of grace supports not Niebuhr's pessimistic rejection of pacifism but rather a Spirit-filled optimism about the possibility of Christian nonviolence.

Chapter 9: The Christian Peacemaker

[1] Quoted in Mary Lou Kownacki, ed., *A Race to Nowhere* (Chicago: Pax Christi, 1980), p. 11.

[2] The best book we know on this is *Hiroshima-Nagasaki: A Pictorial Record of the Atomic Destruction* (Tokyo: Hiroshima-Nagasaki Pub., 1978).

[3] Stationery, books, jewellery, decorative items and tote bags are available from the Fellowship of Reconciliation, Box 271, Nyack, NY 10960.

[4] 'The Weight of Nothing,' quoted in Kownacki, *Race to Nowhere*, p. 85. In quoting this story, we do not in any way mean to imply that peace will be easy or that we will ever abolish 'wars and rumours of wars.'

[5] John R. W. Stott, 'Calling for Peacemakers in a Nuclear Age, Part I,' *Christianity Today*, 8 Feb. 1980, p. 44.

[6] Harvey Cox, 'Let People Cry Out,' *Fellowship*, Sept. 1981, p. 4.

[7] For a brief description of Christian involvement in the antislavery movement, see Jim Wallis, *The Call to Conversion* (Tring, Herts: Lion, 1982). A more detailed presentation is found in Donald W. Dayton, *Discovering An Evangelical Heritage* (New York: Harper & Row, 1976), esp. chap. 2.

[8] Article by Kenneth A. Briggs, *New York Times*, 25 Mar. 1979.

[9]'Anti-Nukes, US,' *Newsweek*, 23 Nov. 1981, p. 44.

[10]Mernie King, 'Peace by Peace,' *Sojourners*, Sept. 1980, p. 24.

[11]'Registration cannot be separated from a draft,' says Senator Mark Hatfield, (Republican Senator for Oregon). 'It's all part of the same programme.' Quoted in the pamphlet, *Register for the Draft? Some Say 'No'* (Philadelphia: American Friends Service Committee, 1980), p. 10.

[12]Eligible members of Sojourners Fellowship, a Christian community in Washington, DC, refused to register. 'The members of Sojourners Fellowship have determined to refuse the call to arms at every point, including registration for the draft,' they said in a statement. 'Further, we advocate that others likewise refuse. Specifically, we encourage young men and women to refuse to register for the draft and support them in their decision. We regard this as our pastoral responsibility, and would invite others who have specific pastoral care for young people to consider it their responsibility as well.' Quoted in *Register for the Draft*, p. 13.

[13]'Non-Registrants,' *Christian Century*, 25 Nov. 1981, p. 1224.

[14]Of the 60 million tax returns filed in 1979 in the States, the IRS counted only one or two thousand in which citizens were protesting tax payments because of war resistance. See John Junkerman, 'Why Pray for Peace While Paying for War?' *Progressive*, Apr. 1981, p. 16. People protest and refuse to pay taxes for many reasons besides war. In the first nine months of 1981, some 21,000 people filed protests, still a tiny proportion of the 95 million tax returns filed in 1981. See 'Evading Income Taxes: The People Challenge the IRS,' *Philadelphia Inquirer*, 28 Nov. 1981, p. 2A.

[15]Taken from the official leaflet on the Peace Tax Campaign, available from the office at 26 Thurlow Rd, Leicester, LE2 1YE.

[16]Quoted in 'Tax Resistance: A Call to Lutherans,' *Vanguard*, Feb. 1982, p. 1.

[17]Congressman Wilbur Mills said of this special tax, 'It is clear that the Vietnam operation and only the Vietnam operation makes this bill necessary' (*The Congressional Record*, 23 Feb. 1966).

[18]We say *most* forms because there are some perfectly legal ways to resist war taxes. One very difficult but perfectly legal method is to reduce income to a nontaxable level. Another legal method is to pay under protest by writing 'paid in protest' on

the cheque and enclosing a letter explaining the reasons for protest.

[19]Cf. Hugo Adam Bedau, ed., *Civil Disobedience: Theory and Practice* (New York: Pegasus, 1969); Carl Cohen, *Civil Disobedience: Conscience, Tactics and the Law* (New York: Columbia Univ. Press, 1971); Robert T. Hall, *The Morality of Civil Disobedience* (New York: Harper, 1971); Daniel B. Stevick, *Civil Disobedience and the Christian* (New York: Seabury Press, 1969); David R. Weber, ed., *Civil Disobedience in America: A Documentary History* (Ithaca, NY: Cornell Univ. Press, 1978); Elliot Zashin, *Civil Disobedience and Democracy* (New York: Free Press, 1971); Howard Zinn, *Disobedience and Democracy* (New York: Random House, 1968).

[20]Donald D. Kaufman's excellent book advocating war tax resistance is called *The Tax Dilemma: Praying for Peace, Paying for War* (Scottdale, Pa: Herald Press, 1978). Kaufman gives many historical examples of Christians refusing to pay taxes which support the military. However, in most of the examples given, the tax was a special levy instituted to support a specific military expenditure, such as the Prussian tax of the 1780s that was used to support military schools (p. 33). To refuse such a special tax would be a clear witness against war and military preparations. But the example is not relevant to contemporary America, where all taxes go into the general fund. Kaufman also cites resistance to buying war bonds (pp. 39–41). Again, this has no relevance to our contemporary dilemma.

[21]We are aware of the ambiguities of even the *civilian* programmes of government. Because a government expenditure is nonmilitary does not necessarily mean that it is good or wise. However, we believe that government budgets still fund many efforts that are both worthwhile and necessary to the functioning of democracy.

[22]It is true that this 'temple tax' went to support the Jewish temple, not the Roman army. However, Jesus certainly did not agree with everything that went on in the temple, as his later cleansing of it showed. Therefore, the fact that Jesus willingly paid this tax showed that he did not find a problem in financially supporting an institution some of whose activities were abhorrent.

[23]Cecil John Cadoux, *The Early Church and the World* (Edinburgh: T. & T. Clark, 1925), pp. 369–70.

[24]In the States, the CBS TV Programme *60 Minutes* (15 Nov.

1981) interviewed three former and one current Internal Revenue Service collection agents. All agreed that the IRS is quite ready to harass and intimidate citizens who are delinquent in tax payment. They described the IRS collection process as 'abusive,' 'a KGB,' 'a little Kremlin,' with 'no sensitivity to the rights of citizens.'

[25] Kaufman, *The Tax Dilemma*, p. 21.

[26] Ibid., p. 25.

[27] For further information on the proposed legislation, see Kaufman, *The Tax Dilemma*, pp. 51–55. One specific proposal is the World Peace Tax Fund. An act giving its provisions has been introduced into the House of Representatives in the States every year since 1972, but has not yet received the votes needed for passage. The bill would set up a special government trust fund which could only be used for non-military purposes. Persons objecting to paying taxes to the military would designate their taxes to this special fund. A 'National Council for World Peace Tax Fund' (2111 Florida Ave NW, Washington, DC 20008) was set up in 1975 to promote this legislation. Its slogan is 'Taxes for peace, not war.' In England, the Peace Tax Campaign is working for similar legislation (26 Thurlow Rd, Leicester, LE2 1YE).

[28] Willard Swartley, 'Answering the Pharisees: A New Testament Study on the Payment of War Taxes,' *Sojourners*, Feb. 1979, p. 20.

[29] One attempt in the States to build a mass war tax resistance movement is the 'Conscience and Military Tax Campaign' (44 Bellhaven Rd, Bellport, NY 11713. Tel: 516/286-8825). People sign a statement that they will refuse military taxes once 100,000 people have signed a similar resolution. The group provides petitions and other materials for the campaign, a campaign packet and a newsletter. As of late 1981, they had 1,350 signers in 47 states.

[30] *Newsletter*, Conscience and Military Tax Campaign, Autumn 1981, p. 3.

Chapter 10: The Church as a Peacemaking Community

[1] John R. W. Stott, 'Calling for Peacemakers in a Nuclear Age, Part II,' *Christianity Today*, 7 Mar. 1980, p. 44.

[2] Ibid.

[3] Cf. Acts 15:1–29, 38–40; 2 Cor 12:20–21; Eph 4:25–32.

[4] Mernie King, 'Peace by Peace,' *Sojourners*, Sept. 1980, p. 25.

[5]You could suggest reading this book or Dale Aukerman's book *Darkening Valley: A Biblical Perspective on Nuclear War* (New York: Seabury Press, 1981) or the study guide *A Matter of Faith* (see appendix D).

[6]See Thomas A. Shannon, ed., *War or Peace* (Maryknoll, NY: Orbis Books, 1980), p. 65.

[7]Samuel H. Day, Jr, 'Captain Coleman's Challenging Job and Why He Decided to Leave It,' *Progressive*, Aug. 1981, pp. 27–31. After a long struggle of conscience, Coleman expressed his decision to leave the military in these words: 'For a Christian it is totally incompatible to take part in the mass murder of millions of innocent people. It is simply wrong.' Ibid., p. 31.

[8]Cf. Ronald J. Sider, *Rich Christians in an Age of Hunger* (London: Hodder and Stoughton, 1978); Doris Janzen Longacre, *Living More with Less* (London: Hodder and Stoughton, 1982); Richard J. Foster, *Freedom of Simplicity* (London: SPCK, 1981); Adam Daniel Finnerty, *No More Plastic Jesus* (Maryknoll, NY: Orbis Books, 1977); Ernest Callenbach, *Living Poor with Style* (New York: Bantam, 1972); Frances Moore Lappé, *Diet For a Small Planet* (New York: Ballantine, 1975).

[9]The three statements are quoted in *Christians at the Crossroads*, a leaflet produced by Christian CND, 11 Goodwin St, London.

[10]Nationwide enrolment in Army ROTC programmes (now 60,000 men and 16,000 women) has more than doubled since 1974. As this book was being written, the Pentagon was planning to open 56 new ROTC campus centres in the fall of 1981. *CCCO News Notes* (Central Committee for Conscientious Objectors), Autumn 1981, p. 5.

[11]Wilmington College in Ohio, for example, offers a peace studies programme to prepare students for careers in organisations dedicated to peacemaking or to help them exercise effective leadership for peace in whatever vocation they choose. Information on the programme is available from Peace Studies Programme, Pyle Centre, PO Box 1243, Wilmington College, Wilmington, OH 45177. Other colleges and seminaries with peace studies programmes are listed in appendix B-3.

[12]Information taken from the brochure produced by the University of Bradford, *The School of Peace Studies*.

[13]In November 1981 over a hundred and fifty US colleges in forty-two states held special teach-ins on the subject 'Avoiding Nuclear Armageddon.' Carl Sagan, the famous astronomer,

spoke at Cornell. Participants at the University of Vermont saw a puppet show on peace. Coordinated events were sponsored by the Union of Concerned Scientists.

Chapter 11: The Christian Witness for Peace in Society

[1] Billy Graham, 'Peace Is a Spiritual Issue,' *The Other Side*, Jan. 1981, p. 19.
[2] Address at Hiroshima, 25 Feb. 1981.
[3] Jim Wallis, *The Call to Conversion* (Tring, Herts: Lion, 1982), pp. 109, 112.
[4] For a discussion of this point, see Ronald J. Sider, 'Words and Deeds,' *Journal of Theology for Southern Africa*, Autumn 1979, pp. 31ff.
[5] Carl Henry made the proposal in a speech to the 1973 meeting of Evangelicals for Social Action held in Chicago, Ill. The substance of the following quotation was confirmed by a letter from Dr Henry to Richard Taylor in Nov., 1981.
[6] John R. W. Stott, 'Calling for Peacemakers in a Nuclear Age, Part II,' *Christianity Today*, 7 Mar. 1980, p. 45.
[7] For many of these suggestions we are indebted to a leaflet by J. Stuart Innerst, 'How to Write a Letter to the Editor,' Friends Committee for National Legislation, Washington, DC.
[8] The *Nuclear War Prevention Kit* (see appendix D) gives more information on news releases.
[9] *Public Papers of the President: John F. Kennedy*, 1 Aug. 1963, item 319A (Washington, DC: Government Printing Office, 1964), p. 610.
[10] Political action can be effective at the local and state levels as well as nationally. In Evanston, Illinois, for example, intensive lobbying by peace groups resulted in the city council's adopting a resolution calling on the United States to enter into an immediate bilateral nuclear weapons freeze with the Soviet Union. See *Fellowship*, Oct./Nov. 1981, p. 20.
[11] Since the early 1940s, the Quakers have maintained a peace lobby in Washington called the Friends Committee on National Legislation. The Mennonites also have a Washington office and a regular newsletter. A number of other churches and inter-religious bodies have similar efforts.
[12] Richard Taylor wrote another book which tells how to organise nonviolent, direct-action campaigns. *Blockade: A Guide to Nonviolent Intervention* (Maryknoll, NY: Orbis Books, 1977).

See also Ed Hedemann, *War Resisters League Organizer's Manual* (New York: War Resisters League, 1981).

Chapter 12: Disarming the Powers

[1] Quoted in *Evangelical Newsletter*, 20 Feb. 1981, p. 1.

[2] Dr Kennan is a historian, former US Ambassador to the Soviet Union, and is widely credited with formulating the US 'containment' policy, a policy of using US power and alliances to contain Soviet expansionism. The quote is from an address he gave on 1 Oct. 1980 to the Second World Congress on Soviet and East German Studies, Garmisch, Germany. See *Disarmament Times*, 3 Dec. 1980, p. 3.

[3] Alva Myrdal, *The Game of Disarmament* (New York: Pantheon Books, 1976), p. 73.

[4] President Eisenhower (1953): The superpowers must 'begin to diminish the potential destructive power of the world's atomic stockpiles.' President Kennedy (1961): 'Mankind must put an end to war or war will put an end to mankind. The risks in disarmament pale in comparison to the risks inherent in an unlimited arms race.' President Johnson (1968): Moscow and Washington will 'pursue negotiations in good faith for the cessation of the nuclear arms race.' President Nixon (1970): 'The nuclear era places upon the two preponderant powers a unique responsibility to explore means of limiting military competition.' President Carter (inaugural address): I hope that 'nuclear weapons would be rid from the face of the earth.' President Reagan (18 Nov. 1981): 'We will seek to negotiate substantial reductions in nuclear arms. . . . My Administration, my country, and I are committed to achieving arms reductions agreements. . . . I believe the time is right to move forward on arms control and the resolution of critical regional disputes at the conference table.' The quotes from Presidents Eisenhower through Carter are taken from William Sloan Coffin, *The Challenge of Disarmament* (New York: Riverside Church Disarmament Program, 1978), pp. 1–2. The quotes from President Reagan are taken from his address to the National Press Club in Washington. (*New York Times*, 19 Nov. 1981, p. A17.)

[5] This estimate is from a talk by nuclear weapons expert Frank Barnaby at the American Friends Service Committee in Philadelphia, 29 July 1981. Actually, the United States will add

seventeen thousand new warheads, but it will remove two thousand, giving a net gain of fifteen thousand.

[6]Robert C. Johansen, *Toward a Dependable Peace* (New York: Institute for World Order, 1978), p. 3.

[7]Ibid., p. 3. For a superb analysis of expenditures, see Ruth Leger Sivard, *World Military and Social Expenditures, 1981* (Leesburg, Va: World Priorities, 1981).

[8]Quoted in *World Federalist Association* (Arlington, Va: World Federalist Assn, 1981), p. 7.

[9]Johansen, *Toward a Dependable Peace*, p. 10.

[10]Ibid., p. 14.

[11]*Billy Graham: A Change of Heart* (Nyack, NY: Fellowship of Reconciliation, 1979), p. 2.

[12]Pope Paul VI's address to the United Nations, 4 Oct. 1965; quoted in *Maryknoll*, Aug. 1979, p. 33.

[13]Roman Catholic Bishop Leroy T. Matthiesen of Amarillo, Texas, recently expressed the unilateral disarmament position as follows: 'If we were a completely Christian nation, it would be possible for us to disarm unilaterally and just trust in the Lord and believe in the power of the resurrection – even if we were destroyed in the process. . . . We're risking all-out destruction now, so why don't we risk all-out peace?' Quoted in Maryknoll Justice and Peace Office *News Notes*, Nov. 1981, p. 14.

[14]Robert C. Johansen, *The Disarmament Process: Where to Begin* (New York: Faculty Press, 1977), p. 5.

[15]In some versions of this proposal, a world police force, supported by all nations, would be used to make sure that no nation violated the disarmament agreement and began to rebuild its war machine.

[16]'In May 1981, a Gallup Poll in the USA reported that 72% of the respondents favored an agreement with the Soviet Union not to build any more nuclear weapons. 80% favored negotiations with the Soviets to try to reach an agreement.' Eugene T. Carroll, 'Wanted Alive: Negotiations!' *Coalition Close-Up*, Newsletter of the Coalition for a New Foreign and Military Policy, Autumn 1981.

[17]In his 1961 farewell address, President Eisenhower issued this sombre warning: 'In the councils of government, we must guard against the acquisition of unwarranted influence, whether sought or unsought, by the military-industrial complex. The potential for the disastrous rise of misplaced power exists and

will persist.' Quoted in George Hunsinger, *Idolatry and Prayer: The Arms Race in Theological Perspective* (New York: Riverside Church Disarmament Program, Nov. 1978), p. 7.

[18]It is not true that the USSR has refused all on-site inspection. For example, during negotiations for the Partial Test Ban Treaty, the Soviets expressed willingness to permit three on-site inspections per year on Soviet soil. The Treaty on Peaceful Underground Nuclear Explosions (signed by Moscow and Washington in 1976) provides for on-site inspections, including provisions to assure that observers from the other country can carry out their functions freely and effectively. In general, however, the Soviet stance has been to oppose inspection.

[19]"US to Add "Cruise" to Naval Force: New Missiles May Hurt Arms Control,' *Philadelphia Inquirer*, 4 Dec. 1981, p. 1A.

[20]Myrdal, *Game of Disarmament*, p. xvii.

[21]Quoted in Bernard T. Feld, 'Words, Not War,' *Bulletin of Atomic Scientists*, Dec. 1981, p. 4.

[22]For a complete list of successful disarmament treaties, along with a fuller description of their provisions, see the US government publication: *Arms Control and Disarmament Agreements: Texts and History of Negotiations* (Washington, DC: Arms Control and Disarmament Agency, 1977).

[23]The United States spent $6 billion on the ABM system before it was scrapped. Undoubtedly many more billions would have been spent if the system had been fully developed. See Paul F. Walker book review, *Bulletin of Atomic Scientists*, Dec. 1981, p. 36.

[24]Herman Will, 'The Churches and Disarmament,' *Engage/Social Action*, Sept. 1978, p. 31.

[25]*Arms Control and Disarmament Agreements*, p. 23.

[26]Ibid., p. 20.

[27]Paul Bennett, *Strategic Surveillance: How America Checks Soviet Compliance with SALT* (Cambridge, Mass: Union of Concerned Scientists, June 1979), pp. 3–4.

[28]Ibid., p. 9.

[29]For example, see Seymour Melman, ed., *Defense Economy: Conversion of Industries and Occupations to Civilian Needs* (New York: Praeger Publications, 1970); Melman, *Planning for Conversion of Military-Industrial and Military Base Facilities* (Washington, DC: US Department of Commerce, Economic Development Administration, 1973); Melman, 'Beating Swords into Subways,' *New York Times Magazine*, 19 Nov.

1978, pp. 43ff.; *The Economic Impact of Reductions in Defense Spending* (Washington, DC: Arms Control and Disarmament Agency, 1 July 1972); Marion Anderson, *The Impact of Military Spending on Machinists Union* (Washington, DC: International Association of Machinists, 1979).

30 'You can't sleep in a missile, you can't wear a missile, you can't drive around in a missile, you can't do a thing with a missile but give it to the government and pray that the government will never find any use for it whatsoever.' Rev. William Sloan Coffin, June 1980 speech at Claremont School of Religion, as recorded on Thesis Theology Cassettes, Pittsburgh, June 1980.

31 Quoted in Mary Lou Kownacki, ed., *A Race to Nowhere* (Erie, Pa: Benet Press, 1981), p. 32.

32 Quoted in *The Freeze Newsletter*, Institute for Defense and Disarmament Studies, Mar. 1981, p. 9. The newsletter is available from the National Freeze clearing house (see appendix B-2).

33 'SALT II: The Only Alternative to Annihilation?' *Christianity Today*, 27 Mar. 1981, pp. 14–15.

34 John R. W. Stott, 'Calling for Peacemakers in the Nuclear Age, Part II,' *Christianity Today*, 7 Mar. 1980, p. 45.

35 Henry Giniger, 'Scientists from 40 Nations Urge Freeze in Nuclear Arsenals,' *New York Times*, 4 Sept. 1981.

36 See Mark Hatfield, *The Age of Anxiety*, Hatfield Backgrounder, no. 193 (June 1981): p. 14.

37 The United States and the USSR followed a somewhat similar process from 1958 to 1963 during their discussions about a nuclear test ban treaty. Both sides placed a voluntary moratorium on nuclear tests for almost three years while experts worked out the details of a treaty to make the test ban permanent. See *Arms Control and Disarmament Agreements*, pp. 33–39.

38 An excellent write-up of the campaign to pass the resolution is found in Randy Kehler and Judith Scheckel, 'Yes! The People Decided: How Voters in Western Massachusetts Passed a Proposal for a Freeze on Nuclear Weapons,' *Sojourners*, Mar. 1981, p. 10.

39 Kennan made the proposal on 19 May 1981 upon receiving the Albert Einstein Peace Prize. The text of his address is available from the Institute for World Order, 777 UN Plaza, New York, NY 10017.

40 Here are some of the key agreements which arms control and

disarmament experts believe would help reverse the arms race:
a) A comprehensive ban on all nuclear tests.
b) A declaration by all nuclear powers that they will not be the first to use nuclear weapons.
c) An agreement to end the production of fissionable materials which can be used in nuclear weapons.
d) The phased reduction of nuclear weapons delivery systems.
e) Balanced reduction of conventional forces.
f) Mutual reduction of military budgets.
g) A total ban on the production and stockpiling of chemical weapons.
h) A freeze on the deployment of troops and bases; not stationing or using troops outside countries where they're now located.
i) A pullback of troops and bases from overseas.
j) Strengthening the Non-Proliferation Treaty.
k) Strengthening international peace-keeping and peacemaking mechanisms.
For a careful analysis of the advantages and disadvantages of many of these proposals, see Robert C. Johansen, *The Disarmament Process*, pp. 111–290.

Chapter 13: Is Nonmilitary Defence Possible?

[1] *For Pacifists* (Ahmedabad, India: Navajivan Publishing House, 1949), p. 4.
[2] Comments by two clergy who represented their denominations at a National Council of Churches 'Dialogue on Disarmament' at Stoney Point Conference Centre, 13–16 Sept. 1979. (It should be stressed that the two clergy were speaking for themselves and not for their denominations or the National Council of Churches.)
[3] 'The Soviet threat is the big lie of the arms race,' wrote Richard Barnet in his article, 'Lies Clearer Than Truth,' *Sojourners*, Aug. 1979, p. 16. See also Fred M. Kaplan, *Dubious Specter: A Second Look at the 'Soviet Threat'* (Washington, DC: Transnational Institute, 1977). Those who minimise the Soviet threat often make the following arguments:
    a) Because the USSR lost twenty million people in World War II, they know the horror of war and are not eager to start a new one.
    b) The Soviets would welcome arms reductions because they realise that money shifted from the military to the civilian

sector of their economy would raise their relatively low standard of living. Like us, they want a better life and more consumer goods. They see a high military budget as a burden keeping them from a better life.

c) Soviet military advances are more a response to Western initiatives than an attempt to gain military superiority. The United States was the first to develop the A-bomb, the H-bomb, the ICBM, the nuclear submarine, cruise missiles, and rockets with multiple warheads. The Soviet Union has always been behind in the arms race. Their military expenditures are a way of playing 'catch-up.'

d) When all weapons systems are counted, the United States and NATO still lead the USSR and the Warsaw Pact in the arms race. The Soviet Union has *not* gained military superiority. We are *not* falling behind them. We now hold, and will continue to hold, the military edge.

e) Soviet weapons are a reaction to the perceived hostility of the world around them. They faced military intervention by the United States and other countries just after their revolution – 'to strangle Bolshevism in its cradle,' in Winston Churchill's words. They have been invaded three times in this century. Now, with NATO to the west, a hostile China to the east and restive satellite nations on their borders, they feel threatened and beleaguered, surrounded by foes, afraid of being attacked. Soviet military power is really their response to outside threats.

f) The early ideological fervour of Communism has dimmed. Current Soviet leaders are not risk takers. They seek coexistence rather than world domination. They are mostly interested in safeguarding their own territory and making sure that neighbouring states are not in a position to attack them.

g) Western fear of Communism has led us to dehumanise the Soviet people and see them as 'totally evil and devoted to nothing but our destruction' (George Kennan, as quoted in *Christian Century*, 8 Apr. 1981, p. 388). Our fear and demonising of the Soviet Union have made us magnify their threat out of all proportion.

[4] *Websters Third New International Dictionary* (Springfield, Mass: G. and C. Merriam, 1961).

[5] In 1944 Communism was represented by a single nation of 180 million people. Today it is represented by approximately 25 nations and almost half the world's population. See 'Soviet Geopolitical Momentum: Myth or Menace?' in *The Defense*

Monitor, Jan. 1980, pp. 11–14. It should be noted that the 25 Communist nations make up fifteen per cent of the total of 163 countries in the world. Also, since some of them (for example, China, Yugoslavia, Albania) are independent of the USSR, it cannot be said that the Soviet Union controls half of the world's population or nations. In fact, exclusive of the USSR itself, Soviet Communism controls or deeply influences only about six per cent of the world's people. See 'Soviet Geopolitical Momentum,' p. 5.

[6]The United States, of course, has not been blameless in using military force and subversion to achieve its national aims. The overthrow of the democratically elected Allende government in Chile, which was assisted by CIA and US corporations with the approval of the administration, is one example of its using power in a way incompatible with democratic values.

[7]'International conflict is inevitable, and political groups or countries will continue to be tempted to impose their wishes by military means. . . . Military action is still believed to be the only effective ultimate sanction for dealing with extreme tyranny and especially with expansionist designs.' Gene Sharp, *Social Power and Political Freedom* (Boston: Porter Sargent, 1980), p. 203.

[8]It should be noted here that some influential Christians take the position that questions of national defence should be of no concern to the Christian. Anxiety about defending one's way of life, they argue, comes from a 'security mentality' which is almost idolatrous, since it places the security of the state above one's obedience to God. 'Our security should come from faith in God,' they say, 'not from reliance on any human "defence system." Our job is not to defend a political system or way of life, but to be faithful.'

We agree that obedience to God is our first obligation as Christians and that our security must come from God. We agree that the search for security, if it remains only on the human level, can become idolatrous. However, as we have argued, we believe that there is a legitimate concern for security and defence which is right for any human group or nation to seek. Christians should support the concern without accepting the need for weapons of mass murder as the basis upon which security is built.

Christians who criticise the 'security mentality' are often at the forefront of defending minorities and Third World peoples against oppressive threats to their rights, culture and freedom. They do not say to the Black person threatened by the Ku Klux Klan, 'Just rely on God for your security.' Rather, they make practical attempts to protect them. Much of the US Civil Rights Movement, in fact, was an attempt to defend the rights of Black people and to secure for Black citizens access to the rights enjoyed by all citizens.

Similarly, when the superpowers invade, oppress or 'destabilise' countries like Afghanistan, El Salvador or Chile, these same Christians are often those who stand up for the rights of these countries to self-determination. They act on the belief that these countries have a right to resist tyranny and to determine their own form of government without outside intervention from the USSR, the United States or any other power.

These and other actions strongly suggest a belief in the validity of defending basic human, economic and political rights. They suggest a belief in the right of a nation to choose its own way of life without outside intervention or oppression.

The desire for national security, it seems to us, is simply the application of these beliefs to *one's own* country and its values and institutions. Just as we should defend *others* against tyranny and oppression, so we should do the same for our own country, if it is threatened by outside, despotic power.

The question, therefore, is not *whether* to defend a nation, but *how*. A desire to defend the values and institutions of one's country does not imply that it is perfect. It does imply that a way of life imposed by an outside power would be drastically less desirable. The imperfect but commendable system of democracy seems to us far preferable to Soviet Communism or to any other system that an outside despot might try to force upon us. 'Government of the people, by the people, and for the people,' though only approximated in the West, is much better than government decreed by a hostile foreign power.

[9]A complete list of books on nonmilitary defence can be found in appendix A-4.

[10]Gene Sharp, *Social Power and Political Freedom*, p. 304. A 1967 report to the cabinet by the Norwegian Defence Research Establishment was entitled 'Non-Military Defence and Norwegian Security Policy.' Similar studies have been written by branches of the Danish, Dutch and Swedish governments. The Swedish Ministry of Defence financed an international confer-

ence on 'Non-Military Forms of Struggle' in Uppsala in 1972. Most of the governmental studies so far are considering nonmilitary defence as a complement to military defence rather than a substitute for it. For details of European efforts and studies, see Gene Sharp, 'Military and Governmental Steps in Investigation of Civilian-Based Defense,' paper produced for the Harvard Centre for International Affairs, 1981.

[11] 'France's Pacifist General,' *Fellowship*, Oct. 1973, p. 11.

[12] Adam Roberts, ed., *Civilian Resistance as a National Defense* (Harrisburg, Pa: Stackpole Books, 1968), p. 210.

[13] Much of the information in this description is taken from the chapter 'Passive Resistance in Hungary, 1859–1867,' in William Robert Miller, *Nonviolence: A Christian Interpretation* (New York: Schocken Books, 1972), pp. 230–43. See also 'Hungary,' in *The Encyclopedia Americana* (Danbury, Conn.: Americana Corp., 1980), 14:585–86.

[14] Miller, *Nonviolence*, p. 237.

[15] Ibid., p. 234.

[16] Ibid., p. 237.

[17] Ibid., p. 238.

[18] Ibid., p. 239.

[19] The account of Norway's resistance is based on the following:

Eivind Berggrav, 'Experiences of the Norwegian Church in the War,' *The Lutheran World Review* 1, No. 1 (July 1948): 42–57.

Odd Godal, *Eivind Berggrav: Leader of Christian Resistance* (London: SCM Press, 1949).

Alex Johnson, *Eivind Berggrav: God's Man of Suspense* (Minneapolis: Augsburg Pub. House, 1960).

Sir Stephen King-Hall, *Defense in the Nuclear Age* (Nyack, NY: Fellowship Pub., 1959), pp. 186–88.

Miller, *Nonviolence*, pp. 251–59.

Roberts, *Civilian Resistance*, pp. 136–72, 250.

Sharp, *Social Power and Political Freedom*, pp. 226–27.

Sharp, *The Politics of Nonviolent Action* (Boston: Porter-Sargent, 1980), pp. 88–89.

[20] Roberts, *Civilian Resistance*, p. 148.

[21] Johnson, *Eivind Berggrav*, p. 147.

[22] Berggrav, 'Experiences of the Norwegian Church,' p. 51.

[23] Johnson, *Eivind Berggrav*, p. 160.

[24] Berggrav, 'Experiences of the Norwegian Church,' p. 44.

[25] Nora Levin, *The Holocaust: The Destruction of European*

Jewry, 1933–1945 (New York: Schocken Books, 1973), p. 392.

[26]Roberts, *Civilian Resistance*, p. 169.

[27]Nora Levin, *Holocaust*, p. 399. For definitive accounts of the Holocaust, including both military and nonmilitary resistance, see Raul Hilberg, *The Destruction of the European Jews* (Chicago: Quadrangle Books, 1961). Information on the Danish resistance is found on pp. 357–63. See also Lucy S. Dawidowicz, *The War against the Jews: 1933–1945* (New York: Bantam Books, 1975). For dramatic examples of Christian nonmilitary resistance to the Nazis, see Philip Friedman, *Their Brothers' Keepers* (New York: Crown Publishers, 1957).

[28]Nora Levin, *Holocaust*, p. 401.

[29]Ibid., p. 435.

[30]Allan A. Hunter, *Christians in the Arena* (Nyack, NY: Fellowship Pub., 1958), p. 40.

[31]John Ferguson, *The Politics of Love* (Greenwood, SC: Attic Press, n.d.), p. 108. The full story of André Trocmé and the resistance of Le Chambon is told in Philip Hallie, *Lest Innocent Blood Be Shed* (New York: Harper & Row, 1979).

[32]Hannah Arendt, *Eichmann in Jerusalem* (New York: Viking Press, 1963), p. 168.

[33]Nora Levin, *Holocaust*, p. 553.

[34]The material on Stephan is from Levin, p. 553. Kiril's action is recounted in Frederick B. Charry, *The Bulgarian Jews and the Final Solution 1940–1944* (Pittsburgh: Univ. of Pittsburgh Press, 1972), p. 90.

[35]Bulgaria, however, did not save some eleven to fourteen thousand Jews in territories outside the country but controlled by Bulgaria. The Jews of these 'annexed provinces' were shipped to Auschwitz and Treblinka in March 1943.

[36]Many fewer died among those who chose nonmilitary resistance than among those who chose to fight Hitler by entering the allied armies. Nevertheless, the suffering and death involved in both forms of resistance show that the defence of freedom requires pain and sacrifice no matter what means of defence are used.

[37]Could the nonmilitary resistance to Hitler have sustained itself if Germany had won the war? We do not know. Many would argue that a Nazi victory would have freed German troops to impose the final solution on the Danes, French and Bulgarians. Others contend that nonmilitary resistance can exercise a power which is even more forceful than military weapons – that a

militarily victorious Hitler could have been defeated in the long run through nonmilitary means.

[38]Quoted in Miller, *Nonviolence*, p. 290.

[39]Much of what follows is taken from Wolfgang Sternstein, 'The Ruhrkampf of 1923: Economic Problems of Civilian Defense,' in *Civilian Resistance*, ed. Roberts, pp. 106–35.

[40]Ibid., p. 112.

[41]Most of the material on El Salvador is from Patricia Parkman, 'Insurrection without Arms: The General Strike in El Salvador, 1944' (PhD diss., Temple University, 1980). For descriptions of nonviolent movements in other parts of Latin America, see Elizabeth Campuzano et al., *Resistance in Latin America* (Philadelphia: American Friends Service Committee, 1970).

[42]Parkman, 'Insurrection without Arms,' p. 69.

[43]Ibid., p. 169. The quote is from an interview with Martínez in the Guatemala City newspaper *El Imparcial*, 12 May 1944, trans. by Patricia Parkman.

[44]Personal conversation with Dr Barbara Krasner.

[45]To the hundreds of angry Black citizens, many of them armed and talking of 'shooting it out' with the police, King said: 'Now let's not become panicky. If you have weapons, take them home; if you do not have them, please do not seek to get them. We cannot solve this problem through retaliatory violence. . . . We must love our white brothers no matter what they do to us. We must make them know that we love them. Jesus still cries out in words that echo across the centuries: "Love your enemies; bless them that curse you; pray for them that despitefully use you." This is what we must live by. We must meet hate with love.' Miller, *Nonviolence*, pp. 302–3.

[46]Martin Luther King, Jr, *Strength to Love* (London: Fontana, 1969).

[47]See chap. six. Some Christians feel uncomfortable using the word 'enemy' in a Christian context. They contend that, if one is really filled with Christ's love, one will no longer see anyone as an enemy. We believe that Jesus was much more realistic. He used the word *enemy* to describe people who 'revile you and persecute you and utter all kinds of evil against you' (Mt 5:11). The New Testament teaches that Christians will have enemies. What was new in Jesus' teaching was not the message that his followers will no longer have enemies, but that his disciples are to love their enemies rather than despise them.

[48]Kenneth Scott Latourette, *A History of Christianity* (New York: Harper, 1953), p. 91.

[49]Cecil John Cadoux, *The Early Church and the World* (Edinburgh: T. & T. Clark, 1925), pp. 531, 251, 253, 555.

[50]Quoted in C. G. H. Macgregor, *The New Testament Basis of Pacifism* (Nyack, NY: Fellowship Pub., 1954), p. 154.

[51]See chap. five, p. 90.

[52]Roland Bainton, *Christian Attitudes toward War and Peace* (Nashville: Abingdon, 1960), p. 73.

[53]Cadoux, *Early Church and the World*, p. 237.

[54]Bainton, *Christian Attitudes*, p. 77.

[55]Jim Wallis, *The Call to Conversion* (Tring, Herts: Lion, 1982).

[56]Cecil John Cadoux, *The Early Christian Attitude toward War* (London: George Allen and Unwin, 1940), p. 82.

[57]Cadoux, *Early Christian Attitude*, p. 72.

[58]Latourette, *History of Christianity*, p. 91.

[59]Apparently, early Christians were quite conscious of the need to give a good example to the heathen by Christian behaviour that embodied sacrificial love even towards enemies. For example, Clement of Alexandria, a leader of the early church, said: 'For when [the heathen] hear from us that God says, "Ye will get no thanks if ye love [only] those who love you; but you will get thanks if you love your enemies and those that hate you," when they hear this, they admire the excess of goodness. But when they see that we do not love, not only those that hate [us], but even those that love [us], they laugh at us, and the Name is blasphemed.' Cadoux, *Early Church and the World*, p. 234.

[60]Kenneth Boulding, quoted in Jerome D. Frank, *Sanity and Survival: Psychological Aspects of War and Peace* (New York: Vintage Books, 1968), p. 270.

Chapter 14: How Nonmilitary Defence Works

[1]Martin Luther King, Jr, *Strength to Love* (London: Fontana, 1969). Dr King uses the phrase 'modern man' in the generic sense. In faithfulness to the original authors, we have usually not changed such terms in quotations.

[2]See, for example, Gene Sharp, *Making the Abolition of War a Realistic Goal* (New York: Institute for World Order, 1981), p. 8. Sharp defines CBD as 'a defence policy which utilises prepared civilian struggle – nonviolent action – to preserve the society's freedom, sovereignty, and constitutional system

against internal usurpations and external invasions and occupations. The aim is to deter and to defeat such attacks.'

[3]We have tried in our own writing to use nonsexist language. One exception, however, is our use of the term *he* or *him* when referring to the invader of a foreign country. We have kept this usage for two reasons. One is that we could not think of any smooth, readable English phrase which would avoid the problem. The other is that, although we realise that women might be involved in an invading force, it is most likely that the majority of the invaders, including the leaders, would be men. The word *he*, therefore, seemed appropriate.

[4]The word *power* is used here in its simplest definition: 'the ability to achieve purpose.' The purpose of the invader is to consolidate his occupation and to achieve his invasion goals, such as economic exploitation or political indoctrination. The purpose of CBD is to resist the invader, to protect the nation's freedom, to restore its sovereignty, and to free it of the occupier. Both the invader and the resister require power to achieve their purpose.

Whereas it is wrong for Christians to use certain kinds of power, biblical faith urges us to use the kind of power that comes from God and that he gives to his followers to accomplish his purposes. (Cf. 1 Chron 29:12; Ps 68:35; Mic 3:8; Lk 24:49; Jn 1:12; Acts 1:8; 2 Cor 12:9; 13:4; Eph 3:20; 2 Tim 1:7.)

[5]Because all or most of the population is involved, CBD has been called 'the most extreme development in the elimination of the distinction between civilians and the fighting forces.' Theodore Ebert, 'Preparations for Civilian Defense,' in T. K. Mahadevan, Adam Roberts, and Gene Sharp, eds., *Civilian Defense: An Introduction* (New Delhi: Gandhi Peace Foundation, 1967), p. 153.

[6]Gene Sharp, *Exploring Nonviolent Alternatives* (Boston: Porter-Sargent, 1970), p. 63.

[7]Gene Sharp, *The Politics of Nonviolent Action* (Boston: Porter-Sargent, 1973), pp. 596–97.

[8]Lt Col Alun Gwynne Jones, 'Forms of Military Attack,' in Adam Roberts, ed., *Civilian Resistance as a National Defense* (Harrisburg, Pa: Stackpole Books, 1967), p. 23.

[9]Jerome Frank, *Sanity and Survival* (New York: Vintage Books, 1968), p. 260.

[10]Patricia Parkman, 'Insurrection without Arms' (PhD diss., Temple University, 1980), p. 169.

[11] A reporter for the *N.Y. Telegram* described how, in May 1930, two thousand five hundred Gandhian demonstrators near Bombay took suffering on themselves rather than react with violence. 'During the morning I saw and heard hundreds of blows inflicted by police, but saw not a single blow returned by the volunteers. . . . Many times I saw the police vainly threaten the advancing volunteers with upraised *lathis* [long, flexible clubs made of bamboo]. Upon their determined refusal to recede, the *lathis* would fall upon the unresisting body, the volunteer would fall back bleeding or bruised, and be carried away on a stretcher.' Quoted in Richard B. Gregg, *The Power of Nonviolence* (Cambridge: J. Clarke, 1960), p. 35.

Gandhi had a deep understanding of suffering's effect on the human spirit. He believed that reason had a limited influence on an opponent. 'Reason has to be strengthened by suffering,' he wrote, 'and suffering opens the eyes of understanding. . . . If you want something really important to be done you must not merely satisfy reason, you must move the heart also. The appeal of reason is more to the head, but the penetration of the heart comes from suffering. It opens up the inner understanding.' Quoted in Sharp, *Politics of Nonviolent Action*, p. 709.

Cecil Hinshaw describes clearly the psychological mechanisms by which suffering love inhibits aggression in *Nonviolent Resistance: A Nation's Way to Peace* (Wallingford, Pa: Pendle Hill, 1956), pp. 37–38. 'To continue a physical attack upon one who chooses from courage to be physically defenceless.' Hinshaw writes, 'to be faced by firm refusal to yield to evil, yet to be met by steadfast love – this is simply more than human nature is prepared psychologically to face.'

[12] Richard Gregg coined the term *moral jujitsu* in his book *The Power of Nonviolence* (p. 43). Just as jujitsu throws an opponent off balance physically, so moral jujitsu throws an opponent off balance morally.

[13] Gene Sharp, *Politics of Nonviolent Action*, pp. 333, 743. See also Craine Brinton, *The Anatomy of Revolution* (New York: Prentice-Hall, 1952), p. 96.

[14] Harvey Seifert, *Conquest by Suffering* (Philadelphia: Westminster Press, 1965), p. 53.

[15] Ibid., p. 54. Seifert relates another incident in which soldiers were shooting directly into a demonstration organised by Gandhi's followers. When those in front fell wounded, 'those behind came forward with their breasts bared and exposed

themselves to the fire, so much so that some people got as many as 21 bullets in their bodies and all the people stood their ground without getting into a panic' (p. 139).

[16] Sharp, *Politics of Nonviolent Action*, p. 147.

[17] Ibid., p. 675. See also Adam Roberts, *Civilian Resistance*, p. 192.

[18] From the report of the Special United Nations Commission on the Hungarian Revolt, cited in Mahadevan, Roberts, and Sharp *Civilian Defense*, p. 203. The ultimate failure of nonviolent resistance in these cases is not necessarily an argument against it. Just as the loss of a military battle is not an argument against the use of military means as a whole, neither should the failure of nonviolent resistance to win all battles be seen as reason to condemn it in general.

In any particular case, the nonviolent approach may have failed because its leadership was weak, because its practitioners were poorly trained, because its cause was not truly a just one, or for any number of other reasons. Nonviolent campaigns that did not achieve their goals because of repressive violence should be studied to see how they might have been conducted more effectively – and perhaps more successfully. On the other hand, we dare not forget the Cross's reminder that nonviolence does not always produce positive results in the short run.

[19] B. H. Liddell Hart, 'Lessons from Resistance Movements,' in Roberts, *Civilian Resistance*, p. 205.

[20] Cadoux, *The Early Church and the World* (Edinburgh: T. & T. Clark, 1925), p. 221.

[21] The examples in the text are of *groups* responding nonviolently to armed groups. Many examples of 'moral jujitsu' acting as a defence in cases of *individual* aggression could also be given. Here is one. A man was hired to kill Dom Helder Câmara, a Roman Catholic archbishop in Brazil who had offended many landowners by taking the side of the poor in disputes over land. The paid assassin was surprised to find the high-ranking church official living in a small, three-room house with no car or servants. The bishop greeted him personally at the door, invited him inside, and asked, 'Do you need me for anything?'

The killer replied, 'No, no, I don't want to have anything to do with you, because you are not one of those that you kill.'

'Kill?' Dom Helder queried, 'Why do you want to kill?'

'Because I was paid to kill you, but I can't kill you.'

'If you are paid,' Dom Helder said, 'why don't you kill me? I will go to the Lord.'

But the man left, saying, 'No, no, you are one of the Lord's.' Mary Hall, *The Spirituality of Dom Helder Câmara* (Maryknoll, NY: Orbis Books, 1980), p. 94.

Many other examples of unarmed individuals conquering their opponents through nonviolent means are given in Allan A. Hunter, *Courage in Both Hands* (New York: Ballantine Books, 1962); and in Allan A. Hunter, *Christians in the Arena* (Nyack, NY: Fellowship Pub., 1958).

[22]Comment made to Richard Taylor by Dr Bernard Lafayette, a top aide to Dr Martin Luther King, Jr.

[23]As we have noted, not all movements of nonmilitary defence have practised this fifth characteristic. Some, in fact, have been carried out with considerable hostility, even hatred, toward the enemy. Similarly, not all theorists of CBD agree that good will needs to be part of a strategy to oppose invasion. Some advocate a negative approach, arguing that the only way to build needed cohesion and solidarity among defenders is to keep sharp boundaries between them and the invaders. In several of the historical cases we have cited, the resisters made no effort to show respect or good will toward their opponents. Instead, they shunned them, ignored them or showed antagonism toward them. Others, like Gandhi in India or Trocmé in France, made good will a part of their resistance.

For a discussion of the pros and cons of these approaches, see Anders Boserup and Andrew Mack, *War without Weapons* (New York: Schocken Books, 1974), pp. 13–18, 21–36. (They lean strongly toward the negative.) Our own position favours the positive approach which corresponds, we believe, with Jesus' life and teachings.

[24]Some understanding of the distinction between loving and liking is essential. In the Sermon on the Mount, Jesus urges us to love those whom we do not like. He says that there is nothing profound in loving 'those who love you' (Mt 5:46). The real challenge is to 'love your enemies and pray for those who persecute you' (Mt 5:44), to 'make friends quickly with your accuser' (Mt 5:25).

Scholars point out that three different Greek words in the Bible texts are translated into the single word 'love' in our English Bible. Two of them, *eros* and *philia*, refer to the kind of love which is based on affection and mutual attraction. When

Jesus said, 'Love your enemies,' however, the Greek word used was *agape*. Agape means 'to deeply care for and will good for someone even when there is no basis for emotional affection.' See Dr Martin Luther King, Jr, *Strength to Love*, p. 44.

[25]The history of nonmilitary movements provides many examples of the practice of good will toward enemies. One striking instance comes from Gandhi's India: 'Shortly after the worst of all riots between Moslems and Hindus, when the Moplah Mohammedans butchered hundreds of unarmed Hindus and offered their prepuces as a covenant to Allah, these same Moslems were stricken with famine. Gandhi [a Hindu] collected funds for them from all over India, and, with no regard for the best precedents, forwarded every *anna* [penny], without deduction for "overhead", to the starving enemy.' Will Durant, *The Story of Civilization* (New York: Simon and Schuster, 1954), p. 628.

The American Civil Rights Movement provides other examples. In Alabama, Birmingham's commissioner of public safety, Bull Connor, unleashed police dogs and opened fire hoses on nonviolent demonstrators and jailed over two thousand Black protesters. When he later became ill and was hospitalised, James Orange, one of the protesters and an aide of King's, learned that Black hospital staff were mistreating Connor. Orange went to the hospital, asked the staff to stop their harassment and took flowers to the commissioner. (Jim Orange related this incident to Richard Taylor in a personal conversation.) See also Flip Schulke, *Martin Luther King, Jr.* (New York: W. W. Norton, 1976), pp. 71–73.

[26]Nonviolent movements often develop written pledges which are handed out to resisters before a demonstration to remind them not to use violence and to show good will toward opponents. A pledge used in the Indian struggle against British rule said: 'If anyone insults an official or commits an assault upon him, a civil resister will protect such official from the insult or attack, even at the risk of her or his own life.' Quoted in Susanne Gowan et al., *Moving toward a New Society* (Philadelphia: New Society Press, 1976), p. 226.

[27]Dr Lewis B. Smedes of Fuller Theological Seminary says of the Christian love found in Paul's 'hymn to love' (1 Cor 13): 'Love believes that the incorrigible liar is of supreme value, that the most corrupt dictator has a redeemable soul, that every killer on Death Row is a person of irredeemable worth. . . . Love

believes that [every] person is of inestimable worth, is redeemable, and can become good.' *Love within Limits: A Realist's View of 1 Corinthians 13* (Grand Rapids, Mich: Eerdmans, 1978), p. 99.

[28] Corrie ten Boom, imprisoned for helping Dutch Jews, found the God-given strength to speak frankly to her Nazi interrogator about the Bible and Christian faith. 'Jesus is the Light the Bible shows to me,' she said to the Nazi lieutenant, 'the light that can shine even in such darkness as yours.' Corrie ten Boom, *The Hiding Place* (Minneapolis: Chosen Books, 1971), pp. 166–68.

[29] Martin Luther King, Jr, *Strength to Love*, p. 42.

[30] Diana Dewar, *All For Christ: Some 20th Century Christian Martyrs* (Oxford: Oxford Univ. Press, 1980), p. 61. The author gives many similar modern examples of martyrdom. See also Allan A. Hunter's *Christians in the Arena* and *Courage in Both Hands* (New York: Ballantine Books, 1962).

[31] Smedes, *Love within Limits*, pp. 85, 91, 120, 131.

[32] Ibid., p. 16.

[33] As we saw in chap. five, the call to follow Jesus is a central theme of the New Testament. This call includes a call to the disciple to take up the cross and suffer as Jesus did. (See Mt 10:38; 16:24; Mk 8:34; 10:38–39; Lk 14:27; 1 Pet 2:21–24; 4:1–2.) 'Only at one point, only on one subject – but then consistently, universally – is Jesus our example: in his cross.' John Howard Yoder, *The Politics of Jesus* (Grand Rapids, Mich: Eerdmans, 1972), p. 97.

[34] Quoted in Smedes, *Love within Limits*, p. 120.

[35] During the American Civil War, the nonviolent Shakers of Pleasant Hill, Kentucky, received protection from a notorious guerilla leader, John Morgan. When Confederate foragers planned to sack the Shakers' well-stocked barns, Morgan prevented them. He told his troops that he knew the Shakers as harmless people who injured no one. He ordered them not to hurt the Shakers in any way. Clarence Marsh Case, *Nonviolent Coercion* (New York: Garland Publishing, 1972), p. 199.

Gene Sharp describes the way in which good will makes it harder for an opponent to use repression: 'Repression against people who are not only nonviolent but also personally friendly . . . will often appear less justifiable than repression of hostile persons. Repression may still be applied, but the impact of the resulting suffering on the opponent group and on third parties is also likely to be greater. . . . An absence of personal ill-will may increase the degree to which the opponent's repression rebounds to weaken his own political position.' Gene Sharp, *Politics of Nonviolent Action*, p. 634.

[36] John Howard Yoder says that 'the unqualified love of the neighbour, including the enemy, to the point of readiness to suffer unjustly at his hands . . . [is] the most appropriate testimony to the nature of God's love and his Kingdom. . . . We love our neighbor because God is like that.' *The Original Revolution* (Scottdale, Pa: Herald Press, 1972), p. 52.

[37] Pitirim A. Sorokin, *The Ways and Power of Love* (Boston: Beacon Press, 1954), pp. 58–60. See also Sorokin, *Altruistic Love: A Study of American 'Good Neighbors' and Christian Saints* (Boston: Beacon Press, 1950).

[38] Hall, *Spirituality of Câmara*, p. 94.

[39] See Rom 5:3–4; 12:12; 1 Cor 13:4; 16:13–14; 2 Cor 4:8–10; 5:1–8; 6:4; Gal 5:22; Phil 1:12–21; Col 1:11; 1 Thess 2:2.

[40] A Christian community caught in the midst of the bloody civil war in Nicaragua in the late 1970s decided to 'place people behind walls of protection by prayer.' Even though they were involved in dangerous areas, helping the wounded, hiding people in their homes and so on, none of the seventy-five community members was killed and only one was hurt. One member 'had his car completely machine-gunned, but didn't have a scratch on his body.' A relative for whom the community had prayed was captured by government troops but was 'the only one spared out of 42 who had their throats cut.' An interview with Carlos Mantica, 'We Were Told to be Ready,' *Pastoral Renewal*, Sept. 1980, pp. 24–25.

[41] Preamble of the Constitution of the United States of America.

Chapter 15: Defending a Nation by Nonmilitary Means

[1] In a speech on 10 Nov. 1948.

[2] King, *Stride toward Freedom* (New York: Harper, 1958), p. 224.

[3] During World War II, the Dutch, Norwegians and Danes kept secret newspapers going during the entire German occupation. Adam Roberts, ed., *Civilian Resistance as a National Defense* (Harrisburg, Pa: Stackpole Books, 1968), p. 144. 'A total of 538 illegal newspapers were published during the five years of Denmark's occupation. In 1944 their combined circulation was over ten million. The largest illegal newspaper reached a

circulation of 150,000 copies in the spring of 1945.' Ibid.,
p. 170.

[4]See Anders Boserup and Andrew Mack, *War without Weapons*
(New York: Schocken Books, 1974), pp. 109ff., for a description of the crucial role played by the media in the Czech
resistance to the Soviet invasion. The authors tell how to
prevent jamming and tracing of clandestine transmitters, how
to supply accurate information to hidden broadcasting stations
and so on.

[5]See Boserup and Mack, *War without Weapons*, pp. 94ff.; and
Roberts, *Civilian Resistance*, pp. 246, 258–61.

[6]For example, the Russians tried to move a trainload of radio-
jamming equipment across the country to silence the Czech
'free radio.' None of the Czech railway workers explicitly
refused Russian orders, but 'a long series of "mistakes" and
"communications failures" so delayed the shipment that the
Soviets eventually had to airlift the equipment.' Boserup and
Mack, *War without Weapons*, p. 46.

[7]The resistance of Norwegian voluntary associations, including
sports clubs, was a key rallying point in the country's resistance
to Nazism during World War II. See Roberts, *Civilian Resistance*, pp. 141–42.

[8]Miller describes the potential of churches as key institutions in
the resistance: 'The more inextricably the nonviolent organisation is enmeshed in the stable and permanent structures of the
society itself, the harder it will be for the enemy to smoke it out
and isolate it. The entire congregation of every parish church,
for example, must be capable of being suspected as a unit of
nonviolent resistance. By this means, the enemy would have to
smash the church as a whole in all its ramifications to get at the
agents of resistance. Such a pattern multiplied throughout the
fabric of society would make for great resilience.' William
Robert Miller, *Nonviolence: A Christian Interpretation* (New
York: Schocken Books, 1972), pp. 109–10.

[9]Nonviolent training proved indispensable to the American civil
rights protesters of the 1960s, who had to maintain their calm
under extreme provocation. Nonviolent training during the
large anti-Vietnam war demonstrations of the 1970s showed
that thousands of people can be trained quickly in the basics of
peaceful protest. For information on nonviolent training, see:
Richard K. Taylor, *Blockade: A Guide to Nonviolent Intervention* (Maryknoll, NY: Orbis, 1977), pp. 139ff; Theodore W.

Olsen and Lynne Shivers, *Training for Nonviolent Action* (London: War Resisters International, 1970); Charles Walker, *Training for Civilian-Based Defense* (Cheyney, Pa: Gandhi Institute, 1982).

[10] Opportunities for such fraternisation inevitably develop after the first wave of invasion has passed. 'Attempts are made to prevent and outlaw fraternization, but eventually such efforts prove fruitless. In time soldiers are marrying girls from the conquered nation, and children are being born whose parents but a short time before were mortal enemies. . . . In [CBD], where deliberate and conscious effort is made to establish understanding and communication with invading soldiers by emphasizing the common humanity which binds occupier and occupied, these contacts become a phase of the struggle to conquer the invader.' American Friends Service Committee, *In Place of War* (New York: Grossman, 1967), p. 56.

[11] This analogy is taken from Miller, *Nonviolence*, p. 104.

[12] 'During the periods of persecution [of the early church], those being examined by the authorities were not left to stand alone. At every opportunity they were surrounded by fellow believers, whose presence emphasised the group standard and lent a resolution born of vital fellowship in common faith. The supporting group was strongly felt to include also a host of heavenly witnesses – God, Christ, and the martyrs who had gone before.' In the US Civil Rights Movement, the same deep comradeship developed. 'The experiences of jail itself – sometimes with 16 or more persons in a cell made for four – helped many persons to experience the sense of joyful, suffering "koinonia" that they had never known in any church.' Harvey Seifert, *Conquest by Suffering* (Philadelphia: Westminster, 1965), pp. 44–45.

[13] Boserup and Mack point out that military commanders try to avoid spreading out their forces and fighting on many fronts at once. 'Concentration of force' is a basic military tactic. Carrying on a battle through CBD, however, would be a way to cause 'maximum strain and overstretch' to the invader's forces. *War without Weapons*, p. 78.

[14] *The World Almanac and Book of Facts*, 1981 (New York: Newspaper Enterprise Assn., 1980), p. 586.

[15] Sir Stephen King-Hall, *Power Politics in the Nuclear Age* (London: Gollancz, 1962), p. 198. King-Hall points out that there are too many positions to be filled in government and

industry and the positions are too technical to be easily fillable. After Germany's surrender in World War II, the Allied occupiers found it necessary to move Germans – including Nazis – back into administrative positions because their knowledge was indispensable to running the government and economy. Likewise, when the Nazis were the occupiers, they could not administer occupied countries with their own personnel. They had to use local collaborationist governments, like Quisling in Norway and Vichy in France. This shows clearly 'that it is impossible to make any profit out of an occupied country unless there is collaboration by the inhabitants' (p. 199).

[16]'They were frightened of their own people, and the evidence suggested that they were making a great effort to prevent them mixing and seeing the contrast between conditions in the East and the West. So they kept shifting their officers and divisions around and did everything of this sort to avoid contact.' Roberts, *Civilian Resistance*, p. 208.

[17]See, for example, Boserup and Mack's chapter 'External Defense: Deterrence and Dissuasion' in *War without Weapons*, pp. 128–39; Gene Sharp's 'Civilian-Based Defense as a Deterrent' in *Social Power and Political Freedom* (Boston: Porter-Sargent, 1980), pp. 234–36; and Sharp's 'Deterrence by Civilian-Based Defense' in *Civilian-Based Defense: A New Deterrence and Defense Policy* (East Boston, Mass: Photocopied manuscript privately printed by the author), pp. 16–18. In the latter study, Sharp makes the important point that 'deterrence . . . is not intrinsically tied to military means, much less to military weapons capacity. Deterrence can occur within the context of strictly nonviolent means. . . . In contrast to military means, this deterrence would not be produced by the threat of massive physical destruction and death to the attacker's homeland. Deterrence would be achieved by the perception that the attacked society could block achievement of the attacker's goals and impose unacceptable costs' (p. 17).

[18]Gene Sharp, *Exploring Nonviolent Alternatives* (Boston: Porter-Sargent), p. 65.

[19]Sharp, *The Politics of Nonviolent Action* (Boston: Porter-Sargent, 1973).

[20]See especially Gene Sharp's detailed treatment in his chapters entitled 'Challenge Brings Repression'; and 'Solidarity and Discipline to Fight Repression,' in *Politics of Nonviolent Action*. See also Boserup and Mack's chapter 'The Ability to

Withstand Repression,' in *War without Weapons*, pp. 82–91. See also index references to *repression* in Seifert, *Conquest by Suffering*, and Roberts, *Civilian Resistance*.

[21] Cf. Mt 10:23; 16:24–28; Mk 4:17; Lk 9:23–27; Acts 12:1–19; 2 Cor 4:8–12; 12:10; 2 Thess 1:4; 2 Tim 3:10–13.

[22] International Fellowship of Reconciliation, 'Report,' July 1980, mimeographed. Available from the Fellowship of Reconciliation, PO Box 271, Nyack, NY 10960.

[23] In a dispute between a nuclear and a non-nuclear power, says Commander Sir Stephen King-Hall, 'the whole weight of world opinion would make it very difficult for the nuclear Power to use its nuclear weapons. It is hard to imagine the USA using a nuclear weapon against Castro even if he attempted to seize the American base in Cuba.' King-Hall, *Power Politics in the Nuclear Age*, p. 108. King-Hall makes a persuasive case for how even totalitarian states have to take world opinion into account.

[24] Jerome Frank, *Sanity and Survival* (New York: Random House, 1967), p. 277.

[25] It might be noted that early American colonists, most of whom resisted Indians 'with musket and shot,' were often massacred and lived in fear of the Indians. Quakers, whose pacifism forbade the use of guns, were largely untouched by marauding Indian bands. A famous Quaker painting shows heavily armed Indians entering a meetinghouse where Quakers were gathered for worship. It is based on an actual incident in which Indians, observing the Quakers' quiet and peaceful manner, came in, sat in silence for a while and then left without harming anyone.

[26] For a description of this possibility, see American Friends Service Committee, *In Place of War*, p. 49.

[27] Nora Levin, *The Holocaust: The Destruction of European Jewry, 1933–1945* (New York: Schocken Books, 1973), pp. 399, 401.

[28] A. J. Muste, *Nonviolence in an Aggressive World* (New York: Harper, 1940), p. 38.

[29] Cf. Sharp, *Exploring Nonviolent Alternatives*, p. 67. For more details on what would be involved in transarmament, see Sharp, *Social Power and Political Freedom*; Bradford Lyttle, *National Defense through Nonviolent Resistance* (Chicago: Shanti-Sena Pub., 1958), pp. 22ff.; Cecil E. Hinshaw, *Nonviolent Resistance: A Nation's Way to Peace* (Wallingford, Pa: Pendle Hill, 1956), pp. 21ff.; Roberts' chapter entitled 'Trans-

armament to Civilian Defense,' in *Civilian Resistance*, pp. 291ff.

[30] For suggestions on needed research, see Theodore Olson, 'An Alternative Defense Strategy for Canada: A Proposal for Joint Military-Academic Research and Experimentation,' (photocopied; Portland, Ontario: Third Annual Ploughshares Summer Workshop, 1979).

[31] Approximately half of all US Senators and many Congressional Representatives are co-sponsoring bills to create the academy. For more information, contact National Peace Academy Campaign, 110 Maryland Ave NE, Washington, DC 20002.

[32] For a description of plans for such an alliance, see American Friends Service Committee, *In Place of War*, pp. 81–82. Regarding mutual assistance pacts, see Sharp, *Exploring Nonviolent Alternatives*, pp. 49, 69.

[33] For a description of how such a nonmilitary defence force might work, see King-Hall, *Power Politics in the Nuclear Age*, pp. 180–81. W. H. Ferry spelt out the rationale for a foreign policy of nonviolence in a letter to the *New York Times*, 18 Jan. 1980.

[34] Daniel Berrigan, *No Bars to Manhood* (Garden City, NY: Doubleday, 1970), pp. 57–58.

About the Authors

Ronald J. Sider studied history and theology at Yale University and received the PhD from that institution in 1969. He is now associate professor of theology at Eastern Baptist Theological Seminary and president of Evangelicals for Social Action. In addition, he is convenor of the Unit on Ethics and Society of the Theological Commission of the World Evangelical Fellowship and a member of the board of Bread for the World. He is also the author of *Rich Christians in an Age of Hunger* and *Christ and Violence* and the editor of *Cry Justice, Living More Simply, Evangelicals and Development* and *Lifestyle in the Eighties*.

Richard K. Taylor studied at Yale Divinity School and Cornell University, and completed a master's degree in social work at Bryn Mawr College in 1962. He has long been active in community development and has worked with the Fair Housing Council of Delaware Valley, the Southern Christian Leadership Conference, the Martin Luther King School of Social Change and Jubilee Fellowship Church in Philadelphia. He is now a consultant on outreach and peace ministries for the Sojourners Community and Evangelicals for Social Action. He is the author of *Economics and the Gospel, Moving toward a New Society* and *Blockade*.

THE CHURCH AND THE BOMB

The report of a working party under the chairmanship of the Bishop of Salisbury

Nuclear weapons and Christian conscience

Does a mushroom-shaped shadow hang over the future of mankind? Or does the 'absolute deterrent' abolish war?

The Church and the Bomb cannot state *the* view of the Church of England, but its contribution to this vital debate is both vigorous and far-reaching. The report combines an analysis of the technical issues, an exploration of the underlying moral questions and detailed recommendations concerning NATO and the British nuclear deterrent.

RICH CHRISTIANS
IN AN AGE OF HUNGER

Ronald J Sider

A biblical study

Famine is alive and well on planet earth. Even the most conservative statistics reflect a horrifying situation. How can Christians respond? What is the biblical perspective?

'This book contains the most vital challenge which faces the Church today. It is one of the most searching and disquieting books I have ever read . . . it calls, above all, for immediate and sacrificial action, if we know anything of God's love in our heart.' *From the foreword by David Watson*

LIVING MORE SIMPLY

Ronald J Sider

Biblical principles and practical models

How should Western Christians live? Dare we
measure our lifestyles by the needs of the poor and
unevangelised rather than by the living standards
of our affluent neighbours?

Here are concrete, practical suggestions for a truly
alternative society.